Maya®
Visual Effects

Maya®
Visual Effects

The Innovator's Guide

Eric Keller

WILEY PUBLISHING, INC.

Acquisitions Editor: Mariann Barsolo
Development Editor: Toni Zuccarini Ackley
Technical Editor: Geordie Martinez
Production Editor: Sarah Groff-Palermo
Copy Editor: Judy Flynn
Production Manager: Tim Tate
Vice President and Executive Group Publisher: Richard Swadley
Vice President and Executive Publisher: Joseph B. Wikert
Vice President and Publisher: Neil Edde
Media Project Supervisor: Laura Atkinson
Media Development Specialist: Kate Jenkins
Book Designer: Franz Baumhackl
Compositor: Susan Riley, Side By Side Studios
Proofreader: Ian Golder
Indexer: Ted Laux
Anniversary Logo Design: Richard Pacifico
Cover Designer: Ryan Sneed
Cover Image: Eric Keller

Autodesk® Maya® Personal Learning Edition (PLE) is a special version of Autodesk® Maya® software, which provides free access to Autodesk Maya for non-commercial use. It gives graphics and animation students, industry professionals, and those interested in breaking into the world of computer graphics an opportunity to explore most aspects of the award-winning Autodesk® Maya® Complete software in a non-commercial capacity. It is available for Windows® 2000/XP Professional and Mac OS® X (Macintosh® PowerPC) operating systems.

Autodesk Maya PLE is based on Autodesk Maya 7.0.1.

Autodesk, Autodesk Maya Press, Maya 8.5, Maya 8, and Maya 7.0.1 are registered trademarks or trademarks of Autodesk, Inc. in the U.S.A and/ or certain other coutries.

Certain content, including trial software, provided courtesy of Autodesk, Inc. c 2006. All rights reserved.

For general information on our other products and services or to obtain technical support, please contact our Customer Care Department within the U.S. at (800) 762-2974, outside the U.S. at (317) 572-3993, or fax (317) 572-4002.

Wiley also publishes its books in a variety of electronic formats. Some content that appears in print may not be available in electronic books.

Library of Congress Cataloging-in-Publication Data

Keller, Eric, 1969-
  Maya visual effects : the innovator's guide / Eric Keller.
    p. cm.
  ISBN-13: 978-0-470-11133-8 (paper/cd-rom)
  ISBN-10: 0-470-11133-X (paper/cd-rom)
  1. Computer animation. 2. Maya (Computer file) 3. Three-dimensional display systems. I. Title.
  TR897.7K42 2007
  006.6'93--dc22

                                    2006101152

Dear Reader

Thank you for choosing *Maya Visual Effects: The Innovator's Guide.* This book is part of a family of premium quality Sybex graphics books, all written by outstanding authors who combine practical experience with a gift for teaching.

Sybex was founded in 1976. More than thirty years later, we're still committed to producing consistently exceptional books. With each of our graphics titles we're working hard to set a new standard for the industry. From the writers and artists we work with to the paper we print on, our goal is to bring you the best graphics books available.

I hope you see all that reflected in these pages. I'd be very interested to hear your comments and get your feedback on how we're doing. Feel free to let me know what you think about this or any other Sybex book by sending me an email at nedde@wiley.com, or if you think you've found an error in this book, please visit http://wiley.custhelp.com. Customer feedback is critical to our efforts at Sybex.

Best regards,
Neil Edde
Vice President and Publisher
Sybex, an Imprint of Wiley

To all the teachers who have inspired and pushed me in my studies of music, art, and science. And to my Mom, who is an inspiration in all three areas.

Acknowledgments

This book owes a lot to the support of the editors at Wiley. What started out as my own goofy idea of a book devoted to Ramp textures has turned into what I hope will be an insightful book on creating effects with Autodesk's Maya. Much of my thanks goes to my technical editor, Geordie Martinez, who kept me honest and constantly challenged my ideas. Most of all he deserves much credit for developing the MEL scripts used in the later chapters. Thanks to Mariann for supporting the concept of the book and allowing me to write about whatever I wanted to, to Toni for putting up with my typing and grammatical skills, to Sarah for dealing with my grouchy emails, to Willem for getting me involved in writing Maya books, and to Dariush for introducing me to everyone at Wiley.

A great deal of thanks goes to all the teachers I've had over the years in music (John A., John C., Sam, Mike, Lisa, Bruce), art (Kevin, John B.), and science (Sat, Dennis, Gael). Thanks to my colleagues who keep me on my toes (Chris V., Nate, Kamal). Thanks to my two co-workers, Daisy and Blue, who interrupt me every few hours for snacks and walks. Thanks to my wife, Zoe, who puts up with these crazy schemes. Thanks to my evil twin, Travis, who calls every day to make fun of me.

About the Author

Eric Keller is a freelance animator working in Hollywood, California, at some of the finer design and effects houses. He got his start in the field of digital visual effects developing animations for scientific visualization at the prestigious Howard Hughes Medical Institute, where he had the opportunity to work with some of the world's leading researchers. He has been working with Maya since version 1 was released and has been an enthusiast ever since. Along with creating animations for molecular visualization, bacterial invasion, and cellular function, Eric has pitched in on numerous animations for film, commercials, and television. He has also written articles and tutorials for industry magazines and websites and contributed three chapters to *Mastering Maya 7*. One of his goals is to bring the quality of feature film animation to the world of scientific visualization. He majored in music at Florida State University and would probably still be playing guitar at weddings if he hadn't accidentally rendered a chrome sphere on his home computer.

If you have questions, you can email him at kellerrific@yahoo.com or check out his website at www.bloopatone.com.

Contents

Introduction   *xv*

Chapter 1   **Texture Effects**   **1**

Creating Animated Lighting Effects with Ramp Textures 2
     Creating the Light Geometry   3
     Shading the Lights   6
     Creating Glowing Lights   8
     Shading the UFO Dome   11

Streaking Energy Effects 12
     Know Your Glows   12
     Creating the Energy Geometry   14
     Creating a Mask with a Second Ramp   15
     Connecting the Ramp to the Motion Path Output Value   15
     Reconnecting the Energy Shader   20

Layering with Multiple UV Sets: The Zombie's Hand. 22
     Creating Multiple UV Sets   23
     Creating the Mask for the Spreading Infection   25
     Creating a Splotch   29
     Bringing the Color Back   29

Abusing Ambient Occlusion: The Sci Fi Scanner. 32
     Creating the Scanner Shader   34
     Tuning the Shader   35

Controlling Particles with Textures: Swimming Bacteria 38
     Creating the Particle and Goals   38
     Creating the Ramps   39
     Adjusting the Ramps   41

Chapter 2   **Particle Effects**   **45**

Particle Instancing and Expressions: Creating a 3D Audio Meter 47
     Using the Instancer   48
     Animating the Meter   54
     Duplicating the Meter   55

Particle Collisions: The Classic Force Field Effect 56
     Creating the Force Field   57
     Creating the Look of the Shield   58
     Ray Gun Impact Effect   59
     Editing the Instances   60
     Animating the Force Field   61

Instancing with Paint Effects: Pushing Up the Daisies 62
     Setting Up Collisions   62
     Creating the Flower   64
     Creating the Flower Object Cycle   65
     Controlling the Growth with Expressions   67

Using Cycle Emission: The Plasma Ball 68
     Creating the Plasma Emitter   69
     Cycle Emission   70

Containing the Particles · · · · · · · · · · · · · · 72
Collision Events · · · · · · · · · · · · · · · · · · · 72
The Secondary Particles · · · · · · · · · · · · · · 72
Polishing the Plasma · · · · · · · · · · · · · · · · 74

Influencing Cameras with Particles 75
Creating the Particle Rig · · · · · · · · · · · · · · 75
Adding Dynamic Motion to the Particles · · · · · 77
Attaching the Camera to the Particle Rig · · · · · 78
Tuning the Motion · · · · · · · · · · · · · · · · · · 79
Creating the Blood · · · · · · · · · · · · · · · · · · 79
Creating the Blood Cell Rotation · · · · · · · · · · 80

Chapter 3 **Rigging for Effects** **83**

The Vibrating Rig: Making a Tentacle Shake 84
Disconnecting the Animated Rig · · · · · · · · · · 84
Creating a Vibrating Joint · · · · · · · · · · · · · · 85
Duplicating the Vibrating Joint · · · · · · · · · · · 87
Adding the Shakers to the Rig · · · · · · · · · · · 87
Reconnecting the Tentacle · · · · · · · · · · · · · 89
Controlling the Vibration · · · · · · · · · · · · · · 90

Inverse Kinematic Splines: Making a Tentacle Climb 92
Drawing the Main Tentacle Curve · · · · · · · · · 92
Adding Joints to the Curve · · · · · · · · · · · · · 94
Animating the Curve · · · · · · · · · · · · · · · · · 95
Adjusting the Animation · · · · · · · · · · · · · · · 96
Creating Joints for the Tentacle · · · · · · · · · · 97
Activating the IK Spline Tool · · · · · · · · · · · · 98
Animating the IK Spline Offset · · · · · · · · · · · 99

Joints and Constraints: The Telescopic Car Suspension Rig 100
Creating the Telescoping Leg · · · · · · · · · · · 100
Creating the Telescopic Rig · · · · · · · · · · · · 102
Setting Limits for the Scale X Attribute · · · · · 104
Creating an IK Handle for the Leg Joints · · · · 105
Creating an Automated Scaling Control · · · · · 105
Duplicating the Leg Rig · · · · · · · · · · · · · · · 107
Placing the Legs · · · · · · · · · · · · · · · · · · · 108
Constraining the Wheels · · · · · · · · · · · · · · 109
Creating Front and Rear Controls · · · · · · · · · 109
Making the Car Move · · · · · · · · · · · · · · · · 110

The Inverse Kinematic Spline Tool and Lattices 114
Setting Up the Lattice · · · · · · · · · · · · · · · · 114
Adding Joints to the Lattice · · · · · · · · · · · · 115
Adding an IK Spline to the Joints · · · · · · · · · 115
Animating the Squashing Effect · · · · · · · · · · 116
Creating a Twist · · · · · · · · · · · · · · · · · · · 118

Chapter 4 **Creative Blend Shape Use** **121**

Blend Shapes and Lattices 122
Revolving a Surface · · · · · · · · · · · · · · · · · 122
Creating a Blend Shape for the Profile Curve · · 123
Setting Up a Control View Camera · · · · · · · · 123
Setting Up Blend Shape Controls · · · · · · · · · 124
Making the Vase Spin · · · · · · · · · · · · · · · · 125
Animating the Sculpting of the Vase · · · · · · · 126

Creating a Blend Shape Control for the Lattice 127
Deforming the Blend Shape Lattice with Joints 127

Blend Shape In-Betweens 129
Working with Blend Shape Targets 129
Painting Blend Shape Weights 131
Creating the Blend Shape Sequence 132
Adjusting the Animation 133
Rigging the Pod 134
Animating the Pod 135
Animating the Eyes 136
Creating the Time Lapse Effect 136

Interactive Blend Shape Rigs 139
Creating the Blend Shape 139
Creating the Interactive Control 140
Duplicating the Rig 142
Editing the Animation 143
Creating an Animated Array of Bricks 144
Having Fun 145

Layering Blend Shapes. 148
Creating the Blend Shapes 148
Animating the Blend Shape with Fractal Textures 150
Creating Controls for the Textures 152
Animating the Blend Shape Transformation 154

Chapter 5 — Paint Effects — 157

Paint Effects and Toon Lines: The Mine Detector Display 158
Creating the Probe and Mine Display 158
Creating the Proximity Warning Display 161
Adding Paint Effects Strokes to the Proximity Display 164
Adding Interactive Control to the Proximity Display 166
Using the Information from the Distance Between Node 169
Duplicating the Mines 171
Animating the Probe 173
Illuminating the Path 174
Animating the Path 175
Finishing Touches 176

Hallucinations in 3D: Using the Smear Stroke. 177
Adjusting the Tree 179
Animating the Tree 179
Framing the Scene 181
Lighting the Scene 182
Using a Smear Brush 183
Tuning the Brush 186
Animating the Tubes 187
Variation Number One 188
Variation Number Two 189
Variation Number Three 189

Paint Effects Strokes and Soft Body Dynamics 191
Animating the Movement of the Bacterium 191
Creating the Soft Body Object 193
Creating Bacterial Pili with Paint Effects 194
Modifying the Weeds Stroke 197
Editing Surface Offset 198
Animating the Bacterial Pili 200

Converting Paint Effects to NURBS   200
Playblast the Animation   201

Taming Paint Effects Brush Strokes: The Test Tube Nerve 204
Creating the Nerve Using Paint Effects   204
Adjusting the Look of the Nerve Stroke   205
Adjusting Branches and Twigs   206
Adjusting Forces   207
Creating a Control Curve   207
Animating the Control Curve   209
Converting the Control Curve to a Soft Body Object   210
Editing the Goal Weights of the Soft Body Curve   215
Controlling the Growth for the Stroke   218
Key Framing Stroke Growth   219
Rendering the Nerve   221

Chapter 6   **Soft Body Springs**   **225**

Soft Body Springs and Geometry: Simulating Magic 226
Creating the Magical Field Geometry   226
Converting the Cube into a Soft Body Object   229
Adding Fields to the Soft Body Object   230
Distorting the Magic Field with a Secondary Particle System   231
Adding a Radial Field to the Distorter Particles   232
Adding Soft Body Springs to the Particles   233
Setting Initial State   236
Rendering the Magical Field   237
Creating a Glowing Edge on the Magical Force Field   240

Soft Body Springs and Particles 244
Creating the Emitters   244
Attaching Springs to the Particles   245
Adjusting the Simulation   248
Adding a Turbulence Field   249
Using the Particle Object as a Paintbrush   249
Setting the Attributes for the paintSprites   250
Creating Particle Sprites   251
Adding Custom Attributes for the Sprites   252
Adding Images to the Sprites   256
Assigning the Images to the Sprites   257
Rendering the Animation   260

Chapter 7   **Rigid Body Effects**   **263**

Rigid and Soft Body Combinations: Dynamic Dents 264
Preparing the Models for Dynamic Interaction   264
Creating the Collision Simulation   265
Adjusting the Simulation   266
Denting a Surface Using Soft Body Dynamics   268
Adding Springs to the Soft Body Object   269
Baking the Rigid Bodies   270
Finishing the Scene   274

Creating Animated Fissures on a Surface 275
Boolean Operations   275
Modeling the Fissure   279
Animating the Fissure   280
Preparing the Scene for Dynamics   282
Separating the Pieces of the Crystal   283

Creating Rigid Bodies from the Separate Pieces   284
Applying Gravity to the Active Rigid Body   284
Adjusting the Dynamics   285
Keyframing the Dynamics   286
Keyframing the Visibility of the Chunks   287

Rigid Body Spring Constraints 289
Creating the Text   290
Renaming the Letters Using MEL   292
Creating the Spring Constraint   294
Adjusting the Spring Constraint   296
Automating the Spring Rig Creation Using MEL   297
Creating a Shelf Button from the Script   300
Completing the Logo Rig   302
Animating the Logo   304
Offsetting the Driven Keys   305
Finishing the Animation   306

Chapter 8   **Hair and Fur Effects**   **309**

Maya Hair: Using Dynamic Curves to Animate a Rope Bridge. 310
Creating the Ropes for the Bridge   311
Converting the Curves to Dynamic Curves   312
Animating the Rope Cut   313
Creating a Hair Constraint   313
Attaching the Stick Constraint to the Second Rope   314
Creating a Plank for the Bridge   316
Attaching the Plank to the Ropes   317
Creating Multiple Hair Constraints   318
Animating the Bridge   322
Finishing Touches   323
Creating a Cache for the Dynamic Curve   323

Maya Fur: The Miracle Lawn 324
Creating Ramps for the Animated Textures   324
Animating the Ramps   326
Rendering the Ramps   327
Creating the Lawn   328
Adding Grass to the Lawn   329
Adjusting the Grass Settings   330
Animating the Length of the Grass   330
Baking the Length Channel   333
Animating the Color of the Lawn   334

Index   *336*

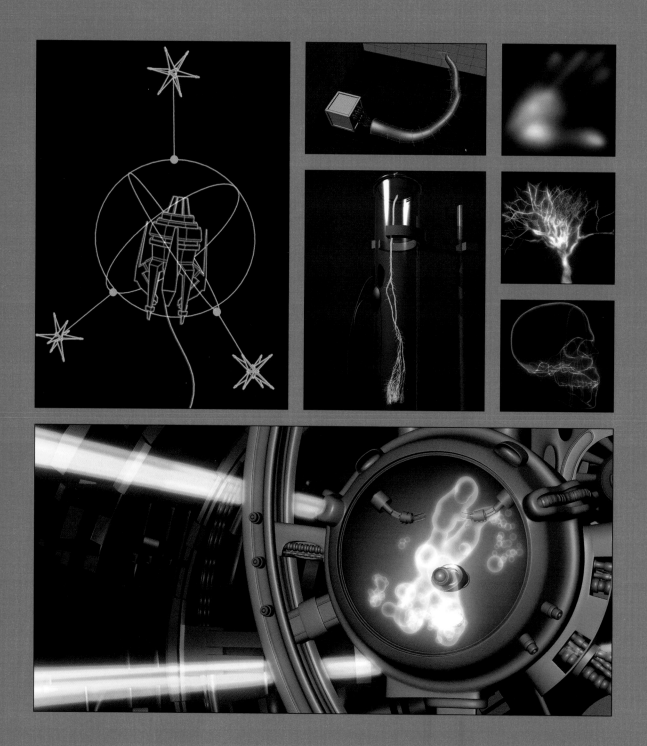

Introduction

One of the things that makes effects animation so engaging is that there are rarely cut-and-dried solutions to any given problem. Most books on computer animation software focus on the most common uses for the tools the software offers. A standard Maya book consists of chapters devoted to modeling cars, rigging characters, and creating plumes of smoke. These are all very important techniques to learn and master, but what happens when you get a job and the art director asks for a squishy kind of energy? Or a fuzzy blob of bacteria that schlorps past the camera? Suddenly you're faced with finding a way to use the Maya toolset in a much less–typical fashion. This book is designed to help you move beyond the basics so that you feel comfortable innovating when creating effects with Maya. Every tool in Maya has three or four common uses and about a billion possibilities for uncommon solutions. That's really what makes it fun.

I've written this book to give you a feel for being part of the production pipeline in a small effects house. Each exercise starts with a request from the art director for a specific effect. We've included small "cocktail-napkin" sketches of each idea. Ideally, the art director should have a nice set of storyboards to guide you—meticulously drawn, developed, and rendered in full color—instead of some chicken scratch on the back of a soggy napkin. However, sometimes the client is hit with a bolt of inspiration in the middle of the night and needs to see it animated, lit, and rendered, by lunch. In these cases, the storyboard often goes out the window and the art director is forced to translate the client's hazy dream into a pile of sticky notes with vague guidelines and some scribbles. This book has a little fun with this particular scenario. In the real world, such a situation does not occur with every project, but it does happen. My hope is that this book will give you the confidence and skills to take on whatever the art director throws at you.

Generally, when you are part of an effects pipeline, even a very small one consisting of just a couple of people, you can count on working with compositors and 2D effects artists who use tools like Adobe After Effects and Apple's Shake to augment, extend, and refine the animations you render from Maya. Sometimes it's much more efficient to create certain effects using 2D software. However, in the interest of helping you achieve a truly deep understanding of what you can do with Maya and how it works, I've written the tutorials as if access to 2D compositing and effects software is unavailable. In addition, no external MEL scripts or plug-ins are needed. In the real world, you would want to take advantage of the thousands of free MEL scripts available on websites such as www.highend3d.com; however, the goal here is to really learn Maya, so any MEL scripts used in the exercises will be the ones you create. Imagine you are the MacGyver of animations, trapped in a basement and strapped to a boiler with Maya, a toothbrush, and a tea cozy as the only tools available to create the effects you need. Some of the tutorials supply the basic models and animation as a starting point, but for the most part, it's up to you and Maya to make the effects happen. As far as the toothbrush and tea cozy go, you're on your own!

In this book, you won't find tutorials about creating explosions, gaseous nebulae, flowing hair, flames, or any other effect that has been covered numerous times in the Maya documentation or in other books. I've worked hard at coming up with original problems and solutions in an effort to help you deepen your knowledge of Maya. Most of these solutions are based on problems I have faced while on various jobs. The examples tend to be geared toward smaller productions, but there is no reason why the same techniques could not be applied to an effect for a feature film.

Who Can Benefit from This Book

This book is targeted specifically at Maya users who feel they have the basics down but want to move to the "next level." It's not meant for beginners. I encourage you to work through a book such as *Introducing Maya 7: 3D for Beginners* or *Mastering Maya 7* before attempting the tutorials in this book. If you are comfortable working in the Hypershade, using the Connection Editor, and navigating the Outliner and Attribute Editor, and if you understand the difference between a shape node and transform node, then you should be at the right skill level for this book. Additionally, if you've worked with other 3D packages and are making the transition to Maya, you should find this book very helpful. Great pains have been taken to present each element of the Maya interface as clearly as possible, but if you find yourself getting lost, you may want to brush up on your basic understanding of Maya before continuing with the exercises in this book.

About This Book

The goal of this book is to teach you techniques for problem solving using Maya. It is unlikely that the animation problems you face in the real world of production will match exactly the solutions given in the exercises. However, chances are they will, in some cases, be close enough so that light bulbs will appear above your head and you'll be able to make the mental connections between the diverse tools available in Maya and come up with your own unique solution.

Specifically, you will learn how to use effects tools such as particles, soft body springs, rigid body dynamics, Hair, and Fur in combination with Maya's other tools such as textures, joints, Inverse Kinematics, lattices, and blendshape deformers. More important, you'll learn techniques, such as creating custom attributes and controls, which will improve the efficiency of your workflow. You'll learn to work faster, smarter, and neater by developing the good habits of an experienced effects artist. Some chapters involve a fair amount of MEL scripting designed to cut the tedium out of setting up effects. The scripting goes beyond the very basics but is still simple enough for a novice scripter to learn. I encourage you to work through the MEL scripts even if it seems a little intimidating. You may not be a world-class coder by the end of the book, but you will learn a few things that may help keep you from having to finish an overdue assignment on a weekend.

This book has a minimum of introductory and explanatory text for each chapter. It's largely exercise-based, and it is a good idea to actually work through the exercises in Maya as you read the book. You certainly can read through the book away from Maya if you want (I learned much of what I know about computer animation reading books on the subway); however, you'll get more out of it if you do the tutorials.

Don't forget the help files! Maya's documentation provides a great deal of background on the Maya toolset and interface. Remember, if you need a refresher on how something works or you need more information, the help files are there for you as part of the Maya interface. The MEL command reference, which is part of the online documentation, is also an essential tool when working with MEL scripts. It contains descriptions of all the available commands as well as the flags associated with them. There are some topics that go beyond the scope of this book, and a review of the help files can come in handy when you need to expand your knowledge.

The first seven chapters require only Maya Complete version 8. I assume that you are learning on a budget and therefore may not have access to the extra modules that come with Maya Unlimited, such as Fur, Hair, Cloth, and Fluids. Even if you are lucky enough to have your own copy of Maya Unlimited, it's not unusual to work on a job at a studio that has only Maya Complete, so it's a good idea to know how much you can squeeze out of Maya without having to rely on the modules that come with Maya Unlimited. Chapter 8 delves into effects created using Maya Hair and Maya Fur. You can always take the techniques described in Chapter 8 and apply them to the exercises from previous chapters.

The Companion CD

The CD that accompanies this book contains the scene files, some MEL scripts, and rendered movies of some of the completed projects. The scene files have been saved incrementally, which means they can serve as a reference point or allow you to skip ahead if you'd like to complete the tutorial quickly. A copy of Maya Personal Learning Edition is also included on the CD. All the scene files are compatible with Maya versions 8 and 8.5, and the folder for each chapter contains a standard Maya project directory structure.

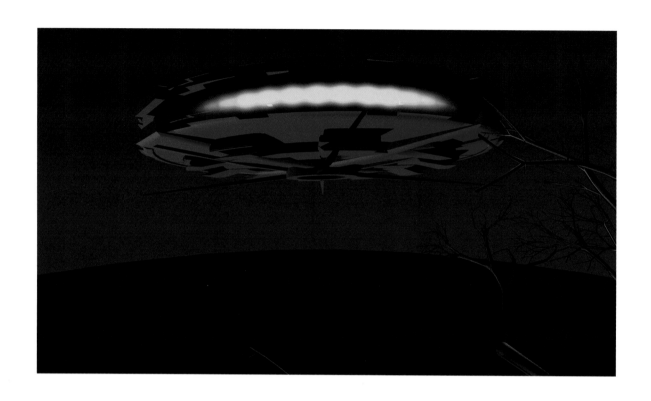

Texture Effects

All too often textures are overlooked as a solution for creating effects. The tendency is to think of them merely as a means for coloring objects. The tutorials in this chapter demonstrate some ways in which engaging visual effects can be created quickly and easily simply by taking advantage of the power that textures offer. The most versatile of all texture nodes—the Ramp texture—will be put to work in many of these examples.

1

Chapter Contents
Creating Animated Lighting Effects with Ramp Textures
Streaking Energy Effects
Layering with Multiple UV Sets: The Zombie's Hand
Abusing Ambient Occlusion: The Sci Fi Scanner
Controlling Particles with Textures: Swimming Bacteria

Creating Animated Lighting Effects with Ramp Textures

In this first scenario, our art director has provided us with a scene consisting of a UFO hovering above a tree-lined hill in the wilderness. Our task is to add some brilliant flashing lights to the craft. Open the scene saucer_v01.mb in the Chapter 1 folder on the CD and take a look at what's going on.

You can see that the saucer model has been roughly animated over a hill. We have a nighttime sky and some scraggily paint effects trees (see Figure 1.1). It looks like a pretty simple scene. The main direction we have been given is to add lights that circle the perimeter of the model as well as something interesting for the dome on top. Yes, directions from some art directors can actually be this vague, depending on the project. We could start by modeling lights from simple spheres and attaching glowing shaders to each one and then use "set driven keys" for them to circle around, but the art director has just instructed us that she needs to post this for client review by lunch time. So let's find a quicker way to do this. Rather than add a bunch of little lights, let's make part of the model one big light and use an animated Ramp texture to create the circling glow.

Figure 1.1: The saucer model hovering over the paint effects trees

To create the glowing effect, we will be using the surface shader. As far as shader types go, the surface shader is just about a simple as you can get. It's basically a shader that does not react to lights or shadows in the scene; it just applies a flat color to an object.

This is why they can be ideal for creating lights on an object as long as those lights are pretty simple. The shader does not emit light in the scene when the scene is rendered with standard Maya software. When a color is placed in the **Out Glow Color** channel, the resulting effect is a very brilliant glow. Its simplicity is why I prefer it for creating the kinds of effects described in this chapter. You can do the same kind of thing with a Lambert or Blinn or any of the other shaders by plugging a color into the **Incandescence** channel; however, this often gives you a few more attributes to keep track of when tuning the glow. It really comes down to how much you want to deal with and the particular effect you are trying to create.

Creating the Light Geometry

First we need to create some geometry which will become our light source.

1. In the Display Layer Editor, turn off the visibility for all of the layers except the UFO_layer to make the scene easier to work with.

2. Rewind the animation to the beginning where the UFO is level with the grid.

3. Take a look at the model. The most obvious place for the lights is in the midsection. It looks like the modeler intended us to use the square polygons that circle the midsection of the model (Figure 1.2).

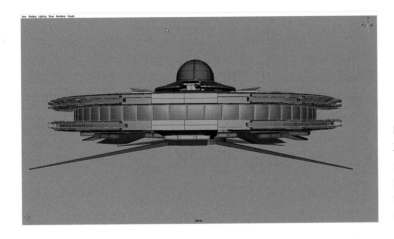

Figure 1.2:
Zooming in on the model shows some square polygons around the perimeter; these will become our perimeter.

4. In the Outliner, expand the UFO group, find the saucer polygon object, and select it.

5. Use the Paint Selection tool to select each of the square polygons that circle the saucer. In Maya 8, the Paint Selection tool has been added to the standard toolbar just below the Lasso tool. When you activate the tool, the saucer section will switch to component mode. In the status line, click the **Select Face Component** button to restrict the selection to polygon faces.

6. When you have them all selected (as in Figure 1.3), double-check that you didn't select anything extraneous; switching to wire frame (hot key = 4) is sometimes a good way to do this.

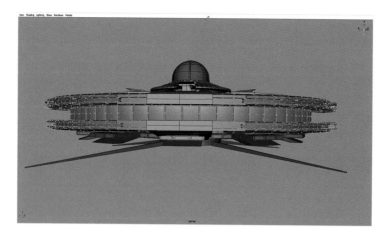

Figure 1.3:
The square polygons around the perimeter of the saucer are selected.

7. We could apply a shader directly to these faces but let's duplicate them and scale them up a little just so we don't have to mess with the main UFO model's UVs. To do this, switch to the Polygon menu set and choose **Edit Mesh > Duplicate Faces > Options**. In the options, make sure **Separate Duplicated Faces** is checked.

8. Click the Apply button. With the object still selected, open the Channel Box (shown in Figure 1.4), select the polyChipOff1 input connection (it may already be selected), and scroll down to find the **Keep Faces Together** attribute. Make sure it is set to on. Find the Local TranslateZ channel about midway up in the Channel Box and set it to 0.1. This will move the duplicated polygons out a little from the surface of the UFO.

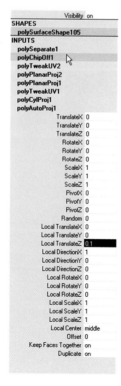

Figure 1.4:
The Channel Box settings for the polyChipOff1 node

9. Switch back to the object selection mode (hot key = F8). In the Outliner you'll see that the saucer object is now a group (Figure 1.5). In the group there is a list of poly objects labeled polySurface1, polySurface2, and so on. If you select poly-Surface1, you'll see that it is the saucer object. PolySurface2 through polySurface59 are the duplicated polygon squares. Select polySurface2 through polySurface59 in the Outliner and use **Mesh** > **Combine** to make them one object.

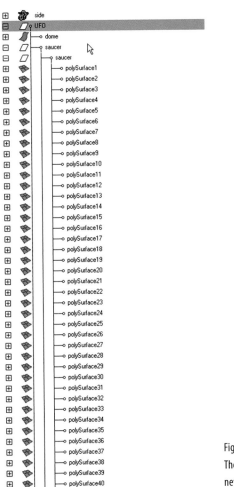

Figure 1.5:
The Outliner showing the
new duplicated faces

10. Select the saucer (which has been renamed polySurface1) and the new poly-Surface60 (at the bottom of the Outliner) and delete history on these objects. The empty transform nodes created when you combined the polygons should disappear from the Outliner.

11. Rename polySurface1 "saucerHull" and polySurface60 "hullLights."

12. Move the hullLights object back into the saucer group.

Shading the Lights

Now we're ready to make some lights.

1. Select the hullLights object and choose **Windows > UV Texture Editor** to open the UV Texture Editor. Press the F key to frame all of the UVs.

2. Select the UVs and choose **Polygons > Normalize UVs**. The UVs stretch to fit the positive coordinate section of the UV grid. The edges may be a bit wavy (see Figure 1.6); you can straighten them out if you'd like, but it really doesn't matter for this purpose.

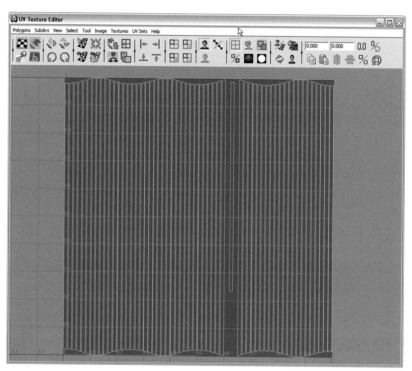

Figure 1.6: The normalized UVs for the hullLights object

3. Back in the perspective window, select the hullLights object again and assign a surface shader to it. Name the surface shader "hullLightsSG."

4. Open the Attribute Editor for the surface shader. In the **Out Color** channel, click the checker button, and in the **Create Render Node** panel, click the **Ramp** button to assign a ramp. Name the ramp "hullLightsRamp."

5. Press the 6 key to switch to hardware texturing in the perspective view. You should see that our UFO has a nice festive array of rainbow-colored lights. We need the color band to go around the saucer hull; to fix that, open the Attribute Editor for the ramp and change it from a **V ramp** to a **U ramp** (Figure 1.7).

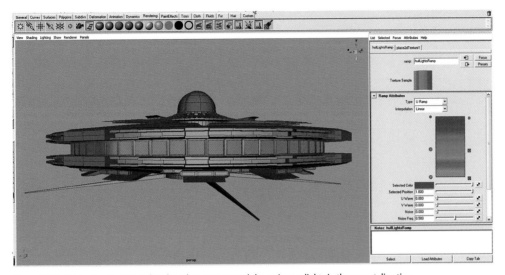

Figure 1.7: Switching to a U ramp makes the colors wrap around the perimeter lights in the correct direction.

6. Much better. Now edit the ramp so that the top is yellowish orange and the bottom is black. Delete the green color in the middle by clicking on the box next to the green area on the ramp display in the Attribute Editor. Move the black color marker halfway up the ramp.

7. Tumble around the model and see how the lights fade from bright orange to black. Animating the lights around the ship is extremely easy.

8. In the Attribute Editor, switch to the place2D Texture node for the ramp texture. Rewind to the start of the animation, right-click over the first field in the Translate Frame attributes (this is the field for the U coordinates' position), and choose **Set Key**.

9. Move to frame 30, change the 0 in this field to a 1, and set another key.

10. Hit the arrow next to the Translate Frame attributes in the Attribute Editor. In the **Post Infinity** menu for the **Anim Curve Attributes**, choose **Cycle**. In each of the boxes under **inTan Type** and **outTan Type**, change the tangent type to linear by typing the word *linear*.

11. Play the animation; you'll see the ramp circle around the ship (Figure 1.8).

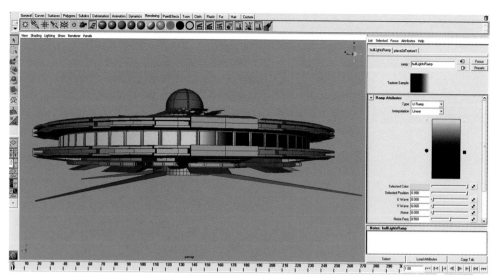

Figure 1.8: The lights now circle around the perimeter of the saucer.

Creating Glowing Lights

Now let's pump these lights up a bit. They look good, but it's kind of Close Encounters of the Blah Kind.

1. Open up the Hypershade and select the hullLightsSG node. Right-click over the swatch and choose **Graph Network**.

2. Select the green line between the hullLightsRamp and the hullLightsSG surface shader. Hit the Backspace key to delete it.

3. MMB drag the ramp over the surface shader, and choose "Other" to open the connection editor.

4. In the Connection Editor, select **Out Color** on the list on the left and **Out Glow Color** on the list on the right. In the perspective window, the lights will turn black. That's OK; they will glow when you render them.

5. Now turn the visibility of the display layers for the background objects back on and render the scene. There are some eerily glowing lights for you! (See Figure 1.9.)

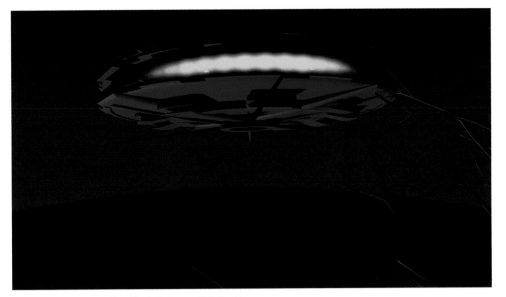

Figure 1.9: The lights now glow like the lights on a UFO should.

When using shader glow in a scene, you may encounter a flickering problem when the sequence renders. This can be fixed by opening up the shader glow node (found in the Hypershade) and turning off the **Auto Exposure** attribute. However, this will make your glowing effects much stronger and blown out. To fix this, render a still with the **Auto Exposure** option in the shader glow node turned on and then open up the output window and make a note of the **Glow Intensity Normalization Factor** value and the **Halo Intensity Normalization Factor** value. Copy these values into a text editor. Then turn off the **Auto Exposure** option on the shader glow node and copy the **Glow Intensity Normalization Factor** value into the **Glow Intensity** field and the Halo Intensity Normalization Factor into the **Halo Intensity** field. The resulting render should match your original render, but if you render an animated sequence, the flickering will be removed. It is important to remember that the shader glow node in the Hypershade sets the overall glow attributes for all incandescent shaders in the scene. Each scene can have only one shader glow node. You can adjust the glows on individual objects by changing the **Glow Intensity** or the **Incandescence** color on their shaders.

After rendering out a quick preview (check out saucer1.mov on the CD), you can see that the lights are looking pretty good. Of course, now the art director pops up behind us and says, "Wow, that's cool, can you add more lights on the bottom? And make the animation of these new lights a little more interesting."

No problem! We can use the same technique but this time will shake it up with some clever use of UV mapping.

Alternative Light Displays

Creating variations on the light displays is easy. In this section we'll see how changing the UV mapping on the light geometry changes the way the lights behave.

1. 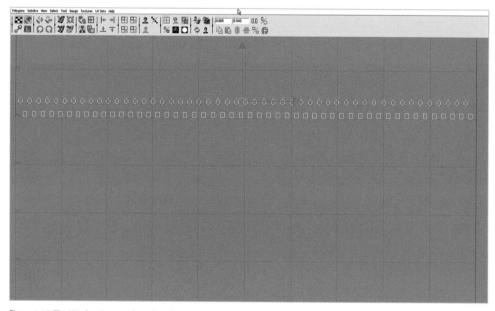 Open saucer_v02.mb from the Chapter 1 folder on the CD. Here we are with the same scene and our perimeter lights are circling around. If you'll notice, on the bottom of the saucer there is a new row of duplicated polygons constructed in the same way as the perimeter lights. In the Outliner, this object is a child of the bottomStructure group. It is named "bottomLights."

2. Select the bottomLights object and open the UV Texture Editor. You'll see that the UVs have been laid out in a horizontal row.

3. Just as with the perimeter lights, assign a surface shader to the bottomLights object and drop a ramp in its **Out Color** channel. Name the surface shader "bottom-LightsSG" and the ramp "bottomLightsRamp." Set the ramp type to **U Ramp**.

4. Adjust the ramp so that it's bright red at the top and fades to black about halfway down.

5. Place some keyframes on the ramp's **Translate Frame** attributes for its place2DTexture node just as you did with the perimeter lights. Remember to set **Post Infinity** to "Cycle". Set the **In Tan Type** and **Out Tan Type** to Linear.

Now the lights move around this bottom section. It is slightly more interesting since the lights follow a path that conforms to the extruded shape of the UFO's bottom section.

6. Select the bottomLights object and open the UV texture editor.

7. Starting on the left-hand side, select the UVs of every other polygon face and move them upward out of the row, but make sure they are pretty much in line (Figure 1.10).

Figure 1.10: The UVs for alternate faces have been selected and moved up in the UV Texture Editor.

8. Once you have two distinct rows of UV faces, select the top row and use the Scale tool to invert the UVs sideways (alternatively, you can use the Rotate tool, just as long as this row of UVs is reversed from its original direction).

When you play the animation, you'll see the lights now alternate so that the sequence goes in two directions at once. You can use the animated ramp technique in conjunction with the UV layout to come up with endless variety of light patterns guaranteed to hypnotize even the most jaded UFO abductees. When you're happy with your light animation, disconnect the ramp from the out color of the surface shader and hook it up to the out glow color just as you did with the perimeter lights.

Shading the UFO Dome

For a final touch to the UFO, we'll add a psychedelic light display for the saucer's dome using another ramp texture.

1. Select the NURBS dome on the top of the UFO. Assign another surface shader to this geometry. Name the new surface shader "domeLightSG."

2. Drop a ramp in the color channel of the dome. Name this ramp "domeRamp."

3. Make sure the ramp is set to **V Ramp**.

4. Adjust the ramp so that it has three bands of lime green alternating with black; make sure the top and bottom are black (Figure 1.11).

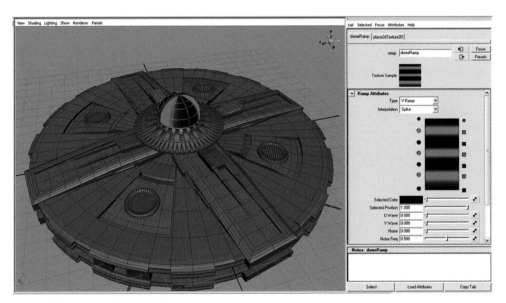

Figure 1.11: The ramp with three bands of green

5. Set interpolation to Spike so the bands are more defined.

6. Move to the place2DTexture node for this ramp and set the second field in the **Repeat UV** attribute to 3; this will increase the number of green bands on the dome.

7. Set the **Rotate Frame** value to 40 so that the bands become kind of a swirl.

8. At frame 0, right-click over the second field in the **Offset** attribute and set a key.

9. At frame 30, change the value to 1 and set another key.

10. Hit the arrow next to the offset value and in the **Anim Curve Attributes**, set the Anim Curve attribute's **Post Infinity** to Cycle, and set the **In Tan Type** and **Out Tan Type** to Linear.

Play the animation. You'll now see the dome swirling with green light—perhaps these aliens hail from some kind of '60s Go-Go planet.

For the bottomLights object and the dome shaders, you can plug the ramps into the **Out Glow** channel just as we did for the perimeter lights. To see a completed version of the scene, open saucer_v03.mb from the Chapter 1 folder on the CD.

Further Study

The exercises in this chapter really highlight the usefulness of the ramp shader and it just barely scratches the surface. The next tutorial takes these ideas to another level. Before moving on you may want to try creating alternative light display patterns by altering the UV layouts of the perimeter and bottomLights. The ramp texture applied to the dome offers up another area of experimentation; see how many variations you can create by playing with the attributes on its place2DTexture node. Try switching it to **a U Ramp** and see what other types of effects that leads to.

Streaking Energy Effects

Fresh from the success of the flying saucer shot, the art director has returned with another job. In this next scenario, a cartoon robot is seen hurtling through space. The shot calls for the robot to leave a trail of streaking, glowing energy in its path. The idea of using particles to create this effect might leap to your mind; certainly that is a viable option, but before we go down the road of tweaking emitters, fields, and goals, let's see what we can get away with using our humble ramp texture.

Know Your Glows

Glowing effects in Maya can be created in many different ways, from Optical Effects and Light Fog to the incandescence channel on a shader. It's a good idea to experiment with different ways of creating glowing effects in Maya. Find the methods that best suit you and develop them over time. Open up the glowTypes.mb scene in the Chapter 1 folder of the CD and take a look at the various settings. These are just a few of the ways glowing effects can be created in Maya.

The glowTypes.mb scene contains five different spheres with different types of glowing and incandescent effects applied. Each sphere has been placed on a different display layer. Turn off all of the layers except the blinnWithIncandescence layer and do a quick render. In the render view, store the rendered image and then go through and render each layer individually. Store the images in the Render View window (in the render view menu, choose **File** > **Keep Image In Render View**) and compare the results using the scroll bar at the bottom of the page. Then turn the visibility of all the layers on and render the spheres together. Note how the glow from one shader can bleed to the next depending on the angle of the camera (Figure 1.12). Take a look at the settings on the shaders applied to each sphere.

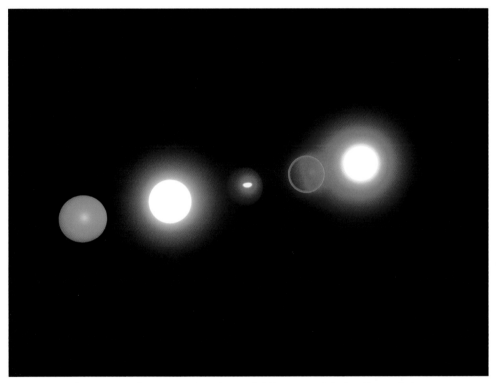

Figure 1.12: The glowTypes.mb scene shows five spheres with different types of glowing effects applied.

Open the robot_v01.mb scene from the Chapter 1 folder on the disc. Set your perspective window to camera1 and play the scene. What you'll see is a little manga-style robot flying along a motion path with the camera following. Set the Time Slider to frame 54 and do a test render. You'll see that he has a toon shader applied to his body and a glowing surface shader applied to the polygons that make up his eye. If you look in the Outliner, you'll see a pfxToon1 object. Select this object, turn its Visibility setting to On, and do another render.

Toon outlines have been applied to the object; this is represented by the pfxToon1 node. They look cool when rendered but they can slow the scene down in the OpenGL display. Once you've seen what the robot looks like with the toon lines, you can open the Attribute Editor for the pfxToonShape1 node and uncheck the **Display In Viewport** attribute, which will hide the toon lines in the perspective window but still allow it to render.

We can take advantage of the robot's motion path curve and use it to extrude a tube that will align itself to the flight path. The energy effect will be a texture applied to this tube. If we leave history on for this tube, then if changes are made to the robot's motion path, the tube will update automatically. Less work for us!

Creating the Energy Geometry

To create the streaking energy we'll first create a tube along the flight path of the robot. This tube will have a glowing texture applied to it in a later step.

1. First let's create the tube. In the Outliner, select the nurbsCircle1 object, Shift+select the motionCurve object, and switch to the Surfaces menu set. Choose **Surfaces > Extrude**. In the options, make sure you check the buttons for **Tube, At Path, Component,** and **Profile Normal**. Make sure **Curve Range** is set to Complete and the **Output Geometry** is NURBS.

2. A NURBS tube now appears along the motion curve. Select this surface and apply a surface shader to its texture. Name the shader "energyTrailSG."

3. Open the Attribute Editor for this new surface shader and click the Apply Texture button next to the **Out Color** channel. From the texture window, choose a Ramp texture. The tube now turns into the familiar red, green, blue rainbow. What a happy flight our robot is having.

4. Name the ramp "energyRamp" and switch its type setting to **U Ramp** so the colors flow along the tube.

5. Adjust the ramp so that it has three thin lines of orange and yellow separated by black (Figure 1.13).

These colored lines will be our energy streaks, but so far they look pretty goofy. They span the entire length of the tube and the robot doesn't even fit in the tube very well. What we want is for the colored streaks to trail behind the robot. We don't want them to appear in front of him.

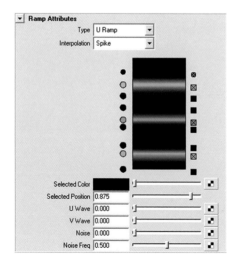

Figure 1.13:
The ramp for the robot's streaking trail of energy

Creating a Mask with a Second Ramp

To hide the parts of the tube that appear in front of the flying robot we'll create a second ramp and use it to mask the colors of the first ramp.

1. Open up the Hypershade, select the energyTrailSG surface shader that has been applied to the tube, and choose **Graph** > **Input And Output Connections** from the Hypershade menu to graph the network.

2. Break the connection between the ramp and the shader's **Out Color** channel (select the green line between the nodes and hit the Delete key).

3. Create a new ramp in the work area and connect it to the shader's **Out Color** channel. Name the new ramp "maskRamp."

We are now back to our happy rainbow tube with the colors appearing in bands along the tube. Open up the Attribute Editor for the maskRamp texture.

Notice that the ramp is a V ramp. That's great—just what we want. We changed the last ramp to a U ramp so that the colors would streak along the tube. This ramp is going to control where those streaks appear on the tube; it will in fact act as a mask and be layered on top of the previous ramp.

4. Delete the blue color at the top of the ramp. Change the green to black and the red to white.

5. Set the **Interpolation** of the ramp to None. If you look in the perspective window, you'll see that half of the tube is white and the other half is black. Select the black color marker on the ramp and move it up and down; notice how the black section of the tube expands and contracts when you do this.

In order to use this ramp as a mask, we want the white area to determine where the streaking energy will appear and the black area to determine where it will be masked. The area in which the streaks appear will then have to grow along the tube at the same rate as the robot flies along the path, so what we need to do next is animate the black part of the tube so that it diminishes in size as the robot flies along the path. We could select the black color marker on the ramp and set keyframes on its **Selected Position** attribute on the ramp, but that is kind of crude. Instead, we'll make a connection between the robot's position and the black marker's position on the ramp. This is amazingly easy.

Connecting the Ramp to the Motion Path Output Value

We'll make a connection between the robot's position on the motion path and the position of the color marker on the maskRamp so that the masking of the energy color is automated.

1. First let's take a look at something interesting: As you move the black marker up and down the ramp, the value in the **Selected Position** field change. When it is toward the bottom of the ramp, the **Selected Position** value is closer to 0; when it is toward the top, it is closer to 1 (Figure 1.14).

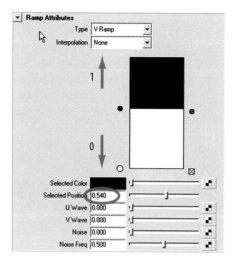

Figure 1.14:
Changing the value in the
ramp's Color Position

2. In the Outliner's Display menu, deactivate the check mark next to **DAG Objects Only**. The Outliner now shows all the nodes in the scene. Scroll down the Outliner and select the motionPath1 node. The motionPath1 node was created automatically when the animator who set up this scene attached the robot to the curve with an animated motion path. Open the Graph Editor with this node selected and select the **U Value** attribute. Take a look at the graph. (You may want to hit the F key to set the focus of the graph on this attribute; it will make it easier to see what's going on.) At the start of the animation, the **U Value** is closer to 0 when the robot is at the start of the path. At the end of the animation, the **U Value** is closer to 1 when the robot is toward the end of the path. The motion path works by animating an object along the U coordinates of a NURBS curve. We can take advantage of this by making a direct connection between the motion path's **U value** attribute and the position of the black marker on the ramp. To do this, we'll use the Connection Editor.

3. Open the Hypershade and graph the input/output connections for the energyTrailSG surface shader on the tube.

4. From the Outliner, drag the motionPath1 node onto the work area of the Hypershade (Figure 1.15).

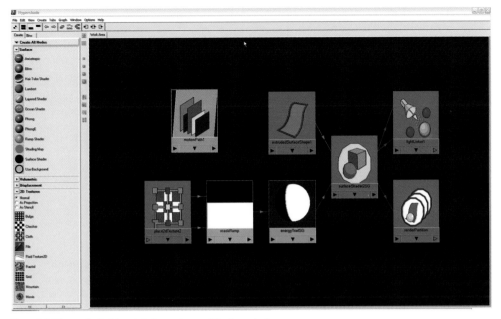

Figure 1.15: The motionPath1 node in the work area of the Hypershade.

5. From the menu at the top of the Hypershade, choose **Graph** > **Rearrange Graph** so everything becomes clearer.

6. In the Hypershade work area, MMB drag the motionPath1 swatch over the maskRamp swatch.

7. From the pop-up menu, choose **Other**.

8. The Connection Editor will open with motionPath1 on the left and maskRamp on the right (Figure 1.16).

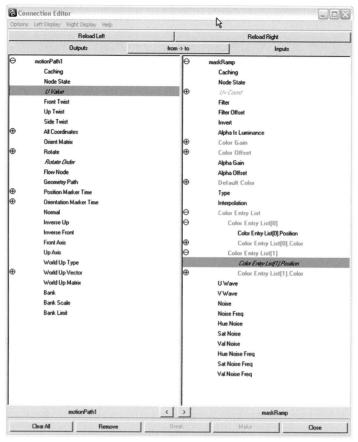

Figure 1.16: You can use the Connection Editor to hook up the motionPath1's **U Value** attribute to the position of the color marker on the maskRamp.

9. Click on the **U Value** attribute under the motionPath1 attribute list.

10. Under the maskRamp attribute list, expand the attribute group labeled **Color Entry List**. This corresponds to the color markers on the ramp. The bottom marker is usually labeled 0, and then additional markers are labeled 1, 2, 3, and so on. Expand the attribute list under **Color Entry List[1]** and **select Color Entry List[1].Position**. This will connect the **U Value** of the motion path to the position of the black marker on the ramp. Close the Connection Editor and take a look in the perspective window (Figure 1.17).

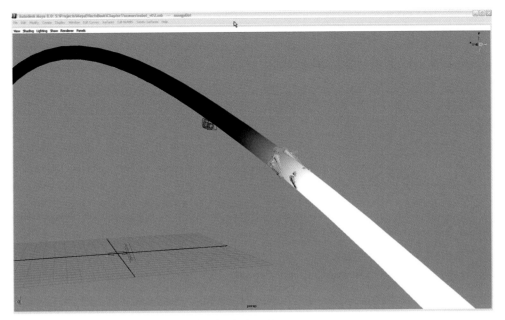

Figure 1.17: The colors on the tube now correspond to the robot's position.

As you move the Time Slider back and forth, you should see the white part of the tube move along with the robot. Making the connection between the two means less work if the timing of the robot needs to be changed later on. The white part of the ramp will always follow the flight of the robot. However, you may notice that at the very first frame of the animation, the entire tube may be white. What happened? At that point of the animation, the robot is at the very beginning of the path, the **U Value** of the motion path is 0, and thus the position of the black marker on the ramp is also 0 and so is the position of the white marker on the ramp. Maya decides to override the black color with the white color when both values are 0. The best way to fix this is to get the **U Value** of the motion path to be just a little above 0 at the start of the animation so that the black and white color positions are not on top of each other on the ramp.

11. Select the motionPath1 node from the Outliner and open the Graph Editor. Select the **U Value** attribute from the bottom of the list on the left.

12. Select the first keyframe on the graph, and in the **Stats** fields at the top of the Graph Editor, change the value in the right field to .001. This will set the keyframe above a value of 0. The tube should turn black. Play the animation and make sure the white part of the tube follows the robot. It may look fairly "steppy" or jerky as it moves, but the rendering will be smooth; it's just the OpenGL display that appears steppy.

Reconnecting the Energy Shader

Now that we have our mask working correctly, we need to reconnect everything in the energy shader.

1. Open up the Hypershade and from the materials area, drag the energyTrailSG surface shader applied to the tube down to the work area using the middle mouse button.

2. Switch to the Textures tab and drag the energyRamp down to the work area.

3. Select the energyRamp, Shift+select the energyTrailSG shader, and graph the input/output connections of the two nodes.

4. MMB drag the energyRamp over the energyTrailSG surface shader and choose **Default** from the pop-up menu. This will automatically disconnect the maskRamp from the **Out Color** channel and replace it with the energyRamp.

5. Open the Attribute Editor for the energyRamp. Take a look at the **Color Gain** attribute in the Color Balance rollout. By default, the **Color Gain** is white, meaning the colors for this texture are at full strength. If we lower this value to gray, the colors will dim—kind of like a brightness control for the colors that make up the texture. If we lower this value to black, the colors will disappear completely. We'll use this property to make our mask.

6. From the Hypershade, middle-mouse-button-drag the maskRamp over the **Color Gain** attribute in the Attribute Editor. This will place this texture in the **Color Gain** channel (Figure 1.18).

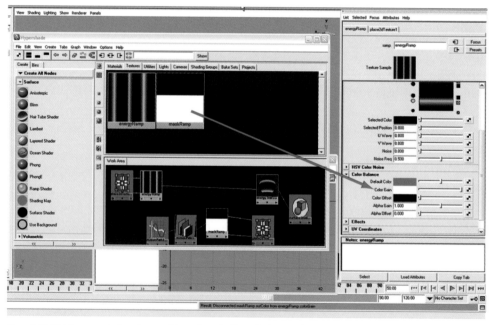

Figure 1.18: Middle-mouse-button-drag maskRamp from the Hypershade on to the color swatch for energyRamp's color gain in the Attribute Editor

Take a look at the perspective window; you can now see that the streaks follow along behind the robot.

Making It Glow

The last thing we have to do is change the texture so that the streaks look more like glowing bands of energy.

1. In the Hypershade, graph the input/output connections for the energyTrailSG surface shader applied to the tube. Select the green line that connects **energy-Ramp.outColor** to **energyTrailSG.outColor** (hold the pointer over the lines connecting the swatches in the Hypershade to see the labels). Hit the Delete key to break the connection.

2. MMB drag the energyRamp texture over the surface shader. From the pop-up menu, choose **Other**.

3. Select **Out Color** from the list on the left side and **Out Glow Color** from the list on the right.

4. Close the Connection Editor and open up the Attribute Editor for the surface shader. Set the **Out Transparency** color to white.

5. From the Hypershade, switch to the Materials tab and select the shaderGlow1 node. Open its Attribute Editor.

6. Turn off **Auto Exposure**, set the Time Slider to 35, and do a test render.

Wow, that robot is really on fire! Let's tone down the effect a little using the attributes on the shader glow node. Try these settings (listed are the settings I adjusted; you can leave the others at their defaults for now):

Glow Type:	Exponential
Halo Type:	Exponential
Threshold:	0
Glow Intensity:	0.18
Glow Spread:	0.025
Glow Eccentricity:	0.085
Halo Intensity:	.033
Halo Spread:	.015
Halo Eccentricity:	0.463

When you're happy with your settings, turn the visibility of the pfxToon lines back on and render the sequence or play the QuickTime of the animation located on the CD. The trail may look a little blocky. To smooth it out you can open the Attribute Editor for the extrudedSurface1 node and increase the settings under Simple Tesselation Options. Open robot_v02.mb from the Chapter 1 files on the CD to see a finished version of the scene (Figure 1.19).

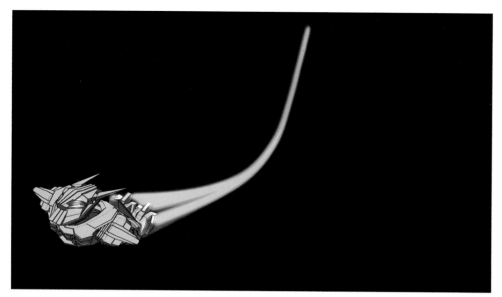

Figure 1.19: A render of the finished robot scene

Further Study

You can use the **Color Gain** on maskRamp to tone down the glow if you still feel that it is too much. You can try setting the **U Wave** value on the energyRamp to 1.0 to add the appearance of the energy twisting around the tube. You can also either add more color bars to the energyRamp or raise its repeat **U value** on the place2D texture node above the value of 1 to get more bands of color in the energy.

Layering with Multiple UV Sets: The Zombie's Hand

On to zombies! Our art director has a new shot involving a close-up on a zombie's hand. The zombie is clearly in the early stages of zombification. We need to add a disgusting black veiny creeping texture that will seal the deal on this shot. Our modeler and texture artists have provided us with a delightful hand model with creepy textures included. However, we will not be using any animated texture file sequences; instead, we are limited to the hand's color texture and a single frame of the black veiny infection texture.

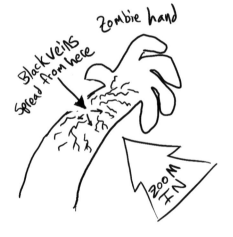

1. Open the zombieHand_v01.mb file from the Chapter 1 folder on the CD and check out the model. Select the hand model and open up the UV Texture Editor.

2. You can see the UVs laid out over the color texture that has been created in a 3D paint program. It doesn't look much like a hand. The main part of the hand is in the upper left and the five fingers are spread around on the right and bottom.

Right-click in the UV Texture panel and choose **UVs** from the marking menu to switch to the UV mode. Drag and select around each piece and note in the perspective window the corresponding pieces of the hand (Figure 1.20).

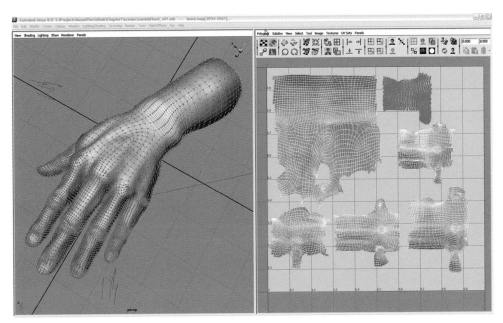

Figure 1.20: Selecting one area of the UVs causes one of the fingers to be highlighted in the perspective window.

This UV layout is OK for texturing but not great for creating our effect. The reason is that the area where we want the infection effect to be—the back of the wrist—is fairly small in this UV layout. So much of the texture coordinates have been devoted to the fingers. We don't want the infection to spread to the fingers in this shot, mainly because as the texture moves over the spaces between the wrist UVs and the finger UVs, the seams will be very obvious. Fortunately there is a way around this—UV sets.

Creating Multiple UV Sets

A polygon model in Maya can have more than one UV set, which adds a great deal of flexibility for creating texture effects (as well as texturing in general). To achieve this effect, we will use a procedural texture to create a mask that will reveal the second color map (the veiny one), gradually creating the effect of a spreading infection. We will use a layered texture in the color channel of the shader applied to the hand and a Ramp texture to create the mask. To maximize the area where the Ramp texture will be applied we will first create a new UV set for the object. This is easy to do, but the Maya interface for UV sets is not the most elegant one around.

1. First let's create a new UV set based on the UV coordinates for the wrist. In the UV Texture Editor, select some of the UVs in the large group in the upper left, the wrist area. With a few selected, you can right-click over them, scroll down in the marking menu, and choose **Select > Select Shell**. All of the UV coordinates for the wrist area should now be highlighted in green.

2. You can copy these UVs into a new empty UV set. To do this, go to the top menu bar in the UV Texture Editor and choose **Polygons > Copy UVs To UV Set > Copy Into New UV Set > Options**. In the options, type the name "infection."

3. All the UV texture coordinates for the fingers should disappear. They still exist; it's just that now you are looking at a whole new UV set with just the coordinates you had selected and copied. Confusing, isn't it? This is certainly an area of the interface that could be improved in future versions of Maya. In any case, just to make things clearer, turn off the texture display in the UV Texture Editor by clicking the face icon in the upper menu area.

4. You can switch back and forth between UV texture sets by choosing **Polygons > Set Current UV Set**. You have to type the name of the UV set into the field. The original set is called "map1," and the new one is called "infection." Try switching back and forth a few times. When you are comfortable with this workflow, switch back to the infection UV set.

5. Now we'll normalize the UVs for the wrist so they fill up the upper-right portion of the UV Texture Editor. Marquee select all the UVs in the wrist area and choose **Polygons > Normalize UVs** to do this (Figure 1.21).

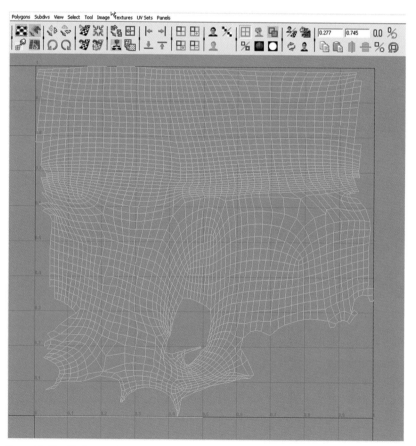

Figure 1.21: The UVs for the infection UV set have been normalized.

Notice that the texture on the hand has not changed in the perspective view. This is because we are editing the coordinates for the infection map but the color texture on the hand's shader is still linked to map1. This is exactly what we want. If the color on the hand has changed and things look really funky, it's most likely because you did not switch to the infection set and you are currently editing the map1 set. You may have to hit Undo a bunch of times or start over to fix this.

Creating the Mask for the Spreading Infection

Now that we have our UV sets created (that wasn't too hard), let's create the spreading mask effect.

1. Open up the Hypershade, select the handSG shader, and graph it in the work area. It's a very simple network: just a color and a bump texture.

2. Create a Ramp texture in the work area and drag it over the handSG group. Choose **Color** from the pop-up menu. This will automatically disconnect the painted color texture from the handSG group. The hand now turned to a happy rainbow color (Figure 1.22). Zombification has been abated! He's cured!

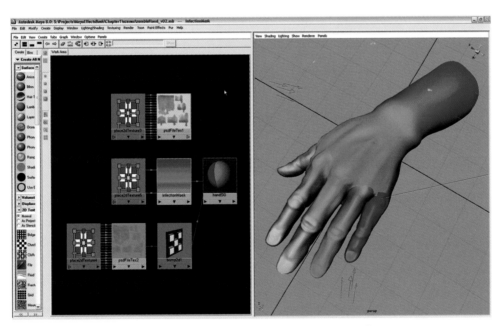

Figure 1.22: The Ramp texture has replaced the File texture applied to the handSG's color channel.

3. The rainbow color on the hand follows the map1 texture coordinates, so you'll notice the seams where coordinates for the fingers start. We'll switch the ramp so that it uses the infection UV coordinates. First change the ramp1 texture's name to "infectionMask" to make things clearer. You can open its Attribute Editor and enter the new name in the box at the top.

4. To assign the infection UV set to the infectionMask Ramp texture, select the hand model and open the Relationship Editor. To do this, choose **Window > Relationship Editors > UV Linking > Texture-Centric**.

5. In the Relationship Editor (Figure 1.23), you'll see the handSG group on the left with a list containing the infectionMask texture and psdFileTex2 texture (that's the texture assigned to the hand's bump channel; we disconnected psdFileTex1 from the color channel). On the right side of the panel you'll see the infection and map1 UV sets listed. If you click on infectionMask or psdFileTex2, you'll see map1 highlighted on the right. Click on infectionMask on the left and then infection on the right to change infectionMask's UV set. You'll see the rainbow colors shift on the hand model in the perspective window. Close the Relationship Editor when you have done this.

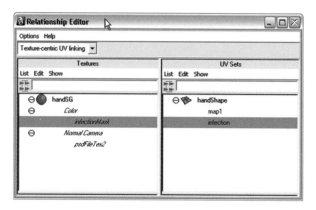

Figure 1.23:
The Relationship Editor allows you to change the UV set for a given texture.

6. Open the Hypershade and graph the network applied to the hand. Notice that there is a new uvChooser node applied to the place2Dtexture node for the ramp. It gets created automatically when you have a shader with multiple UV sets. Click on the infectionMask ramp and open its Attribute Editor.

7. Delete the green color marker; change the red color to black and the blue color to white.

8. We're going to change this black and white gradient to a splotch in the following steps. First, move the white color marker halfway down the ramp.

9. Change Interpolation to None.

10. Change the type of ramp to **Circular**.

Now we have a big black dot that's covering half the hand. If you move the white color marker on the ramp up and down, you'll see the dot grow and shrink. It may be hard to see this because the dot wraps around the hand.

11. In the Hypershade, select the place2D texture node attached to the ramp and open its Attribute Editor. Set the **Coverage** to 0.5 in both U and V. The hand becomes mostly gray. Select the hand and take a look in the UV Texture Editor. Make sure that the Display Image button is turned on.

12. You'll see that the white square with the black dot—our ramp—has moved to the lower-left corner of the texture coordinates for the UVs. We want to move it closer to the upper right. Notice that it's gray outside the white box of the ramp (Figure 1.24).

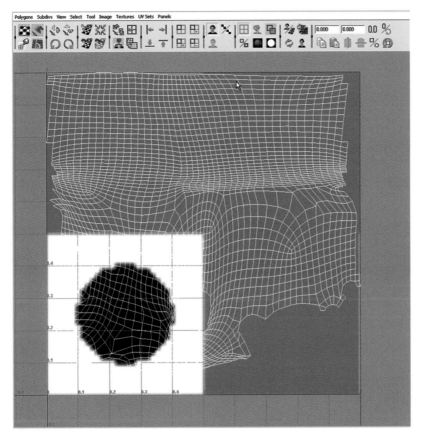

Figure 1.24: The UV Texture Editor with the circular ramp in the bottom left

13. Select the hand in the perspective window and then Shift+select the place2D texture node in the Hypershade. With the hand selected, the UVs in the UV Texture Editor won't disappear and we can see what's going on as we edit the attributes for the place2D texture node.

14. Make sure the Attribute Editor for the 2D texture node is open. In the **Translate Frame** fields, enter some numbers between 0 and 1 and watch what happens to the texture in the UV Texture Editor and the perspective window.

15. Try entering 0.5 for **U** and 0.35 for **V**. That's about where the splotch should be. If these values are not working for you, do some experimentation and try to get the dot to line up on the back of the wrist. Do a quick render of the perspective view, looking at the hand from the top.

We have a nice black dot where we want our splotch, but we also have a mostly gray hand (Figure 1.25).

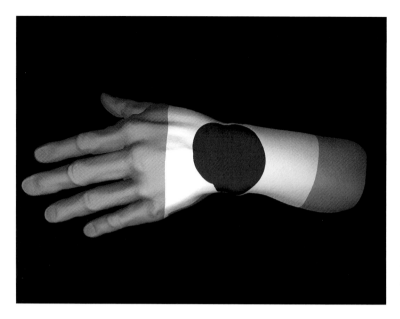

Figure 1.25:
A gray hand with a
minimalist tattoo

16. To get rid of the gray, we need to change the **Default Color** of the Ramp texture. This is the color the texture assumes from the outside of its borders on to infinity. When you lower the coverage of the texture, the **Default Color** becomes visible on the model. To change this, open the Attribute Editor of the ramp, and in the Color Balance folder, set the **Default Color** to white.

17. If you move the white marker on the ramp up and down, you'll see the dot grow and shrink. This is how we'll animate the growth of the infection.

Now we have a white hand with a black dot—looks like a mime caught a case of the black dot plague (Figure 1.26).

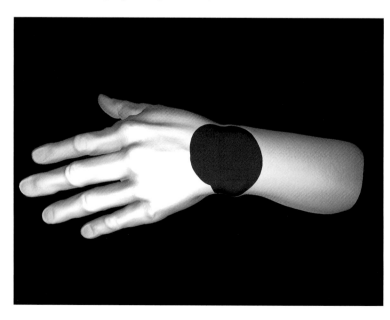

Figure 1.26:
The hand with the
infectionMask applied

Creating a Splotch

These final steps will guide you through the process of making the texture look a bit more real and creepier.

1. To break up the dotlike shape, open the ramp in the Attribute Editor and move the **Noise** Slider up to about 0.2.

2. Set the **Noise Frequency** to 2. Do a quick render.

   That's a nice splotch. As you move the white marker up and down, the splotch will grow and spread just like an infection. Those Ramp textures are handy!

3. Select the black color marker at the bottom of the ramp. In the Hypershade, switch to the Textures tab and find the psdFileTex3 node. With the Ramp texture in the Attribute Editor, middle-mouse-button-drag the icon for the psdFileTex3 node over the selected color for the black marker. When you release it, the texture will be applied to the black part of the ramp.

4. Select the hand model and open up the Relationship Editor for UV linking. Choose a texture-centric view.

5. You'll see the psdFileTex3 listed under Color. Select it and make sure that map1 is highlighted on the right side of the panel when psdFileTex3 is selected. Once you have verified this, move the camera above the hand, make sure the white color marker on the ramp is at halfway, and do a quick render. You should see the ugly black veins on the back of the hand. Move the white color marker down the ramp and render again. The veiny area should shrink.

   This is one of the more important points of this tutorial. You can have multiple UV sets for different textures—even for textures that are connected to other textures. In other words, the Ramp texture is using the infection UV set and the Vein texture (psdFileTex3) is using map1 even though it is plugged into the color marker of the ramp. We could change it but we don't want to—this is exactly what we want.

Bringing the Color Back

Now the ramp acts as a mask for the Vein texture and it's very easy to animate. Time to turn our diseased mime back into a zombie.

1. To get that fresh zombie color back into the hand model, we'll use a layered texture for the color channel. In the Hypershade, go to the Create menu and choose **Create > Layered Texture**. Open the layered texture's Attribute Editor.

2. From the Textures tab in the Hypershade window, middle-mouse-button-drag the psdFileTex1 texture to the right of the green box in the **Layered Texture Attributes**. A blue box will appear representing this texture in the layered texture (Figure 1.27).

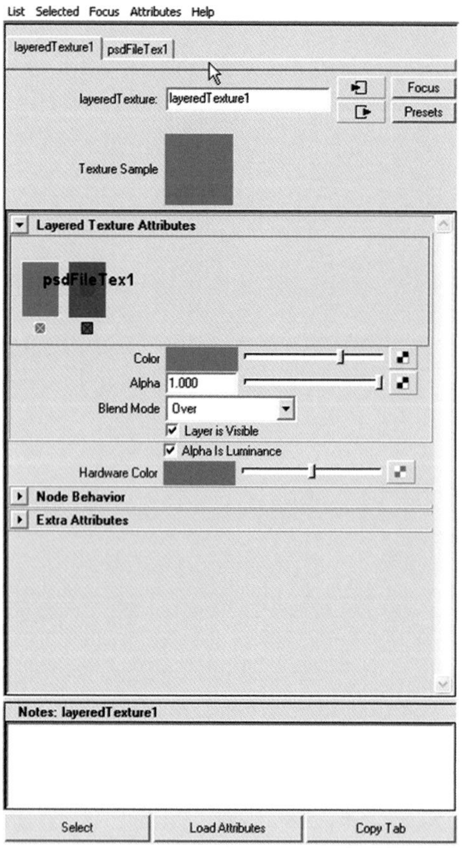

Figure 1.27:
The **Layered Texture Attributes**; the blue box represents psdFileTex1.

3. Click the check box under the green box to delete the green placeholder. Notice that when you hover your mouse pointer over these nondescript green and blue boxes, the name of the texture appears. This is one of the few ways you have to keep things straight with layered textures.

It's also quite easy to create extra layers by accident, either by double-clicking on the layered texture in the Hypershade or by clicking in the gray Layered Texture Attributes box in the Attribute Editor. This may cause your File textures to disappear on the model because they are being blocked by these new textures. If this happens, just delete the new green boxes.

4. Middle-mouse-button drag the infectionMask ramp from the Hypershade to the right of the blue box in the Layered Texture Attributes box.

5. Switch the order of these two textures in the Layered Texture Attributes window by middle-mouse-button-dragging the blue box representing the psdFileTex1 texture to the right of the blue box representing the infection ramp. (Boy, they could give us icons or something here just to make it clearer.)

6. Click on the blue box representing the infectionMask texture. In the attributes below, set **Blend Mode** to Multiply. You should see the psdFileTex1 icon appear in the Texture Sample 1 box above.

7. In the Hypershade work area, select the layered texture (you may have to hover the mouse pointer over the icon to see the name; right now it looks exactly like the psdFileTex1 texture), middle-mouse-button-drag it on top of the handSG shader, and choose **Color** from the pop-up window. This will automatically disconnect the ramp from the color channel and replace it with the layered texture. Do a quick render when it's done.

8. Now our zombie skin color is back, but he's got a black veiny texture growing on his wrist. Select the infectionMask ramp again, and in its Attribute Editor, switch **Interpolation** to **Spike**. This will soften the look of the area at the edges of the infection. Do a quick render—so that there is zombie juice flowing in his veins.

9. Animating this texture is so simple, the undead could do it! Open the Attribute Editor for the infection ramp. Select the white color marker and move it toward the bottom of the ramp to about position .015.

10. Make sure the Timeline is set to frame 1. Right-click over the field for the selected position for the white color and choose **Set Key**.

11. Move the Time Slider to frame 100. Move the white color marker all the way to the top and set another key on its selected position (Figure 1.28).

    You can try rendering the whole sequence or check out the QuickTime file on the CD.

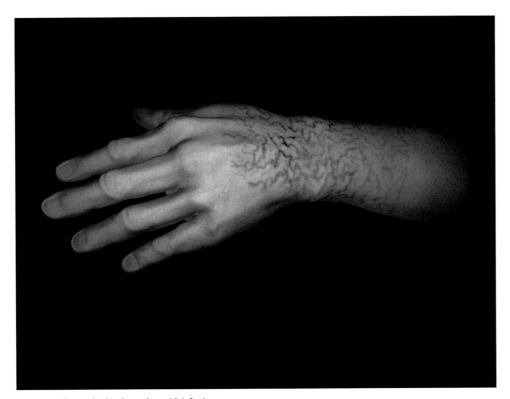

Figure 1.28: The zombie hand complete with infection

Abusing Ambient Occlusion: The Sci Fi Scanner

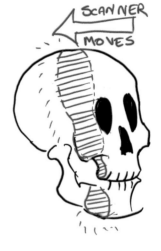

Our indefatigable art director has popped up with a new assignment. She would like to have a shot in which a character's skull is being scanned; we are to create a computer display for the scanning device. A ray of green light passes through the skull highlighting its contours in sort of a cross sectional fashion. Now, there are plenty of ways to create this effect but we're going to try something slightly wacky just to see what happens. We'll be repurposing mental ray's Ambient Occlusion node for something other than its intended function. (BWAH HA HA HA HA HA!)

The Ambient Occlusion texture is commonly used as a quick way to achieve the look of global illumination but without as much calculation. When the Ambient Occlusion node is connected to a shading network, the camera will shoot rays into the scene and test the region within a hemispherical area. If there is geometry within a certain distance of the surface with the occlusion texture applied, or if that part of the surface is occluded (blocked from view) by geometry, then the texture will make that part of the surface appear darker. This simulates the way that, in the real world, when two objects are very close to each other, a certain amount of ambient light is blocked and you get darkness near the edges where the two objects are close. It's kind of like a type of ambient light shadow.

However, we are not going for this particular look. Instead we're going to mess with the settings on the Ambient Occlusion node and take advantage of these properties to create a unique look.

1.　　⊚　Open the skullScan_v01.mb file from the Chapter 1 directory on the CD. Do a quick render from the perspective camera. In the view window, you may want to switch to wire frame just so you can see what's going on.

2.　　There's our skull with an eerie blue glow around it (Figure 1.29). If you look at a graph of the shader applied to the skull, you see that it has a pretty typical x-ray type shader applied to it. This shader uses the Surface Info node to control the positions of colors on a ramp. The ramp is then plugged into the incandescence of the shader. Parts of the geometry that are facing away from the camera at glancing angles will glow and parts that are more perpendicular to the camera are dark. Take a few minutes to examine how the shader works if you're not familiar with this technique.

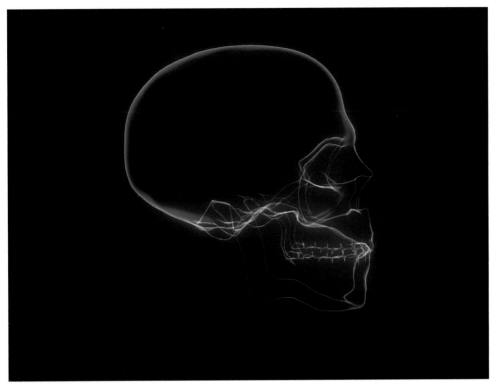

Figure 1.29: A rendering of the scene shows a skull model with fairly typical X-ray style shader applied.

3. Look in the Outliner and expand the scanner group. Along with the skull geometry, there is a hidden plane labeled "slice1." Look in the Channel Box for slice1 and turn the visibility on for this object. If you scrub through the animation on the Timeline, you'll see that the slice1 plane is keyframed so that it continually moves through the skull from front to back. This plane will become our scanner.

4. In the Render Settings window, switch to mental ray and select **Production** from the **Preset Render Settings** menu.

> If mental ray does not appear in the list, open up the Plug-in Manager by choosing **Window** > **Settings/Preferences** > **Plug-in Manager**. In the list of plug-ins, make sure Mayatomr.mll is checked for loaded and auto-load. Now when you go back to the Render Settings window, you should see mental ray loaded.

So think about how the Ambient Occlusion node works. It's essentially shading an object a certain way if geometry is close to it and shading it a different way if geometry is not close to it. The Ambient Occlusion node allows you to alter these parameters and change the distance and the intensity of the effect. Open the Hypershade, create a mib_amb_occlusion node, and take a look at its settings in the Attribute Editor (the mib_amb_occlusion node is found under the **Create** > **Mental Ray Textures** menu in the Hypershade). Open the Attribute Editor for this node. Notice that there are sliders for the **Bright** and **Dark** colors. Who's to say we can't put a light color in **the Dark Color** channel and a dark color in the **Bright Color** channel? It's not like the Maya police are going to show up if we put a texture in these channels, either. I mean, the texture node buttons are right there next to the sliders just crying out to be messed with. OK, so let's mess with them.

Creating the Scanner Shader

1. In the Outliner, expand the scanner group and select the object labeled "slice1."
2. Open the Hypershade, create a Lambert shader, and apply it to slice1.
3. Rename this shader "scannerShader."
4. Open the scannerShader in the Attribute Editor and set the **Transparency Color** to white so that the slice1 object is essentially invisible.
5. Open up the Hypershade and right-click over the scannerShader. Choose **Graph Network** from the pop-up marking menu.
6. Create an Ambient Occlusion texture (you can find this node listed under the Create mental ray textures list). If you've already created one, you can grab it from the Textures tab in the Hypershade and drag it down to the work area.
7. Middle-mouse-button-drag the mib_amb_occlusion texture over the scanner shader and choose **Incandescence** from the pop-up marking menu.
8. Open up the Ambient Occlusion texture in the Attribute Editor. Set the **Bright Color** to black and choose a mid to dark green for the **Dark Color** (0, 0.653, 0 for the RGB values works pretty well).
9. Set the Time Slider to 35 and do a test render.

That's pretty cool but a little intense. In the Attribute Editor for the Ambient Occlusion node, change **Max Distance** from 0 to .25. You might think that a 0 setting would cause it to sample no distance, but in fact it means that the entire scene is sampled. Setting **Max Distance** to .25 will tune the effect a little and give us more detail and less of a blown-out look (Figure 1.30).

You can also try adjusting the spread and the **Falloff** to tune the effect. **Spread** determines the size of the area above the point that is sampled. In this case, a small setting will look slightly brighter than a setting of 1. A lower **Falloff** setting will make the effect more intense for areas where geometry is close together and softer (or in our case, dimmer) for those areas that are farther apart. **Falloff** modifies the **MaxDistance** value so it has no effect unless there is a non-zero setting **in Max Distance**.

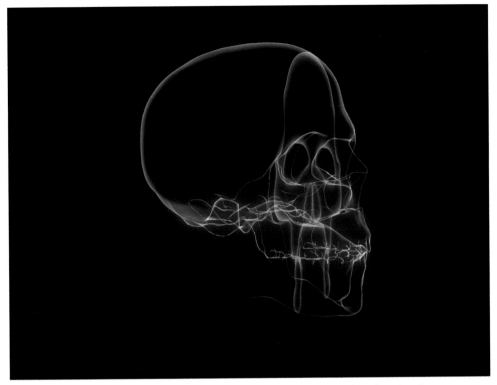

Figure 1.30: The plane intersecting the skull shows up when the Ambient Occlusion node is plugged in to incandescence.

Tuning the Shader

1. In the Attribute Editor for the Ambient Occlusion node, hit the Texture button next to the **Dark Color** attribute (the attribute that you changed to green). In the texture panel, choose Grid.

2. In the attributes for the grid texture, change **Line Color** to a medium green and **Filler Color** to a dark green.

3. Set **U Width** to 0, **V Width** to 0.25, and **Contrast** to 0.85.

4. In the place2D Texture node for the grid texture, set **Repeat U Value** to 0 and **Repeat V Value** to 200 (Figure 1.31).

5. Test render the frame now. Pretty cool. You can render out the whole animation or check out the QuickTime render skullScan.mov on the CD. For a finished example of the scene, open skullScan_v02.mb in the Chapter 1 files on the CD.

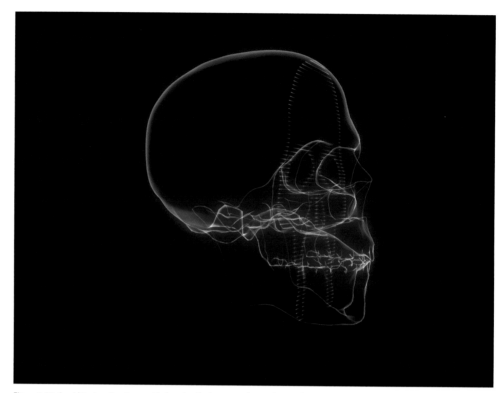

Figure 1.31: A grid texture has been added to the shader network to enhance the scanner look.

Further Study

This technique has a wide range of applications. Try attaching the Ambient Occlusion texture to the incandescence of a shader applied to a wall. In the same way, set a light color for the **Dark Color** attribute and black for the **Bright Color** attribute. Place an invisible hand model near the wall for a very spooky ghostly hand print effect. Check out the spookyHand.mb file on the CD for an example (Figure 1.32).

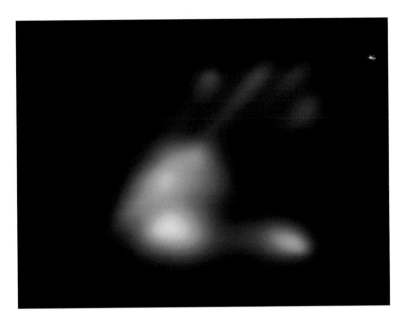

Figure 1.32:
With the Ambient Occlusion node plugged into the incandescence of the wall shader, the hand print only appears when the hand is close to the wall. Mulder?

In Figure 1.33, the geometry behind the text has the same technique applied to its shader to create a glow behind the 3D text.

Figure 1.33:
This same technique can be used to simulate backlighting for logos.

Controlling Particles with Textures: Swimming Bacteria

This last exercise kind of segues to the next chapter on particles. Our art director has presented us with the problem of creating some swimming bacteria to be seen under a microscope. To make the bacteria look like they're alive and kicking, we'll use some ramps to control the direction in which the bacteria are moving. We'll be starting with a blank scene.

Creating the Particle and Goals

Particle motion is commonly controlled through the use of fields, goals, and expressions, or any combination of the three. Almost anything can be a goal for a particle object, even other particles. In this exercise we'll see what happens when two particle objects become each other's goal object.

1. Start a new file, switch to the Dynamics menu set, and create two emitter objects by choosing **Particles** > **Create Emitter** twice.

2. Select each emitter and move them apart at least 10 units on the grid.

3. Go into the Attribute Editor for each emitter and set Type to **Omni**, set **Rate** to 25 particles per second, and make sure **Speed** is at 1.

4. We're going to make a goal for both particles. A goal is like a magnet that attracts the particles; the strength of the magnet is dependent on the goal weight. In this case, we are going to make each particle a goal for the other particle and vice versa. In other words, each individual particle will attract a particle from the other emitter and that particle will attract its opposite. Should be interesting. In the Outliner, select particle1 and then Control+select particle2. Choose **Particles** > **Goal** and open the options.

5. In the options, set **Goal Weight** to 1.0 and make sure that **Use Transforms As Goal** is off. If it is on, then the center of the particle object would be the goal instead of the individual particles and that's not what we want. Click Create to apply these settings.

6. Now select particle2, Control+select particle1, and choose **Particles** > **Goal** to apply the same settings for particle2.

7. Make sure the Time Slider is at least 300 frames and play the animation. Wow, that's not very interesting.

8. The **Goal Weight** for each particle is set to 1, so the particles reach each other in almost no time. In the Channel Box for the particle1 and particle2 shapes, scroll down and set **Goal Weight** for each particle to 0.5. Play the animation and see what happens.

OK, that's slightly more interesting, but not very bacterial. Let's see how we can control the goal weights using some Ramp textures.

Creating the Ramps

The goal weight for the particles will be assigned by the values on a Ramp texture. The initial values will be derived by assigning the goal weight to a random position along the ramp, and from there the weight value will move up the ramp as time goes by. As the goal weight moves through bands of different colors, the value will change. This has some advantages over creating an expression for the goal weight in that it's easier to set up and easier to tune when you need to adjust the animation. However, a few simple expressions will be involved in the setup. First make sure the goal weights for the two particle objects have been set back to 1.0 and proceed with the following steps:

1. Open up the Attribute Editor for particleShape1. In the **Emission Attributes,** set the **Max Count** value for the particle object to 200.

2. We need an attribute that will give us a random initial placement along the ramp for the goal weight of each particle. To do this, we'll create a simple custom attribute. Under the Add Dynamic Attributes rollout, click the General button.

3. In the Add Attribute panel, type **startWeight** for the attribute name.

4. Set **Data Type** to Float (meaning a number that can have a decimal value), and set **Attribute Type** to Per Particle (Array) so that each particle can have a different value assigned. Click the OK button to add the attribute (Figure 1.34).

Figure 1.34: Creating the **startWeight** attribute

5. In the Per Particle Array Attributes list, you should see the new **startWeight** attribute. If it does not appear, click the Load Attributes button at the bottom of the panel.

6. In the blank slot next to the **startWeight** attribute, right-click and choose **Creation Expression**. In the Expression Editor's main box, type the following expression:

```
seed(particleId);
particleShape1.startWeight=rand(0,.5);
```

7. Click the Create button to create the expression. If you get an error message, double-check and make sure you typed it in correctly. This expression just says that as each particle is created (it's a creation expression), it is born with its **startWeight** attribute set to a random value from 0 to .5 (Figure 1.35). The seed attribute ensures that the seed value for the random number generator is consistent so that you'll get the same random values generated each time you open the file. This helps especially when sharing the file with other animators. In this case, the **seed** value is set to the ID number of each individual particle.

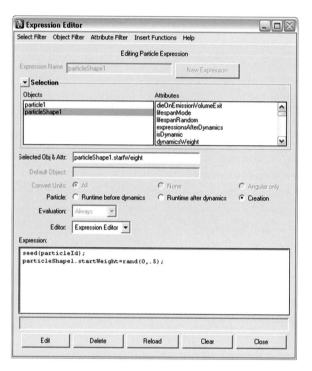

Figure 1.35:
The creation expression for
the **startWeight** attribute

8. Next we'll create the Ramp texture for the goal weight. In the space next to the **goalPP** attribute in the Per Particle Array Attribute list, right-click and choose **Create Ramp** from the pop-up menu. Open the options.

9. In the options, set the **inputV** to **startWeight**.

10. Click OK to add the ramp.

11. Right-click in the same slot again and choose **Edit Ramp**. Edit the ramp so that there are bands of gray and dark gray (almost black) up and down the Ramp texture (Figure 1.36).

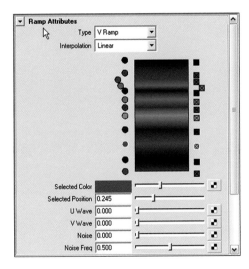

Figure 1.36:
The ramp has a series of gray and dark gray bands; these will determine the value for each particle's goal weight.

12. Go back and repeat steps 1 through 11 for particle2. When you're done, play the animation and note the movement of the particles. Make the goalPP ramp for particleShape2 different from the ramp used for particleShape1.

It's kinda neat but not quite germy enough. The particles are moving about and attracting each other randomly, but it needs something more. First let's see what we can do about the goal weights. It's obvious from the fact that different particles move at different rates that the individual particles have different weights. We can even see what the rates are by changing the particle type.

Adjusting the Ramps

We can see the goal weight value for each particle by switching the particle's Render Type to "numeric". This will help us as we adjust the ramp to create a more natural movement.

1. Under the particle Render Type for particle1, set the type to **Numeric**.
2. Click the Add Attributes For Current Render Type button.
3. In the Attribute Name field, replace "particleID" with "goalPP."
4. Play the animation and try to follow the numbers (Figure 1.37). The higher the number, the faster the particle. These numbers are derived from the values of the colors on the ramp attached to the **goalPP** attribute. You can make sure that these numbers are coming from the ramp by going to the Ramp texture assigned to **goalPP** and deleting all the colors except one. When you play the animation, you'll see that all of the goal weights are now equivalent to the value for the color of that last remaining marker on the map. Actually, since the **startWeightRampPos** value was set from 0 to 0.5, these values are really coming from the lower part of the ramp. There's a reason for doing this.

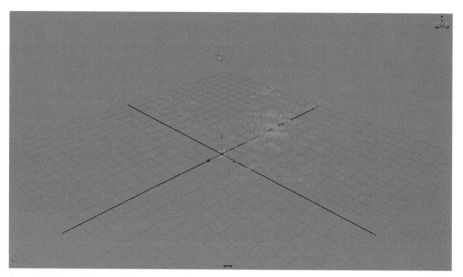

Figure 1.37: The particles set to the numeric render type. The goal weight values for each particle can now be seen.

5. We want to make it so that as time goes on, the goal weight for each particle changes randomly. We can do this by adding another simple expression. Open the Attribute Editor for particleShape1. Right-click over the slot next to the Start Weight value. Choose **Runtime Before Dynamics**.

6. In the Expression box type this:

```
particleShape1.startWeight= particleShape1.startWeight+.01;
```

7. With this expression added to each frame, the **startWeightRampPos** value will move up the ramp in increments of .01. Play the animation and watch the numeric values move up. The numbers will change over time according to the values of the colors in the bands on the ramp. Add this same expression to the **startWeight** attribute of particleShape2.

8. It's kind of cool, there's a springy back and forth motion to the movement of the particles. It needs just a little more to keep the motion random. Does this mean adding more expressions and ramps? Nah, just add a turbulence field. Select particle1 and choose **Fields > Turbulence**. In the options set **Attenuation** to 0 and **Magnitude** to 10.

9. Do the same for particle2 so that each particle has its own turbulence field (Figure 1.38).

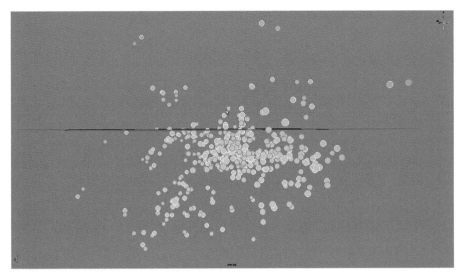

Figure 1.38: The particles set to the blobby surface render type. The ramps on the goal weights make them appear as though they are swimming bacteria.

Now when you play the animation, things start to look germy, in a good way!

Further Study

Applying ramps to per-particle goals is just the beginning. You can use similar techniques on the **rampPosition**, **rampVelocity**, and **rampAcceleration** values as well as your own custom attributes. Here are some suggestions for further tuning the scene you have just created.

1. In the Array Mapper for the ramps applied to the **goalPP** for each particle, set the **Max Value** to 0.5. This will restrict the value range so that none of the weights are higher than 0.5. This may slow down the faster particles. You can also set the array mapper's **Max Values** to different numbers for the ramps applied to each particle just to see what happens. Alternatively, you can adjust the color gain on the ramps to bring the upper limit of the colors down or raise the color offset to boost the lower range.

2. Lower the **Conserve** value for the particles. A setting of 0.8 for each will lead to some wild spiral effects.

3. Randomize the phase values for the turbulence values. To do this, open the Attribute Editor for turbulenceField1, right-click over the **PhaseX** value, and add an expression. The expression turbulenceField1.phaseX=noise(time); is a good one.

4. As we all know, salmonella propels itself through the cytoplasm of a cell by building a tail made of actin filaments; they tend to look like little jets. You didn't know that? Hey, all the cool kids know their microbiology. In any case, you can simulate this effect by turning the particle1 and particle2 objects into emitters and then setting a very low value for each emitted particle's life span.

5. To create the look of the bacteria, you can try particle instancing with a modeled object, or if the bacteria are going to be very small, using blobby surfaces works quite well.

Particle Effects

Particle dynamics are at the heart of creating effects animations. They bring a chaotic sense of spontaneity to computer-generated images that breathes life into a scene. They're also a lot of fun to play with. This chapter dives right in and assumes that you have some working knowledge of particle systems in Maya. Some expressions and even a tiny bit of MEL will be used in these scenes. Mostly we are concerned with how we can use particles in different ways to make difficult effects assignments a little easier.

2

Chapter Contents
Particle Instancing and Expressions: Creating a 3D Audio Meter
Particle Collisions: The Classic Force Field Effect
Instancing with Paint Effects: Pushing Up the Daisies
Using Cycle Emission: The Plasma Ball
Influencing Cameras with Particles

Here are a few things to note before we get going with particle systems. It's good practice to create and use particle disk caches. When you create a disk cache, Maya writes the particle location information for each frame to disk. This improves performance on your machine and also allows you to scrub back and forth on the Timeline when tuning the animation. However, you must also remember to delete and re-create the particle disk cache if any changes are made to the simulation. Otherwise, you may change a parameter on an emitter or a field and wonder why the changes aren't reflected in the animation.

Caches are also useful when working on a network system. You'll get a faster response from a cache on your local system than from one on a network drive; however, if you decide to use a network rendering system, you need to be sure that the render software has access to the particle disk cache or the results can be unpredictable. In addition, you can set the particle disk cache to work only on selected systems; this way, if you have several systems in a scene, you can progressively add the systems to your cache until you have something you like.

If you use random functions in your particle expressions, it's good practice to use the seed function and specify its value. This ensures that the random values will be the same each time the particle system is simulated regardless of which machine it's on. In the last tutorial of the previous chapter, we set the seed function to be determined by the particle's ID for a per-particle array attribute.

```
seed(particleId);
```

It's a good idea to stick this line in your code whenever you're using a random function.

The particle instancer is an extremely powerful tool. I introduce it in several tutorials in this chapter, but I really only scratch the surface of what can be done with the instancer. The instancer allows you to place a copy of a piece of geometry at the location of each particle in a simulation. The instances can be animated in a cycle and even have their rotation and position controlled by a custom per-particle attributes. However, it's important to know that some per particle array attributes, such as color and opacity, will have no direct effect on the instanced geometry. Some additional research and practice may be necessary before you are completely comfortable with the particle instancer.

Finally, in large scenes using a multitude of instanced particles, you may want to explore the use of Level of Detail MEL scripts, which can improve performance by swapping lower-resolution geometry for those instances that are a certain distance from the camera. Scripts like these can be found on the Internet at websites like www.high-end3d.com.

Particle Instancing and Expressions: Creating a 3D Audio Meter

The art director has a commercial project for you for a local chain of car audio specialists. The shot consists of creating an LED audio meter display in 3D. The camera will pan around the LED display, so it really needs to be in 3D as opposed to an animated texture.

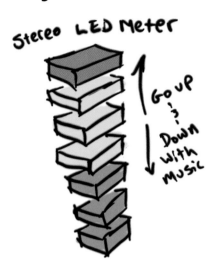

To create this shot, all we really need are some particles, a couple cubes, some lights, and a simple expression. Let's get to it.

1. Open up Maya to a new, empty scene.

2. Switch to the front camera, turn on grid snapping, and from the Dynamics menu set, choose **Particles > Particle Tool > Options**.

3. In the options, set **Particle Name** to audioMeter1. Click the Create Particle Grid check box and set **Particle Spacing** to 1. For Placement, choose With Text Fields. Set **Minimum Corner** to 0 in X, Y, and Z. Set Maximum Corner to 0 in X, 10 in Y, and 0 in Z.

4. In the front view, with the Particle tool active, right-click and hold the button down. In the marking menu that appears, drag upward to the box that says Complete Tool. A tower of 11 evenly spaced particles should appear at the origin. This will become our audio level meter (our meter goes up to 11; that's one more than 10!).

5. Once you have completed your tower of particles, switch to the perspective view and choose **Create > PolygonPrimitives > Cube**.

6. Scale the cube so it's wide and flat (2 x 0.3 x 1).

7. Duplicate this cube three times for a total of four cubes. Name the first one "lightOff," the second "greenLight," the third "yellowLight," and the fourth "redLight."

8. Assign a Lambert shader to lightOff. Make it completely transparent and set **Matte Opacity** to 0.

9. Assign Lambert shaders to greenLight, yellowLight, and redLight. Set the colors of these shaders to green, yellow, and red respectively.

10. Create a locator and name it "meter1." Figure 2.1 shows all the parts of the audio meter.

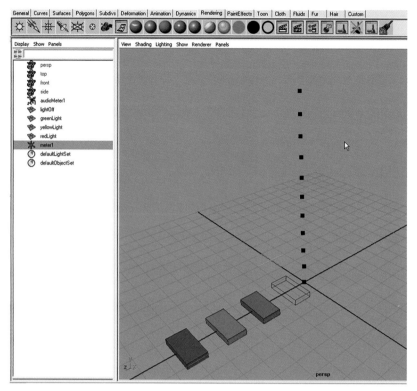

Figure 2.1: The ingredients for the audio meter. The point size on the particles has been scaled up so that they are easier to see.

Using the Instancer

We have all our basic ingredients. We're using particles to create this shot simply because it provides us with a very easy way to swap objects on-the-fly. Essentially, the cubes will be instanced to the particles. We'll use the particles' IDs to determine which colored cube will be assigned to which particle and then we'll use the locator's Y position to determine when the lights are on or off.

1. In the Outliner, Ctrl+select lightOff, greenLight, yellowLight, and redLight, in that order.

2. Choose **Particles > Instancer (Replacement) > Options**.

3. Choose **Edit > Reset Settings** to ensure that the default settings are loaded. Make sure **Cycle** is set to None. The Particle Object To Instance option should be set to audioMeter1Shape (Figure 2.2). There's only one particle object in the scene so far, so this setting will default to the correct option; however, in a scene with more than one particle object, it is important to double-check this setting and make sure the correct particle object—the one you want the geometry instanced to—is selected. Click Create to apply these settings.

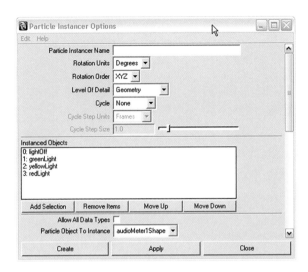

Figure 2.2:
The options for the
particle instancer

The transparent lightOff cube has been used to replace the particles. If you are
in shaded mode, it may look as though nothing has happened—you may want to turn
on Wireframe On Shaded in the perspective window's Shading options just so you can
see what's going on.

4. In the Outliner, select the instance1 node and open its Attribute Editor. In the
instanced object panel you should see that lightOff is at the top of the list in the
0 position. GreenLight is at 1, yellowLight is 2, and redLight is 3. The numbers
are the object index values that we will reference in our expression.

5. Select the audioMeter1 object and open the Attribute Editor for its shape node.
Under Render Attributes, set **Particle Render Type** to **Numeric**; by default the
particleId value will appear in place of the particles (Figure 2.3). The values go
from 0 to 10—that's 11 values total.

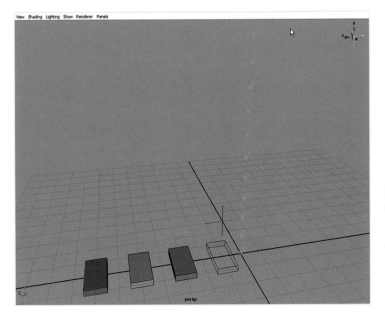

Figure 2.3:
The particles have
been switched to
the numeric ren-
dering type. The
numbers indicate
each particle's ID.

6. Under the **Add Dynamic Attributes** menu, click the General button to create a new attribute. In the Add Attribute panel, enter the name "instanceMe." Set **Data Type** to Float and **Attribute Type** to Per Particle (Array) and leave **Add Initial State Attribute** selected. Click OK to create the custom attribute (Figure 2.4).

Figure 2.4:
The settings in the Add Attribute window for the custom instanceMe attribute

7. In the field next to the new **instanceMe** per particle array attribute, right-click and choose **Runtime Before Dynamics Expression**. The Expression Editor will open up.

8. So the expression we'll make is a basic if statement. It assigns an object index number to each particle based on its **particleId** attribute. This index number will then be used to assign the cubes to the particles. If the **particleId** is 0 or greater but less than 6, then the object index will be 1 (or green); if it's 6 or greater but less than 9, it will be 2 (or yellow); if it's 9 or greater, it will be 3 (or red).

9. First let's get the right-colored cube in the right place. Type the following code into the Expression box in the Expression Editor. While this is not the most elegant way to create this expression, it is very easy to read (see Figure 2.5).

```
if ((particleId >= 0)&&(particleId <= 5))
   {
   instanceMe=1;
   }
else if ((particleId >= 6) && (particleId <= 8))
   {
   instanceMe=2;
   }
else if (particleId >= 9)
   {
   instanceMe=3;
   }
```

Proper expression syntax in Maya requires that you end each command with a semicolon. Sometimes the Expression Editor allows for more space than can be displayed on the printed page in this book. Therefore, you should keep in mind that even though the expressions printed in this book often have line breaks before the end of the command, you do not have to follow suit. Use the semicolons as a guide for where you need to press the Enter key in the Expression Editor at the end of the command.

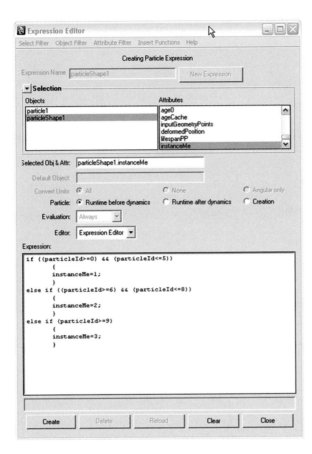

Figure 2.5:
The expression as seen in the Expression Editor

The && means *and*, >= means *greater than or equal to*, and <= means *less than or equal to*. When working in the Expression Editor, you can save some time by just referencing the attribute. If you type instanceMe, the editor will assume you mean audioShape1.instanceMe and you'll see this filled in when you go back to edit the expression. However, if you are creating an expression that references another particle shape's attribute, be sure to write in the full name and attribute or you may get some strange results.

10. Click the Create button to create the expression. If you get an error message, look over what you've written and make sure there are no typos. It happens to everyone.

11. If the expression checks out OK, scroll up to the Instancer (Geometry Replacement) attributes in the particle's Attribute Editor. Under General Options, set **ObjectIndex** to **instanceMe** (Figure 2.6).

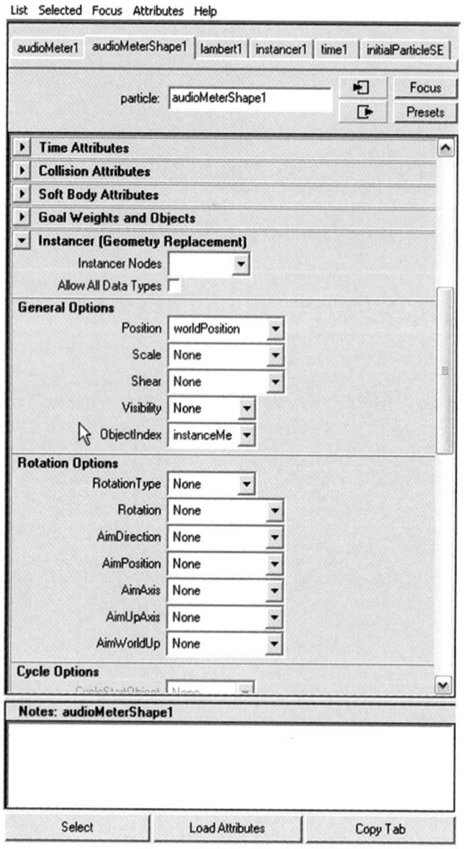

Figure 2.6:
The Instancer options in the particle's Attribute Editor. Setting the object index to the custom **instanceMe** attribute is an easy step to forget!

12. Hit play on the Timeline; the boxes should jump to the right spot. You may see them blink off every time the play marker hits frame 0. If this is the case, copy the whole expression and switch to the Creation expression mode by clicking on the button next to Creation in the Expression Editor. Paste the expression into the Expression box for the **instanceMe** attribute.

Creation expressions calculate at the start of the simulation or when a particle is born from an emitter. We don't have an emitter in this scene since we drew the particles on the grid, so generally speaking we can use a runtime before dynamics expression. However, we get that blinking where the cubes are not instanced according to the expression on the first frame of the animation. Copying the runtime expression into the creation expression area will take care of the blinking.

Runtime expressions calculate on each frame of the simulation. If you set the oversampling (**Solvers > Edit Oversampling Or Cache Settings**) to a number higher than 1, the expression will calculate multiple times per frame based on the oversampling setting.

13. Now that we have the meter with the right boxes in the right places, let's edit it so that the boxes with a Y value greater than the Y value of the locator have their instances swapped out with the invisible noLight object. That way, moving the meter up and down in Y will make animating the meter very easy. Edit the runtime expression on the **instanceMe** attribute so it reads like the following (Figure 2.7):

```
float $meterY=meter1.translateY;
vector $partPos= position;

if ($partPos.y > $meterY)
  {
  instanceMe=0;
  }
else if ((particleId >= 0) && (particleId <= 5))
  {
  instanceMe=1;
  }
else if ((particleId >= 6) && (particleId <= 8))
  {
  instanceMe=2;
  }
else if (particleId >= 9)
  {
  instanceMe=3;
  }
```

The first line creates a variable for the Y position of the meter locator. The second line creates a vector to hold the position of each particle. The first conditional statement we added at the top tests to see if the Y position of each particle is greater than the Y position of the locator. That's all there is to the expression—pretty simple really.

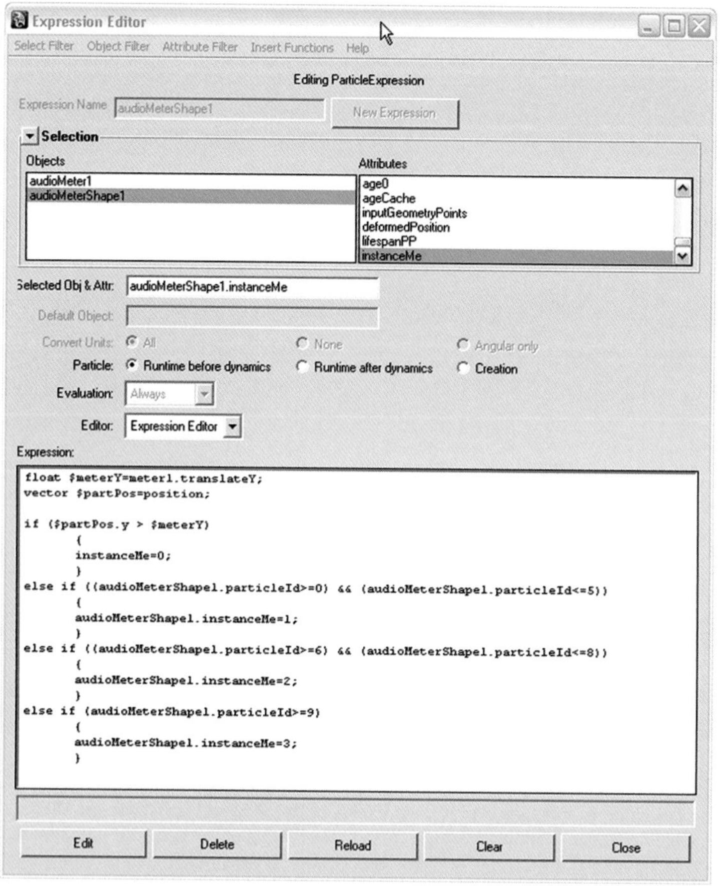

Figure 2.7:
The complete runtime expression for the particle object. Notice that Maya has added audioMeterShape1 to the attributes we referenced when we first wrote the expression.

Maya's expression language does not allow you to directly access a single value from a vector. In other words, if (particleShape1.position.y > $meterY) will not work. You first have to cast the vector into a variable and then access the value through that variable. This is why we created the $partPos variable and then wrote it in the expression as if ($partPos.y>$meterY).

14. Remember to copy the edited runtime expression to the creation expression to eliminate any blinking on frame 1.

Animating the Meter

Animating the meter is very easy, it only requires setting keyframes on the meter locator.

1. Grab the meter locator and set some keyframes on its **TranslateY** attribute. Make sure the interpolation between keys is set to Linear. Animate the locator so that it is moving up and down very rapidly as you might imagine an audio meter would for some thumping music. Keep the keys between 0 and 11.

2. After you've set a few key frames, open the Graph Editor and set the **Post Infinity** options for the curve to Cycle. Play the animation and tune it until you're happy.

Duplicating the Meter

OK, looks like we have a nice animation of a single meter. But wouldn't it be nice if there was more than one meter and if they were colored like an actual audio meter? Well, I reckon it would.

1. Creating more meters is easy. Select the audioMeter1 object and choose **Edit > Duplicate Special > Options**. In the options, click the box next to Duplicate Input Graph.

2. In the Outliner you'll notice that a new particle object and new locator have been created. Move the particle2 object over in X a little so particle1 and particle2 don't overlap.

3. Select the lightOff object, then the greenLight, yellowLight, and redLight objects (in that order!). Choose **Particles > Instancer(Replacement)** with the same settings as before but make sure Particle Object To Instance is set to audioMeter-Shape2.

4. In the Attribute Editor for audioMeterShape, set **Object Index** to **instanceMe** (all of the custom attributes and expressions have been duplicated and updated for this particle when you duplicated the input connections—now that's handy!).

5. If you play the animation you'll see that the two meters move exactly the same. This is because the animation on the duplicated meter object is the same. You can rearrange the keys on its Y translate to mix it up a bit.

6. 🔘 Repeat this process until you have as many meters as you need. To see a finished version of the scene, open audioMeter_v01.mb from the Chapter 2 directory on the CD.

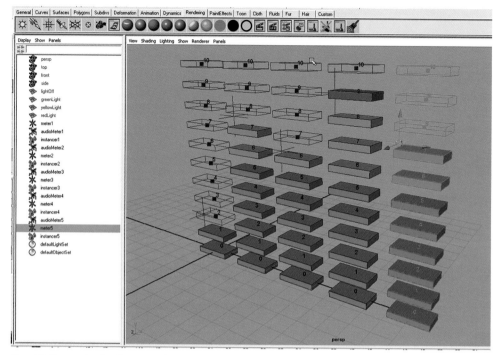

Figure 2.8: The completed audio meter project

Further Study

This setup works pretty well in this particular shot. But what if the art director wanted each audio meter to sway back and forth to the music? You can try duplicating the audioMeter1 object, setting the duplicate as a goal with a weight value of 1, and applying a deformer, such as a lattice, to the duplicate particle object. It will be tricky since you will need to rethink the expressions controlling the relationship between the locator and the instances as well as find a way to make the instanced cubes rotate with the deformation.

Particle Collisions: The Classic Force Field Effect

What science fiction story would be complete without someone trapped behind an invisible force field that seems impervious to all manner of advanced laser weaponry? Well, plenty, but we're going to create an invisible force field effect anyway. We're taking over this shot from a fellow animator who was pulled away for another project. Taking over someone's Maya scene is a lot like wearing their underwear. It can be uncomfortable and disconcerting. This is one reason it is best to keep your scenes neat, clean, and orderly. The same goes for your underwear.

From the Chapter 2 folder on the CD, open the scene called forceField_v01.mb. The scene contains a large room with an elaborate doorway and a somewhat bizarre-looking ray gun. If you play the scene, you'll see that the gun has already been animated and it is shooting particles at the doorway.

Our task involves two effects: The first is to create the force field that appears only when the rays from the gun collide with it. The field should look kind of fuzzy and electric. The second effect is the impact of the gun's rays on the field. They should look like a little flash or pulse and occur right at the point of impact.

Creating the Force Field

For the purpose of this tutorial, the force field will be a bed of particles set to the point style render type. In production, sprites with a slightly more sophisticated look would probably work better, but points will be fine to start out with.

1. Select the shield object from the Outliner. Switch to the Dynamics menu set and choose **Particles > Emit From Object > Options**.

2. Set **Emitter Type** to Surface, **Rate (Particles/Sec)** to 2400, and **Speed** to 0 (Figure 2.9).

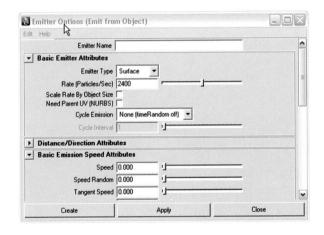

Figure 2.9:
The settings for the surface emitter

3. Rewind to the start of the animation and let it play for about 150 frames. A dense wall of particles should appear in the doorway.

4. At frame 150, stop the animation and select the new particle group (particle2). Change the name of the new particle's transform node to "forceField." The shape node will automatically be renamed "forceFieldShape."

5. With forceField selected, go to the Dynamics menu set and choose **Solvers > Initial State > Set For Selected**.

6. In the Outliner, you'll see that an emitter has been parented to the shield geometry (you may have to expand the shield node to see this). This is the emitter for the forceField particles. Select it, and in its attributes set **Rate (Particles/Sec)** to 0.

7. When you rewind the animation, you'll see the solid wall of particles sitting there at the doorway. We've frozen it in time and stopped its emitter so no more particles will be added.

Creating the Look of the Shield

Now let's get the shield to look a little more dynamic.

1. Select the forceField particle and open the Attribute Editor for its shape node.

2. Scroll down to the Add Dynamic Attributes buttons and click the Color button.

3. In the pop-up window that appears, choose Add Per Particle Attribute and click the Add Attribute button. If Maya is behaving, you'll see a new **rgbPP** field appear in the Per Particle Array Attributes. If it doesn't appear, click the Load Attributes button at the bottom of the Attribute Editor to get the **rgbPP** attribute to appear in the Per Particle (Array) Attributes list.

4. Right-click in the field next to rgbPP and choose **Runtime Before Dynamics Expression**. Since the particles already exist, we won't need to make a creation expression.

5. We will be creating a simple expression that should cause the particles in the field to flicker blue. The **rgbPP** attribute is a vector, so first we'll create a variable that will hold a random number and then we'll use that number for the blue channel in the **rgbPP** attribute. We'll also set the **seed** attribute so that the random numbers generated are consistent each time we run the particle simulation.

6. In the Expression field, type the following:

```
seed(particleId);
float $randB = rand(0.5,1);
forceFieldShape.rgbPP=<<0.5,0.5,$randB>>;
```

$randB is the variable that holds a random number from 0.5 to 1, generated for each frame. Then the **rgbPP** attribute contains a vector where red and green are both 0.5 and the blue channel holds the value contained in the $randB variable.

7. To make the particles move just a little, we will create a similar expression for the **position** attribute. We can add this expression right here in the editor along with the rgbPP expressions. (If you've closed the editor, you can right-click in the field next to position and choose **Runtime Before Dynamics Expression**). Add the following text to the Expression field:

```
float $addRandom=rand(-.001,.001);
position= position+$addRandom;
```

Even though position is a vector, you can add a float to it; it gets added to each member of the vector. In this case, the X, Y, and Z position of each particle has a random number from –.01 to .01 added to it for each frame. This causes them to jiggle slightly. If the scene went on for a long time, eventually the particles in the shield would wander off into space, but it's a short shot so this should be OK.

When you play the animation, the force field has some life to it (Figure 2.10). Since the point particle type retains its size regardless of how close the camera zooms in, the field will seem weaker in closer shots. You may want to zoom out a bit to make the movement and the color changes more obvious.

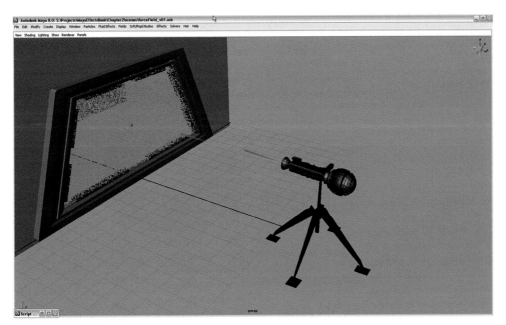

Figure 2.10: The force field is a shimmering blue wall of dots.

Ray Gun Impact Effect

The activation of the force field will be tied in to the impact of the ray gun "bullets." So let's create that effect and then we'll return to the force field to complete the look.

1. Select the rays particle object and Control+select the NURBS shield object. Choose **Particles** > **Make Collide**.

2. When you play the animation now, the rays from the gun bounce off the shield. Let's have them die when they hit the shield.

3. Choose **Particles** > **Collision Event Editor**. Make sure rays is selected in the Objects section at the top of the panel. Leave All Collisions checked and select Emit from Event Type.

4. Set **Num Particles** to 1, Spread to 0, and **Inherit Velocity** to 0. Under Event Actions, check **Original Particle Dies** (Figure 2.11).

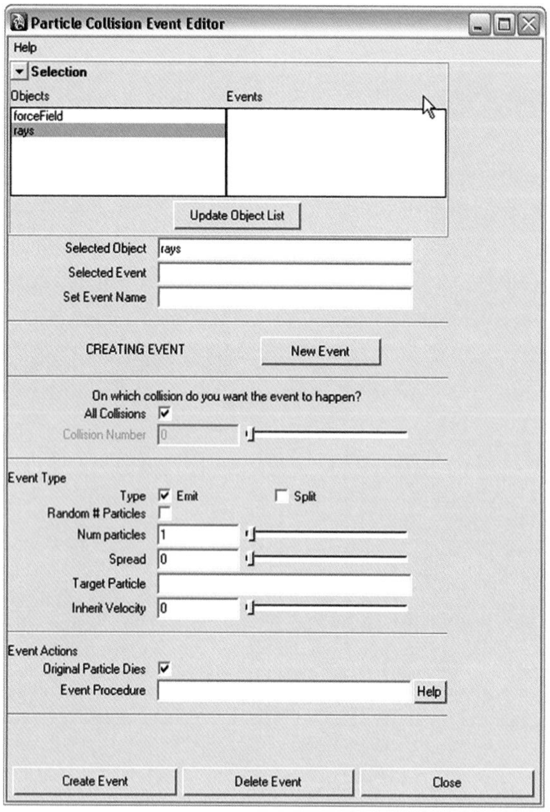

Figure 2.11:
The collision event options

5. Click the Create Event button and close the window. In the Outliner, rename the new particle1 object "impactFlash."

6. In the Outliner, select the object labeled "impact" and turn its visibility on. This is a simple NURBS plane with a circular ramp applied.

7. Select the impact object and then Control+select impactFlash. Choose **Particles > Instancer(Replacement)**. In the options, set **Cycle** to None and make sure **impactFlashShape** is chosen in the **ParticleObjects To Instance** menu.

Editing the Instances

Now when the rays from the gun hit the force field, the impact image appears at the point of impact. Let's make this a little more dynamic. We'll add a ramp to make the flash scale when it appears and we'll shorten its lifespan so each copy doesn't hang around forever.

1. Select the impactFlash shape and open its Attribute Editor. Under Lifespan Attributes, switch the **Mode** to **lifespanPP**.

2. Create a creation expression for **lifespanPP** that reads as follows:

```
seed(particleId);
lifespanPP=rand(0.2,0.3);
```

3. Click the General button to add a new custom array attribute. Name the attribute "scaleMe." Set **Data Type** to Vector and **Attribute Type** to Per-Particle.

4. In the array attributes for impactFlash, right-click in the field next to the new **scaleMe** attribute and choose **Create Ramp > Options**. In the options, set the **inputV** to Particle's Age and choose to map it to a new ramp. Click OK to create the ramp.

5. Right-click over the **scaleMe** field and choose to edit the ramp. In the ramp window, set the bottom and top colors to black and the middle to white. Move the white color down so there's just a tiny sliver of black at the bottom. The top should fade to black (Figure 2.12).

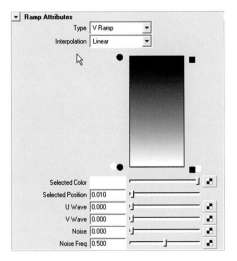

Figure 2.12:
Create a ramp for the
scaleMe attribute.

6. In the Attribute Editor for impactFlash, scroll up to the Instancer (Geometry Replacement) attributes. Under the general options, use the drop-down menu to set **Scale** to **scaleMe**.

Now when you play the animation, the impact spots appear and then scale down quickly. You could have them scale up from 0 if you want; just reverse the colors on the ramp. Of course, that will affect how the force field appears, which is the final task we have to complete.

Animating the Force Field

The last bit is pretty simple.

1. Select the forceFieldShape and open its Attribute Editor. Below the Array Attributes section, click the Opacity button under Add Dynamic Attributes. Choose to add a per-particle attribute.

2. Open up the runtime before dynamics expressions in the Expression Editor. Add the following to the list of expressions:

```
opacityPP=imapctFlashShape.scaleMe;
```

Rewind and play the animation. The force field now appears only when the bullets impact on its otherwise invisible surface. Confound that blasted shield! It's impenetrable!

Further Study

This project has given us a pretty basic force field effect. Try some of these suggestions to improve upon the look of the field.

1. Try varying the look of the impacts on the surface of the force field. You can animate the ramp assigned to the impact surface or create a number of similar impact shapes with different ramps applied. Assign them all to the particle1 instance and then write an expression to randomly choose the instance index when the particle is created.
2. Try creating a hemispherical shield. The flat impact shapes won't work quite as well; you may need to find another solution for that aspect of the animation. The Particle Collision Events Editor may have some helpful options for this.

Instancing with Paint Effects: Pushing Up the Daisies

You come in to work today to find a sticky note attached to your monitor. It says, "Flowers??" and a quick sketch of the shot is scrawled at the bottom. Apparently our director needs a shot of some daisies sprouting up out of the ground. From the chicken scratch on the note you gather that some kind of moving rain cloud is causing the flowers to pop up as the rain hits the field. And here you thought a career in CG would be all orcs and fabulous cyborg babes.

As a Maya artist, whenever you hear "flowers," your mind immediately leaps to Paint Effects. However, you quickly realize that the shot will probably involve a bit more than painting flower strokes all over a surface. No problem! With some particle dynamics, a little bit of MEL, and some expressions, the job will be done in no time.

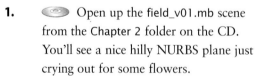

1. Open up the field_v01.mb scene from the Chapter 2 folder on the CD. You'll see a nice hilly NURBS plane just crying out for some flowers.
2. Switch to the Dynamics menu set and create a volume emitter. Set **Shape** to Cube, and in the Channel Box, set **Scale X** to 3, **Scale Y** to 5, and **Scale Z** to 11. Set **Rate** to 16. Rename the particle1 object "seeds."
3. Set some keyframes so that over 200 frames the emitter moves over the field in the X direction.
4. Select the seeds object and add a gravity field. Set the **Magnitude** to 6. Play the animation and make sure that the particles are raining down on the plane (this could be Spain, who knows).

Setting Up Collisions

Now that we have our basic scene set up (Figure 2.13), we'll set up a collision between the plane and the particles. The collision will cause a new particle to be emitted from the point of contact between the plane and our "raindrop" particles. This new particle will become our flowers.

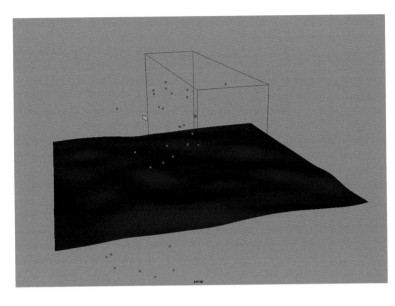

1. Select the seeds object and the plane and choose **Particles > Make Collide**.
2. If you play the animation now, you'll see the raindrops bounce off the plane in all directions. Let's fix that by making a collision event. Select seeds and choose **Particles > Particle Collision Event Editor**. The options will open up.
3. Under **Event Type**, choose Emit. Set **Num Particles** to 1, **Spread** to 0, and **Inherit Velocity** to 0.
4. Under Event Actions, choose **Original Particle Dies**. Click the Create Event button.
5. Play the animation. It's probably very hard to see what's going on. In the Outliner, select the new particle1 object, open its Attribute Editor, and switch its **Render Type** to spheres. Rename it "flowers." Now as you play the animation, you should see spheres appear on the plane as the raindrops fall on it (Figure 2.14).

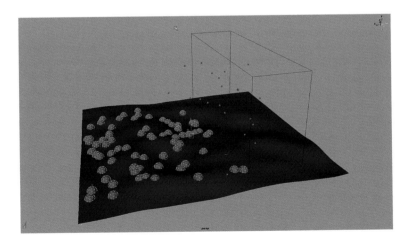

Figure 2.14:
Spheres appear on the field at the point of impact between particle1 and the plane.

Creating the Flower

The next part of this project is slightly tougher. We want to instance a Paint Effects stroke to the second particle—the one currently shown as spheres. But we also want these instanced strokes to grow up out of the ground and remain stationary after they've grown (as opposed to cycling over and over again). If we instanced a growing Paint Effects stroke directly, all the flowers would be growing at the same time instead of when each raindrop hits the plane. To solve this problem, we'll use an animated Paint Effects flower to create a series of flower objects at different stages during their growth—kind of like making an animated clip from a regular piece of keyframed geometry. We'll then instance this series of objects and create a cycle on the instance.

1. Hide everything in the scene so we can see what's going on. Zoom in to the origin of the grid and turn grid snapping on.

2. Open up the Visor (**Window > General Editors > Visor**). Open the Flowers folder on the left side of the Visor and click on the daisyLarge.mel stroke.

3. At the origin of the grid, click and drag for just a heartbeat. Let go and you should see a nice big flower appear (Figure 2.15). You just want one single flower. It will probably grow up a little off center. That's OK, as long as it's pretty close to the origin.

Figure 2.15: A single Daisy stroke drawn at the origin

4. Close the Visor, and in the Outliner, select the strokeDaisyLarge1 node and open its Attribute Editor.

5. To animate the growth of the stroke, click the dasiyLarge3 tab in the Attribute Editor and scroll down to the Flow Animation attributes.

6. Set **Flow Speed** to 12 and click the boxes for **Stroke Time** and **Time Clip** (see Figure 2.16). If you scrub the playhead back and forth on the Timeline, you should see the stroke grow up over the course of 12 frames. (It may switch to a wireframe view to speed up performance. Don't worry if this happens; the flower is still there.)

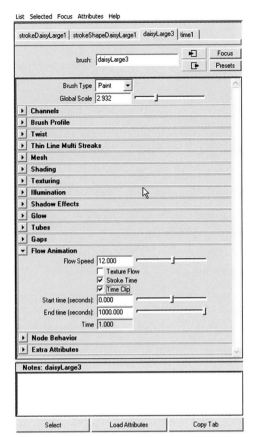

List Selected Focus Attributes Help

strokeDaisyLarge1 | strokeShapeDaisyLarge1 | daisyLarge3 | time1 |

brush: daisyLarge3   Focus
                            Presets

Brush Type Paint
Global Scale 2.932
► Channels
► Brush Profile
► Twist
► Thin Line Multi Streaks
► Mesh
► Shading
► Texturing
► Illumination
► Shadow Effects
► Glow
► Tubes
► Gaps
▼ Flow Animation
    Flow Speed 12.000
                ☐ Texture Flow
                ☑ Stroke Time
                ☑ Time Clip
    Start time (seconds): 0.000
    End time (seconds): 1000.000
    Time 1.000
► Node Behavior
► Extra Attributes

Notes: daisyLarge3

    Select   Load Attributes   Copy Tab

Figure 2.16:
The flow animation attributes
for the Daisy stroke

7. Next let's convert our Paint Effects strokes to polygons. This will ensure that there is less room for weirdness when we instance the object sequence. Select the Daisy stroke and choose **Modify > Convert > Paint Effects To Polygons**. In the options, switch on Hide Strokes. The animation we created for the flower will be carried over to the new polygon flower via history.

Creating the Flower Object Cycle

To create our cycle of objects, we will need to go through each of the 12 frames of the animation and duplicate the flower on each of these frames. We'll end up with twelve flowers each of which is at a different stage in the growth of the flower. This seems fairly repetitive and tedious. Sounds like a job for some simple MEL scripting. Open up the Script Editor or a text editor and go through the next few steps.

1. First we'll set the current time to frame 1.

```
// set current time to frame 1
currentTime -e 1;
```

-e stands for edit. We are editing the current time attribute so that it's now at frame 1.

2. The next few lines are our loop:

```
// loop to create 12 stages of daisy
for ($i=0; $i<12; $i++) {

   //duplicate the daisy group geometry
    duplicate -rr daisyLarge3MeshGroup;

  //move time ahead one frame
    currentTime -e ($i + 1);
  }
```

The first line of the loop sets $i=0, and then as long as $i is less than 12, performs the loop. $i++ is shorthand for $i=$i+1, which increments the loop by 1 until 12 is reached. The loop stops at 12 (Figure 2.17).

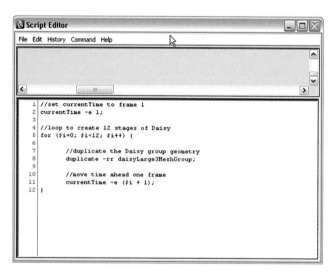

Figure 2.17:
The MEL script in the
script editor

Remember that in the Script Editor, the Enter/Return key on the keyboard ends the line and starts a new line. The Enter key on the numeric keypad executes the script. Don't mix them up when typing a script directly into the Script Editor.

The code inside the loop is very simple. It basically duplicates the daisyLarge3MeshGroup. The -rr flag stands for "return roots only," which means upstream connections will not be duplicated with the new objects. Then the current time is incremented by one frame and the loop is repeated. This continues until the variable $i reaches 12.

3. With the daisy polygon object selected and the script typed into the Script Editor, hit the Enter button on the numeric keypad to run the script. You should see

Maya go to the first frame on the Timeline and then play through the first 12 frames, creating duplicate flowers as it goes. Each new flower is at a different stage of growth in the animation.

If you look in the Outliner, you'll see the new Daisy groups. The next step is to instance them to the flower particle object. Unhide the other objects in the scene and proceed with the next steps.

4. Select the daisyLargeMeshGroup, the original polygon daisy we performed our script on, and hide it.

5. In the Outliner, starting with the daisyLargeMeshGroup1, Shift+select the other duplicated groups in order. Choose **Particles > Instancer(Replacement)**. Open the options.

6. In the Instancer options, make sure **Cycle** is set to None and **Particle Object To Instance** is set to flowersShape. Leave the rest at the default values and click the Create button.

If you play the animation now you should be disappointed. The flowers aren't growing. This is because Cycle has been set to None. If Cycle was on, you'd see each flower grow up, disappear, and then grow up again. This is because the cycle repeats. We want the flowers to grow and then remain grown up. To fix this, we'll use some simple expressions.

Controlling the Growth with Expressions

With a few simple expressions we'll have each flower growing as the seed particle hits the ground.

1. Select the flowers particle object and open the Attribute Editor for its shape node. In the Per-Particle Array Attributes, hit the General button to add a new attribute. Name the attribute "instanceMe" and make sure **Data Type** is set to Float and **Attribute Type** is Per-Particle(Array).

2. Right-click in the field next to the new **instanceMe** attribute (if it doesn't show up, click the Load Attributes button at the bottom of the Attribute Editor). Choose **Creation Expression** from the pop-up menu.

3. In the Expression Editor's Expression field, type this:

```
instanceMe=0;
```

4. Hit the Enter button and then switch to Runtime Before Dynamics. Type this in the Expression field:

```
if (instanceMe<12)
  {
  instanceMe++;
  }
```

This expression says that as long as the **instanceMe** attribute is less than 12, increment the value of **instanceMe** by one. Runtime expressions run every frame. In a way, it's very similar to the loop we created in the MEL script. It's just that the creation and runtime expressions take care of the for($i=0;$i<12;$i++)bit for us.

5. In the Instancer (Geometry Replacement) section of the flowersShape's Attribute Editor, set the **Object Index** value to instanceMe. Set the **Particle Render Type** for flowers to points.

Try running the animation now. You should see flowers pop up when the first particles hit the plane (Figure 2.18).

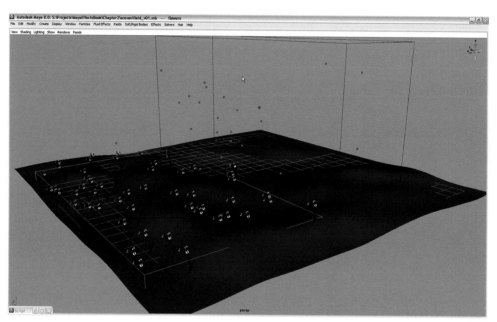

Figure 2.18: The completed daisy project

Further Study

To give the animation some polish, you may want to randomize the Y rotation of the particles as well as the scale so that all the flowers don't look exactly the same. To do this, you can create a per-particle attribute for the rotation and scale values, set a randomizing creation expression, and then set the Rotation and Scale options to these custom values. You can see an example of this in the field_v02.mb scene in the Chapter 2 folder on the CD.

Using Cycle Emission: The Plasma Ball

The next assignment involves some sci-fi energy effects. The shot calls for a ball of plasma moving within a glass containment field that is part of a huge, mysterious machine. The art director would like to see a blob of energy that behaves like it is alive, moving about within the machine's chamber.

The cycle emission attribute on particle emitters is designed so that loops can be created for emitted particles. This is used largely for games when creating a constant loop of something like a fountain of sparks is desirable. Cycling the emission rate can also be used to create some very interesting particle effects. Combined with a turbulence field, cycled emitters can cause particles to behave like tentacles and take on an eerie life of their own. Let's try this out.

Creating the Plasma Emitter

We'll create a volume emitter and place it within the containment shield of the machine.

1.   💿   Open up machine_v01.mb from the Chapter 2 files on the CD. You'll see the model of the machine with the energy chamber on the right side of the frame (see Figure 2.19).

Figure 2.19: The mystery machine model

2.   To speed up performance while working in this scene, you can open up the Display Layer Editor and turn off the visibility for all the layers except the MACHINE layer.

3.   From the Dynamics menu set, choose **Particles > Create Emitter > Options**. Make the emitter a volume and set the **Shape** to sphere. Go ahead and create the emitter; we'll adjust the other settings as we go along.

4.   In the Outliner, expand the mainMachine group. You may want to hide the collisionShield and outerGlass objects so that it's easier to select objects in the chamber.

5.   Switch to the perspective view. Select the particleEmitter1 object and position it so that it surrounds the ball at the end of the generator (Figure 2.20).

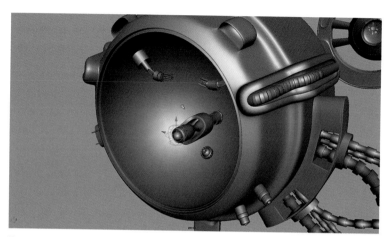

Figure 2.20: The emitter placed inside the containment shield

6.   Scale it down so that it fits around the sphere.

7.   Open the Attribute Editor for the emitter and set **Rate** to 16. Under Volume Speed Attributes, set the **Away From Center** value to 2.

8.   Rename the particle1 object "plasma1." In its Attribute Editor, set **Render Type** to Blobby Surface. Click the button to Add Attributes for Current Render Type and set **Radius** to 0.5.

Play the animation. Particles fly out in a fairly typical style.

Cycle Emission

The Cycle Emission setting will help us create a more interesting movement for the particles.

1.   Open up the Attribute Editor for the particleEmitter and set **Cycle Emission** to Frame (Time Random On). Play the animation. The particles now fly out in a straight line.

2.   In the emitter attributes, turn the **Rate** up to 100. Now we have several streams of particles coming out of the emitter (Figure 2.21).

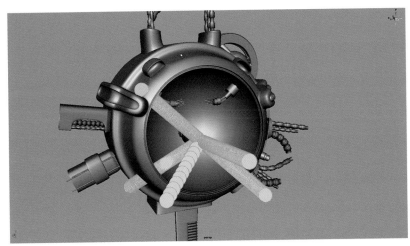

Figure 2.21: Increasing the rate and turning on Cycle Emission causes the particles to fly out in a straight line.

3. Select the plamsa1 particle object and choose **Fields > Turbulence**. Set **Magnitude** to 10, **Attenuation** to 0, and **Frequency** to 1. Now when you play the animation, the streams of particles twist in several directions.

4. To make the movement a bit more dynamic, we can add an expression to one or more of the phase values on the frequency node of the turbulence field. Open the Attribute Editor for the turbulence field. Right-click over the **PhaseX** slider and choose **Create New Expression**. In the Expression field, type this:

```
turbulenceField1.phaseX=noise(time);
```

This will cause the phase of the turbulence field to move from –1 to 1 over time in a semi-random fashion. (It's actually more fractal than truly random.) You can try plugging this expression into the Y or Z phase attributes just to see what happens. When you play the animation, the particle streams start to move about like tentacle arms (Figure 2.22)

Figure 2.22: Adding some turbulence breaks up the straightness of the lines.

Containing the Particles

Now that we have the start of a nice motion for our plasma, let's see if we can try containing them within the chamber.

1. In the Outliner, select the collisionShield object from the mainMachine group and untemplate or unhide it. This is a transparent sphere that will act as our collision object, keeping the particles in the chamber.

2. Select the plasma1 particle object and then Control+select the collisionShield and choose **Particles** > **Make Collide**.

3. Rewind to the beginning of the animation and press play to see what happens. The blobby surfaces bounce around inside the chamber. Not very plasma like.

Collision Events

We'll create a particle collision event that kills the original particle and causes new, smaller ones to appear, as if the blobs of plasma are breaking up when they contact the chamber walls.

1. Choose **Particles** > **Collision Event Editor**. In the panel that opens up, make sure that All Collisions is checked.

2. Set the **event Type** to Emit.

3. Check **Random Number Of Particles**, and set the number of particles to 3.

4. Set **Spread** to 1.0 and **Inherit Velocity** to .5. The new particles inherit half the velocity of the colliding particles.

5. Click **Original Particle Dies**.

Now when the particles hit the walls of the chamber, they burst into a small shower of particles. Those new particles appear as particle2 in the Outliner. Select this particle, rename it "plasma2," and open its Attribute Editor.

Why Emit and not Split? When you choose the Split option for your particle collision event, the new particles that are created in the collision event inherit their lifespan from the original particle. So if the original particle has been hanging around for a couple seconds before it collides, the new particle will be born at a lifespan of 2. This is fine, but that means if a particle floats around for a while before hitting the chamber wall, the new particles may not get created if the age of the original particle is already greater than the lifespan of the new particle.

The Secondary Particles

We'll adjust the settings on the secondary particles so they look like they belong with the original plasma particles.

1. For plasma2, set its **Render Type** to blobby surface. Click on the Add Attributes For Current Render Type button and set Radius to 0.165.

2. Set the **Lifespan Mode** of plasma2 to Random Range with a **Lifespan** value of 0.5 and a **Lifespan Random** value of 0.25.

3. Choose **Window > Relationship Editor > Dynamic Relationships.** In the window, choose plasma2 from the list on the left and turbulenceField1 from the box on the right (under the Fields mode). This will cause the turbulence field to affect the new particles (Figure 2.23).

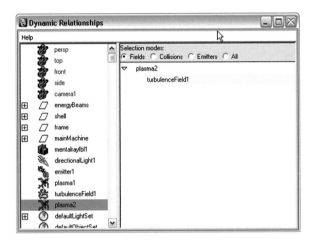

Figure 2.23:
The Relationship Editor connects the new particles to the turbulence field.

4. Select the plasma2 object in the Outliner and Control+select the collisionShield object. Choose **Particles > Make Collide** to keep these new particles inside the chamber.

When you play the animation, things should be looking pretty good. With a few more adjustments we'll have a nice blob of plasma going.

Fixing Particle Collision Problems

If particles are getting past the collision surface, try increasing the **Trace Depth** attribute on the particle's shape node under the **Collision** attribute. If particles are still getting through, you can create a radial field with a negative value so the particles get sucked back into the containment chamber. Finally, you can also open the geoConnector1 tab in the Attribute Editor for plasma2 and increase the tessellation.

Remember that the particle's collision is based on the center of the particle, not the outside of the blobby surface. If the blobby part of the particle is poking through the glass, try either reducing the radius of the blobby surface or scaling down the size of the collision shield object.

Polishing the Plasma

Let's finalize the look of the plasma.

1. In the Outliner, select the plasma1 and plasma2 objects. Open the Hypershade and right-click over the bluePlasma shader. Assign it to the particle objects. The shader is transparent, so this may cause the particles in the viewport to disappear. You can select them or switch to wireframe shading to see what's going on when you play the animation.

2. Open the Attribute Editor for the plasma1 object. Click the General button in the Add Dynamic Attributes section.

3. Switch to the Particle tab and scroll down. Find the **radiusPP** attribute and assign it to the particle.

4. Make a creation expression for the **radiusPP** attribute. In the Expression Editor, type this:

    ```
    seed(partiicleId);
    radiusPP=rand(0.3,0.8);
    ```

5. Do the same for particleShape32, but set the random function to rand(0.15,0.25);.

6. In the Render attributes for both particles, set **Threshold** to 0.2. The Threshold setting causes blobby particles that are close to each other to merge together in a blob. Higher threshold values will make blobbier particles, but they will also cause the blobs to appear smaller. You can see this effect only when you render (Figure 2.24).

    Render out a sequence of the animation from camera1. Or check out the plasmaMachine.mov file on the CD.

Figure 2.24: The completed plasma ball scene

Further Study

Taming particle simulations like this can make you feel a bit like a magician. There are endless ways to create new and interesting movements for your particles; here are just a few suggestions:

1. Try controlling the particles' movements with some goals placed outside the machine.

2. Try adding an expression to make the plasma2 shape's radius scale down over the course of its lifetime.

3. Try adding a ramp to the plasma particles' velocity so that they slow down over time.

Influencing Cameras with Particles

Doctor! Doctor! This patient is keeling over! We can't figure out what's wrong! He needs some CG stat! You've just been assigned a shot to be featured in the pilot of *CSI: Poughkeepsie*. The art director needs a POV shoot from a blood cell hurtling down a blood vessel. The main direction on this shot is to make the camera work dynamic.

Every animator at some point in their career has to do a blood cell animation; it's a rite of passage. It's a staple of medical dramas, drug commercials, and biology education. The trick is how to make something that's been seen a hundred times a bit more interesting.

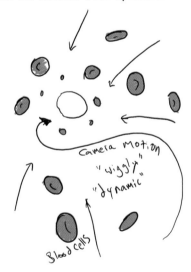

Dynamic camera movement can breathe a lot of life into an otherwise boring shot. A little wiggle and jiggle added to a simple tracking or panning shot can put viewers on the edge of their seat and make the story that much more compelling. There are numerous ways to do this in Maya, and it often becomes a fun challenge to come up with more creative ways to enhance your animated camera moves. In this particular case, we'll see how you can actually use particles as a framework for a camera rig.

Creating the Particle Rig

We'll start with a very simple scene consisiting of a big tube—our blood vessel.

1. Open the bloodVessel_v01.mb scene from the Chapter 2 folder on the CD. Check out the extruded tube. The modeler has been kind enough to leave the original profile curves used to make the model in the scene. That should come in handy.

2. Create a two-node camera by choosing **Create** > **Cameras** > **Camera And Aim**.

3. Create two locators. Name one "aimGoal" and the other "cameraGoal."

4. Select the aimGoal object. From the Animation menu set, choose **Animate** >
Motion Paths > **Attach To Motion Path**. For the time range, use the **Time Slider**
so it takes them 200 frames to reach the end of the curve. In the Attach To
Motion Path Options box, choose **Edit** > **Reset** to set the motion path options to
the default settings. Do the same for the cameraGoal object.

5. Once both locators have been attached to the motion path, set the Timeline to
frame 15 or so, select both locators, and open up the Graph Editor. Hit the F key
to frame the motion path animation curves. Select the motion path keys for the
cameraGoal object and translate them to the right so that they are a few frames
behind the locator goal. In the perspective view, you should see that the cameraGoal locator lags behind the aimGoal locator by just a little bit (Figure 2.25).

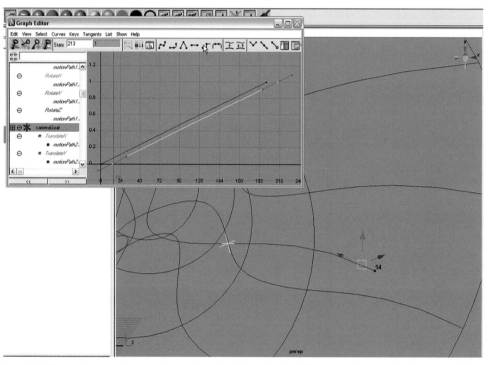

Figure 2.25: Moving the keys for the cameraGoal locator to the right on the Graph Editor causes the cameraGoal locator to trail
behind the aimGoal.

6. Move the Time Slider to the start of the animation. Both locators should be at
the very start of the curve, on top of each other.

7. Switch to the Dynamics menu set, turn curve snapping on, and choose **Particle** >
Particle Tool > **Options**. In the Options, set **Number of Particles to 1. Sketch
Particles** and **Create Particle Grid** should be turned off.

8. In the perspective window, click on the curve and drag the red particle indicator
to the same spot on the curve as the locators. Sometimes curve snapping can be a
little flaky, so this may take a few tries. When you have a particle positioned at
the end of the curve, hit the Enter key on the numeric keypad to create the
particle and drop the tool.

9. Select the particle and switch its **Render Type** to spheres so that it's easier to see.

10. Create a second particle using the same technique, place it in the same spot as the first particle (just duplicating the particle may lead to some weirdness; it's best just to create a second particle). Rename each so that one is called "cameraParticle" and the other is called "aimParticle."

11. Select the cameraParticle and the cameraGoal locator and choose **Particles > Goal**. In the options, make sure **Goal Weight** is set to 1. Do the same for aimParticle and aimGoal.

12. When you play the animation, you should see the particles riding along the motion path on top of their respective locators. It's important to have the particles placed at the same spot as the locators to minimize the movement of the particles at the start of the animation (Figure 2.26).

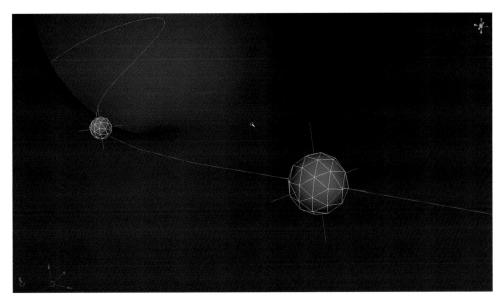

Figure 2.26: The particles are glued to the locators as they fly down the path.

Adding Dynamic Motion to the Particles

Now the fun part: Let's make these particles bounce around.

1. Set the **Goal Weight** value for each particle to 0.3. The **Goal Weight** attribute is listed in the Channel Box toward the bottom.

2. Play the animation now; it looks like the particles are having more fun. Select both the particles and choose **Fields > Turbulence**. Make sure **Attenuation** is set to 0. Set **Magnitude** to 100 and **Frequency** to 3.

3. Set the **Conserve** value of both particles to 0.9. This attribute can also be found in the Channel Box.

4. Play the animation and continue to adjust the **Conserve** of the particles, their **Goal Weight**, and the **Magnitude**, and the **Frequency** attributes of the turbulence field until you get a motion you are happy with.

Attaching the Camera to the Particle Rig

Next we'll use a simple technique to attach the camera and the camera's aim node to the particles.

1. Create two more locators. Name one "cameraPin" and the other "aimPin."

2. In the Outliner, choose **Display** > **Shapes** from the Outliner's menu. Expand the cameraParticle node and select its shape node.

3. Choose **Windows** > **General Editors** > **Connection Editor** to open the Connection Editor.

4. Click the Reload left button to load the cameraParticle's shape node on the left (the outputs) side. Load the transform node for the cameraPin node the right (the inputs) side.

5. Connect the cameraParticle's **World Centroid** attribute to the cameraPin's **Translate** attribute (Figure 2.27).

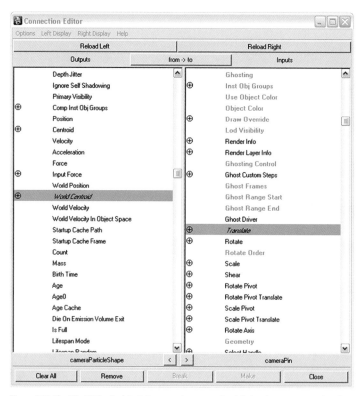

Figure 2.27: The **World Centroid** attribute on the cameraParticle has been connected to the **Translate** attribute on the camera pin locator.

6. Repeat this procedure for the aimParticle and the aimPin objects. When you play the animation, the cameraPin and aimPin locators will be constrained to the particles.

7. The last step is to expand the camera group. Parent the camera to the cameraPin locator and the camera_aim to the aimPin locator. In the Channel Box for the camera and camera_aim, set the **Translate X, Y,** and **Z** values to 0 so the camera and camera_aim objects snap to their pins (Figure 2.28).

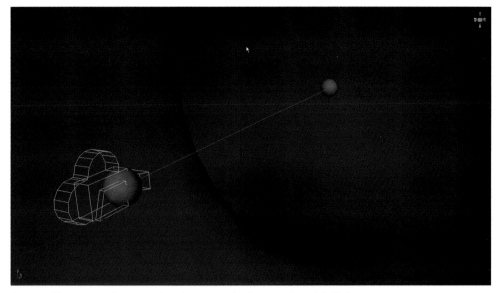

Figure 2.28: The camera and camera aim have been parented to the cameraPin and aimPin locators.

> We could use the Connection Editor to connect the camera and camera_aim directly to the particles, but by parenting them, we still have the option to set keyframes on the camera and aim if we want additional control.

Tuning the Motion

The motion of the camera can be tuned with a little more tweaking of the particle's goal weights and the turbulence settings.

1. Make sure you set both particles back to the point render type so that the camera is not looking inside the particle spheres.

2. Set the viewport to camera one and play the animation. No doubt it will seem too chaotic. To fix this, first set the camera's focal length to 15 so that the tube appears in frame. The shorter focal length of the camera will exaggerate the perspective, which enhances the look.

3. Continue to adjust the settings on the goal weights, the conserve, and the turbulence. The first few frames will be nearly impossible to smooth out. That's OK. We can cut the very beginning out of the shot. Once you are happy with the motion, it's time to make some blood.

Creating the Blood

Our swirling stream of blood cells will be created using Maya's Curve Flow effect and some instanced geometry.

1. Getting blood to flow down the vessel is a snap. Select the curve1 object and choose **Effects > Curve Flow**. In the options, set **the name** to blood, the number of **control segments** to 6, the **subsegments** to 4, and the **emission rate** to 300. Leave **Random Motion Speed** at .5, **Particle Lifespan** at 5, and **Goal Weight** at 1. Click Create to make the curve flow happen.

2. Switch to the perspective window and turn on wireframe. Select the control circle at the very start of the curve. In the Channel Box, adjust its **Scale X** value so that the circle is just a bit smaller than the tube; a setting of 15 should do the trick.

3. Do the same for the other control circles.

4. Once you have them scaled, you'll see a stream of particles flowing down the curve. Switch to the camera view and play the animation (Figure 2.29). Wiiiiiiild!

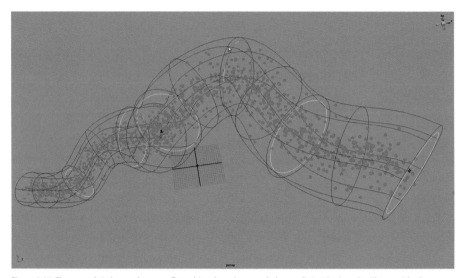

Figure 2.29: The control circles on the curve flow object have been scaled up to fit inside the tube. The particles have been switched to the sphere render type to make them easier to see in this image.

5. Select the bloodCell NURBS object. I think you can guess what's happening next. Yep—choose **Particles > Instancer (Replacement)** to assign the blood cells to this particle. Make sure you have blood_particleShape selected in the Particle Object To Instance To setting.

Creating the Blood Cell Rotation

To finish this animation, we'll add some random rotation to the blood cells.

1. Select the blood_particle and open its Attribute Editor. You'll notice that in the array expressions there are already a bunch of custom attributes and expressions created. These were all created by the curve flow script. You won't have to mess with these at all; don't worry.

2. Hit the General button to add a custom attribute. Name the attribute "rotateMe." Make it a vector, per-particle attribute.

3. Create a creation expression for **rotateMe**. You'll have to scroll down to the bottom of the expression window below all of the other curve flow expressions. Type the following:

```
seed(particleId);
float $rotRand=rand(180);
rotateMe=<<$rotRand,$rotRand,$rotRand>>;
```

The first line creates a random number from 0 to 180. When you place a single number in parentheses after the rand function, Maya assumes the range is from zero to that number. The second line places this random number in the X, Y, and Z values for the particle. Click Edit to add the expressions.

4. Switch to Runtime Before Dynamics, scroll to the bottom of the expression window, and type the following:

```
rotateMe +=10;
```

The += notation is shorthand for saying rotateMe=rotateMe+10, which adds 10 degrees to the rotation for each frame. This means that all the blood cells will rotate in the same direction, but that should be fine for this animation.

5. Hit Edit to add the expressions and then go to the Attribute Editor for the blood particle. Under the Instancer (Geometry Replacement) attributes, go to the Rotation options and set **Rotation** to **rotateMe**. Rewind and play the animation.

It's a vampire's dream come true! You might want to create a Playblast to see the animation in real time. Even though there's not much to it, the jittery camera adds a lot of drama (Figure 2.30). To see a finished version of the scene, open the bloodVessel_v02.mb scene in the Chapter 2 folder on the CD. There is also a blood-Vessel QuickTime movie located in the movies folder.

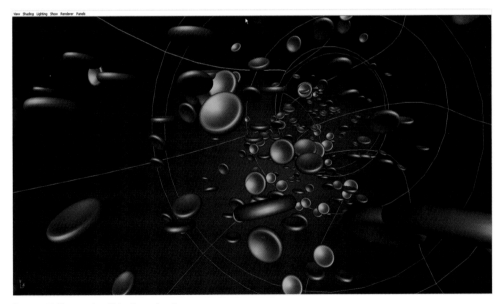

Figure 2.30: The completed blood vessel project

Further Study

The **World Centroid** attribute used to constrain the locators to the particles basically tracks the center of the overall particle object. You can create a large field of particles and use **World Centroid** to keep the camera floating at the center of the particle object. Add some turbulence and vortex fields to the particle and you can create some interesting drifting underwater camera shots complete with particle fishies.

Rigging for Effects

Rigging with the Joint tool is most often associated with character animation, not necessarily effects. However, joints are really just another deformer. Sure they get their own set of menus and a whole bunch of cool options, but when you get right down to it, their main purpose is to deform geometry. In this chapter we'll look at some ways to take advantage of the special properties joints have and use them to create some cool effects.

3

Chapter Contents

The Vibrating Rig: Making a Tentacle Shake
Inverse Kinematic Splines: Making a Tentacle Climb
Joints and Constraints: The Telescopic Car Suspension Rig
The Inverse Kinematic Spline Tool and Lattices

The Vibrating Rig: Making a Tentacle Shake

The art director shows up at your station in a panic. A shot that has already been animated is due for client review in an hour and the original animator neglected to add a shaking effect to a thrashing tentacle. The client specifically requested this in the last meeting and so it's not like it can be left out. How hard would it be to add a sort of spastic shaky effect to the scene? As usual, you say, "No problem," before even looking at the scene. When will you ever learn?

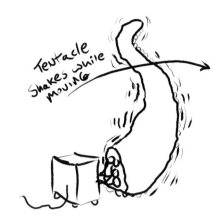

Lucky for you it really is no problem. Open the tentacle_v01.mb scene from the CD and we'll see just how easy it is.

The scene shows a long alien tentacle hooked up to some kind of machine. Apparently some misguided scientists are hard at work trying to revive this severed member. Hit play on the animation and you'll see they were fairly successful at getting it to thrash about. The trick is to get this thing to shake as though electricity were being pumped into it without having to redo the animation (Figure 3.1).

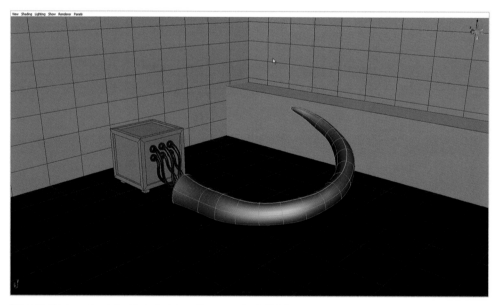

Figure 3.1: The scene already has the tentacle bound to some animated joints.

Disconnecting the Animated Rig

First we'll take apart the original rig that the animator created so that we can implement our electrified shaky rig.

1. Rewind the scene to the beginning. All the joints are in the same position they were in when the tentacle geometry was skinned to the joints.

2. In the Outliner, select the tentacle and switch to the Animation menu set. Choose **Skin** > **Detach Skin**.

3. If you play the animation, you'll see that the joints still move around but the tentacle lies limp on the ground.

Creating a Vibrating Joint

There are many ways to make an object shimmy and shake in Maya. In the previous chapter you saw how particles can be used to add a bumpy motion to an animated camera. In this case, a similar particle rig could be tricky; a much easier method would be the use of an animated Fractal texture applied to a joint.

1. Create a locator and name it "shaker1."

2. Open the Hypershade and create a Fractal Noise 2D texture.

3. Open the Attribute Editor for the Fractal texture. Under Fractal Attributes, click the **Animated** check box. A number of additional attributes will become available.

4. Rewind the animation to the beginning. In the Attribute Editor for the Fractal texture, right-click over the numeric field for **Time** and choose **Set Key** (Figure 3.2).

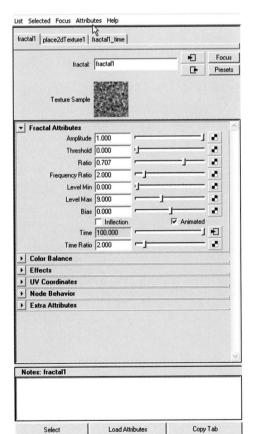

Figure 3.2:
Set keyframes on the
Time Slider to animate
the Fractal texture.

5. Move the playhead for the animation to frame 50 or so, move the slider next to the **Time** attribute in the Fractal texture's Attribute Editor to about 100 or so, and set another key.

6. Click the arrow box to the right of the **Time Slider** attribute and in the fractal1_time attributes, set the **Post Infinity** menu to **Cycle**.

7. In the Outliner, select the shaker1 locator and MMB drag it to the work area in the Hypershade. Make sure that the new fractal1 texture is there as well.

8. Select the fractal1 texture and MMB drag it on top of the shaker1 locator in the Hypershade. From the pop-up menu, choose **Translate** (Figure 3.3).

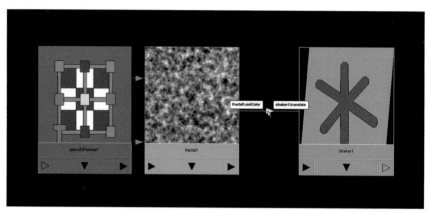

Figure 3.3: The fractal1 texture is connected to the shaker1 locator's translate attribute.

9. Rewind the animation. In the perspective view, zoom in on the shaker1 locator and play the animation. Wow! That thing is bugging out!

10. From the Animation menu set, choose the Joint tool. Click once in the perspective view to create a single joint. Rename it "shakyJoint1."

11. Parent shakyJoint1 to the shaker1 locator. Set the joint's **Translate** values to 0 in the Channel Box so the joint snaps to the same position as the locator (Figure 3.4).

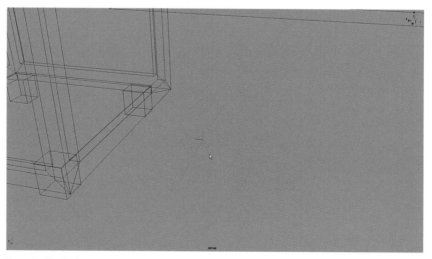

Figure 3.4: The single joint parented to the shaker1 locator

Duplicating the Vibrating Joint

We need to create a similar shakyJoint setup for each of the tentacle_joints, which means repeating the previous steps 17 more times so we have a total of 18 animated Fractal textures, 18 shaky locators, and 18 shaky joints. Luckily we can do this in one easy step.

1. Select the shaker1 locator and use Maya 8's new duplicate special options by choosing **Edit > Duplicate Special > Options**. In the options, set Group Under to World and Number Of Copies to 17 and click on Duplicate Input Graph and Assign Unique Names To Child Nodes (as in Figure 3.5). Click Apply.

Seventeen new shaky locators appear. Each has its own shaky joint and its own animated Fractal texture. You can see this if you open the Hypershade and look in the Texture tab. This is all due to the fact that Duplicate Input Graph was activated.

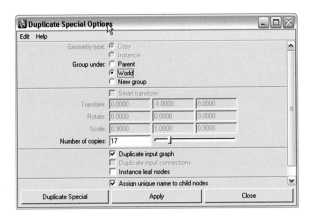

Figure 3.5:
Maya 8 has a new separate options window for Duplicate Special.

Adding the Shakers to the Rig

We'll use a little bit of MEL to complete the task of parenting the shaky joints to the original, animated joints.

1. Our next task involves parenting each shaker joint to its respective tentacle joint (Figure 3.6). To do this we will use a little bit of MEL just to save ourselves some time and trouble. Type the following code into the Script Editor and press the Enter key on the numeric keypad to have it execute:

```
for ($i=1; $i<=18; $i++) {
    parent ("shaker" + $i) ("tentacle_joint" + $i);
}
```

This bit of MEL is a simple loop that parents each of the respective shakyJoints to its respective tentacle_joint. The loop first initializes the variable $i by setting it to 1. The $i++ increments $i by 1 each time it runs, as long as $i is less than or equal to 18. In the body of the loop we append $i to the name of the parent joints and the tentacle_joints so Maya knows which objects to parent to which. It's three lines of code that saves us a whole lot of clicking.

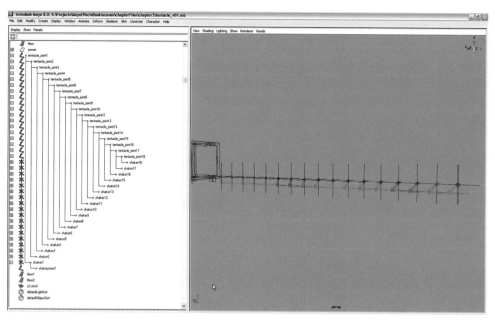

Figure 3.6: The locators are parented to the joints in the original chain.

Notice that each shaker pops into place when you parent it. This is because the translate values already have an input connection (the Fractal texture) that is pretty close to 0, 0, 0 for XYZ. Remember that when you parent an object to another object and then "zero out" its translate values, the child object pops right to the pivot point of its parent. It's as if the parent is now the origin for the child. The Fractal texture, with values being close to 0, 0, 0, is doing this zeroing out of the translate values for us. Very handy.

2. Play the animation. The shaking locators now follow the animation of their parent joints. All of them shake exactly the same way though, which is not what we want.

3. The easiest way to mix up the vibration of the joints is to rotate the place2D texture node attached to each Fractal texture. We could open the attribute for each node and randomly move the slider, or we could put MEL to work for us again and take away some of the tedium. Type the following code into the Script Editor and press the Enter key on the numeric keypad to have it execute:

```
for ($i=1; $i<=18; $i++){
  setAttr ("place2dTexture" + $i + ".rotateUV") (rand(360));
}
```

This is similar to the last bit of code we used in that it is a simple loop that runs as long as $i is less than or equal to 18. In the body of the loop, Maya has to set the rotateUV attribute for each place2dTexture node to a random number from 0 to 360. When you use the rand function with a single number in parentheses, Maya assumes you mean a number from 0 to the specified value; it's the same as writing rand(0,360).

You'll see that when the animation plays, each shaker moves about in a different way.

Reconnecting the Tentacle

Next, we need to reconnect the tentacle to our shaky joints.

1. We will be skinning the tentacle to the new shaky joints, but before we do this, we have to get them as close as possible to the starting position of the tentacle_joints. If you rewind the animation, you'll notice that they are slightly offset from the position of each tentacle joint. This is because the animated fractal is now feeding the translate values for each shaky locator a random value from 0 to 1.

2. Open the Hypershade and switch to the Texture tab. Shift+select all the textures. In the Channel Box, find the **Color Gain R**, **G**, and **B** values. Set them all to 0. The shake locators should pop to the position of the tentacle joints. The fractal textures will turn black when you do this (Figure 3.7).

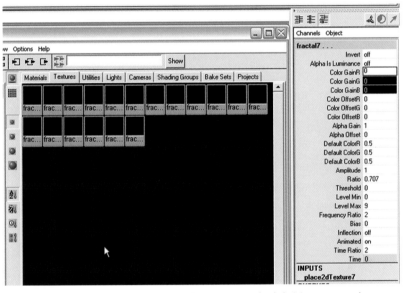

Figure 3.7: Setting the color gain to 0 for the Fractal textures causes the shaky joints to assume the same position as the joints in the original chain.

3. In the Outliner, Ctrl+select each shaky joint. Then Ctrl+select the tentacle. Alternatively, you can save some time by using the MEL select command. Type this into the command line:

```
select -r "shakyJoint*";
```

The r flag stands for *replace*, as in "replace the current section." The asterisk after shakeyJoint is a wildcard that tells Maya to select all the objects whose names start with "shakyJoint." Since our shaky joints are numbered 1 through 18, Maya knows to select all of them. Once they're selected, Ctrl+select the tentacle.

4. From the Animation menu set, choose **Skin > Bind > Skin > Smooth Bind > Options**. In the options, set **Bind To** to Selected Joints, **Bind Method** to Closest Distance, **Max Influences** to 3, and **Dropoff Rate** to 4.

The animation now looks just like it did when we started, but that's good. The only reason it's not shaking is because we turned off the shakiness of the Fractal textures by setting the **Color Gain** values to 0.

Controlling the Vibration

At this point we could turn up the **Color Gain** values on each Fractal texture to get the vibration back; we could even set different values so that the end of the tentacle shakes more than at the base. For now let's create a slider control that takes care of all of the shakers at once. Think of it as a dimmer switch for the shakes.

1. Create a new locator and name it "shakeControl."
2. Open the Attribute Editor for shakeControl and choose **Attributes > Add Attribute**.
3. Name the attribute "**shakeDimmer**." Set **Data Type** to Float, and enter 0 for **Minimum**, 2 for **Maximum**, and 0 for **Default** (Figure 3.8).

You may notice that when we create a custom attribute and name it using the convention "customAttribute," Maya will automatically label the attribute as two separate, capitalized words. However, when we refer to this attribute in an expression, we still need to type it in the Expression Editor using our original "customAttribute" syntax.

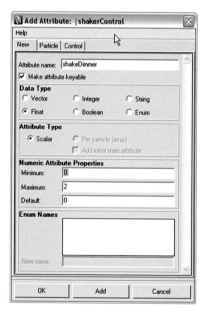

Figure 3.8:
The settings for the custom shake dimmer control

4. Open the Connection Editor and load the shakeControl locator on the left side.

5. Open the Hypershade and select fractal3 (we'll leave fractal1 and fractal2 alone for now).

6. In the Connection Editor, connect the **Shake Dimmer** attribute on the left side to the **Color Gain R, G,** and **B** values on the right. Do this for fractal3 through fractal18 (Figure 3.9).

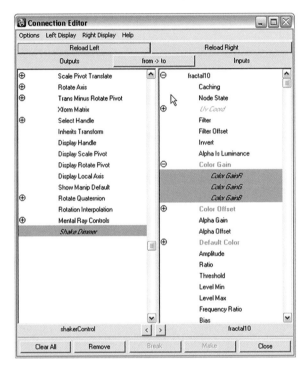

Figure 3.9:

The shakeDimmer

attribute is connected to the Fractal texture's Color Gain R, G, and B.

7. Since fractal1 and fractal2 control the shakers nearest the thick end of the tentacle where the generator model is hooked up, we can leave their **Color Gain** values at 0 or near 0 just so the shaking doesn't get out of hand.

8. Set the **Shake Dimmer** attribute to 0.5 and play the animation. If all goes as planned, you should see the original animation with a bit of quaking added to the movement of the tentacle (Figure 3.10). You can keyframe the **Shake Dimmer** attribute so that the shaking gets worse over time. Setting it at a value between 1 and 2 will create some really crazy shakes.

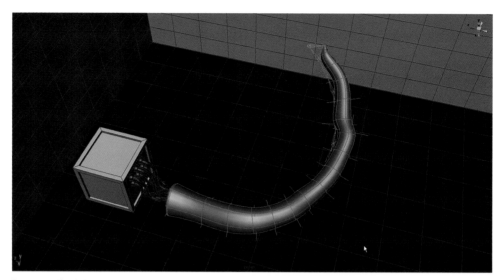

Figure 3.10: The shaking joints add a dramatic deformation to our severed tentacle animation.

Further Study

Try converting the tentacle geometry to a softbody and see how the surface reacts to the shaking. You may want to paint your softbody weights so that the goal values are higher toward the thick end of the tentacle so the model stays intact during the simulation.

Inverse Kinematic Splines: Making a Tentacle Climb

This next shot occurs later in the severed tentaclefilm. At this point, the alien is upset and still holding a grudge against those who have removed its tentacle. In this shot, we see a close-up of a pipe; a tentacle wraps around the pipe as the alien makes its way through the plumbing somewhere beneath the lab.

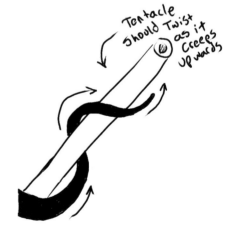

Wrapping a tentacle around a piece of geometry is a pretty straightforward operation. However, we want to add the effect of the tentacle creeping up toward the camera as it wraps around the pipe. To do this, we'll use a combination of regular forward kinematics and the Inverse Kinematic Spline tool.

Drawing the Main Tentacle Curve

1.   Open the tentacleClimb_v01.mb scene from the CD.
2.   We have a simple pipe model and the slimy tentacle. A camera has been set up for the shot. For now, hide the tentacle.

3. First we'll be creating a curve that wraps around the pipe. Later on we will slide the tentacle along this curve using the IK Spline tool. However, if we draw the curve directly on the pipe, we will encounter a problem when the tentacle slides along it; namely, the thickness of the tentacle will cause it to penetrate the geometry of the pipe. To work around this, we'll create an invisible cylinder for our curve that is slightly thicker than the pipe.

4. Create a NURBS cylinder that fits around the pipe up to the bulge at the top of the pipe. Name the cylinder "dummy" and give it 10 spans (Figure 3.11).

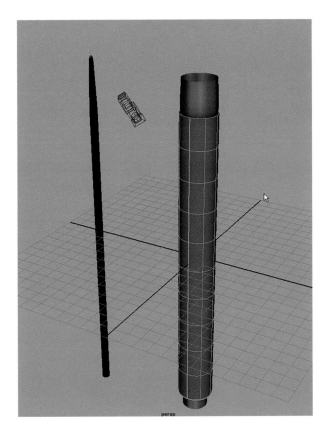

Figure 3.11:
A NURBS cylinder with 10 spans has been placed around the pipe.

5. Select the dummy surface and choose **Modify > Make Live**. Now we can draw a curve on the surface.

6. Choose **Create > CV Curve Tool**. In the options, make sure that **Curve Degrees** is set to Cubic.

7. Turn grid snapping on. Starting from the top of the cylinder, click on the live dummy surface to draw a curve that wraps around the cylinder. With grid snapping on, each time you click on the surface, the new CV should snap to the isoparms of the live surface. Try to draw the curve so that each CV is one span down and two over (see Figure 3.12).

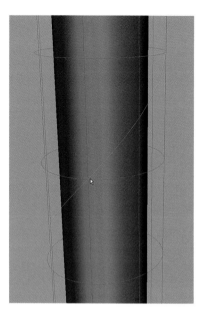

Figure 3.12:
With the dummy surface live
and grid snapping on, we
can draw a curve that spirals
around the pipe.

8. When you've reached the bottom, hit Enter to complete the curve.

Adding Joints to the Curve

We'll add some joints to deform the curve itself; this curve will later become a path for the tentacle to follow.

1. We need to duplicate the curve drawn on the surface. Select Surface Curve and (from the Surfaces menu set) choose **Edit Curves** > **Duplicate Surface Curves**.

2. Rename the duplicated curve "tentacleCurve."

3. In the Outliner, select the dummy surface and hit the down arrow key to make it "unlive." Hide the dummy surface so you don't confuse the tentacle curve with the surface curve. We want to keep the dummy around so we can preserve the history connection between it and the tentacleCurve.

4. Select the tentacleCurve and choose **Edit Curves** > **Rebuild Curves** > **Options**. In the options, set **Rebuild Type** to Uniform and **Parameter Range** to "0 to 1", keep the ends, and set **Number Of Spans** to 12. Make sure it's a **cubic** curve and don't keep the original.

5. Turn on curve snapping, and from the bottom of the curve, start adding joints that follow along to the top. Make a chain of about 18 joints or so. When you've finished making the joints, you should rename them. Select the root joint in the Outliner. Choose **Modify** > **Prefix Hierarchy Names**. In the pop-up window, type **curve_** and hit Enter. The joints will be renamed "curve_joint1," "curve_joint2," "curve_joint3," and so on.

6. Select curve_joint1 and (from the Animation menu set) choose **Skeleton** > **Orient Joints** > **Options**. In the options, choose **Edit** > **Reset** to switch to the default settings; these should work fine (Figure 3.13).

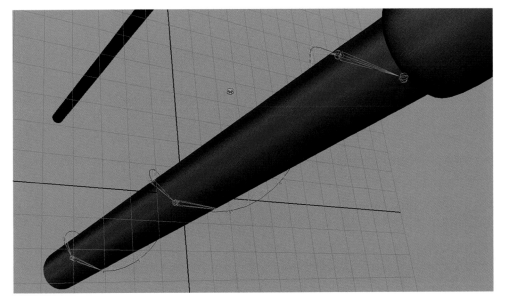

Figure 3.13: The curve joints are drawn on the curve that wraps around the pipe.

7. Select curve_joint1 and the tentacleCurve and choose **Skin > Bind Skin > Smooth Bind > Options**. In the options, make sure that **Bind To** is set **to Joint Hierarchy**, **Bind Method** is set to **Closest In Hierarchy**, and **Max Influences** is set to 3. Go ahead and hit Apply to bind the curve to the curve_joints.

Animating the Curve

Next we'll use the joints to animate the curve coiling around the pipe.

1. Set the range of the animation to 60 frames. Set the playhead to frame 60.

2. In the Outliner, Shift+select all of the curve_joints and set a keyframe on their X, Y, and Z rotational values.

> An easy way to select multiple objects is to use the Sel field located on the right-hand side of the Status line. Just type **tentacle_joint*** in this field and hit Enter. Using the asterisk wildcard will tell Maya to select all of the objects that start with **tentacle_joint**. This can save some clicking.

3. Move back to frame 1. Shift+select joints 2 through 17.

4. Choose the Rotation tool and click on the green circle to rotate the Y axis. Slowly drag to the left so that the chain of joints unwinds (Figure 3.14).

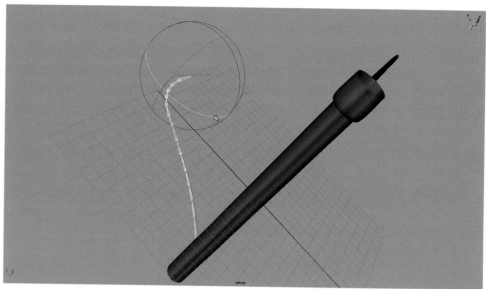

Figure 3.14: Use the rotate tool to unwind the joint chain.

5. Set a keyframe on the rotational values of these joints.

6. Play through the animation. The curve_joints should wrap around the dummy surface over the 60 frames.

Adjusting the Animation

The motion looks pretty good but it's not quite organic enough. To fix it, we'll offset some of the joints' keyframes in time.

1. In the Outliner, Shift+select joints 3 through 17.

2. Open the Graph Editor. Marquee drag around the keyframes at the start of the animation then switch to the Move tool. Hold the Shift key down and MMB drag the keys a few frames to the right.

3. Control+click joint 3 in the Outliner so that it is deselected; joints 4 through 16 should still be selected. Repeat the steps 1 and 2 to move their keyframes to the right.

4. Repeat this process of moving keys and deselecting the parent joint one at a time until you've gone through all the joints up to 17.

5. Reselect all the joints and compare what you see in the Graph Editor with Figure 3.15. It doesn't have to be exactly the same, just similar.

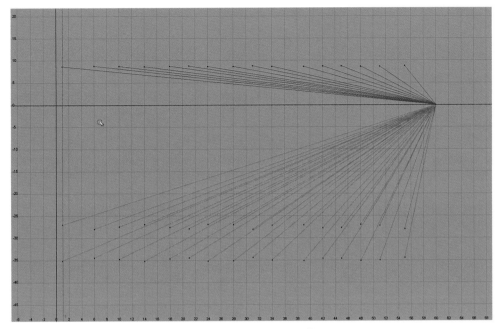

Figure 3.15: The Graph Editor shows how the animation of each joint has been offset in time.

6. The animation looks a bit more natural now.

Creating Joints for the Tentacle

Now that we have our curve looking good, let's put some joints on the tentacle and get it ready for the IK Spline tool.

1. Switch to the side view.

2. Turn the shading display to wireframe so it's easier to see what's going on. You may want to turn the resolution of the tentacle down to rough as well (select the object and hit 1 on the keypad).

3. Turn grid snapping on, and starting from the top of the tentacle, add joints every two units all the way down the tentacle. Hit Enter when all of the joints have been created (Figure 3.16). Use the Prefix Hierarchy command to rename these joints "tentacle_joints."

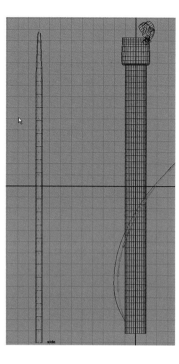

Figure 3.16:
Joints have been added
going down the length of
the tentacle.

4. Smooth bind the tentacle to the tentacle_joints using the settings from the section "Adding Joints to the Curve" earlier in this tutorial.

Activating the IK Spline Tool

The Inverse Kinematic Spline tool allows you to control the rotations of joint in a chain using the CVs on a curve. You can either have Maya automatically create the curve or use an exisiting curve. In this case we'll use the curve we animated coiling around the pipe.

1. From the Animation menu set, choose **Skeleton > IK Spline Handle Tool > Options**. In the options, turn off **Snap Curve To Root** and **Auto Create Curve** (Figure 3.17).

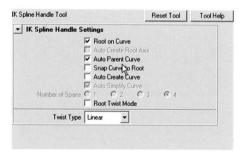

Figure 3.17:
The settings for the IK
Spline Handle tool

2. With the tool active, in the perspective view click on the tentacle_joint at the top of the tentacle, then click on the tentacle_joint at the bottom of the tentacle, and finally, carefully click on the tentacleCurve. The tentacle and its joints should jump over to the tentacle curve.

3. In the Outliner, select the curve_joints and turn off their **Visibility** (Ctrl+h) so that things are a bit easier to see.

Animating the IK Spline Offset

The animation now shows the tentacle wrapping around the pipe. There are a few things we have to fix, though, before we are done.

1. Move to the end of the animation and switch to shaded view.

2. The tentacle is still offset from the pipe. In the Outliner, select the invisible dummy surface. Scale it down in X and Z until the tentacle looks like it's wrapped around the pipe properly. The history connection between the dummy surface and the tentacleCurve allows us to do this.

3. Switch to the camera view. From the Outliner, select ikHandle1. In the Channel Box, find the **Offset** attribute. It should be at 0. Set a keyframe for this value.

4. Move to frame 1 and set **Offset** to .8. Set another keyframe.

5. Playing through the animation from the camera view, you can see that the tentacle now moves up the pipe as it wraps around. I think this motion could be a little more obvious.

6. Move to frame 40 and set **Offset** to 0.5. Set a keyframe here. Now it's looking creepier!

7. You can open the Graph Editor for ikHandle1 and refine the movement of the tentacle's creep (Figure 3.18).

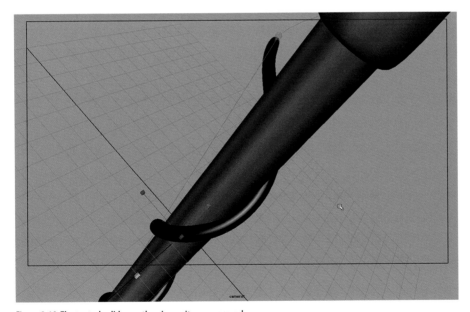

Figure 3.18: The tentacle slides up the pipe as it wraps around.

Further Study

Try a similar animation where the tentacle wraps around pipe with a bend in it. You may have to spend more time refining the animation of the tentacle curve to avoid having the tentacle geometry penetrate the pipe.

Joints and Constraints: The Telescopic Car Suspension Rig

The next shot is for a kids cartoon. It involves a car created by a master inventor. Talk about smooth rides. As this car cruises along a series of rolling hills, the chassis of the car stays level while the wheels stayed glued to the road, all thanks to the super robotic extension suspension invented by our cartoon animator.

To accomplish this task, we need to first create a rig for our robotic extension legs that spans the gap between the car and its wheels. The animator wants to be able to move the car down the roadway and have the legs automatically extend, allowing the wheels to constantly touch the road. We can create a rig composed of joints and constraints to take care of the legs. Once that's done, we'll set up a system where the wheels stick to the road. Then we can connect the legs and the wheels. It's all very simple actually.

Most of the time when joints are used, the animation of the object they deform is based on their rotation. To create our telescopic rig we'll devise a system in which the animation of the legs is based on the scaling of the joints. And it should be noted that the use of the word "telescopic" refers to how the sections of the leg rectract in on themselves similar to how the pieces of a telescope retract in on themselves. In this case it has nothing to do with optics.

Creating the Telescoping Leg

First we'll need to create the geometry for the legs.

1.   🖸   Open up the file extendo-LegCar_v01.mb from the chapter3 folder on the CD.

2.   The car is hovering above the hilly roadway; its wheels are down on the ground. This is the maximum height the car will achieve. You have been instructed to create a telescopic leg that extends from the car down to the wheels. This leg will expand and contract, keeping the car level as it drives over the hills (Figure 3.19).

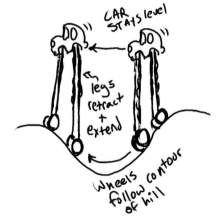

Figure 3.19:
The legs of the car will need
to reach down to the wheels
in the trough between the
hills when fully extended.

3. There is a single piece of geometry named legSection1_1 in the car's left rear wheel well. This will become our telescopic leg.

4. Turn off visibility for all of the display layers except the LEG and WHEELS layers.

5. Switch to the side view and zoom out so you can see the wheels and the leg section.

6. There are about 15 units between the leg section and the wheel. The leg section is one unit tall, so we'll duplicate it 15 times using the new Duplicate Special options.

7. Select the legSection1_1 object and choose **Edit > Duplicate Special > Options**.

8. In the options, set **Geometry Type** to **Copy** and **Group Under to World**. Set **Translate Y** to -1 and **Scale** to 0.9, 1, 0.9. Set **Number Of Copies** to 14. Hit Apply to make the copies (Figure 3.20).

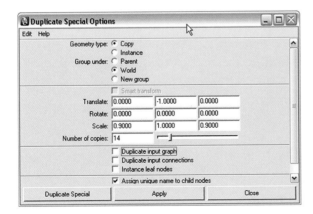

Figure 3.20:
The Duplicate Special
options for the leg section

9. Select all the leg sections and choose **Modify > Freeze Transformations**.

Creating the Telescopic Rig

With our first leg created, we can set up our scale-based telescopic rig to control its extension.

1. From the Animation menu set, choose **Skeleton > Joint Tool > Options**. In the options, turn off **Scale Compensate** (Figure 3.21). **With Scale Compensate** off, all child joints will scale to the same size as their parent joint.

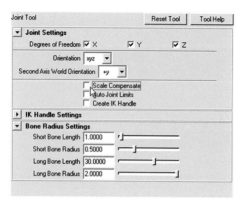

Figure 3.21:
The Scale Compensate
option has been turned off
in the Joint Tool options.

2. Turn on grid snapping and create a joint chain down the length of the leg. Make one joint for each leg section. Place the last joint at the bottom of the final section.

3. Switch to the front view. Select joint1 and move it so that the joint chain is at the center of the leg geometry (Figure 3.22).

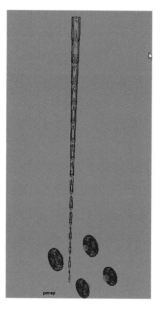

Figure 3.22:
The joint chain at the center
of the leg sections

4. In the Outliner, select joint2 through joint16. In the Channel Box, Shift+select the **Rotate X, Y,** and **Z** attributes. Right-click and choose **Lock Selected**.

5. Select joint1 and choose **Modify** > **Prefix Hierarchy Names**. In the field, type **legSection1_**.

6. This next part is a bit tedious, but that comes with the territory sometimes. Select legSection1_joint1 and Ctrl+select the legSection1_1 geometry. Choose **Constrain** > **Parent** > **Options**. In the options, make sure **Maintain Offset** is checked and that **All** is selected for both **Rotate** and **Translate** (Figure 3.23). The **Weight** setting should be at 1. A parent constraint constrains both the translate and the rotate values. As with a regular parent connection, you can still move the child node. For our purposes, don't move the child nodes. We're using this type of constraint to save time, so we don't need to create both a point and a rotate constraint for each object.

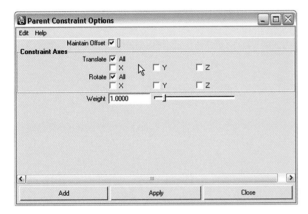

Figure 3.23:
The options for the parent constraint

7. In the Outliner, go down the line and create a parent constraint so that each legSection is constrained to its respective legSection joint. Constrain legSection1_2 to legSection1_joint2, legSection1_3 to legSection1_joint3, and so on. legSection1_joint16 will not need anything constrained to it. Alternatively, you could use a little MEL scripting to automate this process. A simple loop like the ones used in the shaky tentacle tutorial might do the trick. Type the following into the Script Editor:

```
for ($i=1; $i<=16; $i++) {
   parentConstraint -mo ("legSection1_joint" + $i) ("legSection1_" + $i);
}
```

The mo flag in the parentConstraint command stands for "maintain offset." If it's not specified in the command, Maya automatically constrains all axes and gives the constraint weight of 1.

8. When you are done, try rotating legSection1_joint1 to make sure all the geometry has been constrained to the joints. If all the leg sections rotate with the joints properly, good work. You may now ask yourself why we didn't just skin the geometry to the joints. Well, I'm glad you asked.

9. Return legSection1_joint1 to its 0, 0, 0 rotational position and try scaling down in X. You'll see all the section geometry retract just like a telescopic leg should (Figure 3.24). By using constraints instead of binding, we avoid having the geometry scale with the joint. Since we turned off Scale Compensate for the joints, all the child joints scale with the legSection1_joint1 joint, which means this is the only joint we have to worry about animating.

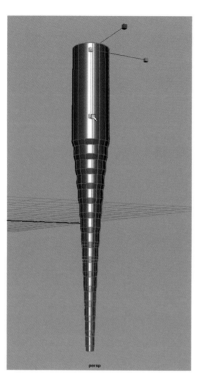

Figure 3.24:
Scaling the top joint causes the telescopic sections of the leg to retract.

Setting Limits for the *Scale X* Attribute

If we scale past 1 in X for the root joint, the sections start to come apart. Let's set some limits to prevent this.

1. Select legSection1_joint1 and open its Attribute Editor.

2. In the Limit Information section, expand the attributes for **Scale**.

3. Click the check box next to **Scale Limit X** and put .01 in the **Min** box and 1 in the **Max** box (Figure 3.25).

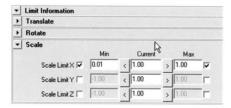

Figure 3.25:
The scale limits are set for the legSection1_joint1 joint.

Creating an IK Handle for the Leg Joints

Next, we'll create an Inverse Kinematic handle so that the leg always points toward the end of the joint chain.

1. Switch to wireframe mode in the perspective view, and from the Animation menu set, choose **Skeleton** > **IK Handle Tool** > **Options**. In the options, switch **Current Solver** to **ikSCsolver**. Turn off **Sticky** (Figure 3.26). The SC solver is a single chain solver. Since we are not concerned about the rotation of the child joints, a single chain solver will do fine (as opposed to the RP, or rotate plane, solver, which adds twist controls to adjust the rotation of the child joints).

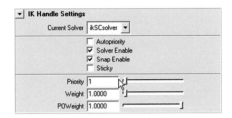

Figure 3.26:
The settings for the
IK Handle tool.

2. With the IK Handle tool active, click on legSection1_joint1 at the top of the joint chain and then click on legSection1_joint16.

3. Create a locator and name it "legWheel_1."

4. Turn on point snapping and place the legWheel_1 locator at the same location as the newly created IK handle at the bottom of the joint chain.

5. With legWheel_1 selected, choose **Modify** > **Freeze Transformations** to zero out its **Rotate** and **Translate** attributes.

6. Select legWheel_1 and ikHandle1 in the Outliner. Choose **Constrain** > **Point** to lock the IK handle to legWheel_1. Select ikHandle1 and turn off its **Visibility** (Ctrl+h) so you don't accidentally select it in the future.

Creating an Automated Scaling Control

Finally, we'll create a control that will automatically scale the leg based on its distance from the wheel.

1. Switch to the side view and choose **Create** > **Measure Tools** > **Distance Tool**.

2. With point snapping on, click on the joint at the top of the chain.

3. Zoom in closely to the legWheel_1 locator on the bottom of the joint chain, and click on it carefully to connect the Distance tool to this locator. You should see two arrows appear between a new locator at the top of the chain and the legWheel_1 locator. The number 15 should appear between the arrows (Figure 3.27).

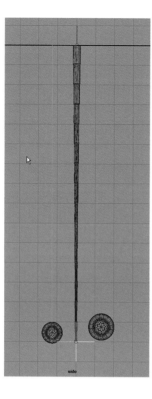

Figure 3.27:
The Distance tool measures
the distance between a
locator created at the top
of the joint chain and the
legWheel_1 locator.

4. Rename Locator1 "legTop_1" and point constrain the legSection1_joint1 joint to legTop_1.

5. Select the legSection1_joint1 joint and scale it down to .01 in X so that the entire leg retracts.

6. Select the legWheel_1 locator and translate it in Y so that it is right at the tip of the bottom of the retracted leg (Figure 3.28).

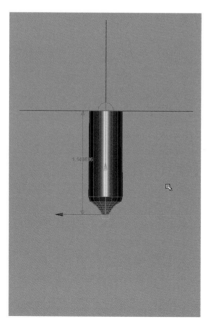

Figure 3.28:
The legWheel_1 locator has
been moved to the bottom
of the retracted leg.

7. In the Animation menu set, choose **Animate > Set Driven Key > Set**. The Set Driven Key window will open.

8. In the Outliner, set the display mode so that shape nodes are available, and then scroll down and choose the distanceDimension1's shape node. Load it as the Driver in the Set Driven Key window.

9. Select the legSection1_joint1 joint and load it as the Driven in the Set Driven Key window.

10. On the right section of the top part of the Set Driven Key window, scroll down and choose the **Distance** attribute.

11. In the bottom right, choose the **ScaleX** attribute.

12. Hit the Key button (Figure 3.29).

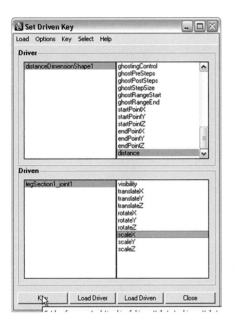

Figure 3.29:
Set Driven Key creates a relationship between the distance dimension's output and the legSection1_joint1 joint.

13. Select the legWheel_1 locator, and in the channel box, set the **TranslateX, Y,** and **Z** values to 0.

14. Select the legSection1_joint1 joint and set the **ScaleX** value to 1.

15. Click the Key button in the Set Driven Key window.

When you move the legWheel_1 locator up and down, the leg should automatically retract.

Duplicating the Leg Rig

Duplicating this rig is easy, by using Duplicate Special, we can avoid having to repeat the process of building the rig from scratch.

1. Select all of the leg geometry and group it. Rename the group "leg_1."

2. Select the leg_1 group and choose **Edit > Duplicate Special > Options**. Set **Group Under to World** and **Number Of Copies** to 1, and check **Duplicate Input Graph** and **Assign Unique Name To Child Nodes**.

3. These Duplicate Special settings will duplicate all of the geometry, the joints, the locators, and the distance dimension. including the set driven keys that automate the scaling. The only thing that will not duplicate is the ikHandle.

4. Hide all the leg1 objects, joints, locators, and so on.

5. Expand the new set of joints associated with leg 2.

6. At the bottom of the joint chain in the Outliner, delete the effector.

7. Create a new IK handle using the steps described in the section "Creating an IK Handle for the Leg Joints" earlier in this tutorial. Hide it and point constrain it to legWheel_2.

8. Make two more duplicate legs using this process. If the newly duplicated legs appear all blue, apply a new shader to them. Sometimes the shading does not duplicate very well. Remember to rename all the joints and geometry associated with leg 2 so that instead of legSection1 they read legSection2. You can use **Search and Replace Names** under the **Modify** menu to do this.

Placing the Legs

The next few steps involve positioning the duplicated legs in relation to the car.

1. When you have four legs, turn the visibility for the CAR layer back on.

2. Place the leg top locators in each of the wheel wells of the car so that legTop_1 is in the driver side front wheel well, legTop_2 is in the driver side rear wheel well, legTop_3 is in the passenger side rear wheel well, and legTop_4 is in the passenger side front wheel well (Figure 3.30).

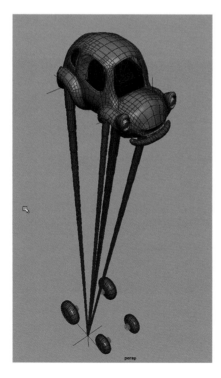

Figure 3.30:
Each leg top locator has been
positioned in the wheel wells
of the car model.

3. Arrange the legWheel locators so that they are at the center point of the cylinder attached to the inside of each wheel (Figure 3.31).

Figure 3.31: The legWheel locators are positioned at the center of each wheel's inner hub.

4. When you have these arranged, select each of the legTop locators and choose **Modify > Freeze Transformations** to zero out their translate values. Do the same for the legWheel locators.

5. You may want to hide the distance dimension objects just to make the scene a bit clearer.

Constraining the Wheels

We'll use parent constraints to attach the wheels to the legs.

1. Select legWheel_1 and then Shift+select the L_front_tire object.

2. Create a parent constraint between the two objects.

3. Do the same for the other three wheels, parent constraining the wheels to the legWheel locators.

Creating Front and Rear Controls

We can create some controls using NURBS curves to make the task of animating the car a bit easier.

1. Switch to the top view and turn on grid snapping.

2. Choose **Create > CV Curve Tool > Options**. Set **Curve Tool Degree** to **Linear**.

3. In the top view window, draw a triangle on the grid using four points.

4. Choose **Modify > Center Pivot** to set the pivot at the center of the triangle.

5. Rename the triangle frontSuspension.

6. Duplicate the triangle and name the duplicate rearSuspension.

7. Scale the triangles down a little bit and move them so that the frontSuspension object is in between the front wheels and the rearSuspension object is in between the rear wheels (Figure 3.32).

Figure 3.32: Two NURBS curves shaped as triangles are placed between the wheels. These will become controls for the front and rear sets of wheels.

8. Freeze their transformations once you are happy with their placement.

9. Parent legWheel1 and legWheel4 under the frontSuspension triangle.

10. Parent legWheel2 and legWheel3 under the rearSuspension triangle.

We could have used locators for the suspension objects, but after a while it starts to look like a mess. The triangles are slightly more visually appealing.

11. Move the front suspension object around, rotating it on its Y axis. You now have a nice control for the car's steering, yet the wheels can also move independently since they are parented under the front suspension control. To return them to their original positions, you can just zero out their transforms.

For an example of the scene up to this point, open the extendoLegCar_v02.mb scene from the chapter 3 folder on the CD.

Making the Car Move

We can connect the car to a motion path to automate its movement across the terrain, then all we have to keyframe are the wheels and the chassis.

1. Select all the leg controls in the Outliner and add them to the LEGS display layer by right-clicking over the LEGS layer in the Layer Editor and choosing **Add Selected Objects**.

2. Turn off the visibility for the CAR, LEGS, and WHEELS layers. Turn on the visibility for the GROUND layer.

3. Select the road object in the perspective view, right-click, and choose **Isoparms**.

4. Select the isoparm at the center of the road. Switch to the Surfaces menu set and choose **Edit Curves** > **Duplicate Surface Curves**. Rename the new curve "carPath."

5. Create a locator and name it "wheelFollow."

6. Switch to the Animation menu set and choose **Animate** > **Motion Paths** > **Attach To Motion Path** > **Options**.

7. In the options, choose **Edit** > **Reset Options**. These should work just fine. We want **Follow** on so the locator rotates to follow the contour of the motion path.

8. Turn the visibility of the other layers back on, and move the playhead so that the wheel follow locator is below the car—around frame 88 or 89.

9. Parent the frontSuspension and rearSuspension objects to the wheelFollow locator.

10. Scrub back and forth on the Time Slider. You should see the wheels climb up and down the hilly road. The legs should point toward the wheels (Figure 3.33).

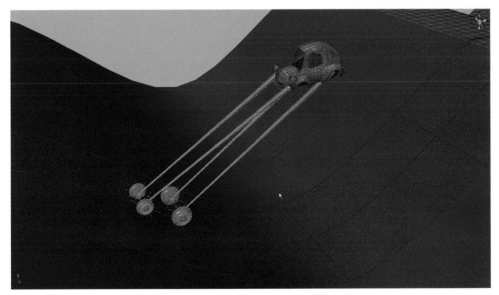

Figure 3.33: The wheels now follow the contour of the road since the suspension objects have been parented to the wheelFollow locator.

11. Set the playhead back to frame 88. Create a new locator and name it "chassis-Control."

12. Place the chassis control at the center of the chassis object. The easiest way to do this is to point constrain the locator to the chassis object (make sure **Maintain Offset** is **Off** in the Point Constraint options). The locator should snap to the center of the chassis. Then, in the Outliner, delete the point constraint from under the chassisControl object. Freeze transforms on the chassisControl.

13. Parent each of the legTop locators to the chassis control locator.

14. Almost there! Create yet another locator and name it "carFollow." Place it at the same location as the chassis control locator.

15. Point constrain carFollow to the wheelFollow object. In the options for the point constraint, turn Maintain Offset on and set Constraint Axes to Z Only.

16. As you scrub back and forth in the Timeline, the carFollow locator should move with the wheelFollow but maintain a level height (Figure 3.34).

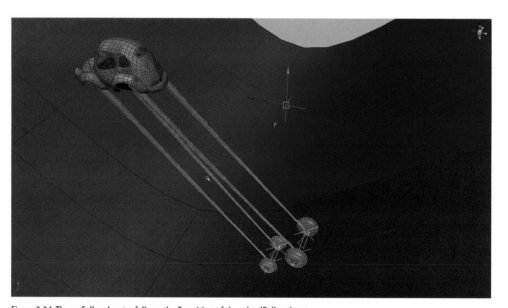

Figure 3.34: The carFollow locator follows the Z position of the wheelFollow locator.

17. Move the Time Slider back to frame 88 and parent chassisControl to the carFollow locator.

18. Parent constrain the Chassis object to the chassisControl locator.

19. As you move back and forth on the Time Slider, the car should remain level while the telescoping suspension legs follow the road. That's one smooth ride!

20. If the car is moving backwards, you can select the wheelFollow locator, open its Graph Editor for the motion path node, and reverse the keyframes so that it's moving in the correct direction.

21. The animator has the advantage of an automated system to control the extension of the legs, but he can also independently keyframe the front and rear suspension and each of the wheels as well as the chassis. This way he can make the legs a little more wobbly as well as move the chassis around as if it's having a

hard time balancing on top of the wobbly legs. Hey, this is a prototype car; it's bound to have a few kinks in it. He will certainly have to make adjustments as the car reaches the crest of each hill. A few keyframes on the chassisControl object should fix these problems.

Check out extendoLegCar_v03.mb for the finished version of this scene (Figure 3.35).

Figure 3.35: Our plucky little car is always level, no matter what the terrain!

Further Study

The telescoping rig created for the legs holds a lot of promise for experimentation. See how you can augment the current rig or repurpose it for other models.

1. Try applying an animated Fractal texture to the movement of the chassis to get a nice shakiness to the car as it putters along.

2. Create a system where the front and rear suspension have their own motion paths to follow. See if you can improve on the controls so that the animator can easily see and select the chassis and wheel controls.

3. See if you can create some custom control objects, like the triangle used for the front and rear suspension, so that the animator can easily access controls for the chassis and each wheel without worrying about clicking or moving the wrong thing.

4. What if, heaven forbid, the art director suddenly decides that the legs need to bend a little to add some squash and stretch? See if you can either design a rig with this built in or alter your current rig. Chapter 4 might hold some clues. A clever use of a blend shape and wire deformers applied to the leg geometry groups might allow you to achieve this.

The Inverse Kinematic Spline Tool and Lattices

A commercial shot requires you to make a soda machine disappear into a black hole in the ground. The client would like the machine to fly up into the air, follow an arc, and then get sucked into the hole top first. The machine should shrink as it goes through the black hole.

Setting Up the Lattice

Instead of skinning the geometry of the soda machine to a joint chain, we'll skin a lattice that deforms the soda machine. This allows for a smooth deformation that's easy to set up. Our first task is creating the lattice.

1. Open the sodaMachine_v01.mb file from the Chapter 3 folder on the CD.

2. The machine has been built as a single polygon object. The modeler has also provided a curve for the machine to follow as it makes its way through the hole (Figure 3.36).

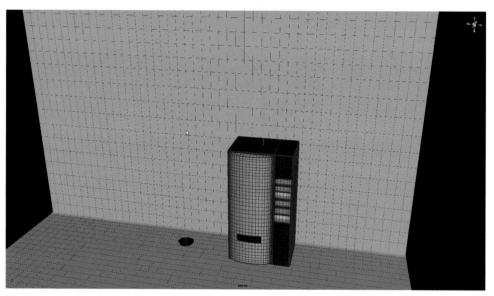

Figure 3.36: The soda machine sits next to a black hole.

3. If you play the animation, you'll see a little hole open up when the curve meets the floor at about frame 20. This hole was created by projecting a circle on the floor, trimming the surface, and then setting keyframes on the scale of the projecting curve.

4. First let's create a lattice around the machine. Switch to the Animation menu set and choose **Deform > Create Lattice**.

5. In the Channel Box for the lattice shape, set the **S, T,** and **U Divisions** to 12.

6. In the Attribute Editor for the ffd1 node, uncheck the **Local** box. This makes the deformation smoother but a little less accurate.

Adding Joints to the Lattice

The next task is creating joints for the lattice.

1. Switch to the front view and turn on wireframe shading.

2. Zoom into the soda machine and turn on grid snapping.

3. Select the Joint tool and reset the settings in the Tools option window. Starting at the bottom of the soda machine, create a joint chain going straight up the center. Make each joint one unit tall so that the resulting chain is 14 joints long.

4. Because of the positioning of the models, the joint chain will be at the same position as the curve (Figure 3.37). Isn't that handy?

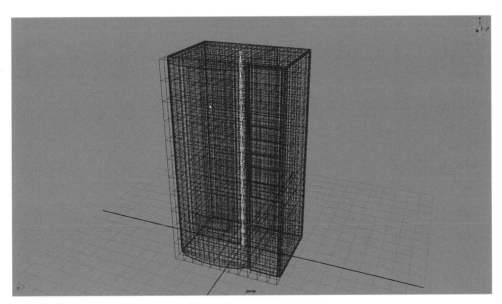

Figure 3.37: The joint chain goes up the center of the machine.

5. Select the joint chain and the ffd1Lattice object in the Outliner (don't select the ffdbase). Choose **Skin > Smooth Bind** to bind the lattice to the joints. In the options, you can use the **Edit** menu to reset the options to the default settings, which should work fine.

Adding an IK Spline to the Joints

An IK Spline can be created for the joints using the motion path curve that already exists in the scene.

1. Choose **Skeleton > IK Spline Handle Tool > Options**. In the options, click **Root On Curve** and **Auto Parent Curve**. Turn off **Snap Curve To Root** and **Auto Create Curve.**

2.   With the IK Spline Handle tool active, move to the perspective window and click on the joint at the bottom of the machine, then the joint at the top, and then the path curve.

3.   Open the Channel Box for the ikHandle1 tool and find the **Offset** attribute toward the bottom of the Channel Box. Leave the value at 0 and set a keyframe at frame 1.

4.   Move the playhead to frame 30 and set the offset to 1. Set another keyframe.

When you play the animation, you'll see the soda machine leap into the air and then go through the hole in the ground (Figure 3.38).

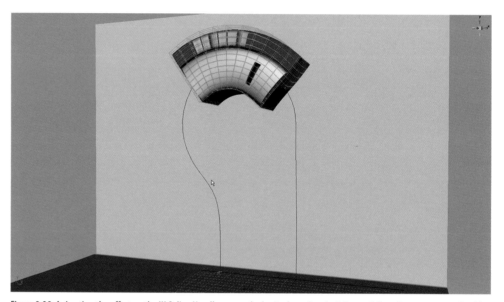

Figure 3.38: Animating the offset on the IK Spline Handle causes the lattice bound to the joints to follow the curve, somewhat like a motion path.

Animating the Squashing Effect

To create the squashing effect, we'll put a second lattice on top of the first lattice that is deforming the machine.

1.   In the Outliner, select the ffd1Lattice object.

2.   Choose **Deform > Create Lattice** to make a new lattice.

3.   In the Channel Box for the new lattice, set the S, T, and U **Divisions** to 6.

4.   In the Outliner, select both the ffd2Lattice object and the ffd2Base object. Move them over to the left so that they are over the hole in the floor. The machine should not deform when you do this. If it does, make sure you have both the lattice and the base selected. Rotate the second lattice and its base object 180 degrees in Z (Figure 3.39).

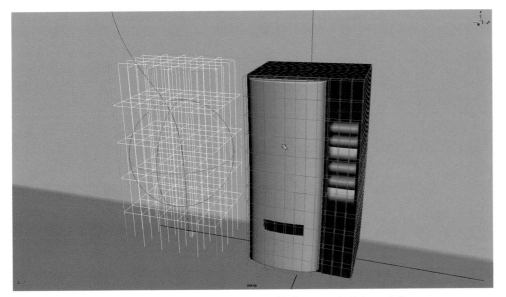

Figure 3.39: The second lattice and its base are moved over the hole, and both are rotated 180 degrees in Z.

5.   Move the playhead to frame 19.

6.   Adjust the second lattice and base so that they are at the same position as the machine. Move them down a little so that they're halfway through the floor.

7.   You may want to hide the first lattice and base just so you don't get confused about what you're looking at.

8.   Select the second lattice and scale it down in X and Z. Scale the lattice base up a little so that the machine looks like it does in Figure 3.40.

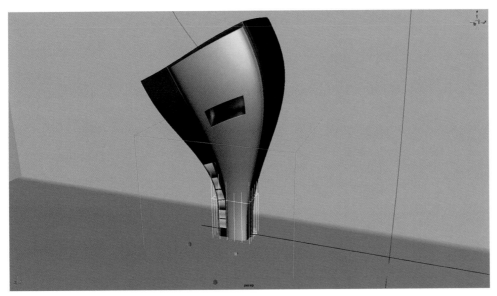

Figure 3.40: The second lattice has been scaled down in X and Z, and its base has been scaled up.

9. Have some fun creating a nice squash effect by adjusting the scale on the second lattice and the size of its base. Right-click over the lattice and choose **Lattice Points**. Select the lattice points and scale them down. It will take some tweaking to get just what you want. Move the animation back and forth and continue to fool around until it looks good.

10. Move to the start of the animation. If you notice that the machine is deformed in a weird way (as in Figure 3.41), it may be that the base for lattice2 has been scaled up too high. Scale it down again until this goes away.

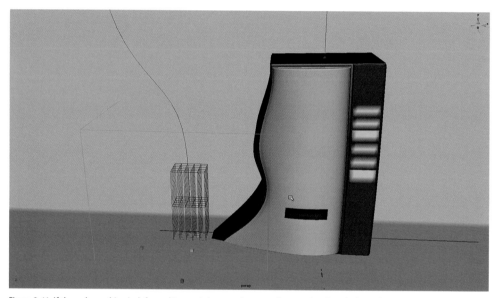

Figure 3.41: If the soda machine is deformed in a weird way at the start of your animation, the base shape for the second lattice may be scaled too high.

Creating a Twist

There are a couple of ways we can add a twist to the soda machine to make its movement a little more interesting.

1. Right-click over the second lattice and choose to select the lattice points.

2. Select the lower rows of lattice points and use the Rotate tool to rotate them in Y about 45 degrees. This should create a nice twisting effect as the machine gets sucked into the hole.

3. You can also set keyframes on the ikHandle's **Twist** and **Roll** attributes to enhance this twisting effect. This may require further tweaking of the lattice to work correctly. The twist control is a lot of fun to play with; experiment with it to get some interesting effects. For this particular shot, however, rotating the lattice points on the second lattice may work better (Figure 3.42).

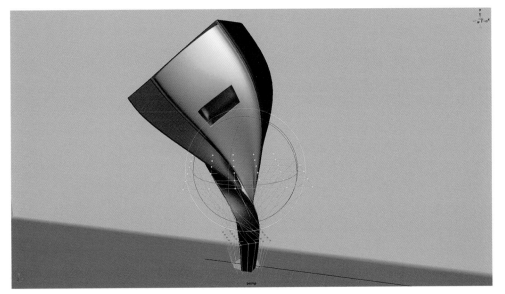

Figure 3.42: Rotating the points of the lattice and adjusting the twist on the IK Spline Handle can create some interesting twisting effects as the machine gets sucked into the black hole.

Further Study

Try selecting the rows of lattice points on the second lattice, attaching some clusters, and adding an animated fractal to the translation values of these clusters to add some shaking as the machine moves through the hole. Who can get enough of that shaking effect anyway?

Creative Blend Shape Use

Blend shape deformers, like joints, are typically associated with character animation—most often for creating facial expressions. In this chapter we'll look at some situations in which blend shapes can be a useful tool for creating other types of animated effects.

Chapter Contents

Blend Shapes and Lattices
Blend Shape In-Betweens
Interactive Blend Shape Rigs
Layering Blend Shapes

Blend Shapes and Lattices

It's no secret why people such as yourself get into 3D modeling and animation—it's all about arts and crafts! In this next shot we'll be creating some CG pottery for another kids cartoon. (You'll have even more fun if you pretend that it is zombie pottery.) In this animation, the pottery spins on a wheel. After a couple seconds, something goes horribly wrong. Such is the case when dealing with zombie pottery.

Revolving a Surface

To create the pottery we'll revolve a surface using a profile curve.

1. Open up a new file in Maya and switch your perspective window to a side view.

2. Choose a CV curve and make sure it is set to cubic under the CV Curve Settings in the options.

3. Draw a profile for a vase a few units from the origin. Make it fairly dense and make sure the last two points at the bottom are at the origin, as in Figure 4.1.

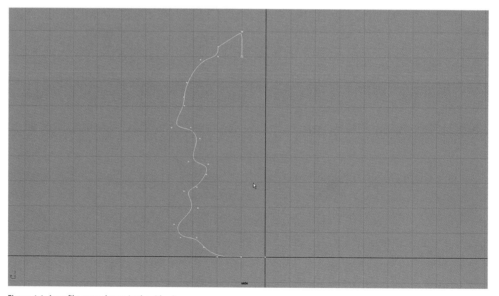

Figure 4.1: A profile curve drawn in the side view

4. Switch to the Surfaces menu set and choose **Surfaces > Revolve > Options**. Reset the options and use the default settings. A pretty little vase should appear.

5. Assign a Blinn shader to the vase so that we get some nice highlights in the perspective window (Figure 4.2).

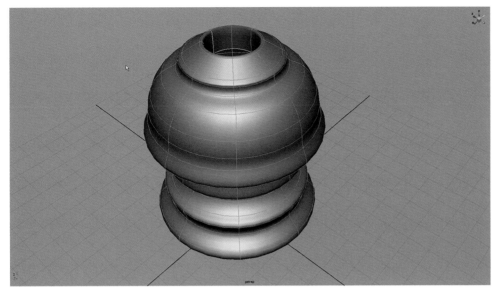

Figure 4.2: The revolved surface makes a spacey vase.

Creating a Blend Shape for the Profile Curve

We want to be able to control the shape of the vase as it spins on the wheel to simulate the effect of fingers shaping it. As long as history is maintained for the surface, any changes we make to the profile curve will be reflected in the revolved surface. We want to be able to edit the curve away from the surface just so that it's easier to see what's going on. If we move the curve away from the origin, the vase will enlarge with it. However, we can move the vase geometry anywhere we want without affecting its shape. We could also create a blend shape for the curve and move that away from both the original profile curve and the vase geometry. Let's try that method.

1.   Select the original profile curve and make a standard duplicate by choosing **Edit > Duplicate**. Rename the new curve "control" and the original curve "vaseProfile."

2.   Move the control curve about 15 units in Z.

3.   Select the control curve and then Ctrl+select the vaseProfile curve. From the Animation menu set, choose **Deform > Create Blend Shape > Options**.

4.   In the options, select the **Local** button and the box next to **Check Topology**; leave **In-Between** unselected.

Remember that the first objects you select will be the blend shape deformers and the last object will be the object they deform. This is important to keep in mind, especially when you Shift+select multiple objects.

Setting Up a Control View Camera

We can create an extra view that focuses on the control curve by making an orthographic camera.

1.   Create a new Camera, and rename it "controlCam."

2. Look through the camera and position it so that the control curve is framed in view.

3. Open up the Attribute Editor for the controlCam. Under the Orthographic Views section, check the box next to **Orthographic**. The camera is now an orthographic camera like the side, front, and top cameras.

4. Parent the controlCam to the controlCurve, and in the perspective view, move the curve farther away from the vase.

5. Set the panel layout to four windows. From the perspective view window, choose **Panels** > **Saved Layouts** > **Four View**.

6. Set the upper-left view to be the Outliner, the upper right to Perspective, the lower left to Side, and the lower right to controlCam (it will be listed in the view window under Orthographic Views). Use Figure 4.3 as a guide.

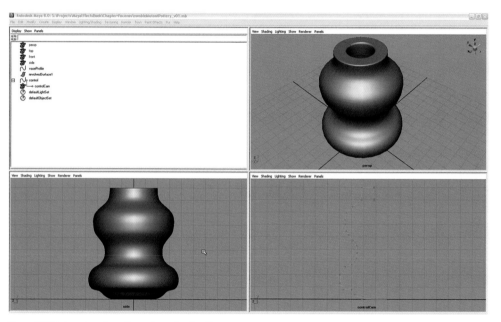

Figure 4.3: This layout configuration makes animating the vase easy.

Setting Up Blend Shape Controls

We'll be using the blend shape applied to the curve as an animation control. We'll apply cluster deformers to the control vertices of the blend shape curve so that we have an easy way to animate the shape of the curve.

1. In the controlCam view, right-click over the curve and choose **Control Vertex** form the marking menu.

2. Select each CV and create a cluster by switching to the Animation menu set and choosing **Deform** > **Create Cluster**.

3. In the Outliner, Shift+select all the clusters and group them. Name the group "controlClusters."

4. In the Outliner, select the vaseProfile curve. In its Channel Box, select blend-Shape1 under the Inputs section. Set the **Control** attribute to 1. This makes the control curve's blend shape strength 100%.

5. Move some of the clusters around in the controlCam view. You should see the shape of the vase update. We now have a handy control mechanism and view for our vase (Figure 4.4).

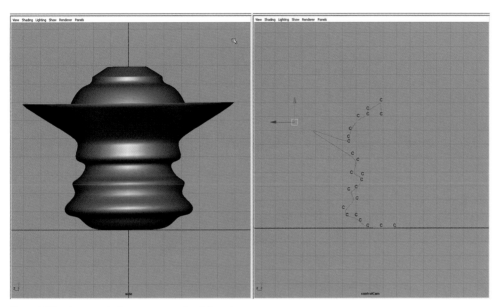

Figure 4.4: The clusters make for an easy control to deform the vase.

Making the Vase Spin

Rather than spin the actual vase object we'll apply a lattice and spin the lattice; this will allow for some flexibility in animating the vase later on down the road.

1. Select the vase geometry and choose, from the Animation menu set, **Deform** > **Create Lattice**. In the Channel Box, set the ffd1LatticeShape's **S**, **T**, and **U Divisions** to 2, 8, 2.

2. In the Outliner, Shift+select both the ffd1Lattice and the ffd1Base.

3. Switch to the Move tool and hit the Insert key on your keyboard to activate editing of the pivot point.

4. Move the pivot point to the base of the lattice, and grid-snap it to the origin.

5. Hit the Insert key again once the pivot point has been positioned.

6. With both the lattice and base selected, switch to the Scale tool and scale both the lattice and the base up a unit or so larger than the vase.

7. In the ffd1 tab of the Attribute Editor, switch the **Outside Lattice** option to **All**.

8. Select the lattice and switch to the Move tool. Hit the Insert key to activate the pivot editing mode. Move the pivot just slightly to the left.

9. In the Channel Box for the lattice, set the **RotateX** to .5. This will give it a slight wobble when it spins (Figure 4.5).

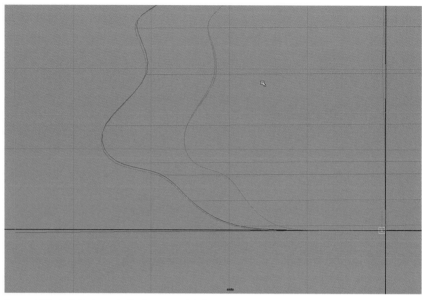

Figure 4.5: The lattice's pivot point has been moved slightly off center and the lattice has been rotated a little in X. This gives the pottery a wobble when it spins.

10. Set the Timeline to 300 frames.

11. On the first frame of the Timeline, set a key for the Y rotation at 0.

12. Move to frame 10 and set the Y rotation to 720. Set another keyframe.

13. Open the Attribute Editor for the lattice. Under the ffd1Lattice Transform Attributes, right-click on the Y rotation channel that's highlighted in orange. Choose **ffd1Lattice_rotateY.output**.

14. In the Attribute Editor for the ffdLattice_rotateY, set **Post Infinity** to **Linear**. Set **InTan Type** and **OutTan Type** to **Linear** as well.

15. In the Outliner, select the vaseProfile curve and hide it.

16. Play the animation and check out the crazy arts and crafts action.

Animating the Sculpting of the Vase

We can now use the clusters on the control curve to animate the vase as if it were being shaped by invisible fingers.

1. Set the Timeline to frame 1. Shift+select all the clusters and use the Shift+W hot key combination to set a keyframe on the translate attributes.

2. Move to different frames on the Timeline, and in the controlCam view, move around the individual control clusters. Set keyframes on their positions. Have fun with setting the keyframes so that the vase looks like it's being shaped over time.

Creating a Blend Shape Control for the Lattice

Blend shapes can be applied to lattices just like they can be applied to geometry; we'll take advantage of this to enhance the animation further.

1. Rewind to the beginning of the animation.

2. Select the lattice and duplicate it.

3. In the Outliner, select the new ffd1Lattice1 and ffd1Base1 objects and move them away from the base. Move them so that you can see them in the control-Cam view.

4. Select the new ffd1Lattice1 and Ctrl+select the original ffd1Lattice. Choose **Deform > Create Blend Shape**.

5. Set the blendShape2 input in the Channel Box for the ffd1Lattice. Set the ffd1Lattice1 attribute to 1 just as we did for the curve blend shape.

Deforming the Blend Shape Lattice with Joints

We'll add joints to the second lattice to make it easier to deform. You should be getting a sense of how you can layer deformers on top of each other to achieve a high level of control over the deformation of your objects

1. In the controlCam view, start from the bottom of the duplicate lattice and create a joint chain going up the center. You may want to use grid snapping to keep the joints in a straight line (Figure 4.6).

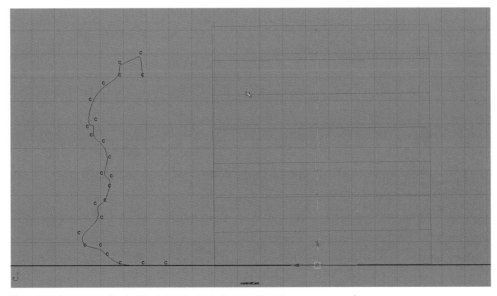

Figure 4.6: Joints are added to the blend shape lattice in the controlCam view.

2. When the joint chain is complete, select the root joint and the duplicated lattice and choose **Skin > Bind Skin > Rigid Bind**.

3. Set the Timeline to 160, select the joints, and set a keyframe on their rotation channels.

4. Move the Timeline to a later frame in the animation. Select the joints parented to joint 2 and start rotating them in X and Z. Set some keyframes and have some fun experimenting with different rotations.

5. Play the animation and watch it in the perspective window. Our zombie pottery has turned into evil mutant pottery. Better get a shotgun in either case. Check out the zombieMutantPottery_v01.mb file on the CD to see a finished version (Figure 4.7).

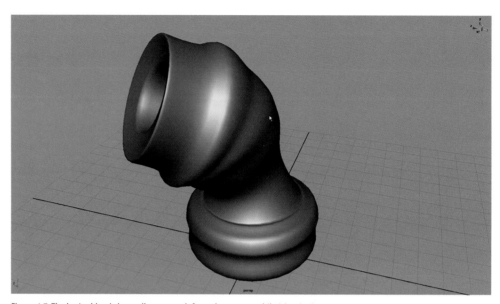

Figure 4.7: The lattice blend shape allows us to deform the pottery while it's spinning.

When layering deformers such as blend shapes, lattice, or joints on a single object, the order in which you apply the deformers will affect how they deform the object. Sometimes if you get unexpected results when you animate the attributes of a deformer it may be a result of the order in which the deformers are applied. You can change the order by opening up the list of inputs for the object. To do this, right-click over the object in a viewport and from the marking menu choose **Inputs** > **All Inputs**. In the List of Input Operations dialog box you'll see all of the deformers applied to the object. To change the order, MMB click on the name of a deformer and drag it up or down in the list.

Further Learning

Clearly pottery is probably not the most exciting thing you'll be animating in your career; however, these principles, simple as they are, can be used for a variety of other techniques.

1. Try this tutorial with a denser lattice. Turn the duplicate lattice into a softbody and apply a turbulence field to the particles to see what happens. Set it up so that the goal weights at the base of the lattice have a higher value than those at the top.

2. Apply some gravity to the softbody particles and see if you can get the spinning vase to melt over time.

Blend Shape In-Betweens

The next shot is a TV network promo for a popular cable channel. The shot calls for a time-lapse-styled animation of a peapod growing. The pod splits open and inside we see a bunch of eyeballs. Ewww gross! The art director wants to know how hard it would be to do this.

Actually it's pretty straightforward and lots of fun. To create this we'll use blend shapes, joints, and a lattice. Blend shapes have two modes: regular blend shape deformers, which are additive, and blend shape in-betweens. The regular additive type are used most frequently for things like facial animation. When you select a number of blend shape targets and then apply them to your model, each blend shape control is independent of the other shapes. When you set two or more blend shapes at full strength, the deformation is added together. So a smile and an open mouth shape result in an open mouth smile.

The in-between blend shape deformer type allows you to select a number of targets and apply them to your model, and the resulting blend shape is a sequence of shapes based on the order in which you select the targets. So instead of getting a smile combined with an open mouth when you animate the value of the blend shape deformer, the result would be a smile and then an open mouth in sequence. How is this useful? We'll see.

Working with Blend Shape Targets

We'll start with a scene that has all the models, including the blend shape targets, created already.

1. Open the peaPod_v01.mb scene from the Chapter 4 folder on the CD. You'll see that the modeler has provided us with a peapod full of eyes (modeled in the open position), the peapod in the closed position, and a small peapod at the start of its growth cycle (see Figure 4.8). There are also some leaves and a stem.

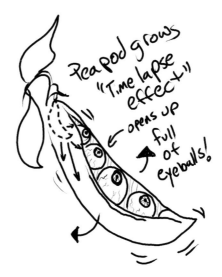

Figure 4.8: The peapod scene with blend shape target models

2. Look through camera1 to see how the shot will be framed.

3. Return to the perspective window. Let's test out how the blend shapes will work before we set up the rig.

4. Turn off the visibility for the Peas display layer to hide the eyes for the moment.

5. In the Outliner, select the pod_closed object, Ctrl+select the pod_start object, and then Ctrl+select the pod_end object. The order of selection is important.

6. From the Animation menu set choose **Deform > Create Blend Shape > Options**. In the options, set **Origin** to **Local** and check the **In-Between** box. Click Create to make the blend shape.

7. Select the pod_end object. In the Channel Box under the inputs for the shape node, select blendShape1. You'll see **pod_start** listed (see Figure 4.9); this is the blend shape control. It actually contains the sequence from pod_start through pod_closed and then ends with pod_end where the pod is open. To test it, choose **Window > Animation Editors > Blend Shape**. As you move the slider up you'll see the peapod first close and then shrink in sequence. For the final animation, we'll just reverse the keyframes for the sequence.

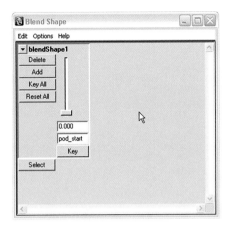

Figure 4.9:
The Blend Shape slider is a
handy control for animating
blend shapes.

Painting Blend Shape Weights

This animation is OK but it might look a lot better if we could have the opening split
in the middle first and then spread to the ends, just to add some drama. To do this
we'll create an intermediate blend shape target between the open and closed shapes by
painting blend shape weights.

1. In the Blend Shape animation control panel, set the slider to 0.5.

2. Choose **Deform > Paint Blend Shape Weights Tool > Options**. The Artisan interface
   will open up in the Tool Settings palette. The peapod will turn white, indicating that
   the value of the pod_start blend shape target for all the vertices of the model is set to 1.

3. Set **Paint Operation** to **Replace** and the **Value** to .5.

4. Start painting around the center of the split in the peapod, The vertices will
   jump to an open position (0.5 = halfway between the pod_closed and pod_end
   states) and the surface around these vertices will turn gray (Figure 4.10).

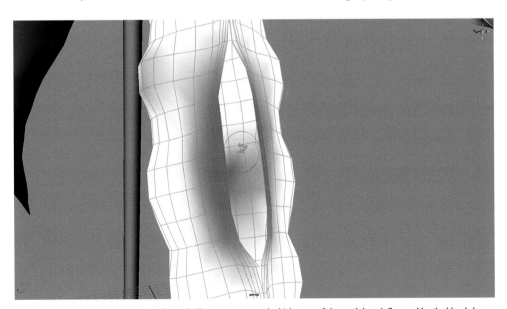

Figure 4.10: The Paint Blend Shape Weights tool allows you to control which parts of the model are influenced by the blend shape
deformer.

5. You may want to move the view inside the peapod to access some of the inner vertices. It takes a little bit of work.

6. When the opening looks similar to Figure 4.10, switch the paint operation to **Smooth** and paint around the vertices that have moved to smooth out the shape.

7. When it looks nice and smooth, set **Operation** to **Replace** and **Value** to 1 and paint any of the vertices on the back of the peapod you may have accidentally painted on the back and sides.

8. If you want to refine the opening, you can try lowering the value of the brush, painting the opening some more, and then smoothing it out until you're satisfied. The closer to zero the value, the larger the opening will be.

9. When you are done painting and the opening looks similar to Figure 4.11, select the peapod_end object and duplicate it.

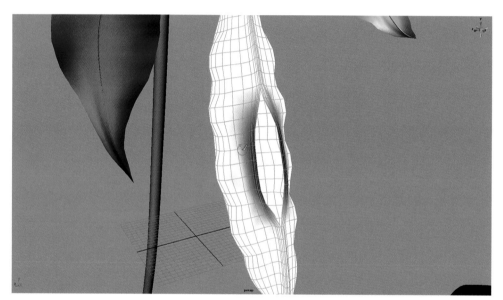

Figure 4.11: The opening has been refined by adjusting the Replace and Smooth values on the Paint Blend Shape Weights tool.

10. Move the duplicate out of the way and rename it pod_split.

11. Select the pod_end object and move the Blend Shape slider all the way to zero so it is back to its original, undeformed, open state.

12. Select all four pod objects (pod_closed, pod_start, pod_end, and pod_split) and delete history on them. This will remove the blend shape deformer on the pod end so that we can use it as a new target in the next blend shape sequence we will build in the following section.

Creating the Blend Shape Sequence

Now that we have all the blend shape targets we need, we'll create a new blend shape sequence that includes the pod_split object.

1. Ctrl+select the pod_split, pod_closed, pod_start, and pod_end objects in that order.

2. Choose **Deform** > **Create Blend Shape** to make the blend shape sequence.

3. Choose **Window** > **Animation Editors** > **Blend Shape** to open the Blend Shape Control window.

4. Move the slider to 1, set the playhead to the beginning of the sequence, and click the Key button.

5. Move the playhead to frame 100, set the Blend Shape slider to 0, and click the Key button.

6. As you play the animation, you'll see the peapod grow, the center will split, and then it will open.

Adjusting the Animation

The animation looks good but it needs a little adjustment to make it more interesting. We'll edit the keys we set on the blend shape deformer using the graph editor.

1. With pod_end selected, open up the Graph Editor. Press the F key to frame the keys on the graph.

2. Adjust the keys so that the peapod grows slowly over time, starts to open, and then pops open. Adjust the handles on the graph to achieve this. You may need to convert the curves to weighted tangents. Try selecting the handles and choose (from the Graph Editor menu) **Keys** > **Free Tangent Weight** to get more control over editing the curve. Use Figure 4.12 as a reference.

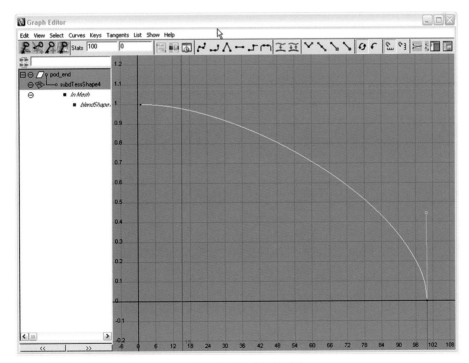

Figure 4.12: The Graph Editor allows you to tune the animation of the blend shape sequence.

Rigging the Pod

Now that we have the sequence animated we can add some additional squirmy motion to the growth using a lattice.

1. Set the playhead at the end of the animation. Turn the visibility for the Peas layer on.

2. In the Outliner, select the pod_end object and the peas group, group them together, and rename the new group "peapod." Add the pod_split object to the blendshapes display layer and turn off visibility of this layer.

3. Select the peapod group and choose **Deform > Create Lattice**.

4. Set the **S**, **T**, and **U Divisions** for the lattice to 4, 8, and 4.

5. Switch to the front viewport to get a side view of the pod. Select the ffd1Lattice and the ffd1Base from the Outliner. Switch to the Move tool, hit the Insert key, and move the pivot point of the lattice up to where the peapod meets the stem (Figure 4.13).

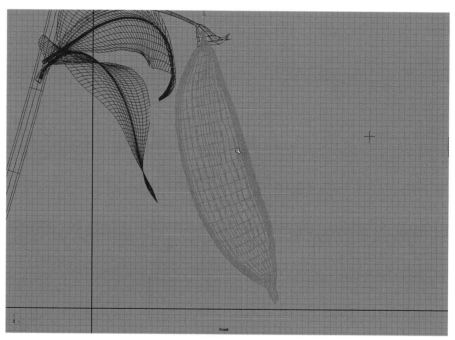

Figure 4.13: The pivot point of the lattice and lattice base have been positioned at the point where the peapod meets the stem.

6. Using the Joint tool, create a series of eight joints moving down the side of the pod in a slight curve; use Figure 4.14 for reference.

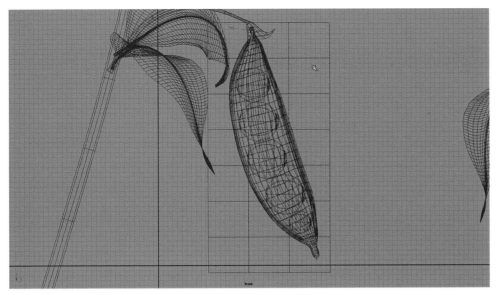

Figure 4.14: Joints have been added to the peapod rig.

7. Switch to the side view and move joint1 so that the chain goes down the center of the pod.

8. Select joint1 and ffd1Lattice. Choose **Skin > Rigid Bind** to skin the lattice.

Animating the Pod

With the lattice rigged we can animated the joints which will, in turn, animate the pod. Its kind of cool to see the pod growing while it's being deformed by the lattice.

1. In the Outliner, select joints 2 through 7. Move the playhead to the start of the Timeline. Turn off visibility for the Peas layer.

2. Switch to the Rotate tool and move it around to get a nice bend in the lattice.

3. Set a keyframe on the rotation channels for these joints. Move ahead 20 or 30 frames, rotate some more, and set another keyframe. We want a nice squirmy motion to the pod, but don't set more than three or four keyframes on the Timeline. Set the last keyframe at frame 90.

4. Open the Graph Editor with the joints selected and set Interpolation to Spline Tangents.

5. If the deformation of the peapod seems a little too harsh, open the Attribute Editor for ffd1Lattice, click on the ffd1 tab, and uncheck the box next to Local. This will make the lattice's deformation a bit smoother.

Animating the Eyes

To add some additional creepiness, we'll make the eyes move around when the pod opens.

1. In the perspective window, use the **Show** menu to turn off visibility for deformers and joints.

2. Turn the visibility for the Peas layer back on.

3. Move to a point on the Timeline right before the peapod starts to split and select the peas group.

4. In the Channel Box, set a keyframe on the **Visibility** channel.

5. Move the playhead backwards in time one frame, set **Visibility** to 0 or off, and set another keyframe.

6. Create a locator and name it "lookAt."

7. Move the locator in front of the peapod.

8. In the Outliner, expand the peas group.

9. Select the lookAt locator and Ctrl+select the pea1 group. Choose **Constrain > Aim > Options**. In the options, reset the settings to the default value and create an aim constraint. Do the same for each of the other pea groups in the pod.

10. Move the playhead to the point where the peas become visible. Move the locator in front of the peapod and set a keyframe on its translation channels.

11. Move the playhead ahead on the Timeline 20 frames or so. Move the lookAtlocator around in space and set a keyframe. Create three or four more keyframes for different positions on the locator so that the eyes are constantly moving around.

12. Play the animation and marvel at its weirdness.

Creating the Time Lapse Effect

OK, the animation is kind of creepy. To really add some flavor, let's create the time lapse effect. This will increase the creepiness by a factor of 10, or 11 even!

1. In the Outliner, Ctrl+select joints 2 through 7, the lookAt locator, and the pod_end object. Open up the Graph Editor.

2. Press F to frame the keys on the graph.

3. Marquee-select all of the keys on the graph.

4. From the menu in the Graph Editor, choose **Curves > Bake Channel > Options**. In the options, set Time Range to Time Slider and Sample By to 3. Turn off Keep Unbaked Keys.

5. Click the Bake button. The curves now have a keyframe set at every third frame.

6. Marquee-select all the curves in the Graph Editor and choose **Tangents > Stepped** to change the interpolation to stepped.

7. When you play the animation, the peapod has the telltale steppiness of a time-lapse film. In the Timeline options, set Playback Speed to Real-Time to really see how the effect will look.

8. In the Outliner, select joints 2 through 7, open the Graph Editor, and frame the selection so you can see the curves for these joints.

9. Start randomly marquee-selecting keyframes and move them up or down. To really get a time-lapse look, you need random pops in the animation where the peapod has moved unexpectedly between exposures. Keep the timing the same, just move values up and down somewhat randomly. Don't go overboard though. Use Figure 4.15 as a rough guide. Your curves will look different as I left the rotation of the joints up to you, but you get the basic idea from looking at the graph.

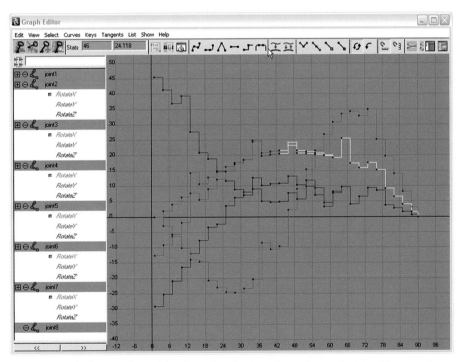

Figure 4.15: Joint keyframes on the graph have been selected and moved up or down randomly to achieve a popping effect in the animation.

10. Do the same thing with the keyframes on the lookAt locator; you can even try a little on the blendshape keyframes. If you decide to render a whole scene like this, you'd probably want to set a similar steppy keyframe style on the intensity of the lights to simulate things like a change in weather during the recording of the time-lapse film. Open peapod_v02.mb from the Chapter 4 folder on the CD to see a finished version. Figure 4.16 shows a rendered version of the scene.

Figure 4.16: A rendered version of the completed "EyePod." That was a long way to go for such a horrible pun!

Further Study

Combining blend shape deformers, lattices, and joints is a great way to achieve a variety of interesting effects. Blend shapes can control growth while joints and lattices control movement. See if you can apply these tools and the time-lapse techniques to an animation of a flower blooming or a snowflake forming.

Interactive Blend Shape Rigs

Our art director is working on a music video and would like some simple abstract animations to show the client. Her vision is something along the lines of simple moving shapes, somewhere between pistons and a piano keyboard. We'll see if we can do something with blend shapes that fits that vague description.

Creating the Blend Shape

First we'll create a single animated brick using a blend shape and a simple control.

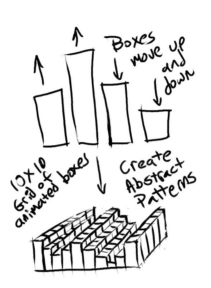

1. Open Maya and start a new scene.

2. Choose **Create > Polygon Primitives > Cube**.

3. Make a duplicate of the cube and move it to the side.

4. Select the top face on the duplicate cube, move it up four or five units, and scale it in a little.

5. Select the top face on the original cube and scale it out a little.

6. Rename the duplicate cube "tall1" and the original cube "short1."

7. Select the tall1 object and then Shift+select the short1 object. Switch to the Animation menu set and choose **Deform > Create Blend Shape > Options**.

8. Reset the options to the default settings and click the Create button to make the blend shape.

9. Select the short1 object. In the Channel Box, click on the blendShape1 node. Highlight the tall1 channel in the Channel Box, and MMB drag left and right in the perspective window to make sure the blend shape is working. You could also use the slider in the **Window > Animation Editors > Blend Shape** window (Figure 4.17).

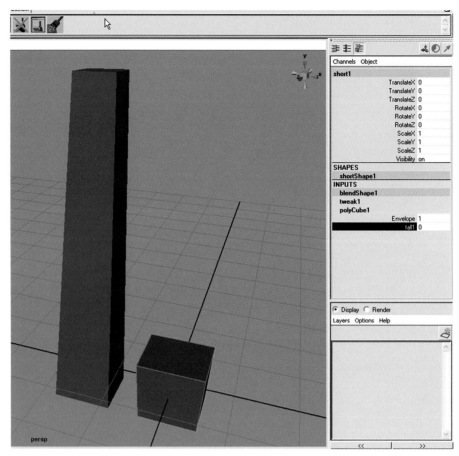

Figure 4.17: MMB-dragging left and right in the perspective window acts as a slider control when the tall1 blend shape deformer is selected in the channel box.

10. The short cube should grow and shrink when you move the slider back and forth. If it's working correctly, delete the tall1 cube. The blend shape deformation controls will not be affected. Set the tall1 value on the blend shape node back down to 0 so that the cube is back at its original, short and squat shape.

Creating the Interactive Control

We'll use the Distance tool to control when the blend shape animates based on the proximity of a locator.

1. Choose **Create > Measure Tools > Distance Tool**.

2. Click twice on the grid to create the two locators used for the tool. The measure indicator should appear between them.

3. Rename one of the locators "pin1" and the other "control1."

4. Select the short1 object and Ctrl+select the pin1 locator. Create a point constraint between these two objects so that pin1 snaps to the short1 object.

5.	Turn grid snapping on and move the control1 locator so that it is two units away from the short1 object—it doesn't matter which axis, as long as the measure indicator is labeled 2 (Figure 4.18).

Figure 4.18: The Measure tool is attached on one end to the short1 cube. The other locator is placed two units away.

6.	Switch to the Animation menu set and choose **Animate** > **Set Driven Key** > **Set** to open up the Set Driven Key window.

7.	In the Outliner, choose **Display** > **Shapes**. Expand the distanceDimension1 node and select its shape node.

8.	Click the **Load Driver** button on the Set Driven Key window.

9.	In the Outliner, go to the **Display** menu and deselect **DAG Objects Only**. Scroll down and choose the blendShape1 node.

10.	Click the **Load Driven** button on the Set Driven Key window.

11.	In the Set Driven Key window, scroll down and highlight the **Distance** attribute in the upper-right section. Choose the **tall1** attribute in the lower right and click the **Key** button.

12.	Move the control1 locator on top of the pin1 locator so that the **Distance** is 0.

13.	Set the blendShape1 node so that the **tall1** value is 1 and the cube is extended and tall.

14.	Click the **Key** button again in the Set Driven Key window.

15.	Turn grid snapping off, select the control1 locator, and move it back and forth through the short1 object. The short1 object should interactively grow and shrink (Figure 4.19).

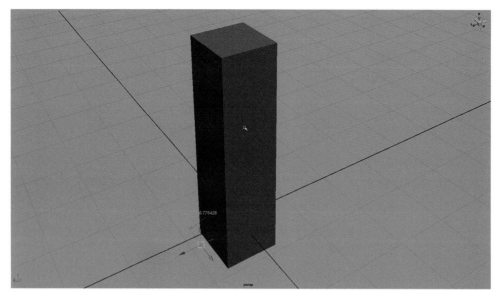

Figure 4.19: The cube grows and shrinks depending on the proximity of the control1 locator.

Duplicating the Rig

Duplicating the object with its input connections allows us to re-create the rig multiple times with just a few clicks.

1. Move the control1 locator so that it is on top of the pin1 locator. In the Outliner, turn off shapes and turn on **DAG Objects Only**.

2. Turn off the **Visibility** for the distance dimension1 object.

3. Select the short1 object, the pin1 locator, and the distanceDimension1 object and group them; leave control1 outside of the group.

4. Name the group "brick1."

5. With brick1 selected, choose **Edit > Duplicate Special > Options**. In the options, set **Group Under** to **World**, set **Number Of Copies** to 9, and check the boxes next to **Duplicate Input Graph** and **Assign Unique Names To Child Nodes**.

6. In the Outliner, Ctrl+select all of the control locators. Group them and name the group "masterControl1."

7. Turn grid snapping on and select each of the bricks one at a time. Line them up two units apart on the grid in numerical order (Figure 4.20).

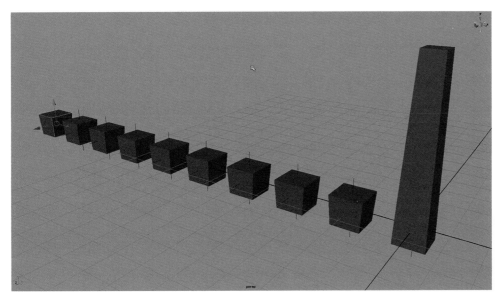

Figure 4.20: All of the brick groups are lined up on the grid two units apart.

8. Select the masterControl1 group and slide it up and down the Z axis underneath the bricks. You should see each brick pop up in a wavelike fashion.

Editing the Animation

To make the motion of the bricks more interesting, we'll edit the driven keys on the Graph Editor.

1. Use the **Display** menu in the Outliner to make the DAG nodes visible again.

2. Shift+select all of the blendShape nodes and choose **Window** > **Animation Editors** > **Graph Editor**.

3. In the Graph Editor, hit the F key to focus on the keyframes. Marquee-select the animation curves. Set Interpolation to Flat Tangents and choose **Curves** > **Post Infinity** > **Oscillate**.

4. Move the masterControl locator back and forth again along the Z axis and see how the animation has been affected.

5. Experiment with the post-infinity settings on the curve. Also, try moving the second key to a different time value; try frame 8 and see how it affects the animation. Experiment with the interpolation of the curve as well as weighted tangents. You can have a lot of fun creating different wave shapes (Figure 4.21).

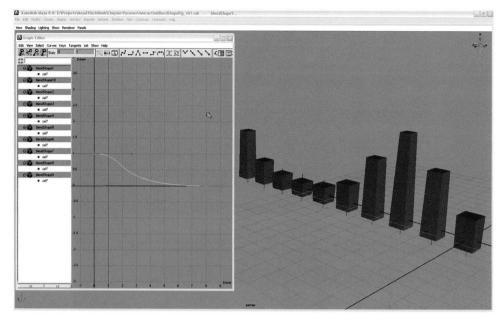

Figure 4.21: Creative manipulation of the driven keys in the Graph Editor helps shape the wave made by the deformed cubes.

Creating an Animated Array of Bricks

We can expand the row of animated bricks into an array by duplicating the group and its input connections.

1. In the Outliner, select the brick groups and the masterControl1 group. Group them together and name the new group "row1."

2. Duplicate the row1 group using Duplicate Special, and open the options for this action. Set **Number Of Copies** to 1 and leave Duplicate Input Graph checked.

3. Move the new row2 group over two units in X. Expand the group and select the masterControl2 group. Move it up and down in Z just to verify that the second group is being controlled the same way as the first.

4. Repeat this until you have a 10-by-10 grid of boxes (Figure 4.22).

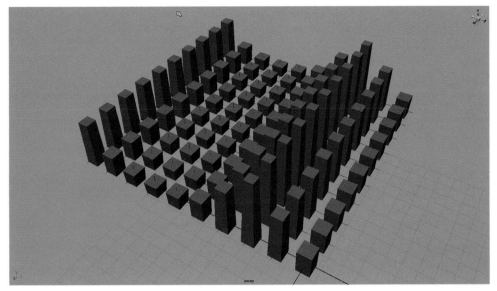

Figure 4.22: Duplicate Special allows you to make multiple copies; each row has its own control.

Having Fun

It's all about experimentation. Once the rig is completed, we can see what effect the master control groups have on the bricks.

1. In the Outliner, go through each of the row groups and move the masterControl groups out from under the row groups.

2. Select all the masterControl groups and group them together. Name the new group "superMasterControl" (Figure 4.23).

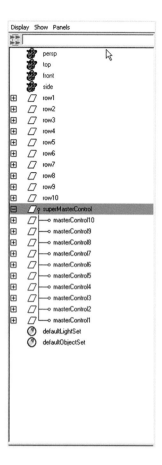

Figure 4.23:
Each masterControl group
has been removed from
the row groups and placed
in a new group called
superMasterControl.

3. Move the superMasterControl group back and forth in Z and see what happens. Try moving it in X or rotating it in Y or Z. You should have some interesting results. Even scaling the group will create some neat effects (Figure 4.24).

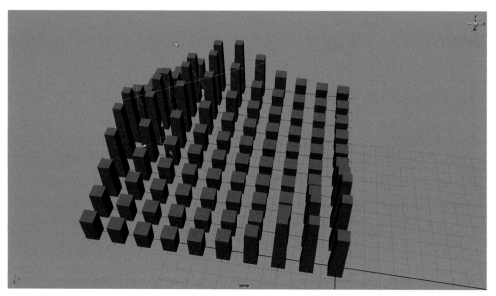

Figure 4.24: Moving the superMasterControl group creates interesting animated patterns in the array of bricks.

4. 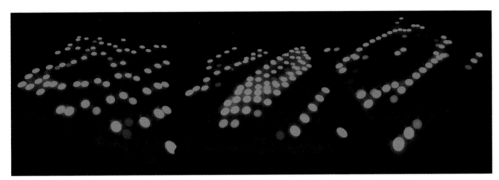 Take a look at the interactiveBlendShapeRig.mb scene on the CD to see a finished version of this animation.

Further Study

The techniques used in this lesson can be used to create an endless variety of abstract animations, at least enough to pad your demo reel. Using a similar combination of blend shapes, measure tools, and set driven keys, see if you can create an interactive blend shape rig for a Venus flytrap or a puffer fish.

Other variations on these techniques can be seen in Figures 4.25 and 4.26.

Figure 4.25: A few stills from an animation using cylinders instead of cubes. The top polygons on each cylinder have been light-linked to a volume light so that they glow brighter as the cylinder grows taller.

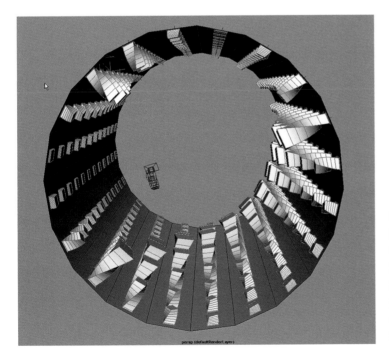

Figure 4.26:
In this version, the polygons that make up a cylinder have been extruded and twisted. A control mechanism similar to the one described in this tutorial has been implemented.

Layering Blend Shapes

A commercial shot for a ridiculously sweet, and possibly lethal, children's cereal has fallen into your lap. The art director would like you to make a bowl of cereal transform into a cartoon-style bomb and then a UFO. She would like to see the transformation from one object to the next be somewhat erratic and spastic (somewhat like the behavior of the children after they eat this stuff). You need to create a rig for the effect that is easy to use so that the animator can take it from there.

Creating the Blend Shapes

⊙ Once again we'll use a scene that has the blend shape targets already prepared.

1. Open the bowl_v01.mb scene from the Chapter 4 folder on the CD. You'll see a pleasant breakfast setting: a bowl, the cereal box, a spoon, a glass, and a jug of milk (Figure 4.27).

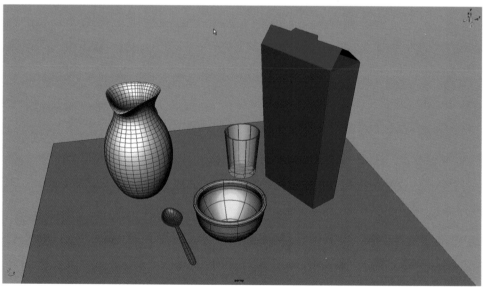

Figure 4.27: A simple setting for the cereal commercial

2. Turn off the visibility of the objects' display layer and turn on the visibility of the blendShapes layer. You'll see the bomb and the UFO model. The bowl, UFO,

and bomb are all NURBS objects. They have been created from the same profile curve, so their topology matches perfectly. This is required for the blend shapes to work properly.

The shot requires the bowl to turn into a bomb and then into a UFO. There are several ways we could do this. The most obvious way would be to create a blend shape sequence as we did for the peapod. However, in order to create the frenetic spastic metamorphosis effect, we will be using an animated fractal texture to control the blend shape weight value. If we use a blend shape sequence, the fractal noise applied to the weight value will cause the bowl to fluctuate between all three states. We want it to fluctuate between only two states at a time. The easiest way to do this is to layer the blend shapes and then create two sets of controls for each blend.

3.   Select the bomb object, then Shift+select the bowl. Switch to the Animation menu set and choose **Deform** > **Create Blend Shape** > **Options**. Make sure the **Local** button is selected and that **In-Between** and **Delete Targets** are not selected. Create the blend shape.

4.   Open the Attribute Editor for the bowl and click on the blendShape1 tab. Rename blendShape1 "bowl2Bomb."

5.   Select the UFO object and Shift+select the bomb object. Create another blend shape with the same settings and name it "bomb2UFO."

6.   Choose **Windows** > **Animation Editors** > **Blend Shape** to open up the blend shape controls. In the options for the Blend Shape window, set the Orientation to Horizontal so both sliders are clearly visible.

7.   Move the slider on the **bowl2Bomb** control to 1. You should see the bowl turn into the bomb (Figure 4.28).

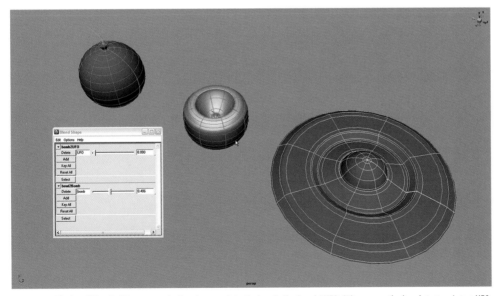

Figure 4.28: The bowl2Bomb slider causes the bowl to turn into the bomb; the bomb2UFO slider causes the bomb to turn into a UFO.

8. Move the slider on the **bomb2UFO** control to 1. Now both bomb shapes turn into the UFO.

9. Set the controls back to 0 and open the Hypershade window.

Animating the Blend Shape with Fractal Textures

Animated fractal textures are a great way to add frenetic energy to an animation. In this case we'll apply the textures to the values of the blend shape deformers.

1. In the Outliner, open the **Display** menu and turn off the **DAG Objects Only** option.

2. Select the bowl2Bomb blend shape and MMB drag it to the work area of the Hypershade. Do the same for the bomb2UFO shape.

3. Scroll down in the **Create Nodes** menu on the Hypershade and click twice on the Fractal texture (under 2D Textures) to create a couple of fractals.

4. Name one of the textures "bowl2BombFractal" and the other "bomb2UFOFractal."

5. Right-click in the work area of the Hypershade and choose **Graph > Rearrange Graph** to make things a bit clearer.

6. MMB drag the bowl2BombFractal texture on top of the bowl2Bomb blendShape node. Choose **Other** from the pop-up menu to open the Connection Editor.

7. On the left side of the Connection Editor, highlight **Out Alpha**. On the right side, expand the **Weight** attribute and highlight bomb, just like what's shown in Figure 4.29. The bowl should change into something between the bowl and the bomb, like a freaky apple.

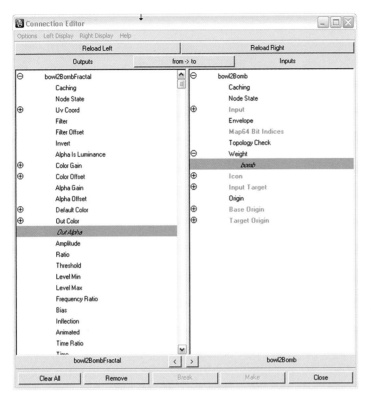

Figure 4.29:
The Out Alpha on the
fractal texture is con-
nected to the bomb
blend shape
Weight attribute.

8. Open the Attribute Editor for the bowl2BombFractal texture. Click the box next to **Animated**.

9. Rewind the animation, right-click over the field next to **Time**, and choose Set Key.

10. Move to frame 200, move the **Time Slider** on the bowl2BombFractal Attributes to 100, right-click, and set another key.

11. Repeat steps 6 through 10 for the bomb2UFOFractal texture (Figure 4.30).

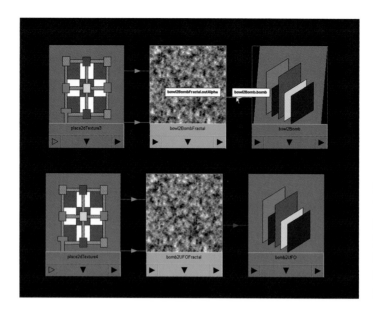

Figure 4.30:
The Hypershade shows the connections between the animated fractal textures and the two blend shape nodes.

Creating Controls for the Textures

If you play the animation now, you should see the bowl spastically morph between the bomb and UFO shapes and the bomb spastically morph between the bomb and UFO shapes. We need to set up a control so that the animator can easily determine which shapes will appear in the sequence.

1. Create a locator and name it "blendControl."

2. Open the Attribute Editor for the blendControl locator and, from the menu at the top of the editor, choose **Add Attributes**.

3. Name the attribute "bowl2Bomb." Set it to **Float** and set a **Minimum** value of 0, a **Maximum** value of 1, and a **Default** value of 0. Click the Add button to create the attribute without closing the Add Attribute Editor.

4. Add three more identical attributes. Name them "bomb," "bomb2UFO," and "UFO" (Figure 4.31).

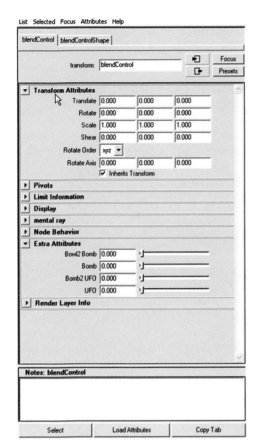

Figure 4.31:
The custom attributes
appear as sliders in the
blendControl's Attribute
Editor.

5. Open the Hypershade and switch to the Textures tab in the upper area.

6. Choose **Window** > **General Editors** > **Connection Editor** to open the Connection
    Editor. Select the blendControl locator and load it on the left side by hitting the
    Reload Left button.

7. In the Hypershade, select the bowl2BombFractal texture and load it on the right.

8. On the left side of the Connection Editor, select the **bowl2Bomb** attribute; on
    the right side, select the **Alpha Gain** attribute.

9. On the left side, select the **Bomb** attribute, and on the right side select the
    Threshold attribute.

10. From the Hypershade, select the bomb2UFOFractal texture and load it on the
    right side of the Connection Editor.

11. Select the **bomb2UFO** attribute on the left and the **Alpha Gain** on the right.

12. Select the **UFO** attribute on the left and the **Threshold** attribute on the right
    (Figure 4.32).

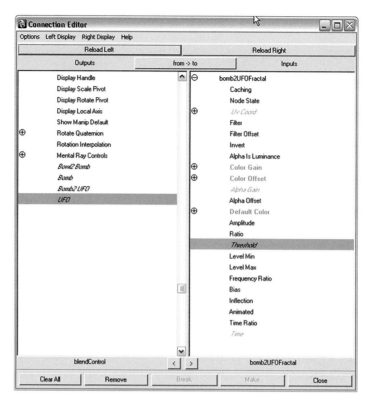

Figure 4.32:
The custom attributes on the blendControl locator are connected to the **Alpha Gain** and **Threshold** attributes of the fractal textures.

Animating the Blend Shape Transformation

With the controls set up, animating the scene is easy.

1. Play the animation. Nothing should happen; all the controls are at 0. Open the Attribute Editor for the blendControl locator and expand the tab under the Extra Attributes folder.

2. With the animation playing, slide up the **bowl2Bomb** attribute. You should see the bowl fluctuate between the bowl and bomb shapes.

3. With the animation playing, slide up the **Bomb** attribute. When the slider is at 1, the bowl has turned completely into the bomb.

4. Now slide up the **bomb2UFO** attribute. The bomb now fluctuates between the bomb and UFO shapes.

5. Slide up the UFO slider and the shape now rests as a UFO, ready to fly off for some sugar-fueled adventures.

6. Set all the attributes to 0 again and set the playhead to frame 30.

7. In the Attribute Editor for the blendControl, right-click over the field for the **bowl2Bomb** attribute and choose **Set Key**.

8. Move to frame 50, set the slider to 1, and set another keyframe on the **bowl2Bomb** attribute.

9. While still on frame 50, set a key on the **Bomb** attribute.

10. Move to frame 60, set **Bomb** to 1, and set another keyframe.

11. Move to frame 90 and set a keyframe on the **bomb2UFO** attribute.

12. Move to frame 110 and set **bomb2UFO** to 1; set a keyframe.

13. While still on frame 110, set a keyframe on the **UFO** attribute.

14. Move to frame 120, set **UFO** to 1, and set a keyframe.

15. Turn the visibility for the blendShapes layer off and turn on the visibility for the object layer. Play the animation and check the results.

16.   To see a finished version, open the bowl_v02.mb file from the CD.

To get the controls to work, we've used the **Alpha Gain** and **Threshold** attributes on the fractal textures as a sort of volume control for the fractal animation. Both **Alpha Gain** and **Threshold** have value ranges from 0 to 1. You can open the Hypershade and zoom in on the textures and see that by turning the **Bomb** or **UFO** controls up, the fractal textures turn white, meaning a value of 1. When the value is 1, the connection to the blend shape node causes the value of the respective blend shape to be 1. The texture is blown out so that the animated fractal texture, while still going on in the background, has no effect on the value of the blend shape. The **Alpha Gain** has a similar but opposite effect. It's not visible in the texture swatch in the Hypershade, but since the **Alpha Gain** is controlling the blend shape, when it's at 0, the fractal animation has no effect on the blend shape; when it's at 1, the fractal animation is at full strength and the spastic morph it clearly visible. The advantage of putting all these controls on the locator is that they can all be edited at once in the Graph Editor.

Further Study

Creating a chain of blend shapes in this manner works well for some situations. Once again we see how the animated fractal texture can create some interesting effects. The following are some suggestions on how to enhance the scene or use these techniques for other projects.

1. Create some particles and set the render type to sphere, fill the bowl with particles, and set the bowl object as a collision object. See if you can get the cereal to fly out of the bowl during the transformation.

2. Apply this effect to models of faces. See if you can re-create something similar to the person-to-agent morph effect from *The Matrix*.

3. To add some springy secondary motion, turn the bowl object into a softbody.

Paint Effects

Paint Effects, as the name suggests, is a powerful tool for effects. It is essentially a procedural modeling and animation tool that is most often used for creating fields of swaying grass, lightning bolts, trees, and other such objects that require mass replication. Paint Effects is kind of like a painting program combined with a particle system. Because of the unique nature of this tool, it can also solve a lot of other effects problems that would be difficult and cumbersome with other Maya solutions. This chapter assumes some knowledge of Paint Effects basics and presents some novel ways to use Paint Effects you may not have tried. Combined with the Toon Lines tool introduced in Maya 7, Paint Effects offers even more flexibility for solving difficult effects problems.

5

Chapter Contents
Paint Effects and Toon Lines: The Mine Detector Display
Hallucinations in 3D: Using the Smear Stroke
Paint Effects Strokes and Soft Body Dynamics
Taming Paint Effects Brush Strokes: The Test Tube Nerve

Paint Effects and Toon Lines: The Mine Detector Display

Our art director has an interesting shot she'd like you to create for a science fiction TV show. The plot calls for our heroes to use a probe ship to navigate a treacherous mine field in space. The art director would like you to create a computer interface display that will help the captain—his brow beading with sweat—guide the probe through the field of invisible mines. The probe will create a path on the screen, and each time it comes within a certain distance of a mine, the display will reveal the mine's position and proximity to the probe so that the course can be altered.

This project has two main objectives: First we must create a nice computerized display for the objects in the scene. We'll use the old vector graphics video games from the '80s as inspiration. Second, we will develop an automated detector system so that the mines are visible when they get within a certain distance of the probe. This will save the animator from having to create numerous keyframes on the visibility of objects; they can concentrate on the animation of the objects in the scene.

Creating the Probe and Mine Display

You can really have a lot of fun creating 3D computer interface designs in Maya. One of the best tools for doing this is Paint Effects's neon brush stroke. Assign it to curves or Toon Lines applied to a surface and suddenly you're taken back to the days of *Tron* (ask your grandparents if you don't know what *Tron* means).

1. ◎ Open the mineField_v01.mb scene from the Chapter 5 folder on the CD. As shown in Figure 5.1, our modeler has given us a simple polygon model for the probe and the mine. There's also a path for the probe to follow. The probe model has a lot of sharp edges on it, which should look great when we apply the neon brush stroke.

Figure 5.1: The probe and mine models

2. Select the probe object, switch to the rendering menu set, and choose **Toon > Assign Outline > Add New Toon Outline**.

3. Black lines appear on the object. Select the new pfxToon1 node that has appeared in the Outliner. Rename it "probeToon" and open its Attribute Editor.

4. Set **Profile Lines** to **Paint Effects** and **Line Width** to .05. Open the attributes for Crease Lines. Set **Crease Break Angle**, **Crease Angle Min**, and **Crease Angle Max** to 0. This will cause our model to have a nice wireframe style display when the Toon Lines are rendered.

5. Set **Local Occlusion** to **Line Surface**. Sometimes when faces are closer together than the thickness of the crease line, they can be visible through the faces of the geometry. The **Local Occlusion** settings, new in Maya 8, prevent this from happening by calculating the occlusion before the scene renders. Normally these calculations are made at render time. Setting **Local Occlusion** to **Line Surface** means that this only occurs on the surface that is generating the Toon Lines. This is fine for our scene.

6. Open the attributes for Screenspace Width Control. Activate **Screenspace Width**. Set **Distance Scaling** to 0, **Min Pixel Width** to 3, and **Max Pixel Width** to 3. This ensures that the Toon Lines are the same thickness regardless of their closeness to the camera. The **Min** and **Max Pixel Width** settings set the range of thickness so that the lines do not become too thin or too thick. Figure 5.2 shows the results of all of these settings.

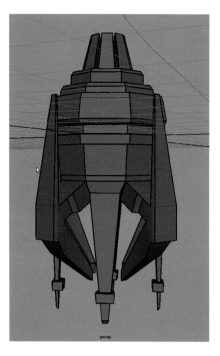

Figure 5.2:
The probe with
Toon Lines applied

7. Choose **Window > General Editors > Visor** to open up the Visor window. In the folders on the left, scroll down and select the glows folder.

8. Select the neonBlue brush so that the icon turns yellow (Figure 5.3). This will make neonBlue the active brush.

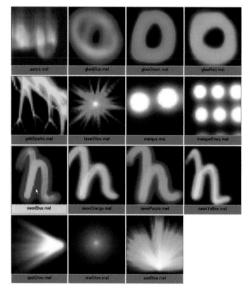

Figure 5.3:
Selecting the neonBlue
brush stroke loads it into
memory as the current
brush.

9. Select probeToon in the Outliner and choose **Toon > Assign Paint Effects Brush To Toon Lines**.

10. Select the probe object and assign a surface shader to it. Leave the color at its default black value. Name the surface shader probeBlack.

The neonBlue Paint Effects stroke has its own set of attributes. Some of these, such as **Screenspace Width**, duplicate settings created for the Toon Lines. It would seem that the Toon Lines settings for Screenspace Width take precedence over the Paint Effects stroke settings. A little experimentation with the settings will help you to understand how the two nodes affect each other. You can leave the Screenspace Width control off in the neonBlue node's attributes.

11. Do a test render and see how the probe looks with the glowing blue Toon Lines. Try adjusting the shading and glow settings in the tab for the neonBlue1 stroke; compare your render with Figure 5.4.

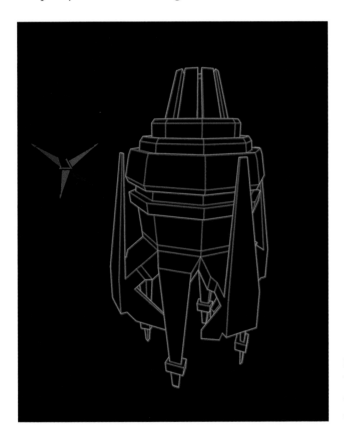

Figure 5.4:
The neonBlue1 brush stroke creates a glowing wireframe outline of the probe object.

12. Repeat steps 2 through 11 for the mine1 object. Name the pfxToon node "mine Toon1" and choose the neonOrange brush stroke to apply to the Toon outlines. You can assign the probeBlack shader to the mine as well.

Creating the Proximity Warning Display

Next we'll create some additional elements for the display that will appear when the mine comes within a certain distance of the probe.

1. Create a NURBS circle and set it to 5 Units in the **ScaleX** and **ScaleZ** attributes. Name the circle "perimeter1."

2. Select the probe and then Ctrl+select perimeter1. Switch to the Animation menu set and choose **Constrain > Point**. The circle should be constrained in all three axes.

3. Create two locators, name the first "traceLoc1" and the second "mineLoc1."

4. In the command line, type **createNode pointOnCurveInfo;** (see Figure 5.5).

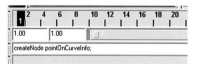

Figure 5.5: You can create a pointOnCurveInfo node by typing a createNode command into the command line.

5. In the Outliner's **Display** menu, turn off the setting for **DAG Objects Only**. Scroll down and find pointOnCurveInfo1 in the list.

6. Open up the Hypershade and MMB drag pointOnCurveInfo1 from the Outliner to the work area of the Hypershade (Figure 5.6).

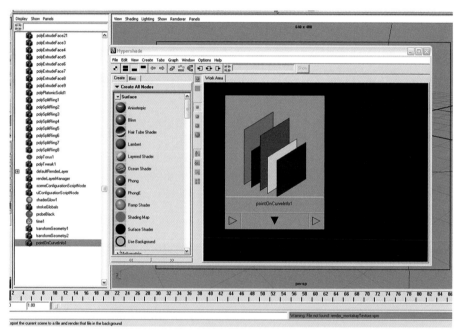

Figure 5.6: The pointOnCurveInfo1 node has been brought into the work area of the Hypershade; from here, connections to other nodes can be made.

7. In the Outliner's **Display** menu, activate the **Shapes Display** option. Expand the perimeter1 object and drag perimeterShape1 to the work area of the Hypershade.

8. In the Hypershade work area, MMB drag perimeterShape1 on top of pointOn-CurveInfo1. Choose **Other** from the marking menu that appears. The Connection Editor will open.

9. In the Connection Editor, scroll down on the left side and highlight the **World Space** attribute. On the right side of the Connection Editor, highlight **Input Curve** (Figure 5.7).

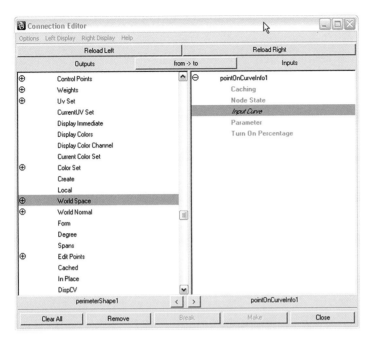

Figure 5.7:
The perimeterShape1
curve's World Space
attribute is connected
to the Input Curve
attribute of the
pointOnCurveInfo1
node.

10. From the Outliner, select the transform node for the traceLoc1 locator and drag it to the work area of the Hypershade.

11. In the work area of the Hypershade, MMB drag pointOnCurveInfo1 on top of traceLoc1. Choose **Other** from the marking menu. The Connection Editor will open again, or these objects will load if it is still open.

12. On the left side, expand the **Result** attributes and highlight **Position**. On the right side, highlight **Translate**. Look in the perspective window; traceLoc1 should now be stuck to the perimeterShape1 circle. You should not be able to move it with the Move tool (Figure 5.8).

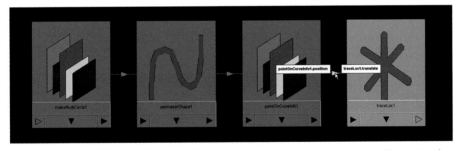

Figure 5.8: The perimeterShape1 node is connected to the input curve of the pointOnCurveInfo1 node. The position of the pointOnCurveInfo1 node is connected to the translate of the traceLoc1 locator.

This technique is one way to constrain an object to a curve. The pointOnCurveInfo1 node is a hidden node that allows you to specify a point on a curve and use it to constrain an object. You can use the parameter attribute of the pointOnCurveInfo1 node to move the object around on the curve. We could use a geometry constraint, but the geometry constraint allows the constrained object to slip around on the curve, which is useful for some operations but not in this case. Another way to go about constraining an object to a curve is to make the curve a motion path for the object and then delete the motion path keyframes. The object will stay locked to the curve. You can still move it around the curve using the **U Value** on the motionPath node.

13. Choose **Create > EP Curve Tool > Options**. In the options, click Linear. Click twice anywhere on the grid to make the curve. Name the curve "line1."

14. Hit F8 to switch to component mode, select one of the CVs on the end of the curve, and choose **Deform > Create Cluster**.

15. Create another cluster for the other CV.

16. Select the mineLoc1 locator and move it out to a place on the grid where you can see it.

17. Point constrain one of the clusters to traceLoc1 and the other to mineLoc1 so that the line1 curve stretches from the mineLoc1 locator to the traceLoc1 locator (Figure 5.9).

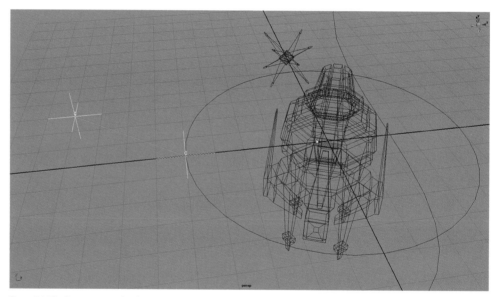

Figure 5.9: The line curve stretches between two clusters. One cluster is point constrained to traceLoc1; the other is point constrained to mineLoc1.

18. Point constrain the mine1 object to the mine1Loc locator.

Adding Paint Effects Strokes to the Proximity Display

We'll add some more neon brush strokes to the proximity display.

1. In the Outliner, select the mineToon1 node. Switch to the Rendering menu set and choose **Paint Effects > Get Settings From Selected Stroke**.

2. Ctrl+select the line1 and perimter1 objects and choose **Paint Effects > Curve Utilities > Attach Brush To Curves**.

3. Name the Paint Effects stroke that is attached to line1 "traceStroke1" and the stroke attached to perimeter1 "perimeterStroke1."

4. In the Outliner, Ctrl+select the two strokes and choose **Paint Effects > Share One Brush**. This will make it so that changing the settings on one stroke will automatically change settings on the other.

5. Open the Attribute Editor for the traceStroke1. Click on the neonOrange tab. Turn on **Screenspace Width**. Set **Distance Scaling** to 0, **Min Pixel Width** to 3, and **Max Pixel Width** to 3.

6. Create a NURBS sphere. Name it "traceDot1."

7. Point constrain traceDot1 to the traceLoc1 locator.

8. Scale it down to 0.25 in all three axes. Assign a surface shader to traceDot1 and make the out color a bright orange. Name this shader "orangeShader." Do a test render and compare the results with Figure 5.10.

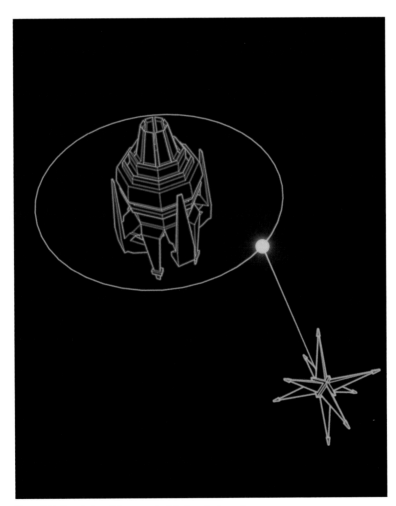

Figure 5.10: A rendering of the computer interface display so far

Adding Interactive Control to the Proximity Display

We'll create an automated system that hides the display when the mine is beyond a certain distance from the probe.

1. In the Outliner, select the mineLoc1 locator.

2. Ctrl+select the perimeter1 circle. Switch to the Animation menu set and choose **Constrain > Aim > Options**.

3. In the options, set **Aim Vector** to 0, 0, –1 and **Up Vector** to 0, 1, 0. Create the constraint. As you move the mine1Loc locator around, the circle should follow and the line1 object between them should remain straight and perpendicular to the perimeter1 circle (Figure 5.11).

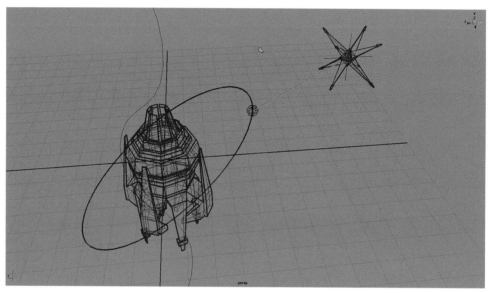

Figure 5.11: The aim constraint between the mine1Loc and the perimeter1 circle causes the line between them to stay straight regardless of the position of the mine.

4. Open the Hypershade, scroll down in the node menu on the left, and click the Distance Between button to create a Distance Between node. This node will play a role similar to the distance measuring tool used in previous tutorials in this book (Figure 5.12).

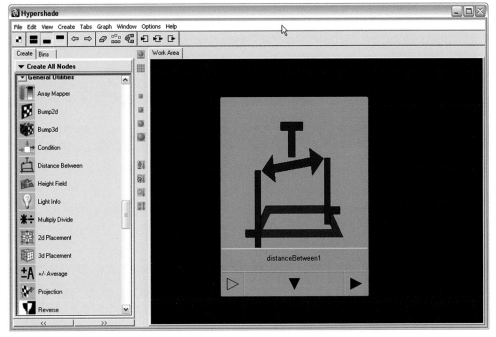

Figure 5.12: The distanceBetween1 node in the Hypershade

5. Make sure that shapes nodes are visible in the Outliner by checking them in the Outliner's **Display** menu. From the Outliner, MMB drag the traceLocShape1 and mineLocShape1 nodes into the work area of the Hypershade. Both of these nodes are parented under the traceLoc1 and mineLoc1 translate nodes of these objects.

6. MMB drag traceLocShape1 on top of the distanceBetween1 node and choose **Other** from the marking menu to open the Connection Editor. Scroll down on the left side of the Connection Editor and highlight **World Position** in the bottom of the list. On the right side, highlight **Point1** (Figure 5.13).

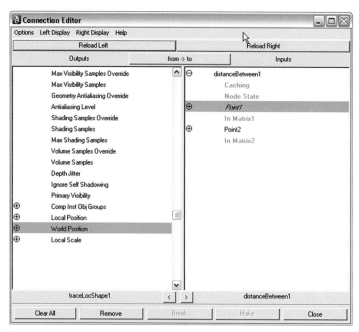

Figure 5.13: The World Position attribute of traceLoc1 has been connected to the Point1 attribute of the distanceBetween1 node.

7. In the Hypershade, select mineLocShape1. Hit the Reload Left button on the upper-left side of the Connection Editor. Select **World Position** on the left again and **Point2** on the right (Figure 5.14).

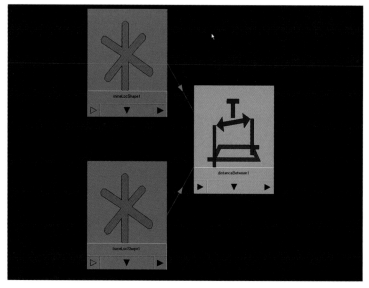

Figure 5.14: The input connections for the distanceBetween1 node in the Hypershade

Using the Information from the Distance Between Node

Now we have a node—the distanceBetween1 node—which will continually give us feedback on the distance in world space between the mineLoc1 locator, which is the position of the mine, and the trace1Loc locator, which is the edge of the perimeter. We'll use one of Maya's utility nodes, the Condition, to control the visibility of traceStroke1.

1. Open the Hypershade (**Window** > **General Editors** > **Rendering Editors** > **Hypershade**) and click on the Utilities tab. Drag distanceBetween1 down to the work area.

2. Open the Outliner and MMB drag the traceStroke1 object into the work area of the Hypershade.

3. Scroll down in the frame on the left side of the Hypershade to the General Utilities rollout. (If you don't see this section, make sure the frame is set to Create Maya Nodes.) Click the Condition icon to create a Condition node. The Condition node is a handy tool designed to change the color of a channel based on a certain condition. However, it can be used in place of an expression to control the behavior of almost any type of node in Maya. Riggers often use the Condition node to control how the joints in a rig behave. The advantage of a utility node over an expression is they calculate faster and they are very easy to use.

4. In the work area of the Hypershade, MMB drag distanceBetween1 on top of condition1 and choose **Other** from the pop-up menu. This, as you may well know, will open the Connection Editor. On the left side of the Connection Editor, highlight **Distance**. On the right side, highlight **First Term**.

5. In the Hypershade, click on condition1 and open its Attribute Editor. Under the Condition Attributes rollout you'll see **First Term** in yellow with a number in it. This is the value given to condition1 by distanceBewteen1. It's the distance between traceLoc1 and mineLoc1. In the **Second Term** field, type 5.

6. Set **Operation** to **Greater Than**. Note the values in the **Color If True** and **Color If False** fields (Figure 5.15). What this says is that if the value of the **First Term** (the distance between mineLoc1 and traceLoc1) is greater than the value of the **Second Term** (5) than the **Color If True** value is 0 for all three fields; otherwise, the value is 1 for all three fields. It's a lot like a conditional statement we might use in an expression.

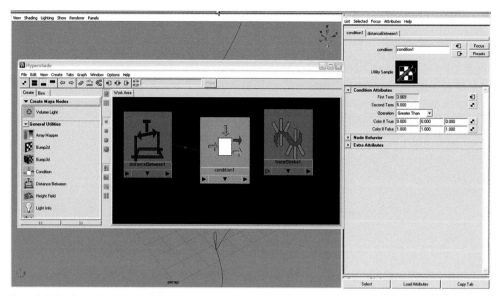

Figure 5.15: The distanceBetween1 node is connected to the condition1 node.

7. In the work area of the Hypershade, MMB drag condition1 over traceStroke1, and choose **Other** from the pop-up menu. In the Connection Editor, expand the **Out Color** attribute on the left and highlight **Out ColorR**. On the right side of the Connection Editor, highlight **Visibility**.

8. In the perspective window, move around the mineLoc1 locator. The Paint Effects stroke should appear only when the mine is less than five units away from the perimeter.

9. Open the Connection Editor and load traceStroke1 on the left. Load perimeter-Stroke1 on the right and connect the visibility attributes so that the visibility of traceStroke1 controls the visibility of perimeterStroke1. Create similar connections so that traceStroke1 also controls the visibility of mineToon1 and trace-Dot1 (Figure 5.16).

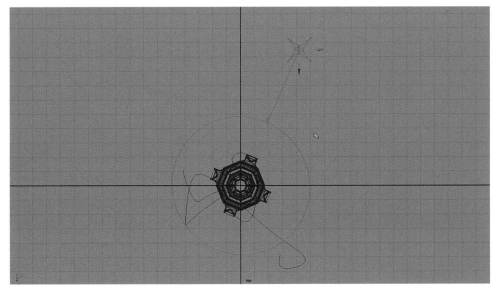

Figure 5.16: The Paint Effects brush strokes on the mine, the circle, and the line between disappear when the mine is more than five units away.

⊙ Moving the minLoc1 locator away from the probe causes the brush strokes on the perimeter and on the mine and the line between them to disappear. This is how our mine detecting probe display will work. The probe is plotting the safe route through the mine field. When it detects a mine, it will display it and then change course. Of course, a mine field with only one mine is not much of an obstacle. To see a version of the scene so far, open mineField_v02.mb from the Chapter 5 folder on the CD.

Duplicating the Mines

To fill up the mine field, we will duplicate the mine with input connections active. This will take a few extra steps, but it shouldn't be too bad.

1. In the Outliner, Ctrl=select mine1, mineToon1, perimeter1, traceLoc1, mine-Loc1, line1, the cluster handles, traceStroke1, perimeterStroke1, and traceDot1. Group them and name the group "mineGroup1" (Figure 5.17).

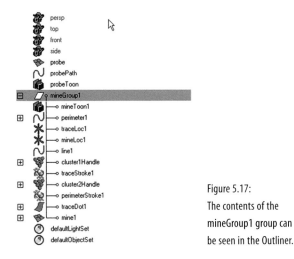

Figure 5.17: The contents of the mineGroup1 group can be seen in the Outliner.

2. Choose **Edit > Duplicate Special > Options**. In the Options, set the **Group Under** attribute to **World** and the **Number Of Copies** to 1. Check the boxes next to **Duplicate Input Graph** and **Assign Unique Names To Child Nodes**.

3. Create the duplicate. You'll notice that under the new mineGroup2 group there is a duplicate probe named probe1. Delete the extra probe1 object.

4. Select the original probe, expand mineGroup2, and Ctrl+select perimeter2. Create a point constraint so that perimeter2 is constrained to the original probe.

5. Select the mineLoc2 locator and move the duplicate mine to another position. If you turn on shaded mode, you may notice that the new mine is transparent. Sometimes Maya forgets to add a shader to an object that has had the Duplicate Special action applied to it. If this happens, open the Hypershade and apply the probeBlack surface shader to this mine. The same problem may have occurred with traceDot2; just apply the orangeShader to this as well.

6. Test out the rig by moving mineLoc1 and mineLoc2 around. Make sure that their associated Paint Effects strokes appear and disappear depending on the distance of the mines from the probe. If everything is working OK, repeat the process a few more times until you have six or seven mines. Or go to the next step and follow the instructions for creating a MEL script that will make the duplicates for you.

7. Select mineGroup2. In the Script Editor, type the following (Figure 5.18):

```
//Duplicate probe groups
//Constrain each new perimeter circle to the probe object

 for( $i=2; $i<6; $i++){
     duplicate -renameChildren -upstreamNodes;
     pointConstraint probe ("perimeter"+$i);
}
//Delete extra probe objects
for($k=1; $k<5; $k++){
  delete ("probe"+$k);
  }
```

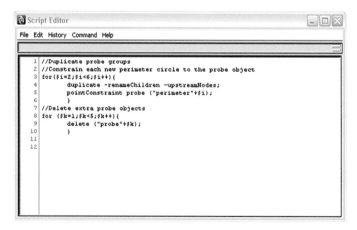

Figure 5.18:
The script as it appears in the Script Editor

8. Hit the Enter key on the numeric keypad to execute the script. The -upstreamNodes flag in the duplicate tells Maya to duplicate the input connections for each new group. The -renameChildren flag tells Maya to assign unique names to the children of the duplicate groups.

9. Select the mineLoc locators in each group and spread them out around the scene so some are activated and some are not. In the Outliner, move the mineLoc locators outside of the mineGroups just to make selection and animation a little easier. Here's another bit of MEL to help automate that task:

```
//Select each mineLoc object and unparent
for ($i=1; $i<7; $i++){
  select ("mineLoc"+$i);
  parent -w;
  }
```

The -w flag in the parent command stands for "world"; we are essentially parenting each mineLoc object to the world instead of the mineGroups. Figure 5.19 shows the scene so far. For a completed version of the scene so far, open mineField_v03.mb from the Chapter 5 folder on the CD.

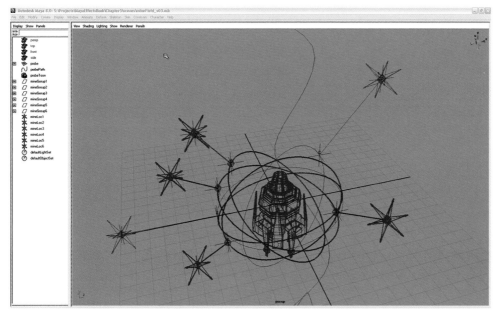

Figure 5.19: The probes have been duplicated with their input connections. Using the mineLoc locators, they have been moved around in the scene.

Animating the Probe

To animate the probe we'll attach it to a motion path.

1. Select the probe object and Ctrl+select the probePath curve. Choose **Animate > Motion Paths > Attach To Motion Path > Options**.

2. In the options, set **Time Range** to **Time Slider**, activate **Follow**, and set **Front Axis** to Y and **Up Axis** to Z. Leave the rest of the settings at their default values.

3. Slowly scrub through the Timeline and position the mines using the mineLoc locators so that they are near the turns in the path of the probe. Position them so that the brush strokes appear right before the probe makes a course correction. You can set keyframes on the mines so that they appear to drift. Rotational keyframes can be set on the mine geometry as well just to make the display a bit more interesting (Figure 5.20).

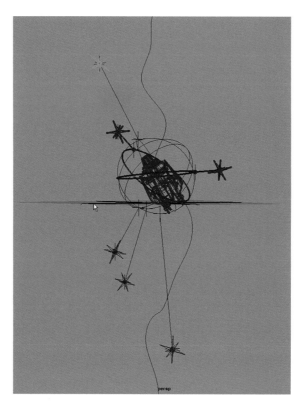

Figure 5.20:
The probe has been attached to the probePath curve as an animated motion path. The mines have been arranged so that they appear at the curves in the path.

Illuminating the Path

Of course, the whole point of this probe is that it's plotting a course through the minefield. Let's add a trace that follows the probe on the path.

1. Switch to the Rendering menu set. In the Outliner, select the probeToon node. Choose **Paint Effects > Get Settings From Selected Stroke.**

2. Select the probePath curve and choose **Paint Effects > Curve Utilities > Attach Brush To Curves.**

3. Rename the new stroke "pathStroke" and open the Attribute Editor for this stroke. Switch to the brush9 tab.

4. Set the **Global Scale** of the stroke to 5. In the Screenspace Width Control rollout, activate **Screenspace Width**. Set **Distance Scaling** to 0, and **Min** and **Max Pixel Width** to 5.

Animating the Path

It's easy to automate the path appearing behind the probe. To do this we'll connect the **U Value** of the motion path to the **Max Clip** attribute of the brush stroke.

1. In the Outliner, uncheck **DAG Objects Only** in the **Display** menu.

2. Scroll down and find the motionPath1 node. Open its Attribute Editor and check the box next to **Parametric Length**. This ensures that the U value output for the motion path is in a range from 0 to 1. The probe may shift a little when you activate this; that should be OK.

3. Choose **Window > General Editors > Connection Editor** to open up the Connection Editor. Load motionPath1 on the left side of the Connection Editor.

4. In the **Display** menu for the Outliner, activate the check box next to **Shapes** so that shape nodes are visible. Find the pathStroke node, expand it, and select the pathStrokeShape node. Load it into the right side of the Connection Editor.

5. Highlight **U Value** on the left side and **Max Clip** on the right (Figure 5.21). This should cause the stroke applied to the curve to trail behind the probe as it makes its way along the motion path.

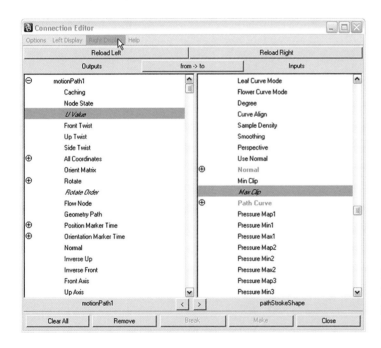

Figure 5.21:
The U value of the motion path node controls the Max Clip value of the path stroke.

The **Min** and **Max Clip** attributes on the brush stroke allow you to determine where the stroke is placed on a curve. These values range from 0 to 1. Tying the motion path's **U Value** to the **Max Clip** is a great way to automate the way in which the stroke is drawn and connect it to an animated object. However the **U Value** of the motion path must be in a range from 0 to 1. This means that when you build your curve for the motion path, you should use the Rebuild function under Edit Curves and make sure that the **Parameter Range** is between 0 and 1. You should also make sure that the motion path node has **Parametric Length** activated; otherwise the stroke won't match up with the object attached to the motion path. You can activate **Parametric Length** in the options when you attach an object to a motion path.

Finishing Touches

To finish the scene we'll add a camera that tracks the probe.

1. Create a camera and name it "renderCam." Set the perspective view to render-Cam and dolly out to a point where you can frame the probe.

2. Group the renderCam and name the group "cameraGroup."

3. Point constrain the cameraGroup to the probe. In the options for the point constraint, make sure that the only axis that is active is the Y axis.

4. Play the animation looking through the renderCam. You should be able to dolly, tumble, and track with the renderCam, but the constraint on the group will keep the camera following the probe.

5. ⊙ If the animation moves too fast, you can open up the Graph Editor for the motionPath1 node and move the keys around. Everything else in the animation will update accordingly, with the exception of any keyframes you may have applied to the mines. To see a finished version of the project, open the mineField_v04.mb scene in the Chapter 5 folder on the CD. You can also take a look at the probe.mov movie to see a rendered version (Figure 5.22).

Figure 5.22:
The completed mine field detector interface display

Further Study

The use of the neon brush strokes with Toon Lines offers endless possibilities for creating interesting sci-fi-styled computer displays. Whether you want to re-create the retro look of *Tron* or the early *Star Wars* or *Star Trek* movies or to create your own vision of computer interface displays of the future, you can really have a ball finding new ways to implement these techniques.

1. Try creating your interface in a 2D drawing program such as Illustrator or Photoshop and then import the paths into Maya. See how you can bring these ideas to life and take advantage of the third dimension.

2. In addition, you can use the distanceBetween and condition nodes to create some interesting interactivity. Think of the holographic gestural displays in movies such as *Minority Report*. See if you can create a display where interactivity occurs when a character's hand comes within a certain distance of the interface.

Hallucinations in 3D: Using the Smear Stroke

You're at your station this morning just wondering what strange and beautiful projects lie in wait when suddenly you feel the hot breath of a panicked art director on the back of your neck. She thrusts a sweaty scribble of an idea into your face and asks, "Can you do this in 30 minutes?" In 30 minutes? No problem! What's the shot?

The shot consists of a nightmarish tree writhing in the netherworld of a tortured soul's inner hell. Really, it's just a 100-frame shot of a tree wriggling around with some kind of hallucinatory effect to make it look cool. Several versions would be greatly appreciated; they need this for a quick client review before going ahead with a finalized shot. That's all? No problem!

As you quickly realize, modeling and rigging a tree will take much longer than 30 minutes, and what about the hallucinatory effect anyway? Don't they have compositors for this kind of thing? Not today apparently. Once again the possibility of using Paint Effects as a solution leaps to your mind. Without further hesitation, you leap to your work station and . . .

1. Start a new scene in Maya and switch to the Rendering menu set.

2. Choose **Windows > General Editors > Visor** and find the treesMesh folder on the left-hand side.

3. Select the oakWhiteHeavy.mel brush (Figure 5.23; if this slows down your system too much, you can also try the oakWhiteMedium brush). At the origin, click and drag for a couple seconds, just enough so that the tree pops up and grows to maturity. You only need a single tree for this shot.

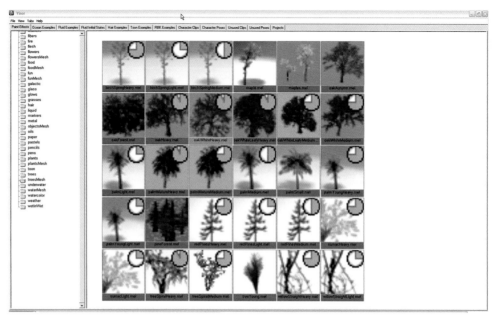

Figure 5.23: The oakWhiteHeavy.mel brush in the Visor

4. With the tree selected, open up the Attribute Editor and switch to the oak-White1 tab. Set **Global Scale** to 10.

5. Open up the attributes rollout for Tubes. In the Growth subfolder, deactivate the **Leaves** check box; we want a nice scary leafless tree. Later on we can easily add a few if we change our minds.

6. ◎ Save the scene as scaryTree_v01.mb (see Figure 5.24).

Figure 5.24:
The Paint Effects oak tree

Adjusting the Tree

Let's make some adjustments to this tree before animating it.

1. In the Outliner, select the strokeOakWhite1 stroke and open the Attribute Editor. Click on the oakWhite1 tab.

2. Expand the Tubes rollout and then the Creation rollout. Adjust the Tube Width 1 and 2 sliders until you get a nice spiky-looking tree. It is entirely up to you and your taste to determine how the tree should look. The Width Scale envelope will allow you to refine the look even further. You can thin out the tips of the branches by adding control points. Use Figure 5.25 as a reference.

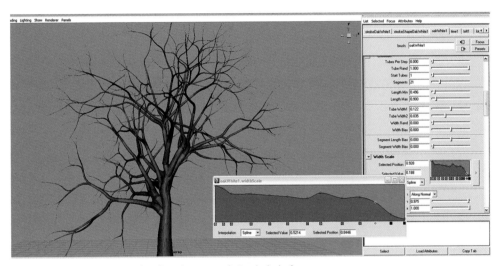

Figure 5.25: The brush settings can be adjusted to custom-design the look of your tree.

3. You can click the arrow button next to the Width Scale envelope to open a larger version of the envelope graph in a pop-up window. It's much easier to edit the Width Scale in this window. This feature is new to Maya 8.

4. Scroll down to the Behavior controls. Open the rollout folder for Behavior and try adjusting some of the controls under Displacement. Adding a little bit of **noise**, **wiggle**, and **curl** should make your tree look more menacing. Raise the values for **Noise** and **Curl** slightly but lower the **Frequency** values so the tree doesn't get too distorted.

    When you have something you like, move on to the next section to add animation. Using Paint Effects is largely an experimental process, so feel free to try adjusting other sliders to see what happens.

Animating the Tree

Using forces will add some creepy life to the tree—no rigging required!

1. To create a constant eerie breathing motion, we will add an expression to the Gravity force. Look in the Forces settings under the Behavior tab in the Attribute Editor for the oakWhite1 brush. Right-click over the field next to Gravity and

choose **Expression** from the pop-up menu. To speed up the playback of the animation, select the strokeOakWhite1 node and in its channel box set the **Draw As Mesh** attribute to **Off**. The tree will appear as a wireframe and allow the animation to play back closer to real time. The render will look the same.

2. In the Expression Editor add the following:

```
gravity=noise(time);
```

3. If you play the animation, you'll see the tree move its limbs up and down wildly. It's a bit too much, so we'll alter the expression. The current noise expression generates semi-random values between -1 and 1. We want to get it in the positive range only, so edit the expression to look like this:

```
gravity=0.5+0.5*(noise(time));
```

4. Now the noise values stay between 0 and 1, but it's still a bit too exaggerated. Edit it one more time to reduce the values by a 10th. Figure 5.26 shows the final result in the Expression Editor.

```
gravity= 0.1*(0.5+0.5*(noise(time)));
```

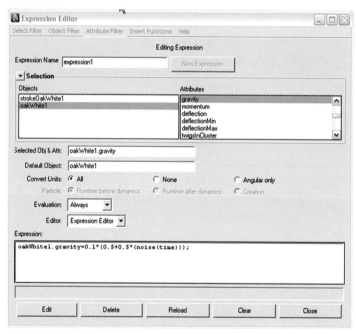

Figure 5.26: The expression applied to Gravity in the Expression Editor

5. Much better. Now let's add a little turbulence to the mix. Open up the Turbulence tab and experiment with the different settings while playing the animation. For a truly creepy look, try using **Local Displacement** with an interpolation set to **Smooth Over Time And Space**. Set the **Turbulence** value to .3, the **Frequency** to .364, and **Speed** to .306. Local displacement works fine for a situation like this in which we just have a single brush. The **Interpolation** setting **Smooth Over Time**

And **Space** works well for slower movements. If we wanted to crank up the **Turbulence** for a really spastic look, we would use **Linear** or **Smooth Over Time**.

6. Open the Spiral settings and add the following expression to the Spiral Max field:

   ```
   spiralMax=0.1*sin(time);
   ```

   This will keep the spiral moving back and forth over time.

7. Play with the Bend settings. You can just give it a static value to keep the branches curled and twisted or add an expression like the one created for `spiralMax`. Try adding this to the `bend` value:

   ```
   bend=0.1*cos(time);
   ```

   Now the `bend` value is the opposite of the spiral value.

8. Play the animation. If you're not getting the willies, you may need to seek professional help.

9. Once the tree stroke has been animated, we can convert it to NURBS. We will convert the stroke to NURBS just in case we decide we want to paint on the tree itself. (You can paint on a stroke that has been converted to polygons, but NURBS have the advantage of inherent UVs. Converting a stroke to polygons requires that you adjust the UVs before you can paint on the converted object, which can be tedious.) In the Outliner, make sure strokeOakWhite1 is selected. The connection to the Paint Effects controls will be maintained as long as history is not deleted. Choose **Modify > Convert > Paint Effects To NURBS > Options**. In the options, make sure Hide Strokes is enabled. Click the Apply button and give your computer a few moments to make the conversion.

Framing the Scene

So far this is pretty straightforward Paint Effects 101 stuff. In a minute we'll get a bit more creative, but first let's get a camera into the scene. The shot calls for a worm's-eye view with the creepy tree towering above.

1. Create a camera and name it "renderCam."

2. Choose **Window > Rendering Editors > Render Settings**. In the Image Size settings, set Width to 720 and Height to 405. Turn off Enable Default Light.

3. In the Maya Software tab, set **Quality** to **Intermediate**. In the Ray Tracing Quality section, enable **Ray Tracing** and keep the default values.

4. Open the Hypershade window. Converting the Paint Effects to NURBS caused Maya to generate a Phong texture for us. This is great except we don't really want a reflective tree. Open up the attributes for phong1 and set **Reflectivity** to 0.

5. In the Perspective view, switch to the renderCam and open its attribute settings. Set **Focal Length** to 15. Use the Dolly Track and Tumble controls to position the camera at the base of the tree pointing upward into the branches, as shown in Figure 5.27.

Figure 5.27: The tree seen through the renderCam. A focal length of 15 increases the creepiness factor.

Lighting the Scene

Now for some classic spooky lighting.

1. Create a spot light, and name it "keyLight." Position it at the base of the tree looking upward; somewhere close to the camera would work nicely. It might be a good idea to select the keyLight and in the perspective window choose **Panels > Look Through Selected**. Then you can use the Dolly, Track, and Tumble controls to position the light just as you did for the camera.

2. Set **Cone Angle** to cover the whole tree; a setting between 70 and 90 should work well.

3. In the Attribute Editor for the light, set **Decay Rate** to **Quadratic** and **Intensity** to somewhere from 30 to 90. Quadratic falloff imitates the way light loses its intensity based on distance, so the proximity of the light to the tree is going to make a big difference in how bright the rendered tree looks. The quadratic falloff also accounts for why **Intensity** may need to be set to a high value before you can see anything in a rendered view. Enable **Ray Traced Shadows**. Set the light color to a pale blue.

4. Do a test rendering and see how the tree looks so far. If the rendering takes longer than 20 seconds, try turning raytracing off and set the light's **Decay Rate** to none and the **Intensity** to 1. The spooky lighting adds a lot to the scene, but don't forget that your art director needs a version of the animation in a hurry.

5. Create a directional light and position it above and behind the tree pointing directly at the camera. Set **Intensity** to 2 and **Color** to a violet or red—sickly green works as well. (See Figure 5.28.)

Figure 5.28: A rendering of the tree with spooky lighting

For our purposes, this 2-point light scheme should work fine. Feel free to experiment with the colors and positions of the lights. If you're a fan of 3-point lighting, feel free to add another light in the scene coming from the side. Adding a file texture to the color of the light is a great way to create the effect of shadows being thrown on the object from somewhere behind the camera. This increases the mystery of the scene. To see a version of the scene so far, open scaryTree_v02.mb from the Chapter 5 folder of the CD.

Using a Smear Brush

Once you have reached a creepiness factor you're happy with and the scene doesn't take more than 10 to 20 seconds to render, we can go on to adding some hallucinatory effects to turn our spooky tree into a truly nightmarish scene.

To create the dream world effect, we will apply a paint brush to the scene and set it to smear so that it distorts the image. We'll try a few variations of this effect just so our art director has some options to show the client.

1. Create a NURBS sphere. Assign a Lambert shader to the sphere and set the **Transparency** so that the sphere is invisible. Name the shader "invisibleSG." You may want to turn on Wireframe On Shaded in the perspective view just so you can see where the sphere is. Name the sphere "distortionSphere."

2. Open the Attribute Editor for the distortionSphere's shape node. Under Render Stats, uncheck all of the boxes; we want to make darn sure the sphere does not appear or affect the render (Figure 5.29).

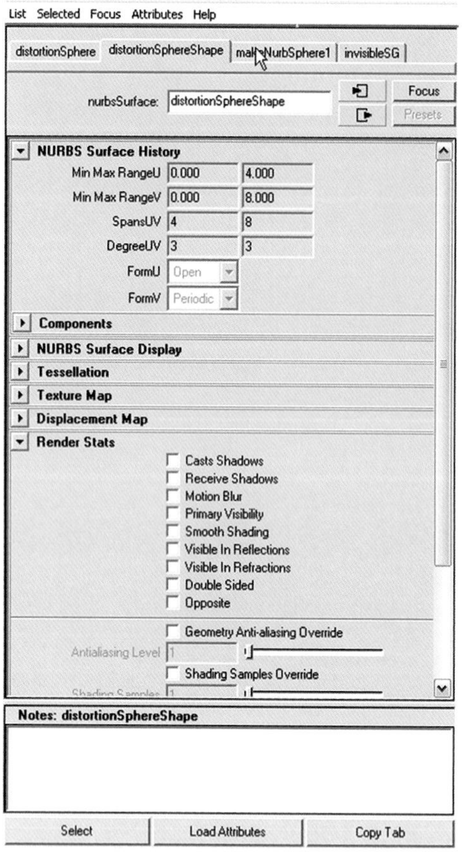

Figure 5.29:
All of the boxes under Render
Stats have been unchecked
just to make sure they do not
affect the render in any way.

3.   Switch to the perspective view. Scale the distortionSphere up and position it so that it surrounds the renderCam. Parent the distortionSphere to the camera and set its **RotateX, Y,** and **Z** attributes to 90, 0 , and 0, respectively so that the camera is looking down the Y axis of the distortionSphere (Figure 5.30).

Figure 5.30:
The distortionSphere
has been parented to
the camera and rotated
so that the camera faces
down the Y axis of the
sphere.

4. Open the Visor (**Windows** > **General Editors** > **Visor**) and click on the Galactic folder on the left-hand side. Select the spaceGasBlack.mel brush.

5. Select the distortionSphere and choose **Paint Effects** > **Make Paintable**. Paint some strokes on the top and sides of the sphere. Don't go too crazy, just enough to partially obscure the camera's view. Use Figure 5.31 as a guide.

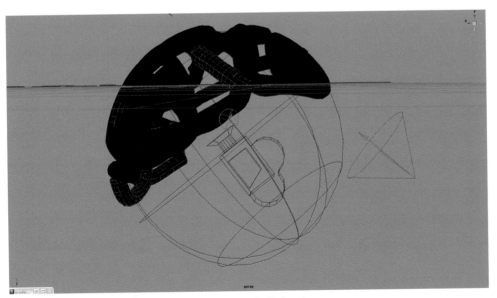

Figure 5.31: The distortionSphere has been painted with the spaceGasBlack stroke.

6. In the Outliner, Shift+select all the spaceGasBlack strokes. Choose **Paint Effects > Share One Brush**. This way if you change the settings for one stroke, all the rest will update.

7. Select one of the strokes and open its Attribute tab. In the settings for **Brush Type** at the top, switch the type to **Smear**.

8. Switch to the renderCam and do a test render (Figure 5.32).

Figure 5.32: The Smear brush setting distorts the image of the tree.

The image looks nicely distorted. Nifty. We can make it much more interesting, though.

Tuning the Brush

As you adjust the settings and create test renders in the render view, be sure to store the images for comparison. To do this, you can choose **File > Keep Image** from the render view window or hit the icon with an arrow pointing into an open box.

1. In the Brush Profile settings, set **Stamp Density** to 16. This will smooth out the brush.

2. Turn **Softness** to 1 to soften the edges of the distortion.

3. Scroll down to the Glow attributes, turn **Shader Glow** up to 0.4 and do a test render. Since the brush has been set to Smear, it is transparent, but the **Shader Glow** setting causes a nice blooming effect wherever the brush distorts the tree (Figure 5.33).

Figure 5.33: The Shader Glow setting on the Smear brush causes highlights on the tree to bloom.

4. Switch back to the perspective view. In the Tubes section of the brush, activate the check box next to **Tube**. The thick strokes now turn into a series of smaller strokes. Set **Tubes Per Step** to 0.2.

5. Set **Length Min** to 0.3 and **Length Max** to 0.6.

6. Set **Tube Width1** to 0.04 and **Tube Width2** to 0.002.

7. In the Width Scale Attributes rollout, set **Elevation Min** to 0 and **Elevation Max** to 1. Keep **Tube Direction** at **Along Normal**.

Animating the Tubes

The tubes of the Smear Brush can be animated to enhance the effect.

1. Move down to the Displacement settings. Set **Displacement Delay** to 0.1. This sets the point along the tube where the Displacement settings below take effect. At a setting of 0.1, the Displacement settings start just above the base of the tube.

2. Use the following Displacement settings:

   - Set **Noise** to 0.15 and **Noise Frequency** to 0.15.
   - Set **Wiggle** to 0.1 and **Wiggle Frequency** to 3.
   - Set **Curl** to 0.5 and **Curl Frequency** to 1.
   - Set **Path Follow** to 0.25.
   - Set **Random** to 0.15.
   - Set **Momentum** to 1.0.

- Set **Turbulence Type** to **World Displacement** and **Interpolation** to **Smooth Over Space And Time.**
- Set **Turbulence** to 0.3, **Frequency** to 0.2. and **Turbulence Speed** to 0.5.
- Set **Bend** to 0.05.

3. Try a test render. These settings are just a guideline. You may want to spend a few minutes experimenting and rendering to see the results (Figure 5.34). When you play the animation, you'll see that the strokes now have a nice wriggling motion. This will make for some cool distortion effects when rendered.

Figure 5.34: The settings on the tubes should make for some interesting distortion effects.

In the next few sections we'll try some variations just to see what happens.

Variation Number One

In this variation the distortionSphere rotates on its Z axis.

1. Save the file under a name like scaryTree_v03.mb and then save it again as scary-Tree_variation1.mb.

2. Select the distortionSphere and rewind to the beginning of the animation. Set a key on the distortionSphere's RotateZ channel.

3. Move the playhead to frame 100, set the **RotateZ** of the distortionSphere to 360, and render another sphere.

4. In the render settings of the scene, set **Frame/Animation Ext.** to **name.#.ext.** Set **Start Frame** to 1 and **End Frame** to 30. Save the scene and then batch render a sequence.

5. When it's completed, use FCheck to view the sequence (Figure 5.35). You can also watch the scaryTree_v01.mov file on the CD.

Figure 5.35: The tubes covering the camera's distortion sphere add frenetic smearing effects to the tree.

Variation Number Two

This variation is a bit more energetic. The distortion sphere scales randomly along its Y axis.

1. Save the scene as scaryTree_variation2.mb.

2. Select the distortionSphere, and in the Channel Box, right-click over the ScaleY field and choose **Expressions**.

3. In the Expression Editor, add the following:

   ```
   scaleY=rand(2,5);
   ```

4. 📀 Save the file and do another test render for 30 frames. As long as File Name Prefix in the render settings is blank, the new sequence should name itself after the Maya scene file, so your previous render will not be overwritten. You can also watch the scaryTree_v02.mov file on the CD.

Variation Number Three

In this variation the Smear Brush is applied directly to the tree itself.

1. Save the scene as scaryTree_variation3.mb.

2. In the Outliner, select the strokeGasBlack strokes. Group them and name the group "cameraDistortion." Hide the cameraDistortion group.

3. Expand the cameraDistortion group, select one of the strokes, and choose **Paint Effects > Get Settings From Selected Stroke**.

4. In the perspective window, marquee-select all the geometry that makes up the tree. Choose **Paint Effects > Make Paintable**.

5. Choose **Paint Effects > Paint Effects Tool**. Start painting randomly all over the tree. Cover the trunk and limbs with the black gas stroke. Don't try to be too neat about it; just cover as much as you can but do leave gaps here and there.

6. In the Outliner, Shift+select the new strokes and choose **Paint Effects > Share One Brush**.

7. Group the strokes and name the group "treeDistortion."

8. Save the file and render out a sequence (Figure 5.36). You can also watch the scaryTree_v03.mov file on the CD.

Figure 5.36: The distortion strokes have been painted directly on the tree.

Further Study

Now you have three variations, you can show the art director several ideas for how to apply this technique in the future. It's unlikely that this shot will be high enough quality for final production, but it works well as a guideline for creating a final animation. You could spend some time converting the tree to polygons and then carefully modeling a nice higher-resolution tree. Then you can rig it with a lattice or bones (or both) and animate it based on the renders you created. Add a nice texture with a displacement map and you're on your way to a production-quality shot. The smear strokes can be used or the renders can be given to the compositor as a rough guide.

Paint Effects Strokes and Soft Body Dynamics

The art director needs a shot of a hairy bacterium swimming past a camera as it makes its way through the goop that makes up the human body. This is for a drug commercial, so naturally scientific accuracy will take a backseat to artistic license. Drug commercials are often much more concerned with persuasion than education.

The bacterium needs to sort of "schlorp" along and it should be covered in icky bacterial hair, known to science types as *pili*. To create the schlorping effect, we'll combine movement through a lattice with a soft body surface. The pili will be created with a Paint Effects stroke.

A soft body surface is essentially a piece of geometry, NURBS or polygonal, that has all of its vertices converted into particles. These particles react to fields, goals, and expressions just like any other particle and their dynamic movements distort the geometry of the soft body. The most common way to apply the soft body is to duplicate the original geometry, convert the vertices of the duplicate surface to particles, and then use the vertices of the original geometry as a goal. Maya takes care of these steps for you when you convert the surface, as we'll see in this exercise.

Animating the Movement of the Bacterium

First we'll tackle the schlorping movement using a lattice.

1. Open the bacterium_v01.mb scene from the Chapter 5 folder of the CD. We see our lone bacterium as a simple polygon surface. This surface was created from a polygon cube that was subdivided with a Smooth operation and then modified using the Sculpt Polygon tool.

2. With the bacterium selected, switch to the Animation menu set and choose **Deform > Create Lattice**. In the Outliner, Shift+select the ffd1Lattice and ffd1Base objects.

3. With both of the objects selected, find the Scale attributes in the Channel Box. Set **ScaleX** to 7, **ScaleY** to 7, and **ScaleZ** to 150. The bacterium should not change; if it does, make sure you are setting the scale on both the ffd1Lattice and ffd1Base objects.

4. Select the ffd1Lattice object and set its **S**, **T**, and **U Divisions** to 2, 2, and 36, respectively. The result of all these settings is shown in Figure 5.37.

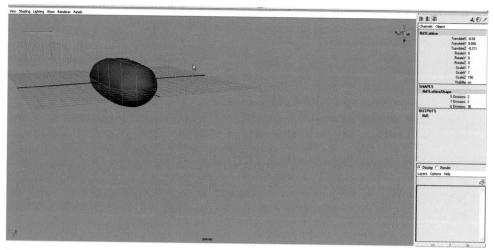

Figure 5.37: The bacterium inside an elongated lattice

5. Select the bacterium object and move it along the Z axis to the far end of the lattice. A setting of –65 in Z should work fine.

6. Set the Time Slider to frame 1. Select the bacterium and, in the Channel Box, right-click over the TranslateZ channel and choose **Key Selected** from the pop-up menu.

7. Move to frame 300 in the Time Slider. Set **TranslateZ** to 65 and set another key on the **TranslateZ** channel.

8. Rewind the animation. Right-click over the lattice in the perspective window and choose **Lattice Point** from the pop-up window. Marquee-select groups of lattice points and scale, rotate, and translate them just enough to create some distortion in the bacterium model (Figure 5.38).

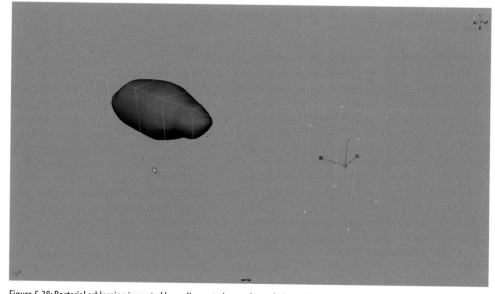

Figure 5.38: Bacterial schlorping is created by scaling, rotating, and translating points on the lattice.

9. Go down the length of the lattice and continue making these tweaks. You can scrub in the Time Slider to see the effect of the lattice tweaks on the bacterium as it moves through the lattice.

10. When you are pleased with the motion, select the lattice and hide it.

Creating the Soft Body Object

By converting the bacterium to a soft body object, we will smooth the effect of the lattice on the geometry and create some fluid secondary motion.

1. Rewind to the start of the animation and select the bacterium. It's important to be at the start of the animation when you convert to a soft body object to avoid having the particles that make up the vertices jump into position at the start of the animation.

2. Switch to the Dynamics menu set and choose **Soft/Rigid Bodies > Create Soft Body > Options**. Set **Creation Options** to **Duplicate, Make Copy Soft**. Uncheck **Duplicate Input Graph**, and check **Hide Non-Soft Object** and **Make Non-Soft A Goal**. Set **Goal Weight** to 0.5 (Figure 5.39). Click Create to make the soft body object.

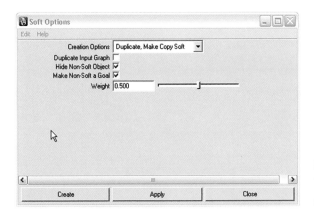

Figure 5.39:
The options for creating
a soft body object

3. Play the animation and check out the schlorping action.

4. In the Outliner, expand the copyOfbacterium object. You'll notice that a particle is parented to the object. These are the particles that make up the vertices of the soft body.

5. Select the copyOfbacteriumParticle object. In the Channel Box, experiment with different settings for **Goal Weight** and **Conserve**; see which settings you like best. A **Conserve** value of 0.98 and a **Goal Weight** value of 0.3 works quite nicely, albeit somewhat cartoony (Figure 5.40).

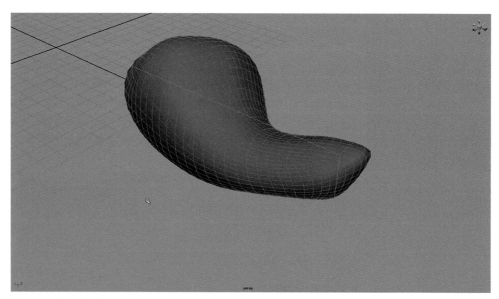

Figure 5.40: The soft body object has a smooth, fluid motion as it moves through the lattice.

6.   To see a version of the file so far, open bacterium_v02.mb from the Chapter 5 folder on the CD.

Creating Bacterial Pili with Paint Effects

The bacterial pili can be created quickly using a Paint Effects brush that we'll modify.

1.   Select the copyOfbacterium object in the Outliner and choose **Windows > UV Texture Editor**. In the Editor, you'll notice that the UVs are all laid out in a standard arrangement for a cube model (Figure 5.41). It's important to make sure your UVs are laid out correctly when using a Paint Effects stroke on a polygon object. If the UVs are overlapping or pinching in weird ways, the brush stroke will not behave correctly. This UV layout is just fine for our purposes.

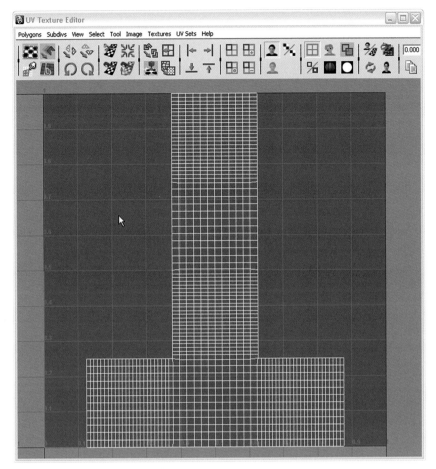

Figure 5.41: The UVs for the bacterium object

2. Close the UV Texture Editor and choose **Windows** > **General Editors** > **Visor**. Scroll down the folders on the left and open the Underwater directory.

3. Click on the tubeWeeds.mel brush so that it turns yellow; this will load it into memory as the current brush (Figure 5.42).

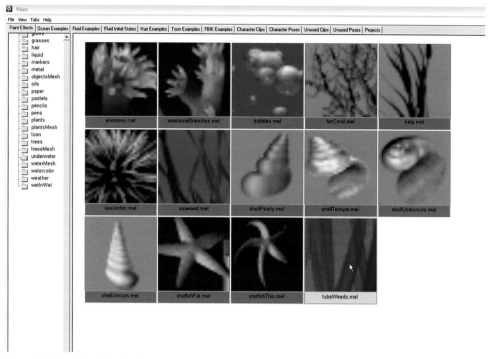

Figure 5.42: The tubeWeeds brush will work well for the bacterial pili.

4. Rewind the animation, switch to the Rendering menu set, select the copyOfbacterium surface, and choose **Paint Effects > Make Paintable**.

5. Start painting the surface of the bacterium with the tubeWeeds brush. Tumble around the model and get every side covered, as in Figure 5.43. It's OK if it takes a few strokes to get it all. To change the brush size, hold the b hot key down and left-mouse-drag left or right; a smaller brush will make smaller strokes.

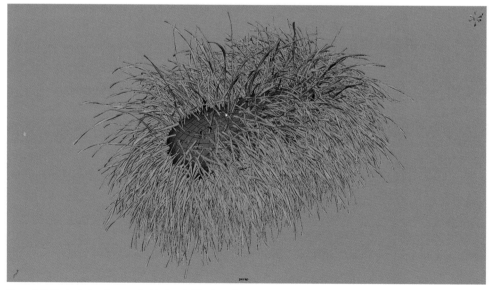

Figure 5.43: The bacterium is covered with the tubeWeeds stroke.

6. In the Outliner, Shift+select all of the tubeWeeds strokes and choose **Paint Effects > Share One Brush**. This will cause the settings for all of the strokes to update when we edit the attributes for one of them.

Modifying the Weeds Stroke

We'll edit the weeds strokes so that they look more like pili and less like underwater plant life.

1. Choose **Modify > Search And Replace Names**. In the pop-up window, type **Tube-Weeds** in the Search For field and **Pili** in the Replace With field. Make sure the All button is selected. This will change the names of the brush strokes.

2. Select one of the strokes in the Outliner. Open up its Attribute Editor.

3. Click on the tubeWeeds tab. (It may have a number associated with it, corresponding to the stroke you picked.) Set **Global Scale** to 1.5. Rename the brush tubePili.

4. In the Brush Profile settings, set **Flatness1** and **Flatness2** to 0. Under the Twist settings, set **Twist Rate** to 0. This will cause the pili to become smooth and round.

5. To make the ends tapered, go to the Tubes rollout, expand it, and find the Width Scale settings. Click the arrow button next to the gray envelope box. This will open up an expanded view of the envelope. Click on the circle in the upper left and drag it down a little. This will make editing the envelope a little easier. The dark area of the box indicates the profile of the tubes that make up the stroke. We'll add some control points to give the tubes a taper.

6. Click again on the right side of the line and drag down again; this will create a second control marker. In the **Interpolation** box, set the option to **Smooth**. Click on the very right to make a third marker and drag all the way down to make a pointy end. Use Figure 5.44 as a reference. You should see the strokes in the perspective view update as you make these changes.

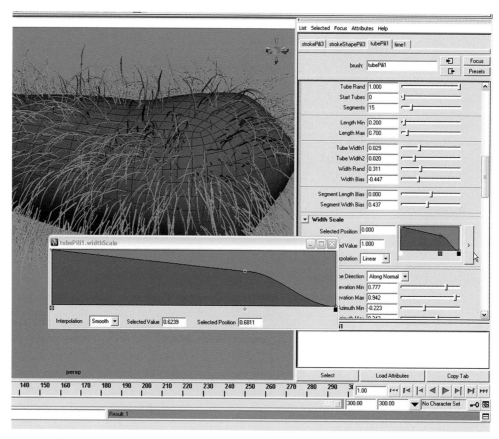

Figure 5.44: The Width Scale attribute controls the profile of the tube. Clicking the arrow button next to the envelope graph opens an expanded view for easier editing.

7. Look above the Width Scale settings and find the **Tube Width1** attribute in the Creation settings. Set this to 0.05 to make the base of the pili a little thicker.

Editing Surface Offset

If you zoom in closely to the surface of the bacterium, you'll notice that some of the pili are floating above the surface (Figure 5.45). This might look weird if we decide to do a close-up shot of the bacterium. To fix this, we'll edit the **Surface Offset** attribute.

Figure 5.45: Some of the tubes appear to be floating above the surface of the bacterium.

1. The **Surface Offset** attribute is found on the shape node for the stroke. Unfortunately, this means if we edit the attribute on one stroke, the others will not automatically update as they do for the brush stroke attributes. We can still use the Attribute Spread Sheet to save some time. In the Outliner, activate the visibility of shapes in the **Display** menu.

2. You can Ctrl+select each of the strokeShapePili objects or you can **stroke-ShapePili*** in the Quick Select box on the status bar. With the strokeShapePili strokes selected, choose **Window** > **General Editors** > **Attribute Spread Sheet**.

3. In the Attribute Spread Sheet, click on the Keyable tab (it may open to this tab automatically). Shift+select the fields in the column under **Surface Offset** and enter –0.1 (Figure 5.46). Hit the Enter key to activate this value. The tubes should no longer float above the surface. Go ahead and close the Attribute Spread Sheet. If the **Global Scale** setting of the brush is higher than 1.5 or if the brush size is large, you may need to enter a higher value for **Surface Offset**.

Attribute Spread Sheet										
Names Layouts Key Layer Help										
Keyable | Shape Keyable | Transform | Translate | Rotate | Scale | Render | Tessellation | Geometry | All										
	Display Percen	Draw As Mesh	Seed	Draw Order	Surface Offset	Motion Blurred	Primary Visibility	Camera PointX	Camera PointY	Camera PointZ
strokeShapePil	100	on	0	0	-0.1	on	on	0	0	0
strokeShapePil	100	on	1	0	-0.1	on	on	0	0	0
strokeShapePil	100	on	2	0	-0.1	on	on	0	0	0
strokeShapePil	100	on	3	0	-0.1	on	on	0	0	0
strokeShapePil	100	on	4	0	-0.1	on	on	0	0	0

Figure 5.46: The Attribute Spread Sheet makes editing attributes on multiple objects much easier.

Animating the Bacterial Pili

Animating the pili involves adjusting the settings in the Behavior tab. Since the bacterium is swimming along in one direction, we can use a general force to create the effect of the pili reacting to its movements.

Expand the rollout under **Tubes > Behavior** and use the following settings (Figure 5.47):

- Under Displacement, set **Noise** to 0.16 and **Noise Frequency** to 0.2.

- Under the Forces settings, set **Gravity** to -0.015. Under Uniform Force, set the third field, the **Z** field, to -0.4.

- In the Turbulence settings, set **Turbulence Type** to **World Force**. Set **Interpolation** to **Smooth Over Time And Space**. Set **Turbulence** to 0.7, the **Frequency** to 0.35, and **Turbulence Speed** to 0.1.

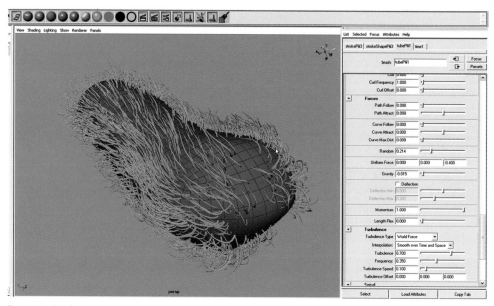

Figure 5.47: By adjusting the behavior settings, we can make the pili react to the movement of the bacteria.

You can experiment with other settings, but this should be enough to get a good motion from the pili. To see a version of the scene up to this point, open bacterium_v03.mb from the cChapter 5 folder on the CD.

Converting Paint Effects to NURBS

We'll convert the strokes to NURBS surfaces so that we can easily apply a shader to the pili.

1. In the Outliner, Shift+select all the strokeTubeWeeds strokes. Choose **Modify > Convert > Paint Effects To NURBS > Options**. In the options, make sure Hide Strokes is selected. Click Convert to make the conversion.

2. In the Outliner, Shift+select the newly created strokeShapeTubePiliSurfaces groups. Open the Hypershade. Right+click over the green bacteriumSG shader and choose **Apply Material to Selection**.

3. Select the copyOfbacterium object and apply the shader to it as well.

Playblast the Animation

It's very likely that all the pili strokes are slowing down the performance of your computer. To get an idea of what the animation looks like without having to render, we'll create a Playblast.

1. In the perspective view, uncheck **NURBS Surfaces** from the **Show** menu so that it's a little easier to move the camera around. Uncheck **Dynamics** as well so that the particles on the soft body are hidden too.

2. Use the tumble, track, and dolly hot keys to position the camera so that you get a clear view of the bacterium as it makes its way through the scene. Try to get close to the bacterium toward the end so you can really see the pili up close. The Playblast will take a while to create, so you may want to focus on just the first half of the animation. Alternatively, you can parent a camera to the bacterium object so that it follows as the bug swims along.

3. At this point, it would be a good idea to create a particle cache for the particles associated with the soft body object. To do this, switch to the Dynamics menu set and choose **Solvers > Create Particle Disk Cache > Options**. In the options, make sure **Particle Systems To Cache** is set to **All**. Go ahead and make the cache. Maya will run through the scene; you won't see it update. When it's finished, you'll be able to scrub back and forth on the Timeline and the particle will update properly because the particle positions have been written to disk.

4. When you're happy with the angle, rewind the animation and turn the visibility of NURBS surface back on in the perspective view.

5. To make a Playblast, choose **Windows > Playblast > Options**. In the options, set **Time Range** to **Start/End**. Set **End Time** to something from 100 to 150, depending on how long you want to wait until the Playblast is done. Set **Display Size** to **From Window**. Setting **Scale** to 0.75 or 0.5 might be a good idea just to make things a bit faster. If it takes forever to make a Playblast, try hiding all the groups of NURBS strokes except for one that is close to the camera. This should speed it up a little. You really just want to get an idea of how the pili will behave when the animation is playing.

6. Click Playblast to start creating the image sequence. Maya will play through the animation and take a screen shot of each frame (Figure 5.48). Make sure you don't cover the window, use a screen saver, or otherwise mess with Maya while the Playblast is being created.

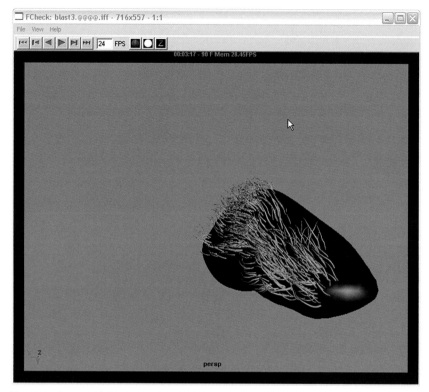

FCheck: blast3.@@@@.iff - 716x557 - 1:1

File   View   Help

24   FPS

00:03:17 - 90 F Mem 28.45FPS

persp

Figure 5.48: Creating a Playblast is a good way to preview the animation before rendering.

The Playblast may take a while. Might be a good time for a cup of coffee.

To see a finished version of the file, open the bacterium_v04.mb scene from the Chapter 5 folder on the CD. To see a rendered QuickTime movie, open bacterium.mov from the movies folder on the CD (Figure 5.49).

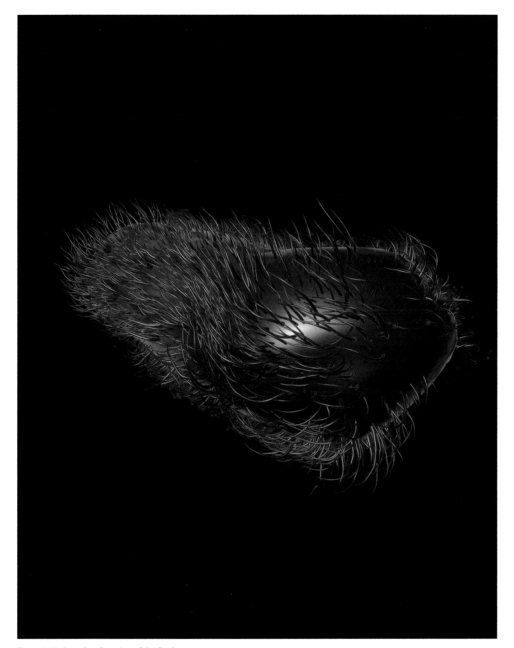

Figure 5.49: A rendered version of the final scene

Further Study

Since the bacterium is swimming along the Z axis, we've been able to easily use the uniform forces settings in the Paint Effects brush strokes options to cheat the look of the pili reacting to the environment. You can try adding a Paint Effects spring to the strokes as well (**Paint Effects > Brush Animation > Make Brush Spring**). This creates a delayed effect in the motion of strokes in relation to the object they are painted on. Applying Paint Effects springs to a scene with many strokes, such as the bacterium scene we just created, may slow your playback time significantly, however, so beware.

Taming Paint Effects Brush Strokes: The Test Tube Nerve

Our scientists are at it again, playing God in the laboratory. When will they ever learn? The art director has returned with a shot for our sci-fi horror film. This time they need an animation of an alien nerve growing in a test tube. Once again Paint Effects comes to the rescue. We'll use a brush stroke to create the nerve and then discover some techniques to control the growth and position of the nerve.

Creating the Nerve Using Paint Effects

First we'll find a suitable brush stroke in the Visor and apply it to our scene.

1.   ⬭   Open the testTube_v01.mb scene from the Chapter 5 folder on the CD. You'll see our test tube experiment set up and ready to grow some alien nerves. Turn on Wireframe On Shaded in the shading options of the perspective view so that the transparent models can easily be seen.

2.   Choose **Windows** > **General Editors** > **Visor** and select the Electrical folder on the left-hand side. Click on the lightningRed.mel stroke so that it turns yellow (Figure 5.50); this will load it into memory as the current brush stroke. How do we know which stroke would make a good nerve? Lots of experimentation and practice. Eventually you get a feel for which strokes work best under certain situations.

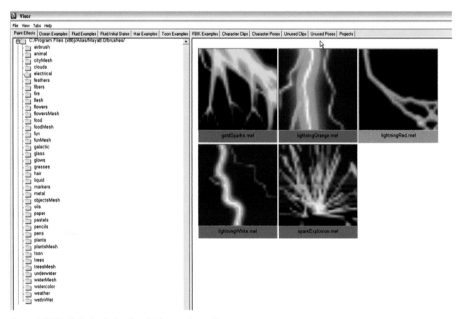

Figure 5.50: The lightningRed.mel stroke is a good start for our nerve.

3. In the Outliner, expand the testTube group and select the liquidSurface object. Switch to the Rendering menu set and choose **Paint Effects > Make Paintable**. Then choose **Paint Effects > Paint Effects Tool**.

4. Hold the left mouse button down and drag for a second or so at the center of the liquidSurface object. When you let go of the mouse button, the lightning stroke should appear (Figure 5.51).

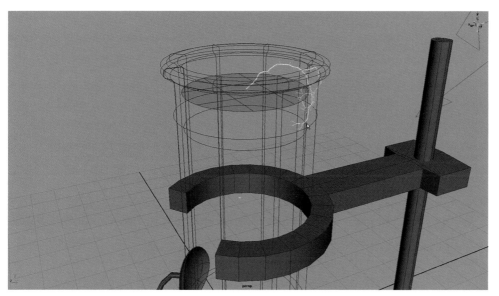

Figure 5.51: The lightningRed stroke painted on the liquidSurface object

5. In the Outliner, rename strokeLightingRed1 "nerve." Turn on **Visibility Of Shape Nodes** in the Outliner using the Outliner's **Display** menu, expand nerve, and rename strokeShapeLightingRed1 "nerveShape."

Adjusting the Look of the Nerve Stroke

We want the nerve to dangle downward into the tube. This requires a fair amount of twiddling with settings and experimentation to achieve.

1. Currently the nerve is popping out of the top of the liquidSurface. To flip it, we need to reverse the Normals on the Paint Effects stroke. To do this, select the nerve stroke and open the Attribute Editor to the nerveShape tab. In the Normal Direction rollout, check the box next to Use Normal. Set the **Normal** fields to 0, –1, 0. These settings worked well for me, but you may need to experiment to get the nerve to grow from the bottom of the liquid surface. Sometimes you can get away with just reversing the surface direction on the NURBS surface (in the Surfaces menu set **Edit NURBS > Reverse Surface Direction**).

2. Select nerveShape and open its Attribute Editor. You'll see a tab labeled lightningRed. This contains the attributes for our brush stroke. Click on this tab. Just to be neat, in the **Brush** field change the name to "nerveBrush."

3. In the Attribute Editor, click on Tubes, then Behavior, then Forces. Set **Path Follow** and **Path Attract** to 0 so that the stroke points away from the liquidSurface.

4. Go up in the Editor and click Creation. Set **Length Min** to 5 and **Length Max** to 6. Set **Tube Width1** to 0.05 to thicken the nerve near the top.

5. Under the Width Scale settings, set **Elevation Min** to around 0.917, **Elevation Max** to 1, **Azimuth Min** to –1, and **Azimuth Max** to around 0.14. We're trying to get the nerve to point downward into the test tube. As was stated earlier, it takes a fair amount of twiddling. If you need to know what each setting does, you can look them up in the Help section. Essentially, these settings control the direction in which the tubes grow from the original Paint Effects path. Arriving at these particular settings is a matter of . . . well, twiddling.

Adjusting Branches and Twigs

Adjusting the branch settings will help us to further refine the look of the nerve. These settings control the place along the length of the brush where the branches split off, as well as their angle, length, and number.

1. Click Growth and then Branches to open the Branches settings.

2. Set **Split Max Depth** to around 6.876, **Split Rand** to around 0.3, **Split Angle** to around 5, **Split Twist** to around 0.5, and **Split Bias** to around 0.488. The nerve may still be poking out of the tube but that's OK; we'll fix it shortly.

3. To make the nerve a little hairier, we'll adjust the twig settings. Set **Num Twigs In Cluster** to 3, **Twig Drop Out** to 0.5, and **Twig Length** to 0.165. The results are shown in Figure 5.52.

Figure 5.52:
The nerve is looking longer and hairier.

Adjusting Forces

If you play the animation, you'll notice that the brush already has some motion built in. We'll modify this to make it slower and more fluid.

1. Set **Turbulence** to 0.25, **Frequency** to 0.4, and **Turbulence Speed** to 1.

2. Set **Turbulence Type** to **Local Displacement**. Local Displacement works fine for a situation like this in which we have just a single brush. If we had a group of brush strokes and we wanted them to react to the force in the same way, such as a bunch of nerves in a tub of liquid, then we would use World Displacement.

3. Set the **Interpolation** to **Smooth Over Time And Space**. The result is shown in Figure 5.53. This setting works well for slower movements. If we wanted to crank up the turbulence for a really jerky look, we would use **Linear** or **Smooth Over Time**.

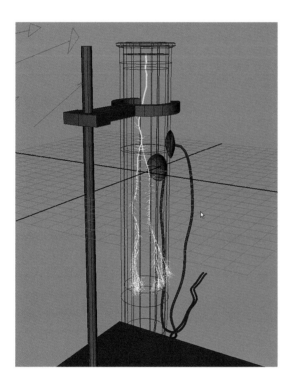

Figure 5.53:
Turbulence has been added to cause the nerve to move over time.

Creating a Control Curve

We can refine the position and movement of the brush by creating a control curve.

1. Switch to the side view and choose **Create > CV Curve Tool**. Starting from the top of the stroke, click five times in the viewport to create a curve. Start the curve close to the root of the nerve brush but have it bend away from the stroke in the Z axis. Use Figure 5.54 as a reference.

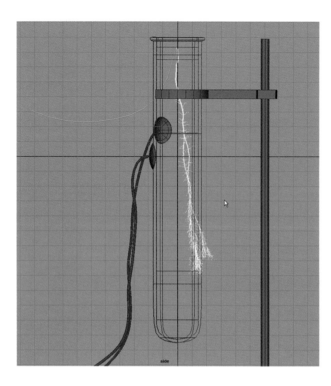

Figure 5.54:
A curve is added to
help control the
shape of the nerve.

2. When the curve is complete, open the Outliner and rename the curve "nerve-ControlCurve." Select the curve and Ctrl+select the nerve stroke. Choose **Paint Effects > Curve Utilities > Set Control Curves**.

3. Open the Attribute Editor for the nerve brush stroke. Under the **Tubes > Behavior > Forces** rollout, set **Curve Follow** to .033 and **Curve Attract** to .04. **Curve Follow** causes the growth of the stroke to follow the curve, whereas **Curve Attract** is more like a force that attracts the stroke.

4. Select the nerveControlCurve and switch to component mode by hitting the F8 key. Select each CV on the curve and position it so that the curve points down into the tube, dragging the nerve stroke with it (Figure 5.55). Don't be too neat about it; the curve should have some small bends in it so that the nerve stroke looks more natural. Make sure the nerve is not intersecting the geometry of the test tube.

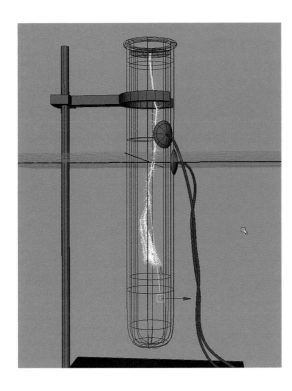

Figure 5.55:
Moving the CVs of the
control curve allows the
shape of the stroke to be
easily altered.

Animating the Control Curve

We can animate the CVs of the control curve to add another layer of movement to the nerve.

1. Select the nerveControlCurve and hit the F8 key to switch to component mode. Switch to the Animation menu set. Starting from the top of the curve, select each CV one at a time and create a cluster deformer by choosing **Deform > Create Cluster**. In the Layer Editor, turn off the visibility of the testTubeLayer to make the selection of the curve's CVs a little easier (Figure 5.56).

Figure 5.56:
Cluster deformers are
added to the CVs of the
controlCurve.

2. We can set keyframes on the cluster deformers to control the movement of the nerveControlCurve. In the Outliner, Shift+select the clusters and group them (Ctrl+g). Name the group "clusters."

3. Select the clusters group in the Outliner and choose **Modify > Prefix Hierarchy Names**. In the pop-up box, type **nerve_**. This is a quick way to rename all the clusters in the group.

4. Switch back to object mode by hitting F8 again. Turn the visibility of the test-TubeLayer back on. Select the lower three clusters and change their position.

5. ⊙ Set some keyframes over the course of the animation while changing the position of the clusters so that the nerve moves around. Just be careful that the nerve does not intersect the test tube surface. To see a version of the scene completed up to this point, open testTube_v02.mb from the Chapter 5 folder of the CD.

Converting the Control Curve to a Soft Body Object

To add even more dynamic motion, we can make the control curve a soft body object to which turbulence and other forces can be applied. We want to convert the control curve to a soft body object which will convert the CVs of the curve to particles. The CVs of a duplicate curve become a goal for the particle CVs of the soft body curve. Then when the CVs of the original curve are animated, there is a delayed springy effect as the soft body control curve is attracted to the duplicate goal curve. The CVs of the goal curve will be animated with clusters just like our current setup.

There are two ways to handle converting this curve into a soft body. We can backtrack through the previous sections of the tutorial before we added clusters to the control curve, convert the control curve to a soft body with a duplicate control curve and then put clusters on that duplicate control curve's CVs, and then animate these clusters, or we can convert the current control curve into a soft body with a goal curve and then use the Hypergraph to switch the new soft body curve to the Paint Effects control curve. In the interest of learning more about Maya, let's try the second method. It's actually quite easy and takes less time than backtracking.

1. Switch to the Dynamics menu set and select the nerveControlCurve. Rewind the animation to frame 1.

2. Choose **Soft/Rigid Bodies > Create Soft Body > Options**. In the options, set **Creation Options** to **Duplicate, Make Copy Soft**. Uncheck **Duplicate Input Graph** and **Hide Non-Soft Object** and check the box for **Make Non-Soft Goal**. Set **Goal Weight** to 1. We'll modify this later with an expression.

3. Select the nerveControlCurve and the copyOfNerveControlCurve. Choose **Windows > Hypergraph Input And Output Connections**. The Hypergraph will open up showing a diagram of the connections between nodes in the scene (Figure 5.57).

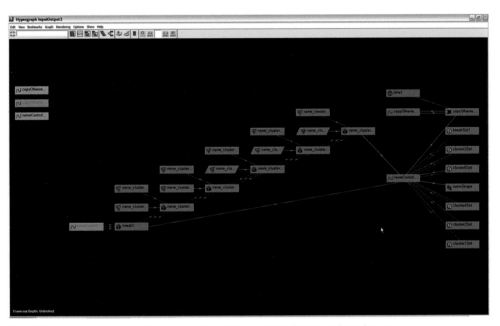

Figure 5.57: The Hypergraph gives a visual representation of the connections between nodes in the scene.

The Hypergraph is an excellent visual representation of what goes on between nodes in a Maya scene. It can be a little intimidating if you've never used it; however, once you become accustomed to it, you'll see that no other window in Maya is more concise about all the various nodal connections in a scene.

Maya 8 has changed the **Window** menu so that you can open up the Hypergraph to either a scene hierarchy display, similar to the Outliner, or an Input Output Connections display similar to the work area of the Hypershade. These view options have always been accessible from the menu bar of the Hypergraph, Maya 8 has just made it a little more convenient to jump into either mode from the main Maya interface. These view modes do not affect the way the nodes behave in Maya. You can also open up both modes at the same time. Some users prefer working in the Hypergraph to the Outliner.

4. A large part of the Hypergraph looks like a web with lines connecting various nodes. Off to the left you'll see three unconnected nodes, two of which are yellow. The nodes in the weblike pattern are the shape nodes; the isolated nodes on the left are the transform nodes for nerveControlCurve and copyOfnerveControlCurve. They are yellow because they are the currently selected objects. The third isolated node is the original shape node for the curve that is now a soft body object. We don't need to worry about this node at this time.

5. To navigate in the Hypergraph, you can use the Alt+MMB key combination to zoom, just like in a viewport, and the Alt+RMB key combination to pan around the window. Zoom in to the nerveControlCurve shapes at the center of the web of nodes.

6. Find the purple line that connects the nerveControlCurveShape to the nerveShape brush stroke. The icons on the boxes indicate what the objects are. The curve nodes have a curve on them and the strokes have are sort of spiky (Figure 5.58). If you hold the mouse pointer over the nodes, you'll see their full names; if you hold it over the lines that connect their nodes, you'll see the connection. This is similar to the Hypershade.

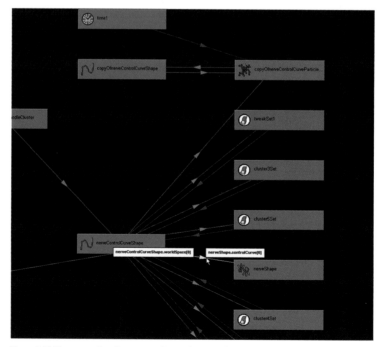

Figure 5.58: The connections between nodes can be seen when the mouse pointer hovers over the line that connects them.

7. The purple line indicates a connection between the **worldSpace** attribute of the nerveControlCurveShape and the **controlcurve[0]** of the nerveShape brush stroke. The zero in brackets indicates which control curve this is; a brush stroke can have more than one control curve. The number in brackets is the index number for each curve.

8. Select the copyOfnerveControlCurveShape that is above the nerveControlCurve-Shape (Figure 5.59) and MMB drag it down on top of the nerveShape brush stroke icon. From the pop-up box, choose **Other**; this will open the Connection Editor.

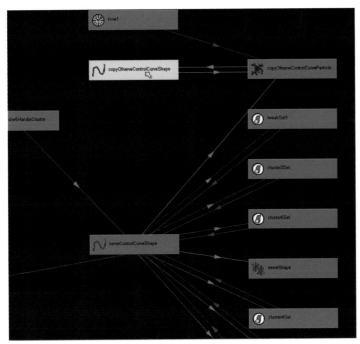

Figure 5.59: The copyOfnerveControlCurveShape is selected; MMB dragging it over nerveShape will allow a connection to be made.

9. From the left side of the Connection Editor, scroll down and highlight the **World Space** attribute. On the right-hand side, find the **Control Curve** attribute. Hit the plus sign to expand the attribute and highlight **ControlCurve[0]**. It's in italics, indicating that it is already connected to something (namely, the original nerve-ControlCurveShape). By highlighting it in the Connection Editor, we are overriding this connection with a new one (Figure 5.60).

Figure 5.60:
The World Space attribute of the copyOfnerveControl-CurveShape is connected to the nerveShape Control-Curve[0] attribute.

10. In the Hypergraph, you can see that a purple line has been drawn between copy-OfnerveControlCurveShape and the nerveShape brush stroke. The line between the original nerveControlCurve shape and the nerveShape brush stroke is now gone. The soft body curve now controls the Paint Effects stroke and the original nerveControlCurve with the clusters is a goal for the soft body curve (Figure 5.61).

Figure 5.61:
The new connection is highlighted in the Hypergraph.

Editing the Goal Weights of the Soft Body Curve

First we'll test the soft body curve to make sure it's working; then we'll create an expression so that the CVs on the top of the curve have a higher goal weight than those on the bottom.

1. In the Outliner, select the copyOfnerveControlCurve object and rename it "SBcurve." Expand the node and rename the copyOfnerveControlCurveParticle "SBcurveParticle." This will help to make the names of the objects in the scene look less like an index for a German philosophy book.

2. In the Channel Box for the SBcurveParticle, set **Goal Weight** to 0.3.

3. Select SBcurveParticle and choose **Fields > Turbulence**.

4. In the Channel Box for the Turbulence field, set **Magnitude** to 10 and **Attenuation** to 0.

5. Play the animation. You should see the nerve sway with the turbulence. The purple curve is the SBcurve, and the blue curve with the clusters is the original control curve. The animation created in "Animating the Control Curve" earlier in this tutorial affects the SBcurve along with the turbulence.

6. Rewind the animation. Select the SBcurveParticle object. In the Channel Box, set the goal weight back to 1.

7. Open the Attribute Editor for SBcurveParticleShape. Set **Particle Render Type** to **Numeric**. By default, the numbers beside the particles in the view window represent the particleId value for each of the particles on the soft body curve. Notice that it starts at the top with 0 and increases in value as it goes down the curve. We'll be using this value to control the weights of the curve (Figure 5.62).

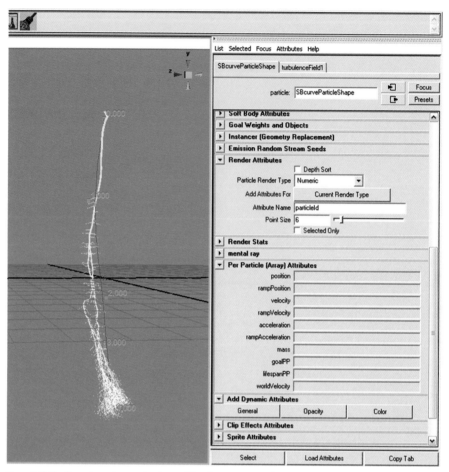

Figure 5.62: The Numeric render type for the particles allows you to see the particleId number for each particle on the soft body curve.

8. Scroll down to the Per Particle (Array) Attributes. Right-click over the field next to goalPP and choose **Runtime Before Dynamics** to open up the Expression Editor.

9. In the Expression Editor's Expression field, type the following:

```
goalPP=0.1*(10-id);
```

10. Hit Create to make the expression active. What this expression does is subtract the particle's id value from 10 and then multiply it by 0.1. This value is now set to the goal weight of that particular particle: 0.1 * (10 − 0) = 1, so the particle with an id of 0 now gets a goal weight of 1; 0.1 * (10 − 1) = 0.9, so the particle with an id of 1 gets a goal weight of 0.9; and so on down the line. Each particle going down the curve has a lower goal weight, allowing its attraction to the original control curve to be weaker; thus it has a slower reaction to the control curve and a stronger reaction to the turbulence.

11. Select and copy the expression in the Expression field. Switch to the Creation Expression mode and paste the expression into the Expression field. By copying this as a creation expression, we ensure that it will be active from the start of the animation.

12. In the **Render Type** attribute for the particle shape, click the Add Attributes For Current Render Type button. In the **attributeName** field, type **goalPP** (Figure 5.63). Now the number next to the particles represents the goal weight for each particle. If you have only a few CVs on your control curve, you may not get much secondary movement as the goal weights. You can edit the expression and change the multiplier to a number like .06 or .05 to reduce the strength of the goal weights overall:

goalPP=.06*(10-id);

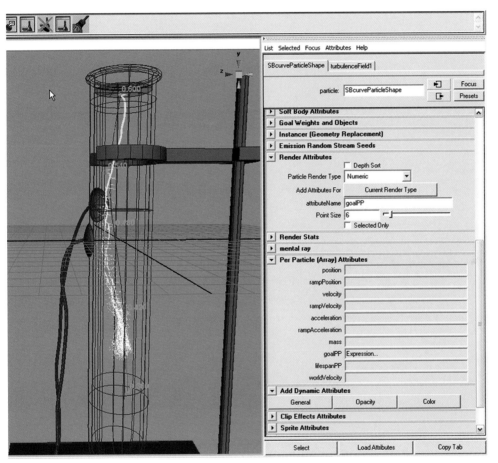

Figure 5.63: The numeric render type has been set to goalPP, allowing the goal weight values to be visible in the perspective view. The expression has been edited to allow for lower values.

To see a version of the scene up to this point, open the testTube_v03.mb scene from the Chapter 5 folder on the CD.

If you decide you need direct control over the goal weights on the soft body particles, you can bypass using an expression and just manually enter the weights. To do this, delete the expression on the **goalPP** attribute of the particles, switch to component mode by pressing F8, and select all the soft body particles. You can then open the Component Editor (**Window** > **General Editors** > **Component Editor**) and change the values in the goalPP column under the Particles tab (Figure 5.64). This might save you time if you have to change things in front of a picky art director.

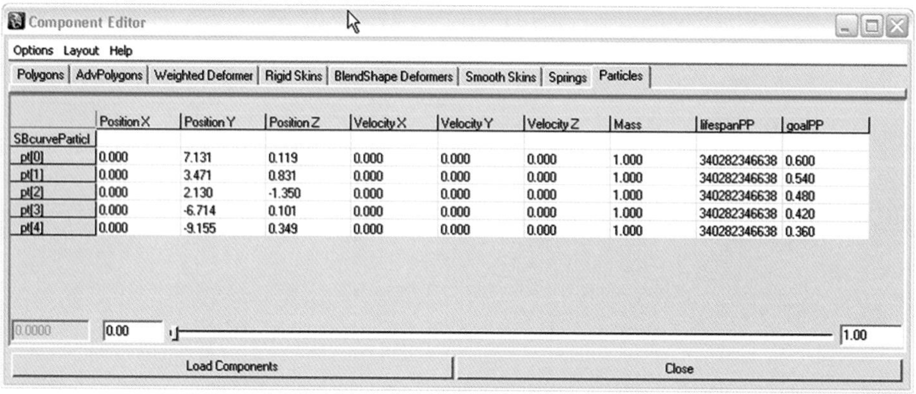

Figure 5.64: The Component Editor allows you to enter the goalPP weights directly.

Controlling the Growth for the Stroke

We want to control the growth of the stroke over time. Maya's Flow Animation settings in the Paint Effects brush stroke attributes will allow you to do this.

1. Select the Nerve brush stroke and open the Attribute Editor. Switch to the nerveBrush tab. Scroll all the way down to the Flow Animation attributes.

2. Set **Flow Speed** to 1, and check the boxes next to **Stroke Time** and **Time Clip**. Uncheck **Texture Flow**. **Stroke Time** animates the growth of the tube over time. **Time Clip** animates the stroke over time, depending on the start time and end time settings. Play the animation to see how the stroke will grow with these settings. Texture Flow controls the animation of textures on the surface of the strokes. We aren't using that for this particular effect, but make a note to experiment with that setting in the future.

3. Set **Start Time** to 3 and play the animation. The stroke won't start growing until the animation has been playing for three seconds. The display of the stroke will look thinner than before; don't worry, Maya has just optimized the display so that playback is faster. It will still render with the settings we created before.

4. Set **Start Time** to 1 and **End Time** to 2 and play the animation. The **End Time** controls when the stroke dies. You can get some great creepy-crawly effects depending on how you set **Start Time** and **End Time** (Figure 5.64).

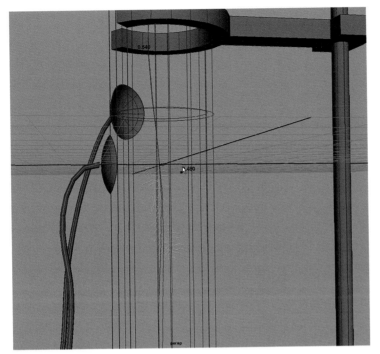

Figure 5.65: The start and end times of the flow animation have been adjusted. Now a section of the nerve creeps by the camera—ick!

5. Set **Start Time** back to 0 and **End Time** back to 1000.

Key Framing Stroke Growth

The Flow Animation settings are useful for getting a basic animated growth out of your strokes, but you just know the art director is going to give you all kinds of crazy instructions on how the nerve should grow. It would be much handier if we could control the growth of the stroke using the Graph Editor.

1. Create a locator and name it "nerveGrowthControl."

2. Open the Attribute Editor. From its menu, choose **Attributes > Add Attributes.** In the **Attribute Name** field, type **grow.** Make sure **Data Type** is set to **Float** and **Make Attribute Keyable** is checked. Click OK to add the attribute.

3. In the Outliner's **Display** menu, uncheck **Dag Objects Only** to display all of the nodes in the scene. Choose **Window > General Editors > Connection Editor** to open the Connection Editor.

4. In the Outliner, select the nerveGrowthControl locator and click the Reload Left button on the Connection Editor to load it on the left side. Scroll down in the Outliner and find the nerveBrush object that has an icon that looks like a paint brush. Click the Reload Right button to load it on the right side of the Connection Editor.

5. On the left side of the Connection Editor, scroll all the way down and highlight the **Grow** attribute. On the right side, find the **Time** attribute in italic and highlight it as well (Figure 5.66). This replaces the current connection to the stroke's **Time** attribute with a connection to the nerveGrowthControl object. The brush will disappear in the viewport.

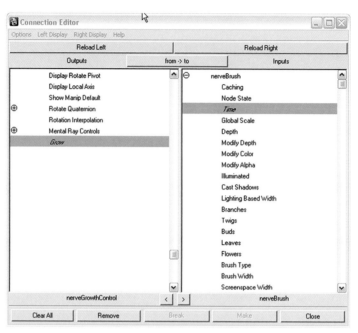

Figure 5.66: The Grow attribute on the nerveGrowthControl locator is connected to the Nerve brush's Time attribute.

6. Rewind the animation and select the nerveGrowthControl object. In the Channel Box, the **Grow** attribute should be at zero. Right-click over it and set a keyframe on this attribute.

7. Play the animation to frame 200. Stop the animation. Type **200** in the field for the **Grow** attribute and set another keyframe. When you play the animation, it should look similar to when you first enabled the **Flow Animation** attributes in the preceding section, "Controlling the Growth for the Stroke." This is because the keyframes on the nerveGrowthControl's **Grow** attribute are consistent with the current frame on the Timeline.

8. With the nerveGrowthControl locator selected, open the Graph Editor by choosing **Window > Animation Editors > Graph Editor**. You'll see the keyframes for the **Grow** attribute on the graph (Figure 5.67). Experiment with moving the keyframes around, adding keyframes, and adjusting the interpolation. Animating the growth of the nerve is now as easy as animating any other common attribute.

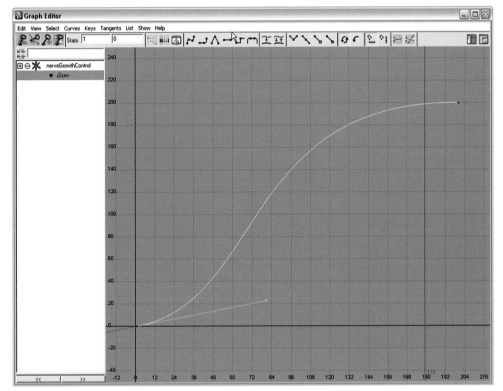

Figure 5.67: Editing the animation of the nerve's growth can be done on the Graph Editor through the Grow attribute on the nerveGrowthControl locator.

Rendering the Nerve

Paint Effects uses its own rendering system within Maya software to render strokes. Unfortunately, this means strokes won't show up behind refracted glass or when using mental ray. To fix this, the strokes will need to be converted to polygons.

1. Select the Nerve brush stroke and choose **Modify > Convert Paint Effects To Polygons**. For this stroke, the default settings should work fine; however, if you get a warning message that says the number of polygons needed for the conversion exceeds the number allowed in the settings, you will have to redo the conversion and raise the polygon limit in the options for converting the brush to polygons.

2. All of our growth animation and turbulence effects will be carried through to the converted stroke. Open the Hypershade and find the nerveBrushShader. This shader was created when the brush was converted. The shading has been carried over from the original red lightning settings. Set **Transparency** to **Black** and lower the **Incandescence** value. Feel free to tweak the shader some more to get a nervy look.

3. If the nerve is hard to see in a render, you may want to adjust the tube creation settings in the nerveBrush stroke's Attribute Editor. The **Tube Width1** and **Tube Width2** settings will carry through to the converted polygon object via history. These are the settings to adjust if you need to make the nerve thicker.

4. Choose **Windows > Render Settings** to open the Render Settings panel. In the Maya Software tab, set **Quality** to **Production** and **Enable Ray Tracing** in RayTracing Quality Settings. Do a test render to see how the nerve looks through the glass. You can adjust the settings on the testTubePhongSG as well as the nerveBrushShader to tune the look of the nerve in the tube. Experiment rendering with mental ray as well.

To see a finished version of the scene, open testTube_v04.mb from the Chapter 5 folder on the CD (Figure 5.68).

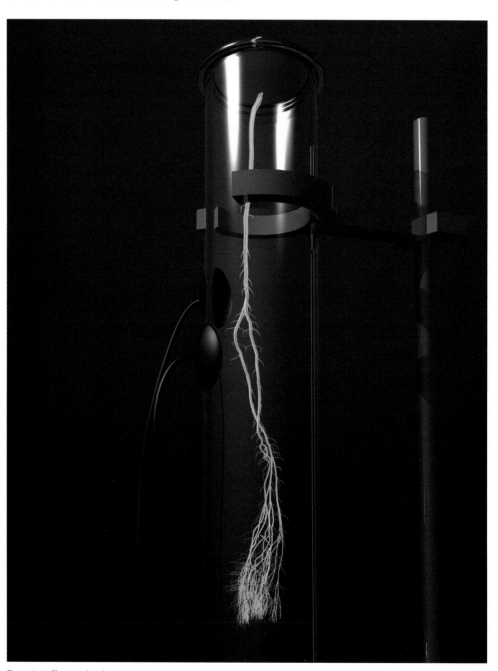

Figure 5.68: The completed nerve scene

Further Study

Once you get a handle on how to adjust Paint Effects brushes, there's really no end to the kind of effects you can come up with. Almost all of the settings in the Attribute Editor for the brush stroke are keyframeable, so it is quite easy to animate the curl of a stroke, the length and number of branches, the thickness of the tubes, and almost anything else. Here are some suggestions for projects you might want to try:

1. Create nerves that grow over the surface of an object. Use the **Path Attract** settings along with control curves to keep the nerve close to the surface.

2. Create a number of control curves for a single brush stroke. Apply nonlinear deformers such as a Bend or a Sine Wave deformer to see how it affects the curve.

3. Use the Distance Between node with set driven keys to cause a curve to grow when another object comes near. (Review the mine detector display tutorial at the beginning of this chapter for tips on how to use the Distance Between node.)

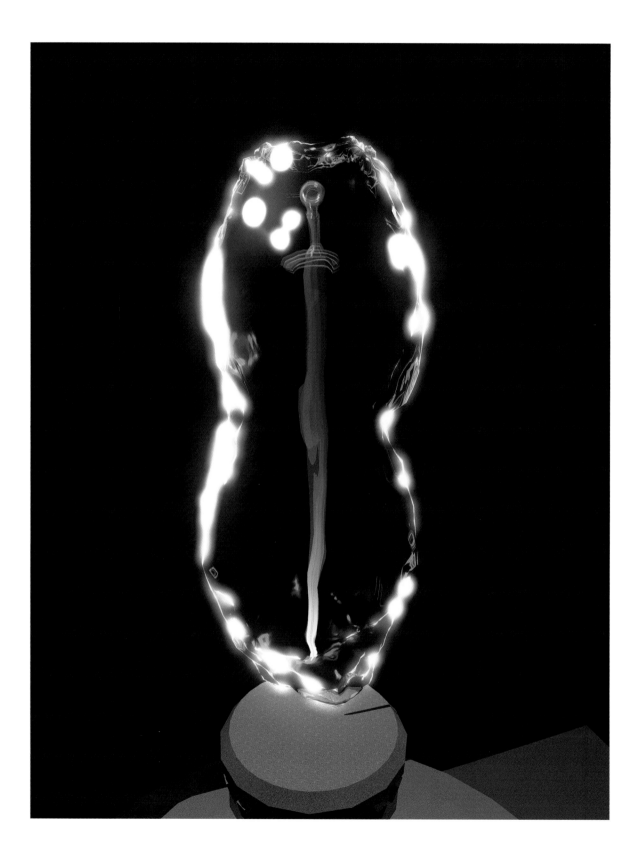

Soft Body Springs

Creating a soft body object involves converting the vertices of an object (NURBS or polygonal), the points of a lattice, or the control vertices of a curve into a particle system. The particle system can then be affected by fields, goals, and expressions just like any other particle system. When this happens, the particle system deforms the geometry, curve, or lattice, creating the effect of secondary or overlapping motion. Essentially, it's a ton of fun. Additionally, you can add springs to the particles of a soft body, which can accentuate the motion of the particles even further. You can add rippling effects across the surface of the geometry or make it stiffer and more rubbery. Springs can also be used to connect non-soft-body objects to particle systems for even wilder effects. In this chapter, we will look at just a few of the myriad possibilities for applying soft body springs to create effects in your Maya scenes.

Chapter Contents

Soft Body Springs and Geometry: Simulating Magic

Soft Body Springs and Particles

Maya has two types of springs, and they are completely unrelated: the aforementioned soft body springs and the rigid body spring constraint. The rigid body spring constraint works with rigid bodies (hence the name) and will be discussed in Chapter 7. Just to make things even more confusing, both types of springs exist on the **Soft/Rigid Bodies** menu. For the duration of Chapter 6, understand that the springs I'll be referring to are the ones created by choosing **Soft/Rigid Bodies > Create Springs** and *not* the ones created by choosing **Soft/Rigid Bodies > Create Spring Constraint**.

Soft Body Springs and Geometry: Simulating Magic

Doesn't it just figure that every time we come across a magical sword that will bless us with invulnerability it's encased inside an impenetrable magical field? In this next shot, you are required to create just such an impenetrable field. The art director would like to see a magical bubble rippling with energy looking somewhat like liquid glass as a sword hovers above a lonely pedestal in some subterranean altar. To create this effect, we'll use a soft body object and some soft body springs.

Creating the Magical Field Geometry

To create the geometry, we want something somewhat spherical that will be able to ripple and bulge evenly without pinching at the poles. For this reason, it's a good idea to use a smoothed polygon cube that's at a fairly high resolution. Creating the geometry is easy.

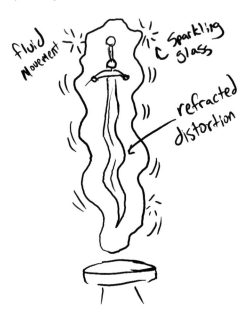

1. Open the sword_v01.mb scene from the Chapter 6 folder on the CD (Figure 6.1).

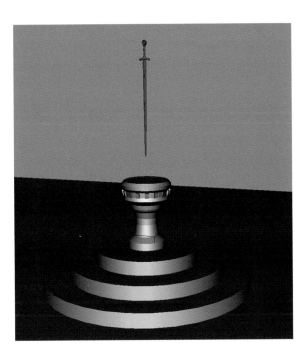

Figure 6.1:
The scene shows a sword
floating above an altar.

2. Choose **Create > Polygon Primitives > Cube** to make a cube. Use the Move tool and translate it along the Y axis so that it's in the middle of the sword. In the Channel Box, under the Inputs section, set the **Subdivisions** settings for **Height, Width,** and **Depth** to 2.

3. In the Channel Box for the cube, set **ScaleX** and **ScaleZ** to 3. Set **ScaleY** to 10. Assign a Blinn shader to the cube and set **Transparency** to a light gray (Figure 6.2).

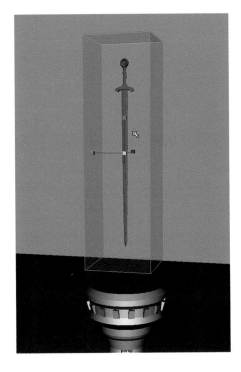

Figure 6.2:
The cube is scaled so that it
encompasses the sword.

4. Switch to the Polygons menu set and choose **Mesh > Smooth**. In the Channel box under Inputs, choose polySmoothFace1. Set **Divisions** to 4 to make a nice dense cube (Figure 6.3).

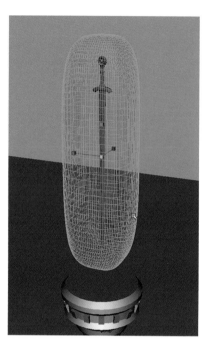

Figure 6.3:
The resolution of the cube has been increased using the Smooth action.

5. With the cube still selected, choose **Mesh > Sculpt Geometry Tool**. Use the Artisan brush tool to push, pull, and smooth the cube into a more organic, less box-like shape. Use Figure 6.4 as a reference.

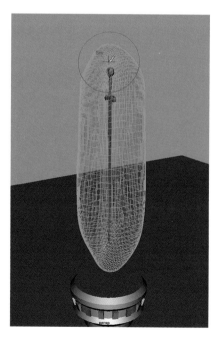

Figure 6.4:
The Artisan tool is used to sculpt the cube into a more blob-like shape.

6. In the Outliner, select the cube and rename it "magicField."

Converting the Cube into a Soft Body Object

Now we have our magic force field and we're ready to convert it to a soft body object.

1. Switch to the Dynamics menu set. With the magicField object selected, choose **Soft/Rigid Bodies > Create Soft Body > Options**. In the options, choose **Duplicate, Make Copy Soft**. Make sure **Hide Non-Soft Object** and **Make Non-Soft A Goal** are selected. When you choose to hide the goal object, Maya turns off the visibility of the object's shape node. If you want to make the object visible later on, you'll have to go into the Outliner or Hypergraph, select the shape node parented beneath the transform node, and turn its visibility back on (Ctrl+H).

2. Set the **Weight** attribute to 1 (this is the particle's **Goal Weight** attribute). Click the Create button to make the soft body. The **Goal Weight** attribute listed in the Channel Box is actually a multiplier for the **goalPP** attribute set on the particle's shape node. If you set **Goal Weight** in the Channel Box to 0.5 and then create an expression to control **goalPP**, you will not get the results you expect. It's a good idea to start off creating your soft body particles with a **Goal Weight** value of 1.

3. In the Outliner you'll see a new object named copyOfmagicField. Parented to this object is a particle labeled copyOfmagicFieldParticle. This is our soft body object and its particles. The particles are the vertices of the soft body object (Figure 6.5).

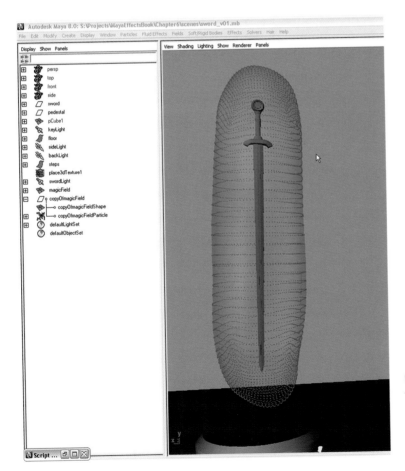

Figure 6.5:
The vertices of the magicField object have been converted to particles.

A Lattice deformer can also be converted into a soft body object. This is an extremely useful option to explore. Lattices generally have fewer points than the object they deform, making it easier and faster for Maya to calculate once they have been converted to particles. Plus you can apply a lattice to a group of objects and then convert the lattice to a soft body for some interesting effects. You can also apply soft body springs to the particles after converting a lattice to a soft body object.

Adding Fields to the Soft Body Object

We'll animate the copyOfmagicField object using fields applied to the particles. We'll do this before adding springs so that we can compare how the object reacts with and without springs.

1. Select the copyOfmagicFieldParticle. In the Channel Box, set **Goal Weight** to 0.5.

2. With copyOfmagicFieldParticle selected, choose **Fields** > **Turbulence**.

3. In the Channel Box for the Turbulence field, set **Attenuation** to 0 and **Magnitude** to 8.

4. Right-click over **PhaseX** and choose Expressions. In the Expression Editor, type the following:

```
phaseX=noise(time);
phaseZ=-1*phaseX;
```

This adds some random motion to the field just to keep it moving (Figure 6.6).

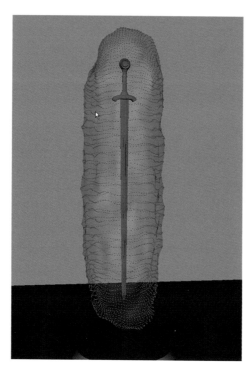

Figure 6.6:
Adding turbulence
helps distort the
copyOfmagicField
object.

Distorting the Magic Field with a Secondary Particle System

The turbulence distorts the field, but it's still fairly typical, so we'll create a more interesting motion using radial fields attached to a secondary particle.

1. Choose **Particles > Create Emitter > Options**. In the options, set **Emitter Type** to **Directional**, **Rate** to 1, and **Speed** to 4. Hit the Create button to make the emitter.

2. In the Outliner, name the new particle1 object "distorter." Select the emitter1 object, and in its Channel Box, set **DirectionX** to 0 and **DirectionY** to 1.

3. In the Channel Box for the emitter1 object, set **TranslateY** to 5 so that it's just below the magic field.

4. In the Channel Box for the distorter particle, set **Particle Render Type** to **Spheres** just to make it easier to see what's going on. If the spheres are too large, you can open up the Attribute Editor, click on the distorter particle's shape node, and click the button labeled Add Attributes For Current Render Type. The **Radius** attribute will now become available in the Attribute Editor and the Channel Box.

5. Set **Lifespan Mode** to **Constant** and **Lifespan** to 4. Wonder to yourself why **Lifespan Mode** is at the top of the Channel Box and **Lifespan** is at the bottom.

6. Play the animation to see the regular stream of particles rise up through the center of the magic field (Figure 6.7).

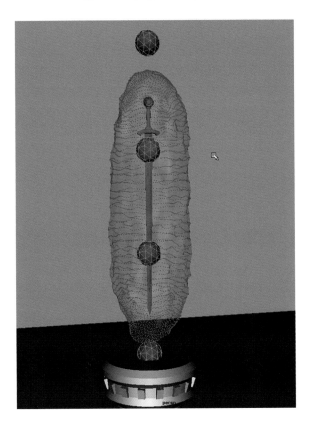

Figure 6.7:
A stream of particles
rises through the center
of the magic field.

Adding a Radial Field to the Distorter Particles

Now we'll use the distorter particles as the source of a field that will deform the copy-OfmagicFieldParticle.

1. Select copyOfmagicFieldParticle and choose **Fields > Radial**.

2. In the Outliner, Ctrl+select the radialField1 object and the distorter particle. Choose **Fields > Use Selected As Source Of Field**. The radialField1 object will become parented to the distorter object.

3. If you play the animation, you'll see the copyOfmagicField object bounce as the distorter particles move through it. We'll adjust the settings on the radial field to refine this motion.

4. Select the radial1 field object. In its Channel Box, set **Magnitude** to 10 and **Attenuation** to 0.2. Set **Max Distance** to 4, **Apply Per Vertex** to **On**, and **Use Max Distance** to **On**. Now we can see a slight throbbing motion applied to the copyOfmagicField object. To make it more fluid, we'll add springs to the object. To see a version of this scene up to this point, open the sword_v02.mb scene from the Chapter 6 folder on the CD (Figure 6.8).

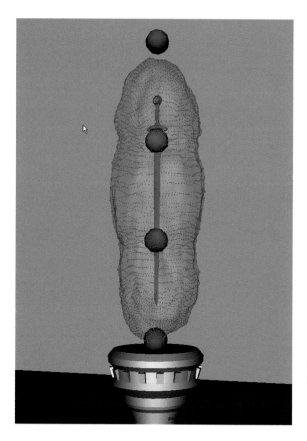

Figure 6.8:
The radial fields attached to each particle distort the force field causing a rhythmic throbbing motion.

Adding Soft Body Springs to the Particles

Springs are drawn between particles in a number of different ways depending on what options you choose when you create them. They cause the particles' motion to become more interdependent since the particles are connected to each other.

1. To get a better idea of what's going on with the scene, select the distorter particle object and the copyOfmagicFieldParticle and hide them both (Ctrl+h).

2. With copyOfmagicFieldParticle selected, rewind the animation and choose **Soft/Rigid Bodies > Create Springs > Options**. In the options, set **Creation Method** to **Wireframe** and set **Walk Length** to 2. This creates springs between particles in a way that resembles a wireframe of the object. The **Walk Length** setting of 2 creates springs on particles that are diagonally across from each other as well as between adjacent particles.

3. Uncheck the settings for **Use Per-Spring Stiffness** and **Use Per-Spring Damping**. Check the box next to **Use Per Spring Rest Length**. Leave **Stiffness** and **Damping** at their default values; we'll change these after the springs have been created. **End1** and **End2 Weight** should be set to 1. Click the Create button to make the springs. It will take a few seconds to create them (Figure 6.9).

Figure 6.9:
The wireframe creation method with a Walk Length of 2 creates a crisscross pattern of springs between the particles on the object.

4. In the Outliner, select the spring1 object and hide it (ctrl+h). This will improve the playback speed on your computer. Play the animation and see if you feel that it has changed at all.

5. It looks slightly different; we'll adjust some settings on the spring1 object. In the Channel Box, set **Stiffness** to 50 and **Damping** to 0.5.

6. Select the copyOfmagicFieldParticle and lower **Goal Weight** to 0.4. Select the radial1 object and set its **Magnitude** to 8, **Max Distance** to 2, and **Attenuation** to 0.5.

7. 💿 You can adjust these settings as well as the **Conserve** attribute on the copyOfmagicFieldParticle and the settings of the Turbulence field until you get some motion that you like (Figure 6.10). **Conserve** is short for "Conserve Energy," meaning that the particles lose energy, or momentum, over time. Lowering this value will cause the particles to slow down over time. The lower the value, the sooner they lose momentum. To see a version of this scene up to this point, open sword_v03.mb from the Chapter 6 folder on the CD.

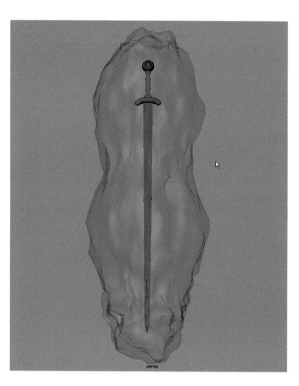

Figure 6.10:
Adjusting the settings on the spring1 object, the Turbulence field, the Radial field, and the copyOfmagic-FieldParticle object helps refine the motion of the magic force field.

8. Save your work and then try setting the **Stiffness** of spring1 to 200. When you play the animation, you should notice that after a few seconds things start to go horribly wrong. See Figure 6.11 for an example of "horribly wrong." Don't worry; your computer is not defective. To fix this you need to raise the sampling rate of the particle solver. Choose **Solvers > Edit Oversampling Or Cache Settings**. Set **Oversamples** to 2. This will cause Maya to calculate the dynamics twice between each full frame. So between frame 1 and frame 2, Maya will calculate the dynamics at frame 1 and frame 1.5. This increase in dynamic accuracy keeps Maya from freaking out when the **Stiffness** or **Damping** values are set to a high value. Sometimes lowering the **Damping** value or the **Conserve** on the particles attached to the springs can prevent the freak-out, but it will change the way the particles behave, which will change the way the effect looks (Figure 6.12).

Figure 6.11:
A high spring stiffness can cause problems if the over-sampling rate is too low.

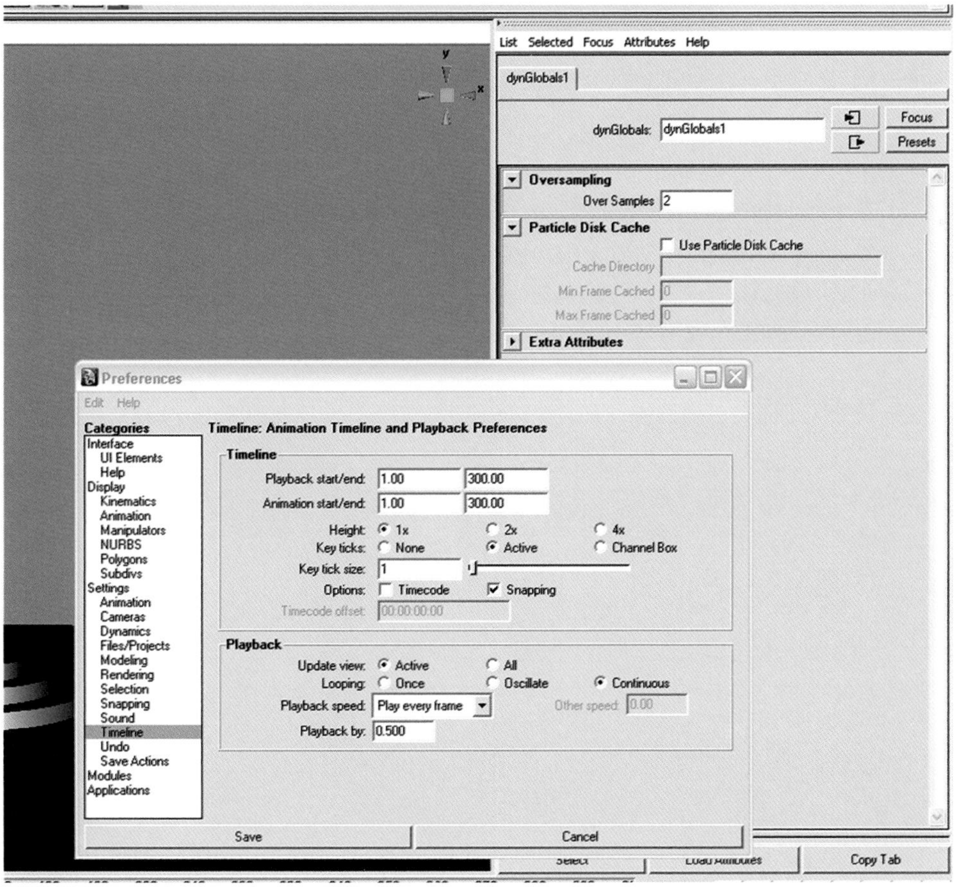

Figure 6.12: Raising the solver's oversampling rate and changing the Timeline's playback settings can fix the problems caused by a high spring stiffness.

Setting Initial State

Once we have a motion that we like for our magical force field, we'll set the initial state of the particles and create a particle disk cache.

1.   Set the **Stiffness** attribute of spring1 back to 50 and set the Playback By setting in the Timeline preferences back to 1. Save the scene.

2.   Rewind the animation and play it until about frame 110.

3.   Choose **Initial State** > **Set For All Dynamic**. When you rewind the animation, frame 1 will now look just like frame 110 and the animation will start from there.

> When you set the initial state of a particle object, there is no "undo." If you decide you don't like the initial state, you'll need to backtrack and reopen the file from a previous version, so remember to save before setting an initial state. If this kind of workflow seems untenable (and it should), you can download a MEL script called dnRemoveInitialState.mel from www.highend3d.com. This script is essential to have when working with particles. However, this script will not work for curve or surface flow particle effects.

4.   When you play the animation, you'll see the magical force field already distorted by the turbulence and radial fields; thus, when our heroes stumble across this most amazing of swords, they won't have to stand around for a few frames waiting for the magical force field to get its act together. (In other words, no run-up is required to get the force field to its distorted shape and you can render the scene starting at frame 1.)

5.   As always, it's essential to create a particle disk cache before rendering. If you plan to render on a distributed network system, make sure the particle disk cache is in a place where all the rendering processors can find it. To create the cache, rewind the animation and choose **Solvers** > **Create Particle Disk Cache**. In the options, you can name the directory where the particle cache will be found. Check the button for All next to Particle Systems To Cache. You can choose to create a cache based on the render settings range or the timeline range (Figure 6.13).

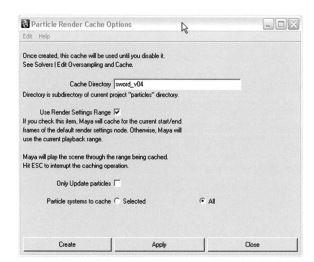

Figure 6.13:
The settings for the particle disk cache

The location of the particle disk cache is relative to your project settings. When you first create your project in Maya (**File** > **Project** > **New**), you can use the default particles directory or specify the path to a particle directory. If you're working on a large project with several artists, you can create your cache on a local drive and then move it to a network drive once you're satisfied with the particle simulation. This way everyone can see the particle disk cache, which saves them the time of having to create a new one. If you move the directory containing the particle disk cache, be sure to update your project settings (as well as the project settings of anyone else working on the scene) so that Maya knows where it is. You can change your project settings by choosing **File** > **Project** > **Edit Current**.

6. Click the Create button to make the cache. You'll see the tick mark on the Timeline play through the animation, but the objects in the perspective window will not update. That's OK. When Maya is finished creating the cache, it will rewind to the start of the animation. You should now be able to scrub through the Timeline back and forth and the animation will update correctly. If you need to change the settings on any of the dynamic objects (particles, fields, or springs), you will need to delete the cache (**Solvers** > **Memory Caching** > **Delete**) to see the changes take effect.

Rendering the Magical Field

To make the force field truly magical, we'll create a refractive shader.

1. In the Outliner, Ctrl+select the distorter and copyOfmagicFieldParticle particle objects and hide them (Ctrl+h).

2. Select the copyOfmagicField object and open its Attribute Editor. Under Render Stats, uncheck the boxes next to Casts Shadows; if you disagree, feel free to leave these settings on.

3. Choose **Window** > **Rendering Editors** > **Render Settings**. Under the Maya Software tab, set the **Quality** to **Production**. Under **Raytracing Quality**, click the check box next to **Raytracing** to turn it on (if it's not already checked). Tumble around the sword and render a frame to see the current state of the shader applied to the magical field (Figure 6.14).

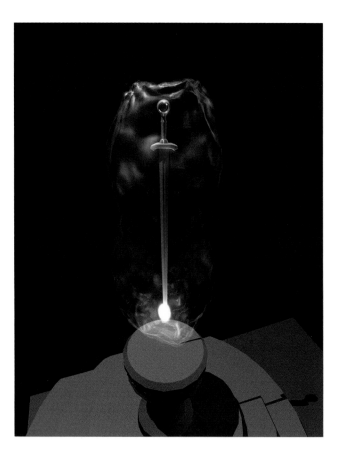

Figure 6.14:
A rendering of the force
field with its unmagical
default Blinn material

4. Select the copyOfmagicField object and open its Attribute Editor. Click on the blinn3 tab and change the name of the shader to "magicFieldSG."

5. Set the **Transparency** slider to white. In the Specular Shading rollout, set **Eccentricity** to .08 and set **Specular Roll Off** to 1.0. Click on the color box next to **Specular Color**. This will open up the Color Chooser. In the V field (value), type 2. This will create very bright specular highlights on the magical field object.

6. Set **Reflectivity** to 0.

7. In the Raytrace Options rollout, check the button next to **Refractions**. Set **Refractive Index** to 1.6 and **Surface Thickness** to 0.1. Render another frame (Figure 6.15).

Figure 6.15:
Activating refractions on
the magical field's shader
creates some interesting
distortion effects.

8.	To enhance the distortion even more, check the box next **to Chromatic Aberration**. This simulates the look of light being divided into its different wavelengths, similar to what happens when it's passed through a prism. This will significantly increase render times, but it gives the transparent object more of a solid glass-like appearance (Figure 6.16).

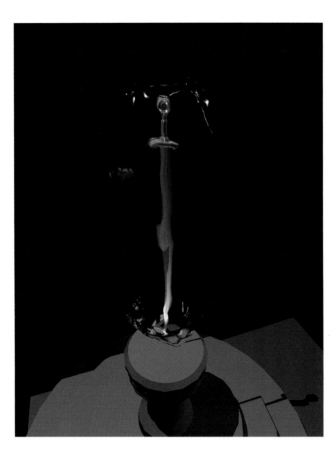

Figure 6.16:
Activating Chromatic
Aberration makes the
surface look more
like glass.

Creating a Glowing Edge on the Magical Force Field

We'll add a nice glowing edge to the field using a Ramp texture. This is a standard technique involving the use of a surface info node to control the color placement on the ramp. The ramp is set so that the edges of the object that face away from the camera have a bright incandescent value while those that are perpendicular to the camera do not.

1. Open the Hypershade and MMB drag the magicFieldSG shader to the work area. From the frame on the left side of the Hypershade, scroll down to the 2D textures and click on Ramp to make a Ramp texture. Rename the ramp "glowRamp."

2. Scroll down to the General Utilities section and click on the Sampler Info button to make a sampler info node.

3. In the work area of the Hypershade, MMB drag samplerInfo1 over the glowRamp and choose Other. This will open up the Connection Editor.

4. On the left side of the Connection Editor, select **Facing Ratio**. On the right side, expand **Uv Coord** and choose **V Coord** (Figure 6.17).

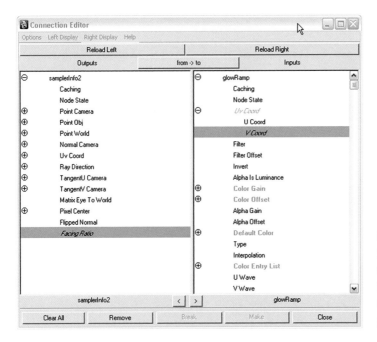

Figure 6.17:
The Connection Editor shows the Facing Ratio connected to the V Coord attribute of the glowRamp.

5. In the Hypershade, MMB drag glowRamp over the magicFieldSG shader. From the pop-up menu, choose **Incandescence**.

6. Open up the Attribute Editor for glowRamp. Change the color of the blue marker to black, delete the green marker, and set the color of the red marker to a pale yellow.

7. Drag the black color marker down, close to the bottom, and set the **Interpolation** to **Spike** (Figure 6.18).

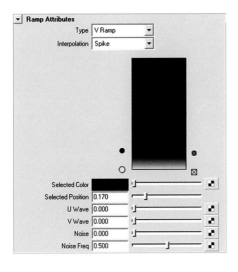

Figure 6.18:
The ramp is adjusted so that the bottom area is yellow and the rest is black. This corresponds to the edges of the object that face away from the camera.

You can achieve the same effect by connecting the Studio Clear Coat node into the incandescence value and adjusting its index; however, the ramp technique offers more visual feedback as well as more options for adding additional bands of color.

8. Move the **Noise** slider to 0.09 and set **Noise Frequency** to 3. Try another test render (Figure 6.19).

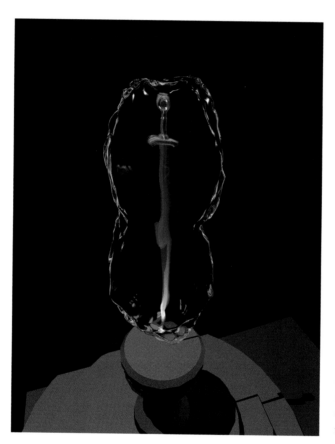

Figure 6.19:
The incandescence settings create a ring of light yellow around the edge of the magical force field.

9. In the Attributes for the magicFieldSG, open the Special Effects rollout and set **Glow Intensity** to .215.

10. In the Hypershade, click on the shaderGlow1 node and open its Attribute Editor. Make sure **Auto Exposure** is unchecked, **Threshold** is at .099, **Glow Spread** is at .042, and **Halo Spread** is at 0.2. Do another test render (Figure 6.20).

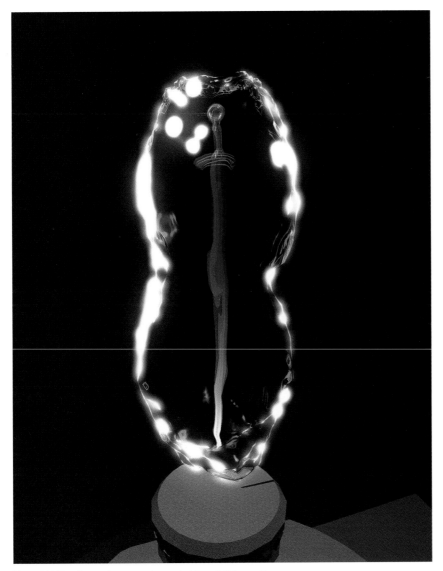

Figure 6.20: The glow settings cause the magical force field to sparkle.

For a finished version of the scene, open the sword_v04.mb scene from the Chapter 6 folder on the CD. To see a rendered animation, open the magicSword.mov file on the CD.

Further Study

The shader settings on the force field are a good start; feel free to adjust them to your own preferences. The field itself is ripe for further experimentation.

1. Try adding additional fields to distort the force field. What happens when the distorter particles fly through the force field on the X or Z axis? See how this affects the shader applied to the object.

2. Try using a similar technique to improve on the force field tutorial ("Particle Collisions: The Classic Force Field Effect") from Chapter 2.

Soft Body Springs and Particles

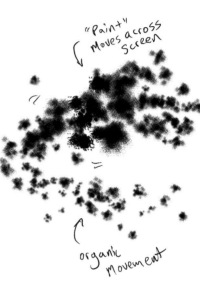

A commercial project needs an abstract background reminiscent of Jackson Pollock but with an organic, living feel. Projects like these are a good opportunity to experiment (provided you have the time). For this one, we'll see what happens when springs connect two independent particle objects. We'll also use particle sprites to create the look of splattered paint. To get an idea of the effect we're going for, view the particleSprings.mov on the CD.

Creating the Emitters

We'll create a couple of emitters and keyframe their rates so that we get a finite number of particles into the scene.

1. Create a new scene in Maya and switch to the Dynamics menu set. Choose **Particles > Create Emitter > Options**.

2. In the options, name the emitter "generator." Set **Type** to **Directional, Rate (Particles/Sec)** to 300, **Speed** to 3, and **Speed Random** to 1.5.

3. Expand the Distance/Direction attributes. Set **Direction X** to 1 and **Spread** to 0.25. Leave the other settings at 0. Click Create to make the emitter.

4. Set the Timeline to 600 frames and play the animation to see the emitter in action.

5. Rewind the animation and open the Channel Box for the generator1 emitter. Highlight the **Rate** attribute, right-click over it, and choose **Key Selected**.

6. Play the animation to frame 120. Stop it and set the **Rate** attribute in the generator1 emitter object's Channel Box to 0. Set another key on the **Rate** attribute.

7. With the generator1 emitter selected, choose **Window > Animation Editors > Graph Editor** to open the Graph Editor. Select the **Rate** attribute on the left side and marquee-select the keys in the graph. Choose **Tangents > Stepped**. This will cause the emitter to stop emitting at frame 120 (Figure 6.21).

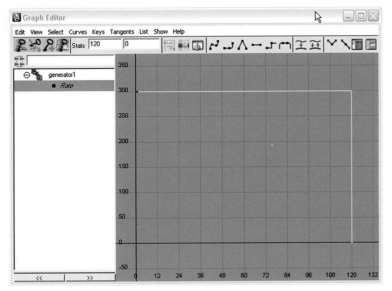

Figure 6.21: The keyframes on the emitter's rate will cause it to stop emitting at frame 120.

8. In the Outliner, select Particle1 and rename it "generatorParticle."

9. Create a second emitter, name it "deformer," set **Type** to **Omni,** and leave the rest of the settings where they are. The only attributes available under Distance/Direction Attributes will be **Min** and **Max Distance**. You can leave them at 0.

10. Set the **X translate** of the deformer1 emitter to 3.

11. Select the new particle1 object and rename it "deformerParticle."

12. Set keyframes on the **Rate** attribute of the deformer1 emitter so that it also stops emitting at frame 120.

Attaching Springs to the Particles

In this context, the springs can be thought of as a type of field. We'll be influencing the motion of one particle object by attaching it to a second using the springs. We can then get all kinds of crazy motion out of the particles by adjusting the settings on the springs.

1. Before creating the springs, we'll increase the oversampling of the solver so that the particles behave correctly. **Choose Solvers > Edit Oversampling Or Cache Settings** to access the oversample settings. In the window that opens up, set **Over Samples** to 2.

2. Select the generatorParticle and open its Attribute Editor. Click on the generator-ParticleShape tab. Expand the Render Attributes rollout and set **Particle Render Type** to **Blobby Surface (s/w)**. Click the Add Attributes For Current Render Type button and set **Radius** to 0.1. Repeat this step for the deformerParticle (Figure 6.22).

List   Selected   Focus   Attributes   Help

| generatorParticle | generatorParticleShape | paint1 | lambert1 | time1 | initialF ◄ ► |

particle: | generatorParticleShape | ⬒ Focus   ⬓ Presets

Lifespan Random 0.000
General Seed 0

▶ **Time Attributes**
▶ **Collision Attributes**
▶ **Soft Body Attributes**
▶ **Goal Weights and Objects**
▶ **Instancer (Geometry Replacement)**
▶ **Emission Random Stream Seeds**
▼ **Render Attributes**

☐ Depth Sort
Particle Render Type [Blobby Surface (s/w) ▼]
Add Attributes For [Current Render Type]
Radius [0.100] ▮———
Threshold [0.000] ▮———

▶ **Render Stats**
▶ **mental ray**
▼ **Per Particle (Array) Attributes**

position [ ]
rampPosition [ ]
velocity [ ]
rampVelocity [ ]
acceleration [ ]
rampAcceleration [ ]
mass [ ]
lifespanPP [ ]
worldVelocity [ ]

▼ **Add Dynamic Attributes**

[Select]   [Load Attributes]   [Copy Tab]

Figure 6.22:
The Radius attribute of the blobby surface becomes available when you click the Add Attributes For Current Render Type button.

3. Select the generatorParticle object. In its Channel Box, set **Conserve** to 0.98. Select the deformerParticle object and set its **Conserve** to 0.95. This will cause them to slow down and overlap in 3D space (Figure 6.23). Once we have the springs set up, we will set the **Conserve** of both these particles back to 1. **Conserve** is short for "Conserve Energy," meaning that the particles lose energy, or momentum, over time. It is a very sensitive attribute and quite useful for tuning the motion of particles.

Figure 6.23:
The Conserve on both particles has been lowered so that they overlap where they stop.

4. Rewind and play the animation to a frame between 108 and 115, before the emitters stop emitting. Select both particle objects and choose **Soft/Rigid Bodies** > **Create Springs** > **Options**. In the options, set **Creation Method** to MinMax, **Min Distance** to 0.1, and **Max Distance** to 0.35. Leave the other settings at their default values (Figure 6.24).

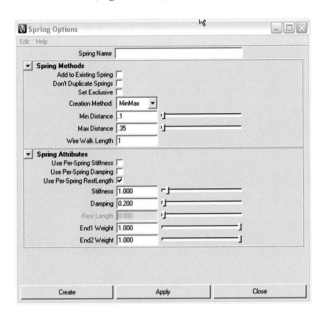

Figure 6.24:
The settings for creating
the springs

5. The MinMax creation method only creates springs between particles that exist within the range specified in the settings. We want a few particles to be free of the springs to create some organic messiness around our main blob of particles. The most important thing to remember is that when you create springs on emitted particles, they will exist only between the particles already emitted in the scene. This goes for applying springs to a single particle object as well as multiple particle objects. If we had applied the springs at frame 1 with the same settings, no springs would be attached to the particles since none have been emitted. Likewise, all particles emitted after the frame where we stopped the simulation will not have springs attached.

6. Rewind the animation, select both particle objects, and set their **Conserve** value to 1. Play the animation and note the way the springs affect the motion of the particles (Figure 6.25).

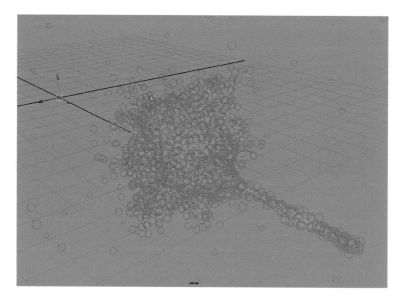

Figure 6.25:
The springs appear on the particles as they are emitted and affect their motion in interesting ways.

Adjusting the Simulation

Even with the **Oversampling** raised to 2, the springs can be very sensitive. If you find that they "freak out" as you edit their settings, lower the spring's **Stiffness** attribute and raise the **Damping** attribute. Small changes will greatly affect how the particles move.

1. Select the spring1 object in the Outliner and hide it (Ctrl+h). This will make the playback a little faster.
2. Try setting the deformer1 emitter's **translateX** value to 5.
3. Set the **Stiffness** of spring1 to 5 and the **Damping** to 0.5. Play the simulation.
4. Try moving the deformer1 emitter above the generator1 emitter. Play the simulation (Figure 6.26).

Figure 6.26:
Repositioning the emitter and adjusting the spring settings gives rise to more interesting variations.

5. Set the **Translate X, Y,** and **Z** values of the deformer1 emitter to 1, –4, and 1, respectively. Set the spring1 **Stiffness** to 10 and the **Damping** to 0.2. Set the **Conserve** of the generatorParticle and the deformerParticle to 0.99 and play the simulation.

Adding a Turbulence Field

Once we have a nice motion created for our particles, we can mix it up even further by adding a turbulence field.

1. Set the **translateX** of the deformer1 emitter to 5, set **translateY** and **Z** to 0. Set the **Conserve** of both particles to 0.99. Set the **Stiffness** of spring1 to 10 and the **Damping** to 0.2.

2. Select both particle objects and choose **Fields > Turbulence**. In the Channel Box for the new turbulenceField1 object, set **Magnitude** to 10 and **Attenuation** to 0.

When you play the animation, a blob forms over the first 200 frames and then spins of into space, slowly twisting. This would make a great undersea blob creature. To see a version of the scene up to this point, open the particleSprings_v01.mb scene from the Chapter 6 folder on the CD.

You can add expressions to the **phaseX, Y,** and **Z** of the turbulence to vary the motion even more (Figure 6.27). Changing the **Magnitude** and **Frequency** values will also create additional variations. Feel free to experiment further. When you're satisfied with the motion, move on to the next section.

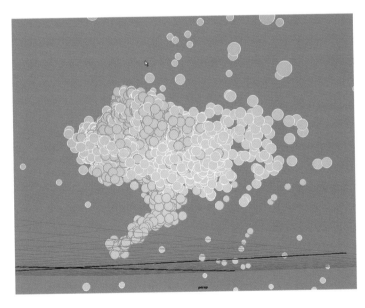

Figure 6.27:
Turbulence adds a writhing motion to the particle blob.

Using the Particle Object as a Paintbrush

We have a very nice simulation going now. This could easily be used to create organic motion for some kind of space cloud creature or microscopic organism. You can apply a shader to the blobby surfaces, adjust the threshold values on the blobby particles, and render some interesting looking animations. The next part of this animation will explore the idea of using our blob as a paintbrush to create an abstract animated Jackson Pollock style composition. You can continue with the scene you have now or start with the particleSprings_v01.mb scene from the Chapter 6 folder on the CD.

1. Select the deformerParticle object and open its Attribute Editor. On the deformerParticleShape tab, open the Render Attributes rollout and set **Radius** to 0. This will make these particles invisible. Sometimes hiding the particle can affect the simulation in strange ways, so this works as a better way to hide the particle.

2. Select the generatorParticle and choose **Particles > Emit From Object > Options**.

3. In the options, set **Emitter Name** to paint. Set **Emitter Type** to **Omni** and **Rate(Particles/Sec)** to 5.

4. Set **Speed** and **Speed Random** to 0. Click Create to make the new particle. This particle will be emitted from the individual generatorParticles, creating a trail of dots as the generatorParticles move through space.

5. In the Outliner, expand the generatorParticle object. You'll see the new paint emitter parented to it. Select the new particle1 object and rename it "paintSprites." Rewind and play the animation (Figure 6.28).

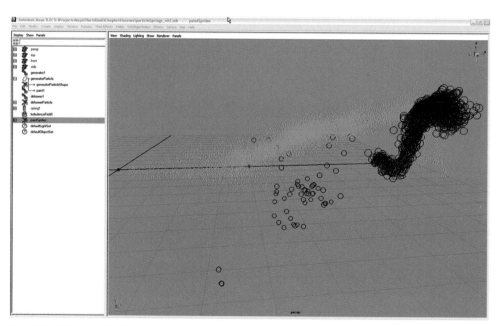

Figure 6.28: Adding an emitter to the generatorParticle causes it to leave a trail of new particles as it moves through space.

6. Select the generatorParticle and set its **Radius** value to 0, just as we did for the deformerParticle in step 1 of this section.

Setting the Attributes for the paintSprites

We'll create some expressions to control how the paintSprite particle object appears in the scene.

1. Select the paintSprites particle and open its Attribute Editor. Click on the paintSpritesShape tab and expand the Lifespan Attributes rollout.

2. Set **Lifespan Mode** to **lifespanPP Only**.

3. Scroll down to the Per Particle (Array) Attributes and right-click over the field next to **lifespanPP**. Choose **Creation Expression** from the pop-up window.

4. In the Expression Editor, type the following:

```
seed(particleId);
lifespanPP=rand(0.1,3);
```

The seed attribute is assigned to each particleId value. This is a handy way of ensuring that each time the animation is played, the same random values are generated, even when the animation is played on a different machine. It's a good idea to include this line whenever you use a random function in a per-particle expression. The lifespanPP value is set to a random value between 0.1 and 3 seconds. Now the particles die off, giving the appearance of a dense cloud crawling through space.

Creating Particle Sprites

Particle sprites are essentially two-dimensional cards attached to each particle. The cards are constrained so that they always face the camera. A texture is mapped to the cards, allowing you to greatly expand the versatility of your particle objects. You can even apply animated textures to the particles. In this case, we'll be applying different still images to the particles to create the effects of paint splatters in space.

1. Select the paintSprites object and open the paintSpritesShape tab. Under the Render Attributes rollout, set **ParticleRender Type** to **Sprites**. The cloud of dots now turns into a large number of green squares (Figure 6.29).

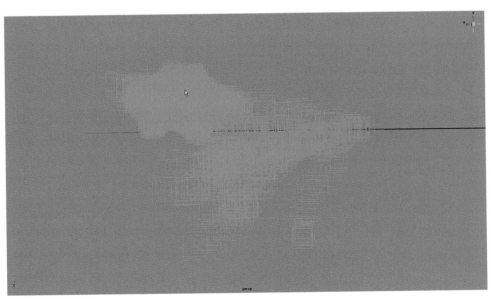

Figure 6.29: The paintSprites particle has been set to the Sprites render type.

2. Select the check box next to Depth Sort. This will ensure that those sprites closest to the camera will appear in front. Tumble around the scene and observe how the sprites continually face the camera.

Adding Custom Attributes for the Sprites

We'll add some attributes to help randomize the size and rotation of the sprites.

1. Under the Add Dynamic Attributes rollout, click the General button. In the pop-up window, click on the Particle tab. Select **spriteScaleXPP** and hit the Add button. Do the same for **spriteScaleYPP** and **spriteTwistPP** (Figure 6.30).

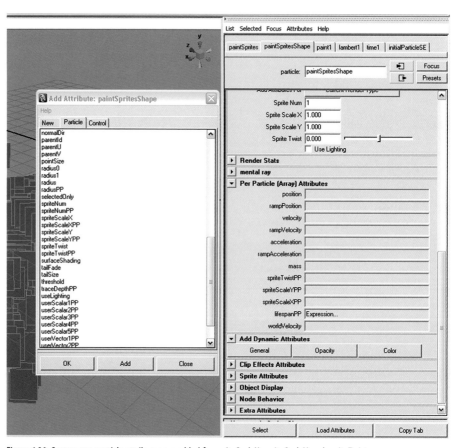

Figure 6.30: Custom per-particle attributes are added for spriteScaleX, spriteScaleY, and spriteTwist.

2. Scroll down to the Per Particle (Array) Attributes and right-click over the field next to **spriteScaleYPP**. Choose **Creation Expression** from the pop-up window. Add the following lines to the expressions in the Expression field (Figure 6.31):

```
spriteScaleYPP=rand(0.1,1);
spriteScaleXPP=spriteScaleYPP;
spriteTwistPP=rand(-180,180);
```

Figure 6.31: Three new expressions have been added to the Creation expressions for the paintSprites particle.

ScaleX and **YPP** control the width and height of each sprite card; in this case a random size is assigned at the creation of the particles. The **Twist** value is the rotation of each particle.

3. Next we'll create a ramp that will cause each particle to shrink over time. Click the General button in the Add Dynamic Attributes rollout and switch to the New tab. For the **Attribute Name**, type **scaleRamp**, set **Data Type** to **Float** and **Attribute Type** to **Per Particle (Array)**. Click the OK button to add the attribute.

4. In the Per Particle (Array) Attributes section, right-click over the field next to **scaleRamp**. (If **scaleRamp** does not appear, click the Load Attributes button at the very bottom of the Attribute Editor.) Choose **Create Ramp > Options**. In the options, make sure **Input V** is set to **Particle's Age**. Click OK to add the options.

5. Right-click in the same field again and choose **Edit Ramp** (Figure 6.32). In the Attribute Editor for the ramp, delete the gray marker in the middle. Select the white color marker at the bottom and move it up a little (Figure 6.33).

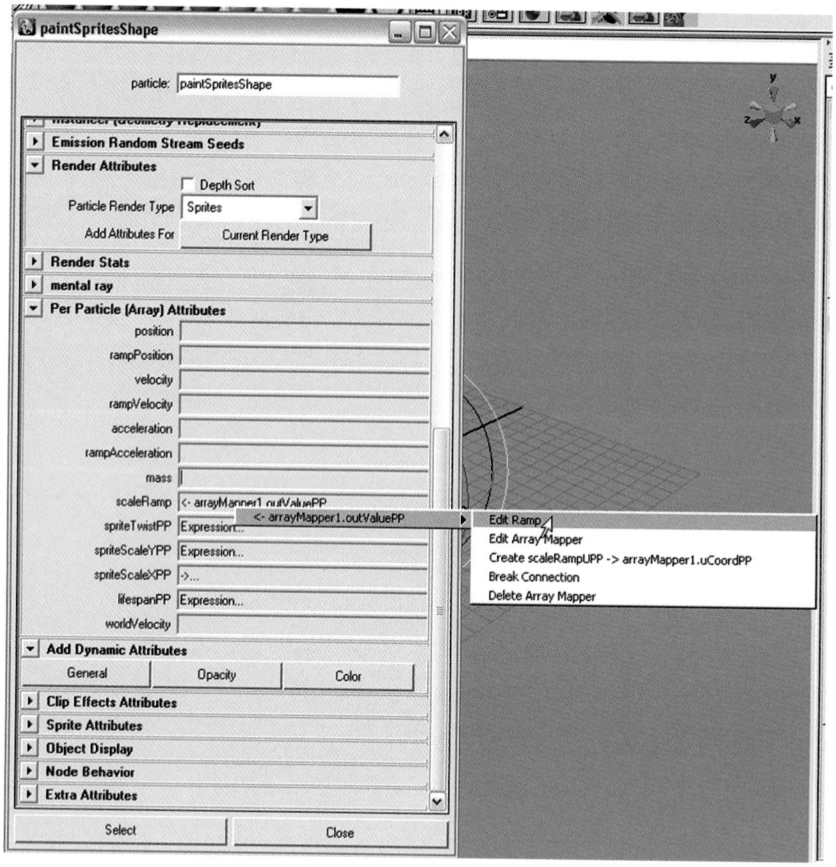

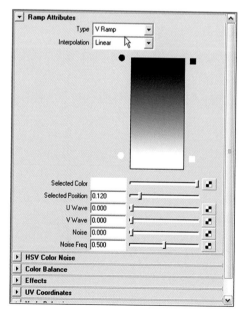

Figure 6.32: Right-click over the scaleRamp field and choose Edit Ramp to open the ramp in the Attribute Editor.

Figure 6.33:
The ramp will control
the scale of the sprites
over time.

The ramp won't do anything until we plug it into an expression. The ramp starts at a value of 1 (white) and moves upward to a value of 0 (black). The color of the ramp is based on the age of the particle, so when the particle is born, the value is 1, and it gradually moves down to 0 right before the particle dies. We'll use these values as a multiplier for the scale of the sprite so that each sprite is born with the random **scaleYPP** value assigned to it according to the creation expression. Then as the animation plays and the particle ages, this value will be multiplied by the values from the ramp, causing it to get smaller and smaller until it dies. Let's add the expression that will do this.

6. Right-click over the **spriteScalePP** field and choose **Runtime Before Dynamics Expression**. In the Expression field, type the following:

    ```
    spriteScaleYPP=spriteScaleYPP*scaleRamp;
    spriteScaleXPP=spriteScaleYPP;
    ```

    When you play the animation, you'll see the sprites shrink over time (Figure 6.34).

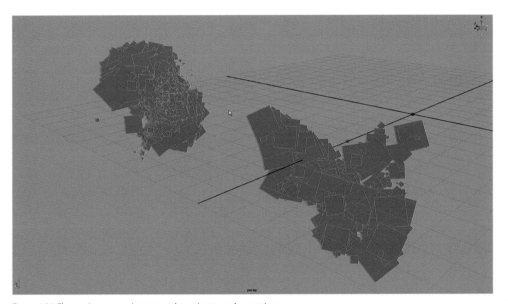

Figure 6.34: The runtime expression causes the sprites to scale over time.

7. We'll add one more attribute and expression to make the sprites turn slowly. Repeat step 3 to create a new attribute. Name the attribute "spinMe."

8. Right-click over the field next to **spinMe** and choose **Creation Expression**. In the field, add the following to the expressions:

    ```
    spinMe=rand(-3,3);
    ```

9. Click the Edit button to include the expression. Switch to the Runtime Before Dynamics mode and add the following to the expressions listed in the expression editor:

    ```
    spriteTwistPP=spriteTwistPP+spinMe;
    ```

10. Click the Edit button and then play the animation to see the results. To see a version of the scene so far, open the particleSprings_v02.mb scene from the Chapter 6 folder on the CD.

Adding Images to the Sprites

The final section of this tutorial deals with adding images to the sprites to get the look of splattered paint. We'll use Paint Effects to generate the images.

1. Choose **Window** > **Paint Effects** to open the Paint Effects interface.

2. Switch to canvas mode by choosing **Paint** > **Paint Canvas**.

3. It's important that the images applied to the sprites are small since they will take up a fair amount of memory. To change the canvas size, choose **Canvas** > **Set Size**. In the pop-up window, set both sliders to 64.

4. To set the background color, choose **Canvas** > **Clear** > **Options**. In the options, set **Clear Color** to a dim gray so that it can be seen in the Paint Effects window. Hit the Clear button to apply.

5. In the Paint Effects window, use the Alt+right mouse button combination to zoom in on the canvas.

6. Choose **Window** > **General Editors** > **Visor** to open the Visor. From the folders on the left-hand side, choose Pens. Select the ink.mel brush.

7. In the Paint Effects window, click on the black square next to the C slider. Change the color to bright red (Figure 6.35).

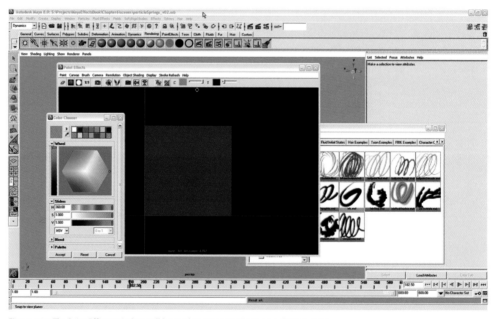

Figure 6.35: The Paint Effects window will be used to generate the images for the sprites.

8. Paint some red dots on the Paint Effects canvas. Use the b hot key to vary the size of the brush. (Hold down the b key and left-button-drag left or right to change the size of the brush.) Avoid painting near the edges.

9. When you have something you like, click the white circle button in the upper-left corner of the Paint Effects window. This displays the alpha channel of the image. Click the colored circle button to switch back to a colored view of the canvas (Figure 6.36).

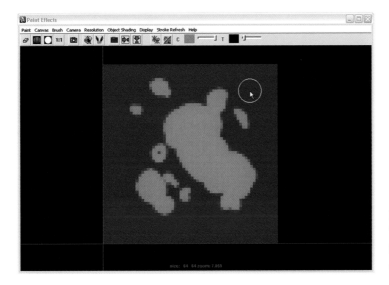

Figure 6.36:
The paint splatter
in the Paint Effects
window

10. Choose **Paint** > **Save Snapshot** to save the image. Name the image splat.1.iff and save it to the sourceimages directory of the current project. It is important to use the *filename.#*.iff format when saving the image so that Maya can read it properly when we use it as a sprite image.

11. Choose **Canvas** > **Clear** (or hit the eraser icon in the upper-left corner) to clear the image so that you can start a second one. Make six more images like this one. Make red, white, and yellow paint splats. Name the images splat.2.iff, splat.3.iff, splat.4.iff, and so on.

Assigning the Images to the Sprites

We'll set up another expression to randomly assign the images to the sprites.

1. Select the paintSprites particle object and assign a Lambert shader to the object. Name the shader "spriteSG."

2. Open the Attribute Editor for spriteSG, and click the checkered button next to the color channel to assign a texture to the color. In the pop-up Create Render Node window, click the File button.

3. In the Attribute Editor for the file1 node assigned to the color channel, click the folder icon next to Image Name. In the file browser window, find the project sourceimages directory in which you saved the splat images. Choose splat.1.iff for the file texture.

4. The red paint splat image will now be applied to all of the sprites, making the scene look like a scene from *Kill Bill, Vol. 1*. Notice that the transparency has already been taken care of when the image was loaded. This is one of the advantages of using the IFF file format for sprite images (Figure 6.37).

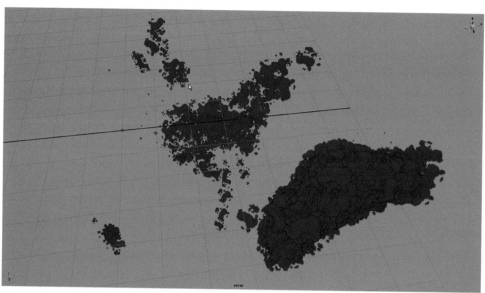

Figure 6.37: The splat.1 .iff file has been applied to the sprites in the scene.

5. Open the Attribute Editor for the spriteSG shader. Click on the file1 tab to open the File texture. Expand the Interactive Sequence Caching Options rollout and click the check box next to Use Interactive Sequence Caching. Set **Sequence Start** to 1, **Sequence End** to 7, and **Sequence Increment** to 1. This defines the parameters for the file image sequence Maya will use for the sprites. The range 1 to 7 corresponds to the seven images created in Paint Effects.

6. Click on the Use Image Sequence check box in the File Attributes window. This will load the images for the Interactive Sequence Caching. You'll get a warning saying that some images don't exist. That's OK; you can ignore the warning. Nothing will have changed yet. We have one more expression to add to get the images to assign themselves randomly.

7. Select the paintSprites particle object and open its Attribute Editor. Click on the General tab to add one more per-particle attribute. In the Add Attribute window, click on the Particle tab, and select the **spriteNumPP** attribute from the list. Click the Add button to add it (Figure 6.38).

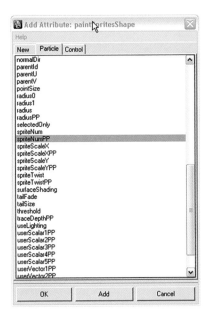

Figure 6.38:
The spriteNumPP
attribute will control
how the images are
applied to the sprites.

8. Right-click in the field next to **spriteNumPP** in the Per Particle (Array) Attributes section of the Attribute Editor. Choose **Creation Expression**. Add the following to the creation expression:

```
spriteNumPP=rand(1,7);
```

9. Play the animation. The red, white, and yellow paint splats should appear on the sprites (Figure 6.39).

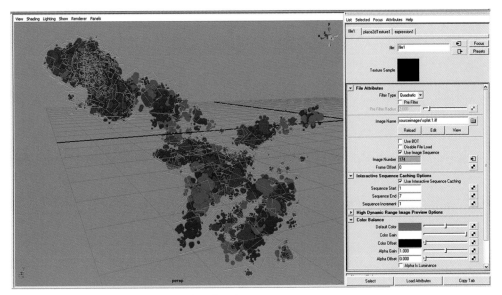

Figure 6.39: Different images are applied randomly to the sprites.

Rendering the Animation

Sprite animations require the Hardware rendering engine as opposed to Maya Software or mental ray. We'll set the animation up for rendering.

1. The colors on the paint splats are looking kind of dull. To fix this, open up the Attribute Editor for the paintSprites particle object. Click on the paintSpritesShape tab. In the Add Dynamic Attributes rollout, click on the Color button. In the pop-up window, choose Add Per Object Attribute. Click the Add Attribute button.

2. The sprites all turn black. In the Attribute Editor, open the rollout for the Render Attributes. Type 1 in the fields for **Color Red, Color Green**, and **Color Blue**. (If these fields aren't there, click the Load Attributes button at the bottom of the Attribute Editor.) The colors should now appear bright just like the original images you created (Figure 6.40).

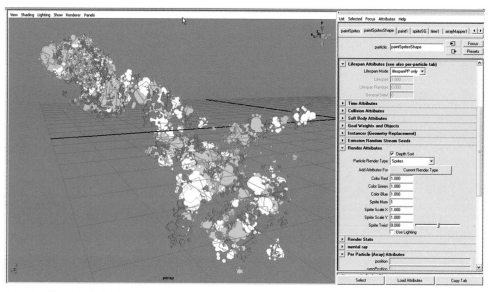

Figure 6.40: The original colors have been restored to the sprites.

3. As always, it's a good idea to create a particle disk cache before rendering. This scene is long and has a lot of particles, so make sure you have plenty of disk space before making a cache. The cache I created for this scene (600 frames) came out to 8.5 gigabytes! You may want to reduce the length of the Timeline before making the cache if you're concerned about space. To create the cache, choose **Solvers > Create Particle Disk Cache > Options**. In the options, set **Particle Systems To Cache** to **All**. You can choose to base the cache on the length of the Timeline or the frame range on the render settings. Click Create to make the cache; it may take a while to create.

4. You can either position the camera to capture as much of the scene as possible or animate it to follow one particular blob of paint. Be aware that the sprites may rotate if they get extremely close to the camera. Once you're happy with the camera view, open up the render settings.

5. Choose **Window > Rendering Editors > Render Settings** to open up the Render Settings Editor window (that sentence is just pure poetry). Switch the Render Using menu to Maya Hardware. Choose your desired resolution and frame range just as you would for any other render. In the Maya Hardware tab, set the Preset to Production Quality with Transparency. You can adjust the other settings as you see fit. There are no lights or shadows in the scene, so it should render quickly even at a high-quality setting. You can preview the render by switching to the Rendering menu set and choosing **Render > Render Current Frame**.

6. Once you have the settings adjusted, you can render out a sequence or view the particleSprings.mov scene on the CD. To see a finished version of the scene, open the particleSprings_v03.mb scene from the Chapter 6 folder on the CD. The particle disk cache will not be included in the scene.

Further Study

Applying springs to particles is a great way to create a different look for your particle motions. Simply applying turbulence and other fields can get a little old after a while, so it's nice to find new ways to shake up your particle simulations. This tutorial only scratches the surface.

1. Try combining an emitted particle with springs with a collision surface. See if you can make a blob of particles crawl across the floor.

2. Connect springs between an emitted particle and a particle grid.

3. Try connecting springs to an emitted particle to form a curve.

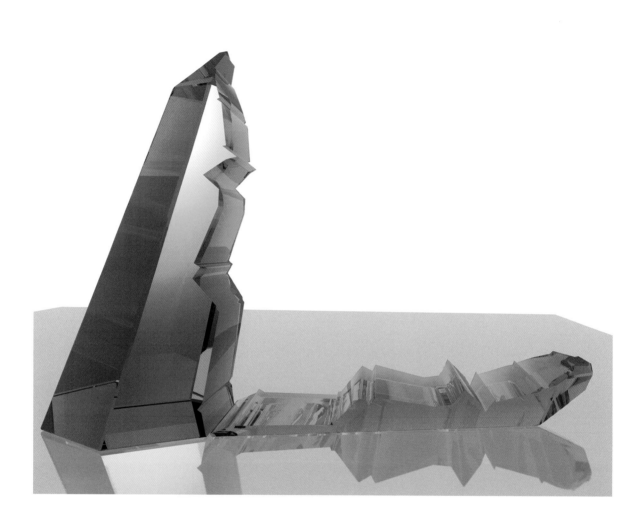

Rigid Body Effects

Maya's rigid body dynamics are a set of tools that allow you to simulate interactions between hard surfaces. Maya calculates the physical effects of objects reacting to forces, other objects, and different types of constraints, saving you time on what would otherwise be a very difficult animation to keyframe. However, rigid body dynamics can be a little tricky. The system isn't perfect, so it's best to think of a rigid body dynamic simulation as a starting point. Once you have your simulation working properly, it's usually a good idea to "bake" the dynamics into keyframes, which can then be edited and refined in the Graph Editor.

In this chapter we'll take a look at a few examples of animation that can benefit from using rigid body dynamics.

Chapter Contents

Rigid and Soft Body Combinations: Dynamic Dents
Creating Animated Fissures on a Surface
Rigid Body Spring Constraints

Rigid and Soft Body Combinations: Dynamic Dents

A kids cartoon requires a shot in which a submarine has sunk to the ocean floor. It lands on a steep slope and slides downward, leaving an impression in the ground behind it as it slides to its demise. This particular animation is for previsualization—it is essentially a rough 3D storyboard that will be used as a guide for the final animation. This means you won't have to worry about using detailed models or textures; you're just trying to get an overall sense of the shot so that the director can focus on things like timing and camera angles.

Preparing the Models for Dynamic Interaction

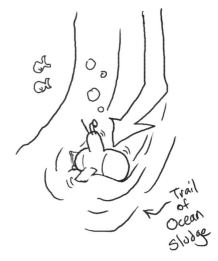

We'll set up the models so that our dynamic simulation is a little easier for Maya to calculate.

1. 💿 Open the submarine_v01.mb scene from the Chapter 7 folder on the CD (Figure 7.1). The scene consists of the submarine model and the ocean floor. The submarine is a single piece of polygon geometry. The ocean floor is a NURBS surface.

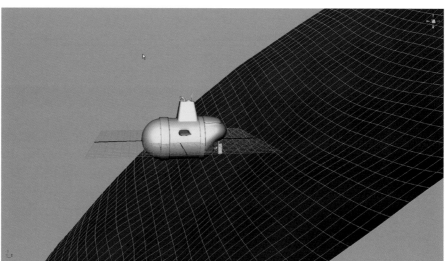

Figure 7.1: The scene shows the submarine and the ocean floor geometry.

2. Open the Outliner for the scene. You'll see a third polygon object labeled "submarineProxy." Select this object, and in the Channel Box, set its **Visibility** to 1 to unhide it. The modeler was kind enough to include a less-detailed version of the submarine for making the dynamic collisions a little faster (Figure 7.2).

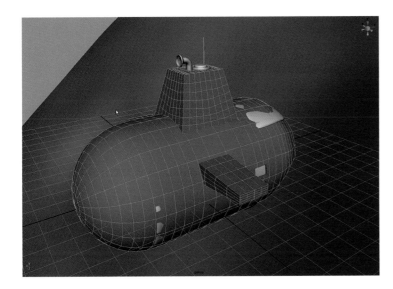

Figure 7.2:
A less-detailed proxy object has been included in the scene.

3. Select the submarineProxy and Ctrl+select the sub object. Switch to the Animation menu set and choose **Constrain** > **Parent** > **Options**. In the options, make sure that **Maintain Offset** is unchecked. Click Create to make the constraint. This will constrain the translation and the rotation of the sub object to the submarineProxy object. This is not always necessary when setting up objects for rigid body collisions, but since the original sub object has some details built into the model, using a lower-resolution proxy object should help keep the dynamic collision calculations from slowing down the simulation too much or from creating weird and unexpected motion.

4. Select the submarineProxy object and assign a Lambert shader to it. Name the new shader "proxySG."

Creating the Collision Simulation

We'll set up our basic collision between the submarine and the ocean floor.

1. Switch to the Dynamics menu set. Select the oceanFloor object and choose **Soft/Rigid Bodies** > **Create Passive Rigid Body**. A passive body is a dynamic object that is not influenced by dynamic fields but can act as a collision surface for active rigid bodies. You can also constrain active rigid bodies to a passive rigid body surface.

2. Select the submarineProxy object and choose **Soft/Rigid Bodies** > **Create Active Rigid Body**.

3. In the Channel Box for the submarineProxy object, set the **TranslateY** channel to 30 and the **TranslateZ** channel to 32.

4. Select the submarineProxy object and choose **Fields** > **Gravity** > **Options**. In the **Edit** menu of the Options dialog box, choose **Reset Settings**. The default settings for the gravity field are a good starting place. Click the Create button to make the field. Rewind and play the animation to see how the objects interact.

Adjusting the Simulation

Currently the simulation looks like a plastic toy bouncing down a hill. We need to make it look like a heavy submarine sinking to the bottom of the ocean and sliding down the hill. There are a number of ways to accomplish this. We can adjust the settings on the objects or the gravity field or even add other fields to the simulation. After each step in this section, play the animation and make a mental note of the changes.

1. Select the submarineProxy object and open its Channel Box. Under the rigid-Body1 node, find the **Bounciness** attribute and set it to 0.1. This will tone down the bounce when the submarine hits the floor.

2. Set **Mass** to 100, and set **Damping** to 0.5.

3. Set **Dynamic Friction** to 0.5. **Dynamic Friction** determines how much a moving object resists movement against another rigid body surface. Both the submarineProxy object and the oceanFloor object have this attribute and adjusting both will affect the simulation. Just to keep things simple, we'll focus on adjusting the **Dynamic Friction** of the submarineProxy object for now.

4. Set **Static Friction** to 0.25. **Static Friction** determines how easily an object starts sliding once it makes contact with another rigid body surface. If you turn **Static Friction** up on our current simulation, it will cause the submarine to tumble and roll as it slides. This may be what you want, maybe not. Keep it in mind as we continue to tune the simulation (Figure 7.3).

Figure 7.3:
The settings are adjusted on the submarineProxy object's rigidBody1 input node.

5. Select the gravityField1 object and set its **Magnitude** to 6 to get it to start looking like the action is happening underwater.

6. If the submarine gets stuck on the ground, you can try rotating or repositioning the submarineProxy object at the start of the animation. You can also adjust the **Static Friction** and **Dynamic Friction** settings on the rigidBody 1 node. Or you can try changing the way Maya calculates the dynamics. To do this, open the Attribute Editor for the submarineProxy object, click on the tab for rigidSolver, and choose among **MidPoint, Runge Kutta,** and **Runge Kutta Adaptive** for **Solver Method. MidPoint** provides the fastest and least accurate dynamics calculation, **Runge Kutta** is slower and more accurate, and **Runge Kutta Adaptive** is the slowest and most accurate method. You can also raise the value of **Rigid Body Solver Step Size,** which will cause the rigid body solver to increase the number of calculations it makes per frame. This is a good way to increase the accuracy of the simulation without changing **Solver Method.**

7. You can also raise the **Collision Tolerance** value under the Rigid Solver Attributes rollout for the rigidSolver node (Figure 7.4).

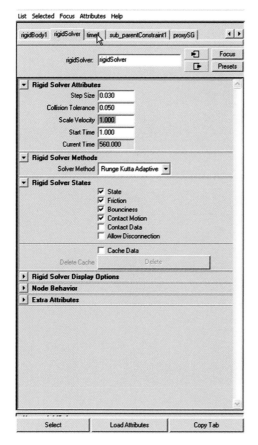

Figure 7.4:
The settings for the rigidSolver node

8. ⊙ Finally, select the submarineProxy object and choose **Fields** > **Drag** to create a drag field. Select the dragField1 object, and in its Channel Box, set **Magnitude** to 60 and **Attenuation** to 0. Make sure **Use Max Distance** is off. To see a version of this scene up to this point, open submarine_v02.mb from the Chapter 7 folder on the CD.

Denting a Surface Using Soft Body Dynamics

To create the effect of an impression of the submarine at the point of impact on the ocean floor, we'll add a soft body surface.

1. Select the oceanFloor object and duplicate it (**Edit** > **Duplicate** or Ctrl+d). Rename the duplicate surface "oceanFloorSB."

2. Use the Move tool and translate oceanFloorSB up along the Y axis a little bit above the original oceanFloor surface.

3. When you duplicate a rigid body object, a duplicate rigidBody node will also be created. To delete this unnecessary node, open the Outliner and turn on the display shapes option from the Outliner menu (**Display** > **Shapes**). Expand the oceanFloorSB object and select the rigidBody2 node; the icon is a bowling ball hitting some pins (Figure 7.5). Hit the Delete key to delete this node.

Figure 7.5: The oceanFloor object has been duplicated and moved up in the Y axis. The Outliner shows the duplicated rigidBody node.

4. Rewind the animation. Select oceanFloorSB and choose **Soft/Rigid Bodies** > **Create Soft Body** > **Options**. In the options, set the Creation options to Make Soft; the other options will become unavailable. You can leave **Weight** at 1; it doesn't do anything in this case.

5. In the Outliner, expand the oceanFloorSB object and select the oceanFloorSBParticle object. Ctrl+select the submarineProxy object and choose **Particles > Make Collide**.

6. Play the animation. When the submarine hits the soft body copy of the ocean floor, the particles controlling the vertices drag the geometry downward through the original ocean floor object. They keep going for as long as the animation is playing (Figure 7.6).

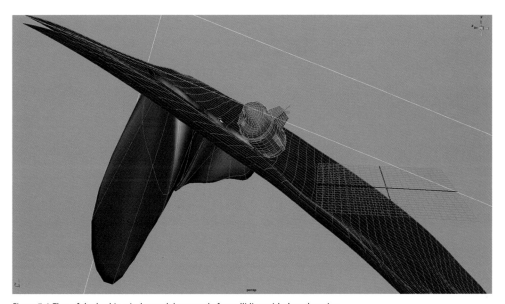

Figure 7.6: The soft body object is dragged downward after colliding with the submarine.

7. To stop the constant downward drag of the particles on the soft body object, select the oceanFloorSBParticle object and open its Channel Box. Set the **Conserve** value to 0.8.

8. To create some stretching in the oceanFloorSB object, open its Attribute Editor and click on the geoConnector1 node. Raise the **Friction** attribute to anywhere from 0.5 to 1.

Adding Springs to the Soft Body Object

It would be interesting if the ocean floor reacted more to the submarine's impact. By adding soft body springs to the soft body object, we can have the ground bunch up at the leading edge of the impression created by the sliding submarine.

> Note that springs and spring constraints are not the same thing. Springs are dynamic connections between particles. A spring constraint is a rigid body constraint created between two rigid bodies. We'll take a look at spring constraints in the last tutorial in this chapter.

1. Rewind the animation and select the oceanFloorSB object. Choose **Soft/Rigid Bodies > Create Springs > Options** (not Create Spring Constraint!).

2. In the Springs Options window, set **Creation Method** to Wireframe. Set **Wire Walk Length** to 2. You can leave the rest of the settings at their default values.

3. It will take a few seconds for the springs to be created. Once they appear, you may want to select the spring1 node in the Outliner and hide it; this will speed playback a little. Play the animation to see what effect the springs have on the motion of the ocean floor.

4. To increase the drama of the effect, you can raise the spring **Stiffness** to 50 and lower the **Damping** to 0. You can also translate the original oceanFloor rigid body object downward along the Y axis so that the submarineProxy object sinks deeper into the oceanFloorSB object (Figure 7.7).

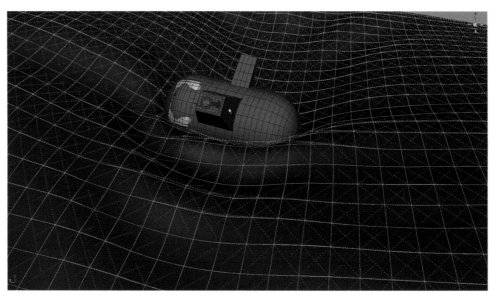

Figure 7.7: Adding springs to the oceanFloorSB object causes the ground to bunch up in the area just below the impact of the submarine.

5. The danger with using springs is that they can make the ocean floor look a little rubbery. To mitigate this you can adjust the spring1 object's **Stiffness** and **Damping** attributes, as well as the **Friction** attribute on the oceanFloorSBParticle object. To see a finished version of the scene up to this point, open submarine_v03.mb from the Chapter 7 folder on the CD.

Baking the Rigid Bodies

Baking the rigid body simulation into keyframes before rendering is always a good idea. It not only allows you to tune the animation using keyframes on the Graph Editor, it also ensures that your rendering will produce predictable results. You could bake the rigid dynamics before adding the soft body object; however, if you decide that you want to change the simulation after adding the soft body dynamics, you'd have to backtrack to a version of the scene before you added the soft body object.

1. Once you are happy with the motion, save the scene and then save it again as a new version; this way you can go back to the previous version if you need to adjust the simulation.

2. You can create a cache for the rigid body dynamics just as you can for particles. Creating a cache means the simulation data are written to disk, allowing you to scrub back and forth on the Timeline. If you make changes to the simulation, you'll need to delete the cache to see the changes take effect. To create a cache for the rigid body dynamics, select one of the rigidBody objects from the Outliner and open its Attribute Editor. Click on the rigidSolver tab and click on the box next to Cache Data in the Rigid Solver States rollout, then play through the animation. To delete the cache, just hit the Delete button next to the Delete Cache label (Figure 7.8).

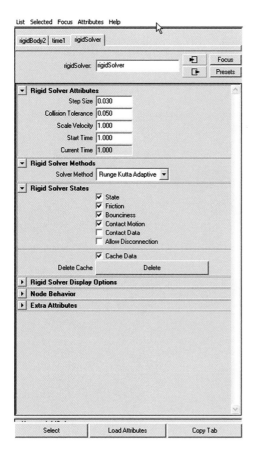

Figure 7.8:
The rigidSolver Attribute Editor contains the settings for creating a rigid body cache.

3. Select the submarineProxy object. In its Channel Box Shift+select the attributes highlighted in yellow, namely, all the translate and rotate attributes. Choose **Edit > Keys > Bake Simulation > Options**. In the options, set **Hierarchy** to Selected and **Channels** to From Channel Box. Set the **Time Range** to Time Slider and **Sample By** to 1. Check the boxes next to **Keep Unbaked Keys** and **Disable Implicit Control**. Uncheck **Sparse Curve Bake** (Figure 7.9).

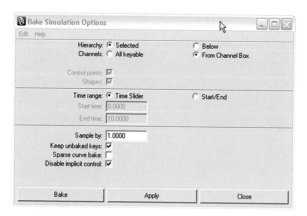

Figure 7.9:

The settings for the Bake Simulation Options

4. Click the Bake button to bake the motion to keyframes. Maya will play through the animation and convert the simulation.

5. When the baking operation is complete, select the submarineProxy object and open the Graph Editor (**Windows > Animation Editors > Graph Editor**). You'll see the keyframes on the various translation and rotation channels for the submarineProxy object (Figure 7.10).

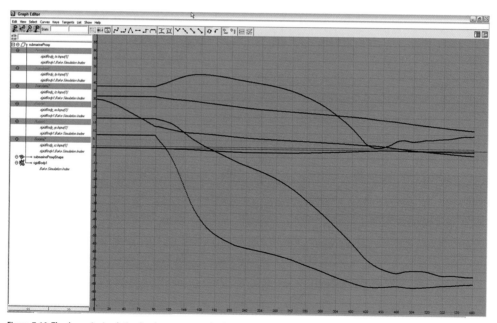

Figure 7.10: The dynamic simulation has been converted to keyframes through the Bake Simulation operation.

6. Once this has been completed, you can open the Outliner and select the rigid-Body1 and rigidBody2 objects as well as the gravityField1 and dragField1 objects and delete them (Figure 7.11).

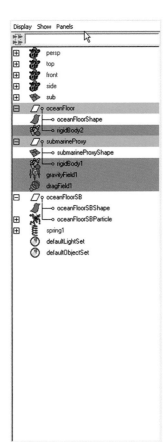

Figure 7.11:
The rigid body nodes can be
deleted once the simulation
has been baked into
keyframes.

7. You can delete the original oceanFloor object as well.

Baking a simulation applies to any object that has an incoming control other than keyframes. This
includes driven keys, expressions, the constraints, and connections made through the Connection Editor.
You could have just as easily selected the sub object that is constrained to the submarineProxy object and
baked its animation into keyframes. This would allow you to delete the submarineProxy object. However,
until you create a cache for the particles controlling the motion of the oceanFloorSB object, you'll need to
keep the submarineProxy object around as a collision object.

8. It's a good idea to simplify the animation curves applied to the submarineProxy
object. Currently, it has a keyframe on every single frame of the animation, which
will make it hard to work with if the animation needs to be changed. Select the
submarineProxy object and open the Graph Editor. From the Graph Editor menu,
choose **Curves > Simplify Curve > Options**. Set **Time Range** to Time Slider, and
Simplify Method to Classic. Set **Time Tolerance** and **Value Tolerance** to 0.1
(Figure 7.12). Click the Simplify button to perform the operation. The resulting

curves will now have fewer keyframes, making them more manageable to edit if changes need to be made. Simplifying the curves won't work correctly unless the rigidBody nodes attached to the objects have been deleted.

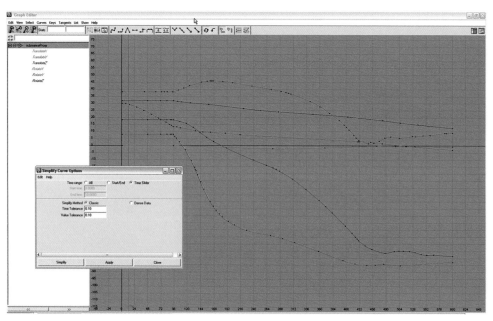

Figure 7.12: The simplified animation curves as they appear in the Graph Editor

Finishing the Scene

A few more operations need to be performed before the scene is ready for rendering. Most previsualizations can get away with a hardware rendering (or even a Playblast). Before we render or hand this scene over to anyone else to work on, we want to make sure it's nice and clean. You can open the submarine_v04.mb scene from the Chapter 7 folder on the CD if you'd like to start from a scene that has been completed up to this point.

1. In the Outliner, select the oceanFloorSBParticle object and choose **Solvers > Create Particle Disk Cache > Options**. In the options, set the Cache Directory to submarine_v04. This will create a directory in the Particles folder of your current project if it doesn't already exist. Set **Particle Systems To Cache** to Selected. (There's only one particle system in the scene, so it doesn't really matter which option you pick.)

2. Rewind the animation and click Create to make the cache. Maya will play through the scene. Just the Timeline will update; the action in the perspective window will not change. Once it's finished, you can scrub back and forth in the Timeline and the animation will update correctly. If you need to make changes to the action of the soft body, you'll need to delete the cache before the changes are reflected in the scene.

3. In the Outliner, select the submarineProxy object and hide it so that you can see the yellow submarine in all its glory (Figure 7.13).

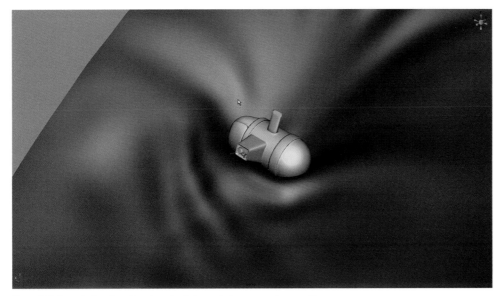

Figure 7.13: Our unlucky submariners have landed on a sludgy spot on the ocean floor.

Further Study

These techniques can be used for a variety of effects. Try some of the following and see how they might be applied in your own projects:

1. See if you can combine rigid body collisions and a duplicate soft body object to simulate the creation of a dent in a car when it's struck by a small meteor (or two).

2. See if you can use these techniques to create footprints left by a large monster or tire tracks left by a vehicle. You may need to link the deformation of the object to an animated bump or displacement map if you need a higher level of detail left in the tracks.

3. Use the Particle Collision Event Editor to create bubbles or clouds of silt when the submarine collides with the oceanFloorSBParticle object.

Creating Animated Fissures on a Surface

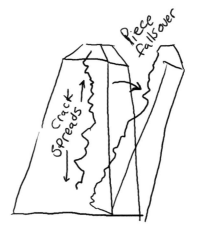

This next shot is for a commercial. The art director would like to have a fissure appear on the surface of a crystal and spread along the surface. Then a large chunk of the crystal falls off and lands on the ground. You'll want to use rigid body dynamics to animate the chunk falling off the crystal, but that's the easy part. The tricky part is animating the fissure on the surface. To do this, you'll use an animated Boolean operation.

Boolean Operations

Performing a Boolean operation on a piece of NURBS or polygonal geometry involves using one piece of geometry to edit a second piece of geometry. There are three results of this type of operation: union, difference, and intersection. Creating a union means the two pieces of geometry are fused together into a single piece. Creating a difference means one piece of geometry cuts a hole into the second. The intersection results in a piece of geometry created from the overlapping area of the two objects. The two pieces of geometry have to be of the same type (NURBS or polygon only). See Figure 7.14 for examples of the three Boolean operations.

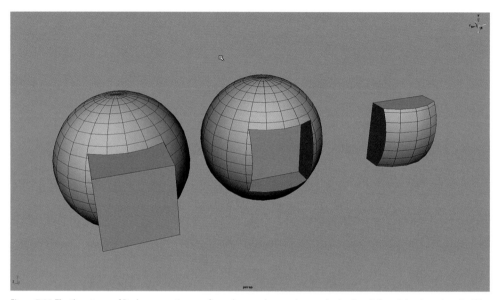

Figure 7.14: The three types of Boolean operations performed on a polygon sphere and cube: from left to right, the union, the difference, and the intersection.

The cool thing about Maya's Boolean operations is that they can be animated using history. So we can create a piece of geometry for our crack and animate it intersecting with the crystal. The unfortunate thing is that the topology of the geometry created with Booleans can be a little messy; we have to be very careful when animating the geometry to avoid weird artifacts that can show up when the scene is rendered.

1.   Open the crystal_v01.mb scene from the Chapter 7 folder on the CD. Switch to the renderCam and start a render. This scene uses mental ray, so you'll want to make sure the mental ray plug-in is loaded or you will get an error. Figure 7.15 shows the result.

Figure 7.15: A rendered view of the crystal_v01.mb scene from the renderCam

Our crystal has been modeled and textured using a basic dielectric material, which is a great material for creating glass surfaces. This scene doesn't look too bad considering it's lit with a single directional light. The floor uses a basic Blinn with a little bit of reflection blur. You'll notice that there are no shadows. The dielectric material does not work with shadows, which is unfortunate, but this setup should work fine for right now.

2. Create a polygon cube and name it "fissure." Set its **ScaleX** and **ScaleY** values to 65. Set its **ScaleZ** value to .07. Set **TranslateX** to 7, **TranslateY** to 31, and **TranslateZ** to –12.

3. In the Channel Box under the Inputs section, set **Subdivisions Height** to 24.

4. In the Outliner, select the crystal object and Ctrl+select the fissure object. Switch to the Polygons menu set and choose **Mesh > Booleans > Difference**.

5. You'll notice that the fissure object has disappeared. In the Outliner, a new object named polySurface1 has appeared. This is the result of the Boolean operation. Select it and rename it "crystalDifference."

6. In the Outliner, you'll see that the fissure object now has transfom1 parented beneath it. To see the fissure object, select transform1 and open its Attribute Editor. Click on the fissureShape tab and under the Object Display rollout, uncheck the box next to **Intermediate Object** (Figure 7.16).

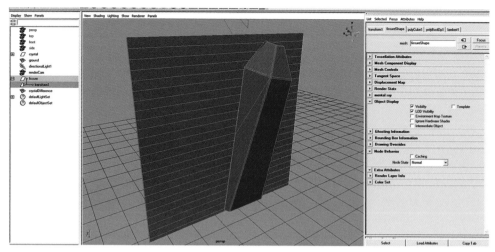

Figure 7.16: The visibility for the fissure object has been restored; this will make animation easier.

7. Assign a Lambert shader to the fissure object and set its transparency to white. Name the new shader "transparentSG" and make sure that the shading options in the perspective window are set to Wireframe On Shaded.

8. Select the fissure object and translate it back and forth along the X axis. You'll notice that the topology of the crystal object updates as the fissure object passes through it. A thin cut appears at the intersection of the fissure cube and the crystal. This will become the fissure on the surface of the object. You'll also notice that the faces of the crystal triangulate themselves at certain points during the intersection and the shader on the polygon changes (Figure 7.17). To fix the shading problems, select the crystalDifference object and reapply the crystalSG shader to it.

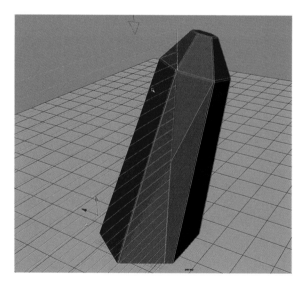

Figure 7.17:
The shader on the faces
of the crystal changes
as it intersects with the
fissure object.

To see a version of the scene up to this point, open the crystal_v02.mb scene from the Chapter 7 folder on the CD.

Modeling the Fissure

This next part is a lot of fun. Now that we have the Boolean difference operation set up to properly slice the crystal, we can turn our bland straight cut into a jagged crack by moving the vertices of the fissure object.

1. Select transform1 and set its **TranslateX, Y,** and **Z** values to 0 so that it's intersecting the crystalDifference object.

2. Switch to the side view in the viewport and set the shading mode to Wireframe.

3. Select the fissure object and hit the F8 key to switch to component mode. Marquee-select around the groups of vertices on the fissure object and move them around to make a jagged cut that travels down the crystal. Figure 7.18 shows how this process works. Be careful to not overlap the vertices of the fissure object; this will cause errors with the Boolean operation and the crystal will disappear.

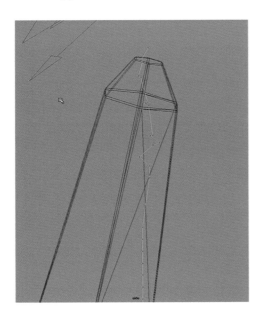

Figure 7.18:
Groups of vertices of the fissure object are moved back and forth to make the fissure more jagged.

4. Switch to the front view and move the fissure object along the X axis so that it no longer intersects the crystal object.

5. To make the crack gradually appear as the fissure object moves through the crystal, we'll adjust the model. Marquee-select groups of vertices and translate them in X away from the crystal. The farther from the crystal they are, the later that part of the crack will appear; for example, to make the crack start at the bottom, make sure those vertices are closer to the crystal. In Figure 7.19 the model has been adjusted so that the crack will start in the middle of the object. Be careful not to move the vertices up or down on the Y axis or the crack will move in strange ways as it forms.

Figure 7.19: Groups of vertices of the fissure object are moved back away from the crystal. This will make the crack appear to grow along the surface of the crystal as the fissure object moves through the crystal object.

6. Marquee-select the vertices on the side of the fissure opposite the crystal and move them in X to extend the length of the fissure object. We need to completely divide the crystal object with the fissure object once the animation of the crack is complete.

To see a version of the scene up to this point, open crystal_v03.mb from the Chapter 7 folder on the CD.

Animating the Fissure

Animating the fissure is easy; however, it's a good idea to keep a close eye on the crystal geometry for any problems that might appear in a rendering of the scene.

1. Rewind the animation and select the fissure object. Position it on the X axis so that it is not intersecting the crystal. Highlight the **TranslateX** attribute in the Channel Box, right-click, and choose **Key Selected** from the pop-up menu.

2. Set the playhead at frame 220 on the Timeline. Move the fissure object along the X axis so that it completely divides the crystal, and set another keyframe (Figure 7.20).

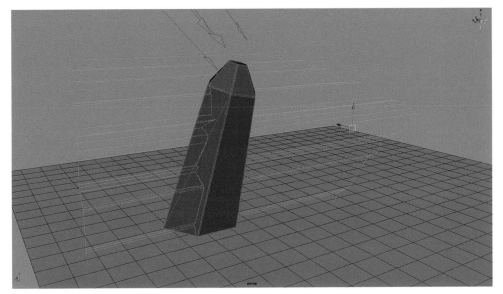

Figure 7.20: The fissure object is moved so that it divides the crystal object.

3. Hide the fissure object and play the animation. The crack now appears on the surface of the crystal and spreads over the course of 220 frames.

4. To make the animation more interesting, select the fissure object and open the Graph Editor. Add keyframes to the **TranslateX** animation curve and edit them so that the fissure moves at a less-even pace (Figure 7.21).

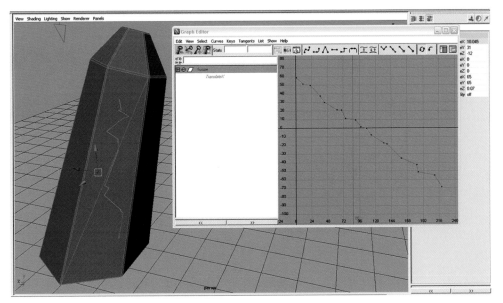

Figure 7.21: Adding keyframes to the fissure object's animation curve makes the scene more interesting.

Preparing the Scene for Dynamics

At this point, it is very important that we make sure the animation of the fissure is behaving properly. Once we add dynamics to the scene, it will be harder to go back and edit the way the fissure forms in the crystal.

1. Switch to the renderCam and play through the animation. Look for any problems on the geometry as the fissure forms on the surface. If you see dark triangles appearing or other strange topology problems, try editing the vertices on the fissure object until the problems go away.

2. Make sure the crack is not too thin and that it separates the two parts of the crystal completely. If the interior faces of the two pieces overlap each other, you will get interpenetration errors when you apply rigid body dynamics. At this stage, you can fix this by adjusting the vertices of the fissure object just to make sure that it is not so thin that the interior faces of the object are too close or overlapping (Figure 7.22).

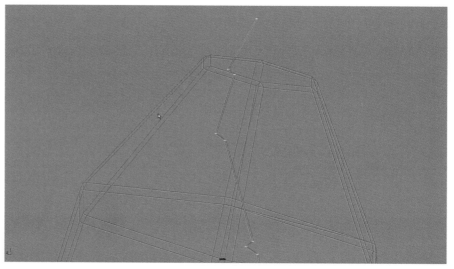

Figure 7.22: The vertices of the fissure object have been adjusted so that the interior faces of the crystal object are not too close together or overlapping; this will ensure that the dynamics calculate properly.

3. Create a few test renders to make sure the crystal renders OK (Figure 7.23).

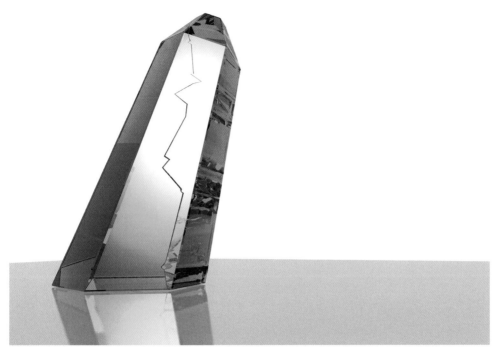

Figure 7.23: A test render shows how the fissure will look on the surface of the crystal.

To see a version of this scene up to this point, open crystal_v04.mb from the Chapter 7 folder on the CD.

Separating the Pieces of the Crystal

To apply dynamics to the scene, we'll duplicate the object and separate it into two polygon objects.

1. Move the playhead on the Timeline to frame 300 and select the crystalDifference object.

2. Duplicate the object by choosing **Edit > Duplicate** (or Ctrl+d). Hide the crystalDifference object.

3. Switch to the Polygon menu set. Choose **Mesh > Extract > Options**. Make sure **Separate Extracted Faces** is checked and leave **Offset** at 0. Click Extract to perform the action.

4. In the Outliner you'll see that the duplicate crystalDifference1 object now has two polySurface nodes below it. Rename the crystalDifference1 group "crystalDynamic" and rename the large polySurface object "largeChunk" and the smaller one "smallChunk."

5. Select the two chunks and delete history on them. The empty transform node in the group should disappear (Figure 7.24).

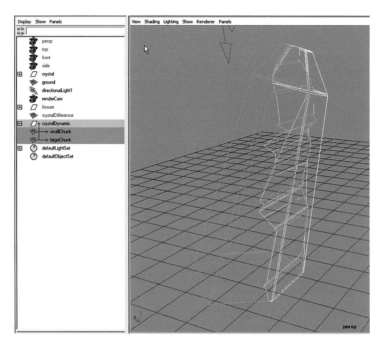

Figure 7.24:
The duplicate crystal object has been separated into two polygon objects. The two objects have been renamed in the Outliner.

Creating Rigid Bodies from the Separate Pieces

The next part of the scene requires that the smaller piece of crystal falls off the larger piece and bounces on the ground plane. To do this, we'll convert the pieces into rigid bodies and then apply a gravity force.

1. Switch to the Dynamics menu set. Select the ground object and choose **Soft/Rigid Bodies > Create Passive Rigid Body**.

2. Select the largeChunk object and convert it to a passive rigid body as well. This object is not going to move or react to forces, so it's fine to make it a passive body. If we change our mind, we can easily convert it to an active rigid body. To do this, select the largeChunk object, open its Channel Box, and under the rigidBody input node, set the **Active** attribute to On. The body will then react to forces. This attribute can be keyframed, as we'll see a few steps down the road.

3. Select the smallChunk object and choose **Soft/Rigid Bodies > Create Active Rigid Body**.

Applying Gravity to the Active Rigid Body

To cause the small piece of crystal to fall over, we'll add a gravity field to the rigid body.

1. Rewind the animation, select the smallChunk object, and choose **Fields > Gravity > Options**. In the Option box for the Gravity field, choose **Edit > Reset Settings** to make sure the default settings are applied. Click the Create button to make the field.

2. Play the animation. If all goes well, the smaller chunk should fall over and bounce against the ground plane. If you get an error message, it may be that the rigid bodies are interpenetrating each other. Solving this problem at this stage of the project may be tricky considering how we created the rigid body objects. The best way to fix this is to backtrack to the section "Preparing the Scene for Dynamics" and adjust the vertices on the fissure object. You'll have to repeat the steps for duplicating, separating, and converting the object to rigid body dynamics. To see a version of the scene up to this point, open the crystal_v05.mb scene from the Chapter 7 folder on the CD.

Adjusting the Dynamics

The crystal is now falling apart properly, but the smaller chunk is a little on the bouncy side.

1. Select the smallChunk object and open up its Channel Box. Under the rigidBody3 input node, scroll down and set the **Bounciness** attribute to 0.1 and **Damping** to 0.5.

2. You can change the way the piece falls by adjusting the **Center Of Mass** attribute. Switch to the side camera and turn on the wireframe display mode (hot key = 4). You can see a little *X* at the center of both the smallChunk and largeChunk objects. This is a visual representation of the **Center Of Mass** (Figure 7.25).

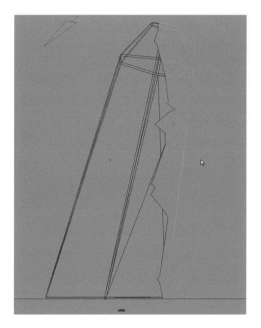

Figure 7.25:
A small *X* at the center of each rigid body shows the location of the center of mass.

3. You can change the position of the **Center Of Mass** by adjusting the values for **Center Of MassX, Y,** and **Z** in the Channel Box. If you are using the crystal_v05.mb scene, try setting **Center Of MassY** to 47.5 and **Center Of MassZ** to –2.5. Play the simulation and see the difference in the way the smallChunk falls off the largeChunk (Figure 7.26).

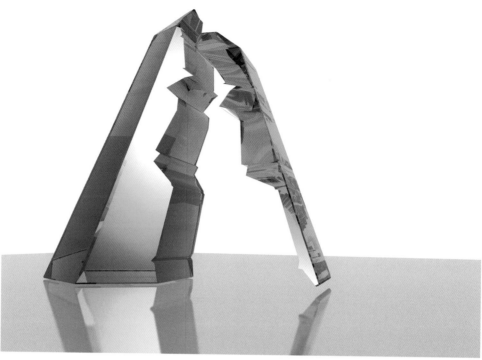

Figure 7.26: Changing the position of the center of mass causes the smallChunk to fall off the largeChunk in a different way.

4. You can try adjusting **Mass, Damping, Center Of Mass, Static** and **Dynamic Friction** (on the ground, the smallChunk, and the largeChunk), and **Bounciness** to alter the way in which the smallChunk falls off the largeChunk. You can also add a Drag field if you feel the need to slow smallChunk down as it falls off; this can help to make it look more massive.

Maya's Shatter effect (**Effects** > **Create Shatter** > **Options**) is a good tool for breaking up a piece of NURBS or polygon geometry into shards. It even has options for converting the shards automatically to soft or rigid bodies (wouldn't it be interesting if the crystal turned to Jell-O?). However, it does suffer from limitations. First, you can't easily animate the cracks appearing in the object the way we have with our crystal. Second, if you convert the shards to rigid bodies, some additional work will be required to get them to collide with each other properly. Converting them to rigid bodies with collisions on (which the Maya documentation recommends not doing) is sure to cause interpenetration errors, which will hang Maya up if not crash it altogether. However, the shards do look more realistic and interesting than the crack we created using our Boolean method. If you have the time and patience, you could most likely combine the two methods to create a more interesting animation. It would be cool to see the smallChunk break into tiny bits when it collides with the ground or crumble as it slides off the largeChunk.

Keyframing the Dynamics

The animation is almost complete; however, we need to time the dynamic simulation so that it occurs after the crack has been made.

1. Rewind the animation, select the crystalDifference object, and unhide it (Ctrl+H).

2. Select the smallChunk object and open its Channel Box. Under the rigidBody3 input node, scroll down and find the **Active** attribute. Set it to Off by typing **0** into the field (Figure 7.27).

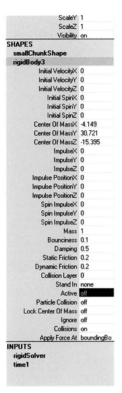

ScaleY	1
ScaleZ	1
Visibility	on
SHAPES	
smallChunkShape	
rigidBody3	
Initial VelocityX	0
Initial VelocityY	0
Initial VelocityZ	0
Initial SpinX	0
Initial SpinY	0
Initial SpinZ	0
Center Of MassX	-4.149
Center Of MassY	30.721
Center Of MassZ	-15.395
ImpulseX	0
ImpulseY	0
ImpulseZ	0
Impulse PositionX	0
Impulse PositionY	0
Impulse PositionZ	0
Spin ImpulseX	0
Spin ImpulseY	0
Spin ImpulseZ	0
Mass	1
Bounciness	0.1
Damping	0.5
Static Friction	0.2
Dynamic Friction	0.2
Collision Layer	0
Stand In	none
Active	off
Particle Collision	off
Lock Center Of Mass	off
Ignore	off
Collisions	on
Apply Force At	boundingBo
INPUTS	
rigidSolver	
time1	

Figure 7.27:
The Active attribute is set to Off; this will keep the small-Chunk object from reacting to the gravity field.

3. Right-click over the Active field and choose **Key Selected** from the pop-up menu.

4. Set the Timeline to frame 230 (or at least 10 frames after the crack has fully formed in the crystal). Set the **Active** attribute to On by typing **1** into the field; set another keyframe on this attribute.

Keyframing the Visibility of the Chunks

When you play the animation now, you'll see the smallChunk fall off the largeChunk after the crack has formed. However, things look a little strange because both the crystalDifference object and the crystalDynamic group are visible. To fix this, we'll keyframe the visibility of the objects.

1. Select the crystalDynamic group and hide it (Ctrl+h).

2. Set the Timeline to a few frames before the keyframes on the **Active** attribute of the small chunk; try frame 225.

3. Select the crystalDifference object. In its Channel Box, right-click over the **Visibility** attribute and choose **Keyframe Selected**.

4. Type **225.5** in the field at the very right of the Timeline (or add 0.5 to whichever frame you chose in step 2 of this section).

5. Select the crystalDifference object, and set **Visibility** to On by typing a **1** into the Visibility field.

6. Set another keyframe on this attribute.

7. Select the crystalDynamic group, and set a keyframe on its **Visibility** attribute.

8. Use the field at the right to set the current frame to 226. Set the **Visibility** of the crystalDynamic group to On and set another keyframe.

Swapping out the visibility of two identical objects is not the most elegant solution, but it should work OK. I prefer to do this on half frames (frame + 0.5) to avoid any blinking in the render. If you keyframe the visibility on whole frames, you may only see this blinking when an animation has been rendered out for video and converted to fields. Sometimes you can cheat this effect by switching camera angles between the point where the fissure is complete and when the smallChunk starts to fall over. An image of the final animation is shown in Figure 7.28. To see a finished version of the scene, open crystal_v06.mb from the Chapter 7 folder on the CD.

Before rendering the scene, it would be a good idea to bake the simulation on the dynamic objects. To do this, follow the steps described in the section "Baking the Rigid Bodies" of the Dynamic Dents tutorial that starts this chapter. To see a rendered sequence, open the crystal.mov QuickTime from the movies folder on the CD.

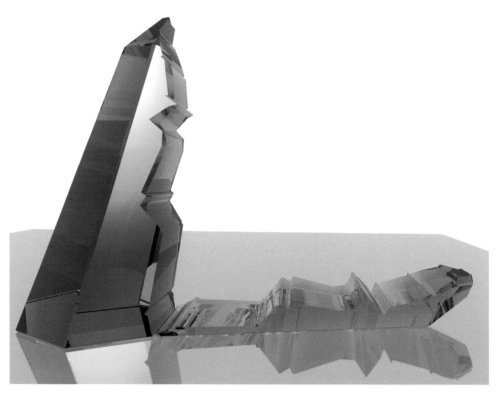

Figure 7.28: A render from the final version of the scene

Further Study

This exercise should give you some ideas on how to create more complex dynamic animations. Here are some suggestions on how you can use and expand these techniques:

1. Create an animation where a laser beam cuts a circle in a thick wall of glass or ice. Have the circular section pop out of the hole and bounce on the ground. You can connect the translation of the Boolean cutting object to the progress of the laser beam as it makes a cut in the glass.

2. See if you can create a crack that splits in two or three directions, or one that starts from inside the crystal.

3. Create an animation of a road being split in two by an earthquake. See if you can add an animated texture map to the split to give it more detail.

Rigid Body Spring Constraints

Three-dimensional flying text animations are nearly unavoidable when you work as a freelancer in the industry. I often wonder about the first director who decided his film needed to have a giant 3D logo soaring through space. I picture some guy in the 1920s hoisting steel letters with a crane above a Chaplinesque set...but I digress. The art director has a fairly simple job for you: Krandle Productions needs a new animation for its logo. The shot calls for the individual letters to fly into the frame from above the camera and bounce into place with a springy, comical action.

To create this effect, we'll use the rigid body spring constraint on some 3D letters. The effect itself should be very simple to pull off; however, *Krandle Productions* is 18 letters long, meaning we have to repeat our setup 18 times. This is a good opportunity to practice some MEL scripting. We also want to make our setup flexible. As you know, flying logos are technically easy, but there's almost always a billion and a half changes the client will want to see before it settles on that particular version that just screams "Krandle Productions."

The MEL scripting in this chapter is really just a taste of what MEL can do. MEL is an extremely powerful tool; in fact, you could say that Maya is MEL. The Maya interface actually operates through a series of MEL scripts. In fact, all of Maya is really made from MEL. The authors of the earliest versions of Maya created the MEL scripting language because at the time C++ (one of the most common programming languages) could not achieve the complex 3D operations they needed. Through MEL scripts, you can create your own tools and do things that you couldn't do otherwise by using only the regular Maya toolset.

The MEL scripts in this exercise are mostly focused on speeding up your work flow. The whole idea behind including MEL scripts in this tutorial is to help you appreciate how much scripting can improve your Maya skills and speed things up for you. This is by no means an extensive lesson covering all aspects of MEL. I would encourage you to consult the Maya help files for complete descriptions of each command. When I work with MEL, I have the help file open at all times. Maya 8's documentation has improved a lot, and you can now easily access all the commands. To open the help files, you can always hit the F1 key on your keyboard or choose **Help > Maya Help** from the main menu. You can use the search function in the help browser to quickly search for a command or click the Commands link on the left side of the browser (Figure 7.29).

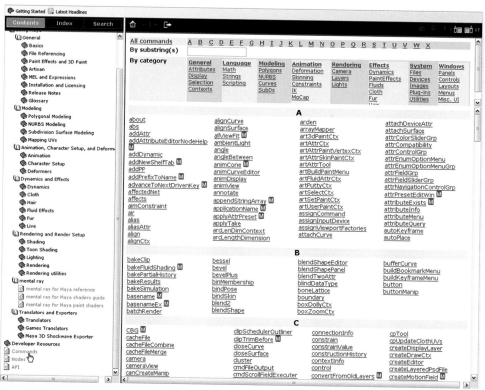

Figure 7.29: Maya's documentation includes a complete list of MEL commands.

In addition to the documentation, there are a number of books devoted to MEL that are worth checking out. This exercise offers fairly brief descriptions of the commands, coding style, and proper syntax. I do not expect you to become a MEL scripting whiz by the end of it, but I do hope that if you're not already incorporating MEL into your working habits, this exercise will convince you to do so. Let's get to it.

Creating the Text

Maya's text creation tools are pretty good for creating basic letters. You can use the Text tool to create the letters directly in Maya or you can easily import curves from Adobe

Illustrator or EPS files and use the Bevel Plus tool to turn the imported curves into 3D objects. For this exercise, we can get away with using the standard Maya Text tool.

1. Start a new scene in Maya and choose **Create** > **Text** > **Options**.

2. In the Text field type **Krandle Productions**. You can choose the other options as you see fit. The following options are the ones used in the examples for this exercise:

   - Font: Arial Black
   - Type: Bevel
   - Create Bevel: At Start and At End
   - Bevel Width: 0.1
   - Bevel Depth: 0.1
   - Extrude Distance: 0.5
   - Create Cap: At Start and At End
   - Outer Bevel Style: Convex Front Edge
   - Inner Bevel Style: Same as Outer Style

3. Once the letters have been created, select them in the perspective and switch to the Polygons menu set. Choose **Mesh** > **Separate**.

4. Choose **Edit** > **Delete All By Type** > **History** to delete the history on the letters.

5. In the Outliner, select the group node named polySurface1 and rename it "logoGroup" (Figure 7.30).

Figure 7.30: The letters have been created and separated. The polySurface1 group has been renamed logoGroup in the Outliner.

Renaming the Letters Using MEL

Now we need to rename each object in the group so that it matches the letter it represents (i.e., polySurface2 should be renamed "k," polySurface3 should be renamed "r," and so on). We can do this manually, but instead let's warm up with a little MEL scripting, which will make things less tedious and provide us with some useful techniques we can apply in the future.

1. First, let's combine the two parts of the *i* into one object. Select the geometry that makes up the *i* and the dot to the *i* and choose **Mesh > Combine**. A new polySurface1 object will be created and placed outside of logoGroup. Delete history on this object (**Edit > Delete By Type > History**), rename it "i," and in the Outliner, MMB drag it back into the group. Make sure that you place it between the t and the second o object.

2. Open up a text editor such as Notepad, WordPad, or text edit (on the Mac). We'll do our coding in a text editor and then copy and paste it into the Script Editor. This makes it easier to modify the code as we go along.

3. In the text editor, type the following:

```
//Create an array containing the letter names
string $logoLetters[]={"k","r","a","n","d","l","e",
"p","r1","o","d1","u","c","t","i","o1","n","s"};
```

> Proper expression syntax in Maya requires that you end each command with a semicolon. Sometimes the Expression Editor allows for more space than can be displayed on the printed page in this book. Therefore, you should keep in mind that even though the expressions printed in this book often have line breaks before the end of the command, you do not have to follow suit. Use the semicolons as a guide for where you need to press the Enter key in the Expression Editor at the end of the command. Maya ignores white spaces and returns in MEL scripts; only lines that end in a semicolon are considered complete. You can take advantage of this to make your code more readable for users.

4. The string variable we just created is an array. Think of an array as a box containing a bunch of data. In this case, the data are the names of the letters. These letters will become the new names for the polySurface objects in the logoGroup.

5. The order of the data in the array is important. Each entry in an array is given an index number starting with 0. So *k* is in the 0 position, *r* is in the 1 position, *a* is in the 2 position, and so on. You need to have the brackets when you create an array. The brackets in an array are there to hold a number indicating the size of the array (e.g., $selectedNumbers[18]). By leaving the brackets empty, you're telling Maya to figure out the size of the array. It's perfectly fine to leave the brackets empty even when you know how big the array is. The only time you would need to have a number between the brackets is when you're creating a runtime script and you need to reserve a certain amount of memory space for incoming values. This is not a runtime script, so you can leave the brackets empty.

6. Add this to the next line of script in the text editor:

```
string $selectedLetters[]=`ls -sl`;
```

This command creates another array. The command is in two parts. The first part of the command is to create an array named $selectedLetters. Note that the brackets are there but have no number inside. This is because we don't know offhand how many items will be in the array since the array will be created based on user input. The user input in question is the second part of the command, the "list selected" command. Notice that it is in back quotes (the key just below the Esc key on most standard keyboards). The back quotes are a way of nesting a command inside another command. So what this line says is, "Create an array named $selectedLetters and put whatever the user currently has selected into this array." It's important to remember that Maya will put the currently selected objects in the array in the order in which they were selected. The first object selected will be in position 0 of the array, the second will be in position 1, the third will be in position 2, and so on.

7. Add this next line to the code in your text editor:

```
for ($i=0;$i<size($logoLetters);$i++){
    rename $selectedLetters[$i] $logoLetters[$i];
}
```

This is a loop. The part of the line in parentheses creates a variable named $i and sets it to 0. Then it says as long as $i is less than the size of the $logoLetters variable (in this case, the size is 18), keep going through the loop. The $i++ notation is shorthand for incrementing a number by 1. (The programming language C++ is programming geekspeak for saying it's "one more" than the original programming language known as C.) The second line in the loop is the action that will be performed as long as $i is less than the size of $logoLetters. It basically renames each item in the $selectedLetters array after the items in the $logoLetters array. So the item at position 0 of $selectedLetters (namely, polySurface2) will be given the name in position 0 of the $logoLetters array (namely, *k*). As it goes through the loop, the $i variable is used to match the position of one array to the other. Each time it goes through the loop, $i is incremented by one until it hits 18 (the size of our $logoLetters variable), and then the loop ends. Let's try it and see if it works.

8. Select the text in Notepad and copy it. Switch to Maya. In the Outliner, select the polySurface2 object, then Shift+select polySurface3 through polySurface20. (Remember that the order of the selection counts!)

9. Open the Script Editor and paste the text copied from Notepad into the lower portion of the Script Editor. Hit the Enter key on the numeric keypad to execute the text. If there are any typos in the script, you will get an error message. If not, you should see that all the objects in the logoGroup have been properly renamed (Figure 7.31).

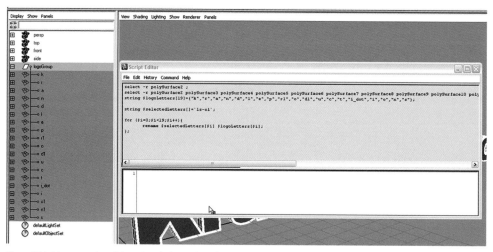

Figure 7.31: After execution of the script, the letters have been successfully renamed.

So you may be thinking, "Wow, it would have taken a lot less time to just rename the letters manually." Maybe. However, the more MEL scripting you do, the faster you get and the more you become aware of how much MEL can help you eliminate tedious repetitive tasks. What's more, you can save this script and reuse it in the future anytime you need to rename a bunch of objects. Once you feel more comfortable with MEL scripting, you might want to try editing it so that the $logoLetters array accepts user input to create the letter names. You also may want to create an error message or some kind of reminder so that the user knows to select the letter objects in order before executing the script. If you do a lot of logo work, this kind of script can become very handy. Later on in this chapter we will be using arrays a lot in a very similar way. Make sure you have a clear understanding of the concepts explained so far in this chapter before moving on. To see a version of the scene so far, open the krandle_v01.mb scene from the Chapter 7 folder of the CD.

Creating the Spring Constraint

First we'll create a spring constraint rig for one of the letters using standard Maya tools. Once you understand how this will work, we'll write a script to automate the process.

1. Marquee-select all the letters and choose **Modify > Center Pivot**. This will place the pivot point at the center of each letter.

2. Assign a Blinn shader to the letters, name it "logoSG," and set its color to white.

3. Create a polygon cube and name it "activeCube1." Make sure that it has only one division for Height, Width, and Depth.

4. We want to place the cube at the center of the letter *K*. One way to do this is to point constrain the cube to the letter and then delete the point constraint. This ensures that the pivot points of the two objects are at the same place. Select the letter *K* and then Ctrl+select the activeCube1. Switch to the Animation menu set and choose **Constrain > Point**. The cube should pop to the center of the letter *K*.

5. In the Outliner, expand the activeCube1 node, select the activeCube1_pointConstraint node, and hit the Delete key to delete the node.

6. Select activeCube1 and choose **Modify > Freeze Transformations**. This ensures that when the cube's translate channels are set to 0, it will be at this position (Figure 7.32).

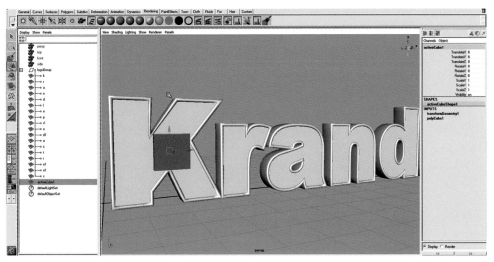

Figure 7.32: The activeCube1 object has been placed at the center of the K object using a point constraint.

7. Duplicate activeCube1 and name the duplicate "passiveCube1."

8. Set the **TranslateY** value of passiveCube1 to 10 and choose **Modify > Freeze Transformations**.

9. Switch to the Dynamics menu set. Select activeCube1 and choose **Soft/Rigid Bodies > Create Active Rigid Body**.

10. Select passiveCube1 and choose **Soft/Rigid Bodies > Create Passive Rigid Body**.

11. Select passiveCube1 and Shift+select activeCube1. Choose **Soft/RigidBodies > Create Spring Constraint** (Figure 7.33).

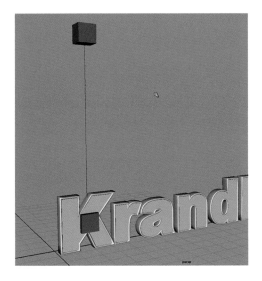

Figure 7.33:
A spring constraint has been created between the two cubes.

12. Play the animation. Wow! Nothing happens!

Adjusting the Spring Constraint

After creating the spring constraint, we can adjust the settings to make it springy.

1. Before playing with the spring, let's constrain the letter *K* to the active cube. Select activeCube1 and then Shift+select the letter *K*. Switch to the Animation menu set and choose **Constrain > Point**.

We could have converted the letter *K* to an active rigid body and used a spring constraint between it and passiveCube1; however, sometimes, depending on what forces you apply to the active rigid body, it can start rotating in a way that's hard to control. This way we can keep the *K* from rotating unexpectedly by using a point constraint between it and the active object.

2. Select the spring constraint and take a look at the Channel box. The **Spring Rest Length** is set to 10. By no small coincidence, that is the distance between activeCube1 and passiveCube1. When you create a spring constraint, the default **Spring Rest Length** value is set to the distance between the two objects connected by the constraint. Set the **Spring Rest Length** to 5 and play the animation. Now the cube (and the K) bounce up and down in a springy fashion.

3. Set the spring **Damping** to 1 and play the animation. Now the spring stops bouncing a bit sooner.

4. Set **Spring Stiffness** to 25. Now the spring has a faster motion to its springiness (Figure 7.34).

Figure 7.34: Adjusting the settings on the spring constraint changes the behavior of the spring.

5. Set **Spring Rest Length** back to 10, **Spring Damping** to 0.1, and **Spring Stiffness** back to 5.

6. Select activeCube1. In its Channel box set the **Collisions** attribute to 0 or Off. This will keep the cubes from banging into each other when the spring is activated.

We'll be working with these attributes again down the road, so keep them in mind as we go forward. To see a version of the scene so far, open the krandle_v02.mb scene from the Chapter 7 folder of the CD.

Automating the Spring Rig Creation Using MEL

That's our basic rig. There's not much to it. We now have a choice. We can repeat the steps in the preceding section, "Creating the Spring Constraint," 17 more times, or we can write a script to automate the process. The nice thing about writing a script is that it becomes a handy tool we can use again and again in the future, especially if the art director says, "Oops! The client kinda changed the font. How hard would it be to do everything over again?" Art directors only say things like this on a Friday night when you have a hot date lined up.

1. Before writing the script, it's a good idea to know what the script is going to do. Actually it's kind of essential. What we want is an action that we can store on the shelf as a shelf button. When we select an object, or in this case all of the logo letters, and click our custom shelf button, we'll perform another loop in which the following should happen:

   a. An array variable will be created containing the currently selected object.

   b. A for loop will start, and each time it runs, the following steps will be executed. The number of times the loop runs is based on the size of the selection.

   c. The pivot point of the object will be centered. (By default, text objects have their pivot point at the origin. We need to center the pivot point for each object for the script to run properly.)

   d. A cube will be created and named "activeCube_*the name of the current selected object*." So if the letter *e* is selected, a cube named activeCube_e will be created.

   e. The activeCube will be placed at the pivot point of the currently selected object.

   f. The transforms on the activeCube will be frozen so that its translate values will be 0 in X, Y, and Z.

   g. The active cube will be duplicated and named "passiveCube_*the name of the object originally selected*." Again, if the letter *e* was selected when the script was executed, the new cube will be named passiveCube_e.

   h. The passiveCube will be moved up 10 units in Y and its transforms will be frozen.

   i. The two cubes will be selected and grouped.

   j. The activeCube will be converted to an active rigid body.

   k. The passiveCube will be converted to a passive rigid body.

   l. A spring constraint will be created between the two objects.

   m. The original selection will be constrained to the active cube.

Writing a descriptive list like this one is a good way to start your script. It will help you solve problems and keep track of what's going on. Plus, you can copy these lines and use them as comments in the script, just to save a little typing.

2. Open up your text editor and let's start writing the script. The first lines are easy. We'll create a variable array containing the currently selected object:

```
//Create array variable containing the currently selected object
string $currentSelection[]=`ls -sl`;
```

Note the "list selected" command in back quotes; we've created a variable containing the results of the "list selected" command.

3. We'll use the size command to get the number of selected objects contained in the $currentSelection variable. We'll set our loop to run based on the size of $currentSelection.

```
for ($i=0; $i<size($currentSelection); $i++){
```

4. The first command in the loop centers the pivot of the selected objects:

```
//first center the pivot of the object to avoid
//collision with other objects
CenterPivot $currentSelection[$i];
```

5. The next few lines create the first cube:

```
//create a cube "activeCube" + the name of $currentSelection
string $activeName = "activeCube_" + $currentSelection[$i];
print ("the name of the active cube is: " + $activeName +"\n");
string $activeCube[] = `polyCube -name $activeName`;
```

The first two lines of this part of the script are designed to give the user of the script some feedback. It's always nice to know what's going on while the script is running, and it makes it easier to debug if something goes wrong. In this case, we are creating a variable named $activeName. The contents of the variable are printed in the next line so that while the script is running, each time it goes through the loop we'll see "the name of the active cube is activeCube_k, the name of the active cube is activeCube_a" and so on. The \n notation tells Maya to print the next statement on the following line. Then, of course, we use the poly-Cube command to make the cube. Once again we've combined two commands into one by first creating the string array variable $activeCube[] (note the brackets) and then inserting the polyCube command as the contents of that variable. We've also used the $activeName variable to name the activeCube.

6. The next few lines place the cube at the pivot point of the original selection:

```
//place the activeCube at the pivot point of $currentSelection
delete `pointConstraint $currentSelection[$i] $activeCube[0]`;
```

This is yet another example of how to nest one command inside another. The delete command may throw you off, so let's break it down a little. Rather than create the point constraint on one line and then delete it on the next, you can save some typing and do both tasks in a single line.

Think from inside the back quotes out. The pointConstraint command creates a point constraint between the activeCube object (the object at position 0 of the $activeCube array) and the original selection (the object at position 0 of the $currentSelection array). Then, after the constraint is created and the active cube is at the position of the original selection, the point constraint itself is deleted. When you use the pointConstraint command, you list the object doing the constraining first and then the object being constrained second. We're deleting it because further on down the road, we'll constrain the original selection to the active cube.

7. Next we'll select the active cube and freeze its transforms:

```
//select and freeze transforms on the activeCube
makeIdentity -apply true $activeCube[0];
```

8. Now we'll duplicate the activeCube and rename it passiveCube:

```
//duplicate the activeCube, rename the duplicate
string $passiveCube[] = `duplicate $activeCube[0]`;
//capture the passiveCube's new name in a short variable
//so we don't have to type long variable names
string $passiveName =`rename $passiveCube[0]
("passiveCube_" + $currentSelection[$i])`;
```

These lines are both examples of a command used to create the contents of a variable.

9. The passiveCube is now moved up 10 units in Y and the transforms are frozen:

```
//move passiveCube up 10 units and freeze transforms
setAttr ($passiveName + ".translateY") 10;
makeIdentity -apply true $passiveName;
```

10. The two cubes are selected and grouped. The group is renamed. This will help to keep the Outliner nice and neat:

```
//group the two cubes and rename the group
select -add $activeCube[0];
group -name ("springGroup_" + $currentSelection[$i]);
```

Since the passive cube remained selected at the end of step 9, we can just add the active cube to the selection and group them together.

11. Next we'll convert the two cubes to rigid bodies:

```
//select the cubes and convert them to rigid bodies
string $activeRigid = `rigidBody -active $activeCube[0]`;
string $passiveRigid = `rigidBody -passive $passiveName`;
```

12. The next step creates the spring constraint:

```
//Create the spring constraint between the two cubes
constrain -spring $passiveName $activeCube[0];
```

13. And finally, we'll constrain the original selection to the activeCube:

```
//constrain the original selection to the active cube
pointConstraint $activeCube[0] $currentSelection[$i];
}
```

14. Once you've typed all of this into your text editor, review it closely for typos and double-check that the lines end in semicolons (except for comment lines). Copy it from the text editor and paste it into the Script Editor. Shift+select all of the letters in the perspective window and hit the Enter key on the numeric keypad. To see the completed code, open the springRig.mel script from the scripts directory on the CD.

This script is a fair amount of work, but now you have something you can use every time you want to replicate this setup. If you haven't done much scripting, some of this may seem confusing. Try writing the script anyway, even if you don't understand every line. The Command reference in the Maya online documentation is a huge help, and you should refer to it anytime you don't understand a command. (Use the search function to find the command you need explained.) The more you work with scripts, the more you'll understand how they work and it will start to feel natural. Just like learning French! (Unless you are French, in which case it's just like learning Portuguese.)

Creating a Shelf Button from the Script

Creating a shelf button from the script is easy, and once you have the button, you can just click it whenever you want to run the script. You can also easily assign it to a hot key.

1. Once you're sure the script is working properly, make sure all changes are made in the code written into your text editor. Save the script to your scripts directory as rigidSpringRig.mel.

2. Copy the script and paste it into the work area of the Script Editor.

3. Make sure the shelf currently displayed is one to which you would like to save the script. The Custom shelf is a good choice.

4. Highlight the text in the Script Editor and choose **File > Save Script To Shelf** (Figure 7.35).

```
5     string $currentSelection[]=`ls -sl`;
6
7     for ($i=0; $i < size($currentSelection); $i++){
8
9         //first center the pivot to avoid collision with other objects
10        CenterPivot $currentSelection[$i];
11
12        //create a cube "activeCube" + the name of the current selection
13        string $activeName = "activeCube_" + $currentSelection[$i];
14
15        print ("the name of the activeCube is: " + $activeName +"\n");
16        string $activeCube[] = `polyCube -name $activeName`;
17
18        //place the activeCube at the pivot point of the $currentSelection
19        delete `pointConstraint $currentSelection[$i] $activeCube[0]`;
20
21        //select and freeze transforms on activeCube
22        makeIdentity -apply true $activeCube[0];
23
24        //duplicate the activeCube, rename the duplicate
25        string $passiveCube[]=`duplicate $activeCube[0]`;
26        //capture the passiveCube's new name in a short variable
27        //so we don't have to type long variable names
28        string $passiveName = `rename $passiveCube[0] ("passiveCube_"+$currentSelection[$i])`;
29
30        //move passiveCube up 10 units and freeze transforms
31        setAttr ($passiveName + ".translateY") 10;
32        makeIdentity -apply true $passiveName;
33
34        //group the two cubes and rename the group
35        select -add $activeCube[0];
36        group -name ("springGroup_" + $currentSelection[$i]);
37
38        //select the cubes and convert them to rigid bodies
39        string $activeRigid = `rigidBody -active $activeCube[0]`;
40        string $passiveRigid = `rigidBody -passive $passiveName`;
41
42        //create the spring constraint between the two cubes
43        constrain -spring $passiveName $activeCube[0];
44
45        //conastrain the original selection to the activeCube
46        pointConstraint $activeCube[0] $currentSelection[$i];
47    }
```

Figure 7.35:
The script is selected and saved to the shelf from the Script Editor.

5. A pop-up box will ask you to input a name for the shelf button. The name should be short enough to fit on the shelf button but descriptive enough so that you know what it means. This is often a losing battle, which is why it's a good idea to create custom icons for your shelf buttons. There are instructions on how to do this in the help files.

6. Once you've created your shelf button, select one of the letters and click the button. A new spring rig should appear attached to the letter.

7. If the button works OK, open the Shelf Editor by choosing **Window > Settings/Preferences > Shelf Editor**. You can edit commands in the Shelf Editor, change the name of your shelves, and delete buttons you no longer use (Figure 7.36). Click the Save All Shelves button to make sure your new button appears the next time you open Maya.

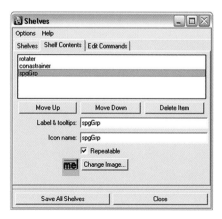

Figure 7.36:
The script is selected and saved to the shelf from the Script Editor using the Shelves dialog box.

Completing the Logo Rig

Much of the work on animating this scene will be devoted to adjusting the settings on the springs. Rather than having to deal with selecting and adjusting each of the 18 springs, we'll set up a control mechanism so that they can all be controlled by adjusting the settings on a single node. To do this quickly, we'll write a few more shorter scripts.

1. Select each letter in the logo in order and click on your new shelf button to complete the spring setup. Make sure to remember to group the original activeCube1 and passiveCube1 you created before writing the script. Rename them "activeCube_k" and "passiveCube_l." Name the group "springGroup_K."

2. In the viewport, marquee-select all of the lines representing the spring constraints. Group them together (Ctrl+g) and name the group "springConstraints" (Figure 7.37).

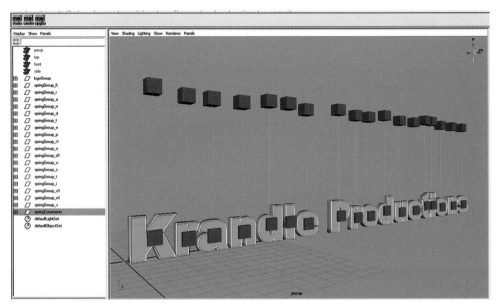

Figure 7.37: The spring constraints are selected and grouped.

3. In the Channel Box for the springConstraints group, highlight all of the attributes except **Visibility**. Right-click and choose **Lock And Hide Selected**. We won't need to move the springConstraints group, and this makes the Channel Box nice and clean so that we can add some custom attributes.

4. Open the Attribute Editor for the springConstraints group. From the menu in the Attribute Editor, choose **Attributes > Add Attributes**. In the Attribute Name field, type **stiffness**. Make sure that **Make Attribute Keyable** is selected. Set **Data Type** to Float. Leave the rest of the settings at their default and click the Add button to add the attribute.

5. Add two more attributes with the same settings. Name one "damping" and the other "restLength" (Figure 7.38).

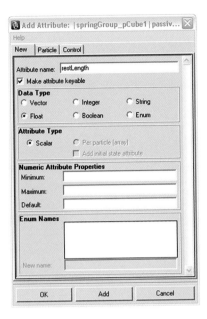

Figure 7.38:
Custom attributes are added
to the springConstraints
group.

6. We can use the Connection Editor to connect the **Stiffness, Damping,** and **Rest Length** attributes of the springConstraint group to each of the spring constraints, or we can write a quick MEL script to do it all at once. Let's try the MEL script. In your text editor, type the following:

```
//use MEL to select all the rigidSpring constraints
select -r "rigidSpringConstraint*";

//create a list of the selected items using an array
string $allSpringCons[] = `ls -sl`;

//connect stiffness, damping, and rest length of each
//spring constraint to attributes on the group node

for ($i=1; $i<size($allSpringCons); $i++){
    connectAttr -f springConstraints.stiffness
    ($allSpringCons[$i] + ".springStiffness");
    connectAttr -f springConstraints.damping
    ($allSpringCons[$i] + ".springDamping");
    connectAttr -f springConstraints.restLength
    ($allSpringCons[$i] + ".springrestLength");
}
```

Hit the Enter key on the numeric keypad to execute the script.

7. Select the springConstraints group and set **Stiffness** to 5, **Damping** to 0.5, and **Rest Length** to 5. Play the animation. The letters should bounce up and down a few times before coming to rest. You can select each spring constraint

and double-check that the **Stiffness, Damping,** and **Rest Length** attributes are highlighted in yellow, indicating an incoming connection. To see a version of the scene so far, open the krandle_v03.mb scene from the Chapter 7 folder on the CD.

Animating the Logo

To make the animation a bit more interesting, we'll create a custom control object to animate the on/off state of the springs using driven keys.

1. Create a locator and name it "animationControl."

2. Select the animationControl locator and create a custom attribute named "springRelease." Set its **Minimum** to 0, its **Maximum** to 18, and its default value to 0.

3. Switch to the Animation menu set and choose **Animate > Set Driven Key > Set.** This will open the Set Driven Key dialog box.

4. Select the animationControl locator and click the Load Driver button.

5. Marquee-select all the lines in the viewport representing the spring constraints. In the Channel Box, scroll down and find the **Constrain** attribute. Set it to 0, or Off. The lines representing the springs should become dotted lines (Figure 7.39).

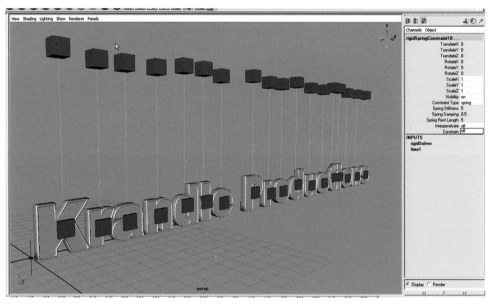

Figure 7.39: The spring constraints become dotted lines when the Constrain attribute is turned off.

6. Click the Load Driven button at the bottom of the Set Driven Key window to load the springs.

7. In the Set Driven Key window, select animationControl in the upper-left panel and springRelease in the upper-right panel. In the lower-left panel, Shift+select all of the spring constraints. In the lower-right panel, select **Constrain.** Click the Key button to set a key.

8. Select the animationControl locator, and in its Channel Box, set the **Spring Release** attribute to 1.

9. Shift+select the spring constraints, and in the Channel Box, set the **Constrain** attribute to 1, or On. Click the Key button at the bottom of the Set Driven Key window.

Offsetting the Driven Keys

In our current setup, changing the **springRelease** attribute on the animationControl locator from 0 to 1 will cause all of the spring constraints to go from off to on. This is not very interesting. We'll use the Graph Editor to offset the driven keys on the spring-Constraints so that as the **springRelease** attribute moves from 0 to 18, each spring will be activated in a wavelike fashion. This work flow is a fast way to set driven keys on a large number of objects instead of setting them on each individual object.

1. Marquee-select all of the spring constraints and open the Graph Editor by choosing **Window > Animation Editors > Graph Editor**.

2. Hit the f key to focus on the curve, then zoom out a little (Alt+RMB) so that you can see more of the graph. The X axis of the Graph Editor usually represents time, but in this case, since we're using driven keys, the X axis represents the value of the **springRelease** attribute on the animationControl locator. So as **springRelease** moves from 0 to 1, the **Constrain** value of all of the springs move from off to on. We want to offset each individual spring constraint's **Constrain** value by one value on the graph so that as we animate the **springRelease** attribute, each spring fires in succession.

3. On the left-hand side of the Graph Editor, Ctrl+click the rigidSpringConstraint1 node to deselect it; the others should remain selected.

4. Marquee-select the keyframes in the Graph Editor. Hit the w key on the keyboard to switch to the Translate tool, and move the keys one value to the right along the X axis (Figure 7.40).

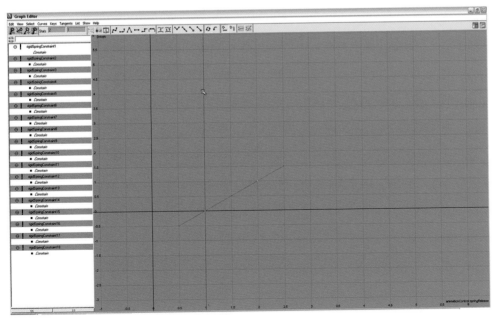

Figure 7.40: The driven keys for the spring constraints appear on the Graph Editor.

5. Ctrl+click rigidSpringConstraint2 on the left-hand side of the Graph Editor to deselect it. Marquee-select around the keys on the Graph Editor and move them another value to the right along the X axis of the Graph Editor.

6. Repeat this process, deselecting one of the rigidSpringConstraints and moving the keys for the rest until you've moved them all. If you reselect all of the rigid-SpringConstraints on the left side of the Graph Editor, it should look like Figure 7.41.

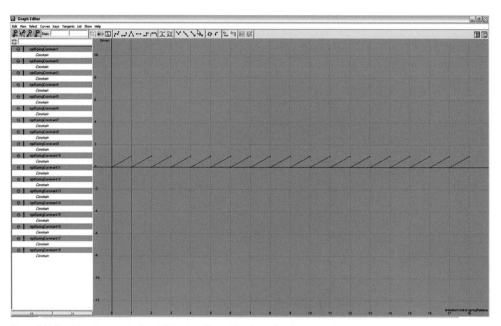

Figure 7.41: The driven keys on the Graph Editor have been offset for each spring constraint.

Finishing the Animation

Finally, we can start animating. Hey, it's a lot of setup, but now the scene is very flexible and changes can be made quickly. Plus, you've got some handy MEL scripts out of the process.

1. Rewind the animation. Select the animationControl object and set the **springRelease** value to 0. Set a keyframe on this attribute.

2. Set the playhead to frame 40 and change the value for **springRelease** to 18. Set another keyframe.

3. Hide all the groups except for the logoGroup. Rewind and play the animation. The logo should start moving up and down in a wavelike fashion as each spring becomes activated (Figure 7.42).

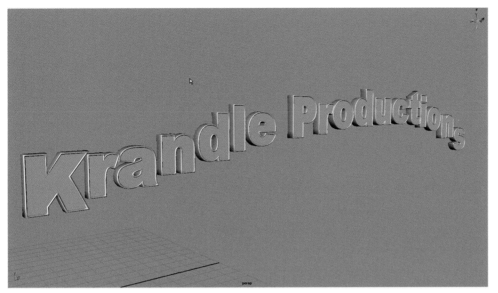

Figure 7.42: The logo moves as a springy wave because of the springs attached to each letter.

4. 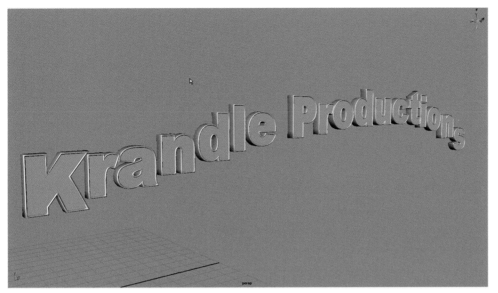 Experiment with the settings on the springConstraints group. Adjust the animation curve for the **springRelease** attribute and see how it affects the animation. To see a completed version of the scene, open krandle_v04.mb from the Chapter 7 folder on the CD.

Further Study

This exercise leaves you at the starting place for creating an interesting logo animation. Combine the animation with some camera moves and dynamic lighting that will really impress the client.

1. Try converting the letters to active rigid bodies; see what happens when the letters collide with each other.

2. Create a script where each active cube is being pulled from opposite sides by spring constraints attached to two different passive cubes. Then create an animation where each letter vibrates as though it's been attached to a string on a musical instrument.

3. Keep an eye out in the future for more opportunities to use MEL scripting to speed up your work flow. Not every Maya animator out there uses MEL scripting as much as they could. The better you get at it, the more of an edge you'll have on the competition.

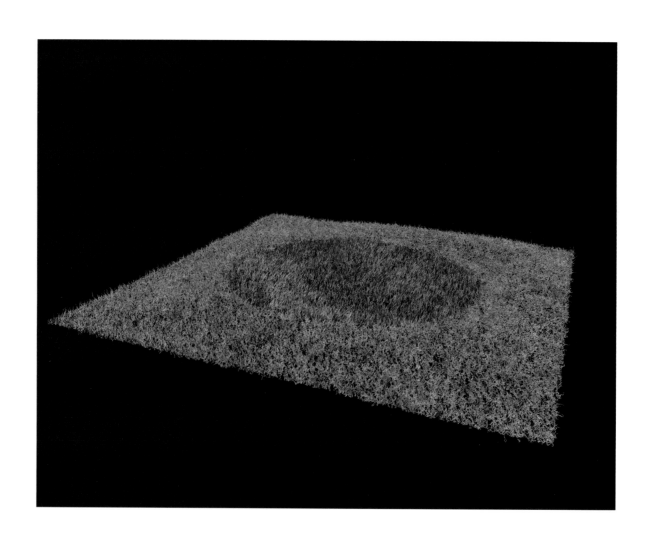

Hair and Fur Effects

Maya Unlimited is an extended professional version of Maya that adds several powerful modules to the standard Complete package. These include Cloth, Live, Fluid Effects, Fur, and Hair. This book has focused mostly on what you can achieve with the standard Maya Complete package because most individual artists as well as smaller companies can only afford Maya Complete. However, I wanted to have one chapter devoted to effects you can achieve with a couple of the Maya Unlimited modules. There are several books dedicated to Maya Unlimited effects, including Learning Maya 7: Maya Unlimited Features *(Sybex, 2006), which is part of the Autodesk Learning Tools series. If you're fortunate enough to have access to a copy of Maya Unlimited, I hope this chapter will give you some ideas on innovative uses for these tools. If not, read through this chapter anyway. You never know when you might get lucky and find yourself at a workstation with Maya Unlimited loaded on it.*

Chapter Contents

Maya Hair: Using Dynamic Curves to Animate a Rope Bridge
Maya Fur: The Miracle Lawn

This chapter is by no means a comprehensive guide. Further study will be required to achieve a deeper understanding of these tools and techniques. Maya's online documentation is always a good place to start. In keeping with the spirit of this book, we'll be looking at nonstandard applications of the Maya Unlimited tools.

Maya Hair: Using Dynamic Curves to Animate a Rope Bridge

Maya Unlimited's Hair module is so much fun to play with that it alone justifies getting a copy of Maya Unlimited if you can afford it. What makes it so much fun is the ability to use the Hair module to convert NURBS curves to dynamic curves. It's true that you can get a lot of mileage out of converting a curve to a soft body and even more when you add soft body springs. However, the Hair module gives you an additional level of dynamic realism. Dynamic curves can float, flop, and fly in the wind in ways that you just can't replicate using soft body dynamics. I highly recommend that after working through this tutorial, you go back to some of the previous chapters and see what you get when you add dynamic curves to Paint Effects, Inverse Kinematic spline rigs, and motion path animations. This particular tutorial looks at ways to use the Hair module to create and animate a rope bridge.

This tutorial covers a lot of ground and moves pretty quickly. We will revisit MEL scripting techniques designed to cut down the time spent on repetitive tasks. This is undoubtedly the most challenging tutorial in this book, but once you work through it and think about the techniques, you'll find you have a much deeper understanding of how to use MEL to create complex setups quickly. You may want to read through the tutorial "Rigid Body Spring Constraints" in Chapter 7 just to make sure you're comfortable with using these MEL scripting techniques. OK, let's get to it.

The art director has an animatic that requires a shot of a rope bridge. An animatic is a kind of animated moving storyboard that directors use when working out how an effects shot will be set up. Animatics created through the use of computer graphics are common for both live action and fully CG productions. Generally they don't need a whole lot of texturing, lighting, or detail. The main focus is on working out the action, timing, and framing.

So here's the catch: This rope bridge will span a chasm. It's your standard series of wooden planks suspended between two ropes. The ropes will be cut on one side by an escaping character (we don't need to worry about animating the character). First one rope will be cut, causing the bridge to tilt; then the second rope will be cut, causing the bridge to fall and collide with the chasm wall on the opposite side.

To achieve this effect we'll use dynamic curves created using the Hair module. We'll also use special Hair constraints along with our standard point, aim, and orient constraints.

Creating the Ropes for the Bridge

The first task is to create a pair of curves, which will be converted into dynamic curves to serve as the ropes for the bridge.

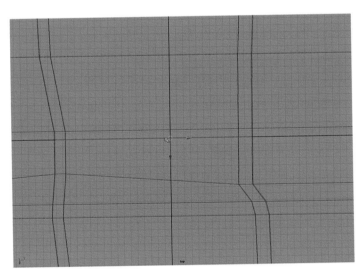

ropes are cut on oneside.

Cut rope
1 first.

1. Open the bridge_v01.mb scene from the Chapter 8 folder on the CD. You'll see a polygonal chasm ready for a rope bridge.

2. In the viewport, switch to the top view and set the shading to wireframe (hot key = 4).

3. Turn grid snapping on and choose **Create > EP Curve Tool.** Click on the grid once, close to the edge of one side of the chasm, and then again on the opposite side. Press the Enter key to create the curve (see Figure 8.1). The EP (or edit point) Curve tool is a quick way to draw a curve in a scene; it requires only two points.

Figure 8.1:
An edit point curve spans the chasm.

4. Switch to the front view and move the curve up along the Y axis until it is level with the sides of the chasm.

5. Rename the curve "ropeBase1."

6. Duplicate the curve (hot key = Ctrl+d). Set the **TranslateZ** of ropeBase1 to 3 and the **TranslateZ** of ropeBase2 to 0.

7. Select both curves and choose **Modify > Freeze Transformations.**

Converting the Curves to Dynamic Curves

Making the curves dynamic is pretty darned easy.

1. Switch to the Dynamics menu set. Select both curves and choose **Hair > Make Selected Curves Dynamic > Options**. In the options, uncheck the box next to **Attach Curves To Selected Surfaces** and leave **Exact Shape Match** checked. Click the Apply button to make the curves dynamic.

2. In the Outliner, expand hairSystem1OutputCurves. Rename the curves "rope1" and "rope2."

3. In the Outliner you'll see a node labeled hairSystem1. When you open the Attribute Editor for this node, you can access all of the dynamic settings applied to the two dynamic curves. Expand the Dynamics rollout and then the Solve rollout. Set **Stiffness** to 0.

4. Rewind and play the animation. Nothing happens. This is because our original curves have only one span each, but that's OK; we can fix that. In the Outliner, expand the hairSystem1Follicles group and select follicle1 and Shift+select follicle 2. Open the Channel Box, and toward the bottom, set the **Fixed Segment Length** attribute to **On** and the **Segment Length** to 1. This determines the number of CVs sampled from the input curve. Rewind and play the animation; now the curves drop down and sag beneath the original curves (Figure 8.2).

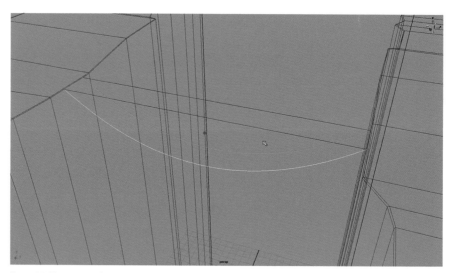

Figure 8.2: The ropes sag beneath the original curves.

5. Stop the animation once the hairs have settled. Select rope1 and rope2. Choose **Hair > Set Rest Position > From Current**. Rewind and play the animation; the curves will sag again a little lower. Once they have settled, choose **Hair > Set Start Position > From Current**. This will cause the curves to start in their sagging position. To see a version of the animation up to this point, open bridge_v02.mb from the Chapter 8 folder on the CD.

Animating the Rope Cut

We'll create some keyframes to animate the cutting of the ropes.

1. In the Outliner, expand the hairSystem1Follicles group and select follicle1.

2. Open the Channel Box for follicle1 and look for the **Point Lock** attribute. By default, it should be set to Both Ends. Rewind the animation, right-click over **Point Lock**, and choose **Key Selected**.

3. Set the Timeline to frame 150. (Don't worry if the curves start to act funny. A hair system is like any other dynamic system; eventually you'll have to create a cache before you can jump around on the Timeline. For now you can ignore the erratic behavior of the ropes; it's not hurting anything.) Set **Point Lock** to Tip and set another keyframe.

4. Repeat these steps for follicle2 but set the second **Point Lock** keyframe to frame 250.

5. Rewind and play the animation. The first rope should become detached from one side of the canyon and fall starting at frame 150. The second rope should fall at frame 250 (Figure 8.3).

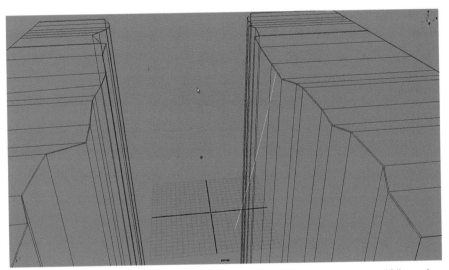

Figure 8.3: When the animation is played, the curves become detached from one side of the chasm and fall toward the other.

Creating a Hair Constraint

Before we create the planks that span the bridge, we'll do a test case with a single plank so that the workflow is clear. Once we have everything working correctly, we'll use some MEL scripts to quickly set up a number of wood planks for the bridge. The first step involves creating a hair constraint.

1. Rewind the animation. In the Outliner, expand the hairSystem1OutputCurves group and select rope1.

2. Switch to the Dynamics menu set. Choose **Hair > Create Constraint > Stick**. A locator will appear above rope1. Rewind and play the animation. This time when the first rope becomes detached from the chasm wall, the constraint holds the center of the rope, preventing it from falling (Figure 8.4).

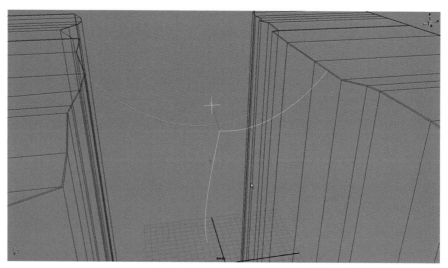

Figure 8.4: The stick constraint holds the rope suspended in space after it detaches from the chasm wall.

Attaching the Stick Constraint to the Second Rope

So the trick is how to get the stick constraint to become attached to rope2 so that it appears as if rope1 is hanging from rope2. There are a couple ways to do this. In the tutorial "Paint Effects and Toon Lines: The Mine Detector Display" in Chapter 5, we used the pointOnCurveInfo node to attach a locator to a curve. Another way to do this is to attach a locator to a curve using a motion path and then delete the keyframes applied to the U value of the motion path, which keep the locator from moving along the curve. In this case, we can attach the stick constraint to rope2 using the motion path method, which requires fewer nodes and less setup than the pointOnCurveInfo node method.

1. Rewind the animation. Select the locator that represents the stick constraint, and Shift+select rope2. Switch to the Animation menu set and choose **Animate > Motion Paths > Attach To Motion Path > Options**. Choose **Edit > Reset Settings** from the menu at the top of the option box. This will reset the options to their default values. Make sure that the check box next to **Follow** is selected. This will not have any effect on the constraint, but later on when we create the plank, we can orient the plank to the constraint so that the plank's rotation matches the bend in the curve. Set **Front Axis** to **Y** and **Up Axis** to **Z**. Click the Apply button to attach the constraint to rope2.

2. In the Outliner, open the Display menu and uncheck **DAG Objects Only**. This way the Outliner will show all the nodes in the scene.

3. Scroll down the Outliner and select the motionPath1_uValue node (Figure 8.5).

Figure 8.5:
The motionPath1_uValue
node is selected in the
Outliner.

4. Hit the Backspace key on your keyboard to delete this node. This will delete the keyframes set on the motion path.

5. In the Outliner, select the motionPath1 node and open its Channel Box. In the Channel Box, set **U Value** to 0.15. The constraint will be repositioned a little further down along rope2.

6. Rewind and play the animation. Now when rope1 becomes detached, it hangs from rope2 (Figure 8.6).

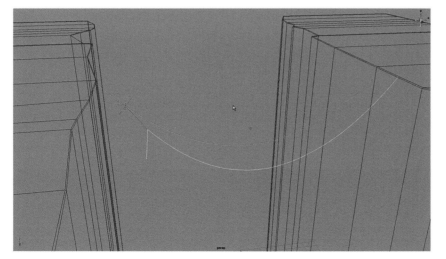

Figure 8.6: Rope1 now hangs off of rope2.

Creating a Plank for the Bridge

So now we have the basic setup for a single constraint. Next we'll create a plank and see how we can attach it to the ropes.

1. Create a locator and name it "plankPin1."

2. Attach plankPin1 to rope1 using the technique described in steps 1 through 6 of the preceding section ("Attaching the Stick Constraint to the Second Rope"). Set the **U Value** of the new motionPath2 node to 0.15, and make sure you attach the locator to rope1 and not rope2. It should end up opposite from the stick constraint locator attached to rope2 (Figure 8.7).

Figure 8.7: The plankPin1 locator is attached to rope1 opposite from the stickConstraint.

3. Create a polygon cube. Name it "plank1." Set its **ScaleY** attribute to 0.25 and its **ScaleZ** attribute to 3.5.

4. Switch to the top camera in the viewport. Select plank1 and choose the Move tool (hot key = w). Hit the Insert button on your keyboard to activate the pivot point. Move the pivot point along the Z axis so that it's close to the end of the plank. Use Figure 8.8 as a guide.

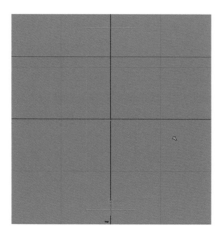

Figure 8.8:
The pivot point of plank1 is moved to one end of the plank.

Attaching the Plank to the Ropes

We will attach the plank to the ropes using constraints.

1.   Select plankPin1 and Shift+select plank1. Switch to the Animation menu set and choose **Constrain > Point**.

Now the tricky part is to get the plank to look like it's attached to both ropes. If you play the animation you'll see that the plank follows the position of the plank pin but its orientation remains constant, causing it to look kind of like it's floating (Figure 8.9). To get the plank to look as though it spans the distance between the ropes, we'll create an aim constraint so that the plank is always oriented toward the hair constraint locator attached to rope2. However, we need an up vector for the aim constraint so that as the rope falls and the objects attached to the ropes change their orientations, the aim constraint does not get confused about which way is up. To solve this problem, we'll create another locator and use this locator as the up vector for the aim constraint. The new locator will be parented to the plankPin1 locator so that as the ropes fall, the up vector of the aim constraint updates correctly.

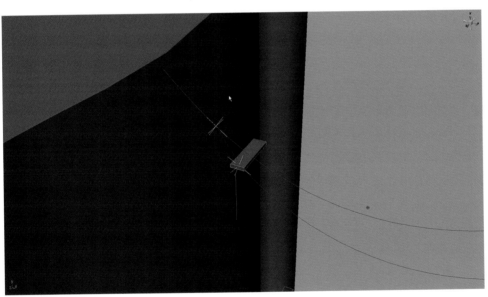

Figure 8.9: The plank is attached to the ropes but its orientation is incorrect.

2.   Create a locator and name it "upVector1."

3.   Parent upVector1 to the hair constraint and then set its **Translate** and **Rotate** attributes to 0 so that it moves to the same position as plankPin1.

4.   Set the Z translation of upVector to 3.

5.   Select the hair constraint, and then Shift+select plank1. From the Animation menu set, choose **Constrain > Aim > Options**. In the options, make sure **Maintain Offset** is unchecked. Set **Aim Vector** to 0 0 –1, **Up Vector** to 0 1 0, and **World Up Type** to Object Up. In the **World Up Object** field, type **upVector1**. Make sure **Constrain Axes** is set to **All** and **Weight** is at 1. Click Apply to make the constraint (Figure 8.10).

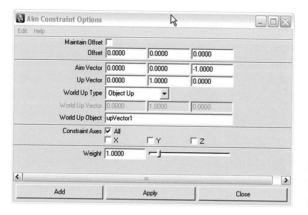

Figure 8.10:
The options for the aim constraint

The plank is now oriented correctly and should continue to look that way as the ropes fall to the other side of the chasm (Figure 8.11).

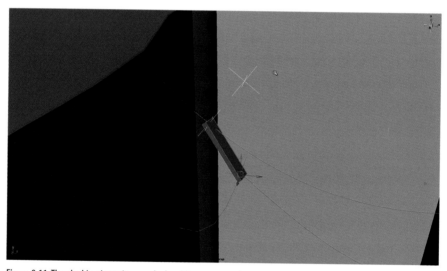

Figure 8.11: The plank's orientation now looks a bit more natural.

To see a version of the scene so far, open the bridge_v03.mb scene from the Chapter 8 folder of the CD.

Creating Multiple Hair Constraints

So now we have the basic setup for the plank. To create multiple planks spanning the gap between the two ropes, either we can repeat the preceding steps multiple times or we can set it up quickly using some MEL scripting.

1.   Let's start with a semiblank slate. Open the bridge_v04.mb scene from the Chapter 8 folder on the CD.

2.   Open a text editor such as Notepad, WordPad, or text edit (on the Mac). Type the following into the text editor:

```
for ($i=0; $i<10; $i++){
```

```
//commands go here
```

```
}
```

This is the start for our basic loop. We will be creating 10 planks between the two ropes, so the loop stops right before it reaches 10. All the commands will be placed between the curly brackets of the loop where it says commands go here.

3. Type these lines between the curly brackets of the loop:

```
// sets U param on rope
float $ropeUpos = ($i * 0.1)  + .05;
```

This line creates a variable named $ropeUpos. This variable will be used to set the **U value** of the motion paths we'll be using to attach the hair constraints to the rope. If you recall, for the test case using a single plank, we attached the hair constraint to the rope using a motion path, deleted the keyframes on the motion path, and then manually inputted a **U value** for the motion path that placed the hair constraint at a certain point along the rope curve. We will be including those actions later in the script, but first we're creating a variable named $ropeUpos that will hold the **U value**. So the first time the loop runs, $i=0, so $ropeUpos = (0 * 0.1) + 0.05 = 0.05. The next time the loop runs, $i=1, so $ropeUpos = (1 * 0.1) + 0.05 = 0.15 and so on until the loop stops when $i reaches 10.

4. Type these lines next:

```
// create all 10 hair constraints
select -r rope1;
createHairConstraint 2;
```

The first command selects rope1, the second command creates a stick constraint.

5. Then add these lines:

```
// get the name of the hair constraint transform
string $hairConstTransName[] = `pickWalk -d up`;
```

We need to get the name of the hair constraint we created in step 4 so that we can refer to it later in the script. The createHairConstraint command does not return the name of the hairConstraintShape, so to retrieve it we use the pickWalk command to tell Maya to move up one node—just like hitting the up arrow key when you have something selected in the Outliner—and then place the name of that node into a variable named $hairConstTransName. Since we know that after creating the hair constraint in step 4 the shape node of the constraint is selected, we can use the pickWalk command to move up one node to the hair constraint's. Alternatively, you can use the listRelatives command with the -p flag to get the name of a node's parent.

6. This next line creates the motion path, which will attach the hair constraint to rope2.

```
// attach the hair constraint transform to rope 2
string $motionPathNode1 = `pathAnimation -follow true -fractionMode true
-curve rope2 $hairConstTransName[0]`;
```

The follow and fractionMode flags for the motion path are set to true. The fraction mode will ensure that the parameterization of the curve is set so that the constraints are spaced out correctly when we assign the **U value** later on in the script. The curve flag tells Maya which curve we want to attach the constraint to.

7. Next we delete the keyframes applied to the motion path. We have to do this before setting the U value of the path. If you get confused, refer back to the section "Attaching the Stick Constraint to the Second Rope" earlier in this tutorial.

```
// must delete the animation curve automatically created with this
select -r ($motionPathNode1 + "_uValue");
delete;
```

8. And now we can use the $ropeUpos variable we created in step 3 to set the position of the hair constraint along the rope.

```
// with animation curve now gone set the motionpath U value
setAttr ($motionPathNode1 + ".uValue") $ropeUpos;
```

9. The hair constraint is all set, so now we have to create a locator for our plank pin. Type this as the next lines in the script:

```
int $plankPinNum = $i + 1;
string $loc1[] = `spaceLocator`; // pin
```

The first line creates a variable that will allow us to name the plank pin correctly; the second line actually creates the locator.

10. We need to create a second locator so that the aim constraints we use to orient the planks have an up vector that behaves predictably.

```
// created an UpVector for every plank so the rotations stay proper
string $loc2[] = `spaceLocator`; // upVector
```

11. Now we rename the locators just to make sure that the names are unique to the scene.

```
// dynamically capture plankPin rename just in case there's
// already one with that name
string $plankPin = `rename $loc1[0] ("plankPin" + $plankPinNum)`;
string $upVectorLoc = `rename $loc2[0] ("upVector" + $plankPinNum)`;
```

12. The upVector locator is parented to the hair constraint and moved three units along the Z axis. Note the way the point and orient constraints are created and deleted in the same line so that the upVector locator has the same position and orientation as the hair constraint. This technique was used in the Rigid Body String Constraints tutorial from Chapter 7.

```
// First put it in the right translation and orientation
delete `pointConstraint $hairConstTransName[0] $upVectorLoc`;
delete `orientConstraint $hairConstTransName[0] $upVectorLoc`;
parent $upVectorLoc $hairConstTransName[0];
```

```
// put the upvector inside the hairConstraint and move it UP in the +Z
// so it is always on the upside of the plank
setAttr ( $upVectorLoc + ".translateZ") 3;
```

13. These next lines repeat steps 6, 7, and 8, but this time we are attaching the plankPins to rope1.

```
// place plankPin on other side
string $motionPathNode2 = `pathAnimation -f 1 -fm 1 -c
rope1 $plankPin`;

// must delete the animation curve automatically created with this
select -r ($motionPathNode2 + "_uValue");
delete;

// with animation curve gone you can set the motionpath U value
setAttr ($motionPathNode2 + ".uValue") $ropeUpos;
```

14. We need to duplicate our original plank object.

```
// duplicate the master plank and use it for this set
string $dupPlank[] = `duplicate -n ("plank" + $plankPinNum)
-rr plank1`;
```

15. And point-constrain the duplicate plank to the plankPin.

```
// point constrain it to the plankPin
string $ptCons[] = `pointConstraint $plankPin $dupPlank[0] `;
```

16. And finally, we can aim-constrain the plank to the hair constraint using the upVector locator to determine the up vector for the constraint.

```
// aim constrain it using the upVec locator and it will fix the
// rotations
string $aimCons[] = `aimConstraint -offset 0 0 0 -weight 1
-aimVector 0 0 -1 -upVector 0 1 0 -worldUpType "object"
-worldUpObject $upVectorLoc
$hairConstTransName[0] $dupPlank[0]`;
```

Don't forget to close the loop using the curly bracket }.

17. Copy these lines from your text editor and paste them into the Script Editor. Hit the Enter key on the numeric keypad on your keyboard to execute the script. To see a completed version of the script, use the Script Editor or a plain text editor to open the bridgePlanks.mel script from the script folder of the CD. It's a good idea to go through the toil of writing out the script yourself. Troubleshooting for typos is a pain in the neck, but it will force you to examine the script closely. After a while, scripting will become more natural.

Animating the Bridge

To finish the animation, we have to keyframe the cutting of the ropes and create a collision surface so that the ropes don't penetrate the chasm wall when they fall.

1. Rewind and play the animation. When the first rope is cut, the planks should hang off of the second rope (Figure 8.12). When the second rope is cut, both ropes and the planks should fall toward the opposite wall of the chasm.

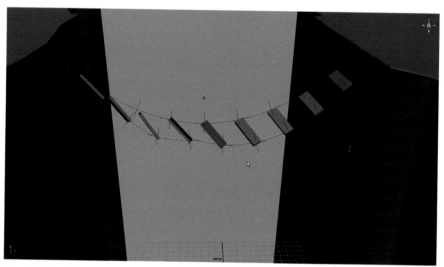

Figure 8.12: The planks hang off the second rope before falling to the opposite side of the chasm.

2. We can create a collision cube to prevent the hair from penetrating the chasm geometry. Select rope1, and from the Dynamics menu set, choose **Hair > Create Constraint > Collide Cube**. Select the cube, and scale and rotate it so that it matches the orientation of the chasm wall. Do the same for rope2. It's OK if the cubes overlap. See Figure 8.13 for reference.

Figure 8.13: The collision cube is positioned on one side of the chasm.

Finishing Touches

To change the behavior of the rope bridge, you can adjust the settings on the hairSystem1 node.

1. In the Outliner, select the hairSystem1 node and open its Attribute Editor. Open the Dynamics rollout.

2. Experiment with different settings for the **Stiffness, Gravity, Damp,** and **Drag** attributes. Note how they affect the movement of the bridge.

3. Under the Forces rollout, try raising the value on the **Turbulence** attribute.

To see a version of the scene so far, open the bridge_v05.mb scene from the Chapter 8 folder on the CD.

Creating a Cache for the Dynamic Curve

Much like particle systems and rigid bodies, simulations using the Hair module should be cached once you decide the animation is acceptable. This will ensure that other animators working on the scene get the same results you do and that there are no problems during rendering.

1. To create a cache, select the hairSystem1 node and choose **Hair > Create Cache > Options.**

2. In the options, set **Cache Time Range** to **Start/End**. Set the start frame to 1 and the end frame to 700. Set the **Sampling** attribute to Over. You can increase the **Rate** value for the oversamples if you'd like, but a setting of 1 should be fine for now.

3. Rewind the animation and hit the Create button to create the cache. The cache for a hair system is stored in RAM until you save the scene. The cache file is written to the Data folder of the current project and it ends in the .mchp extension. You can copy this file to a network directory if other users are working on the same scene or if you are rendering using a distributed network rendering system. When you open the Attribute Editor for the hair system, you'll see a tab

labeled cache_hairSystemShape1. This new tab contains settings that will allow you to change which cache file you are using for the scene.

4. You can find settings for appending, truncating, or deleting the cache under the **Hair** menu.

Further Study

This exercise introduces you to just a few of the effects you can create with the dynamic curve feature in Maya's Hair module. Any curve you have in a scene can be made dynamic. Curves with surfaces lofted between them, IK spline curves, curves that emit particles, and curves with Paint Effects brushes applied to them are just a few examples. Here are a few more ideas on how you can expand the rope bridge lesson:

1. Try adding dynamic rope rails to the bridge.

2. See if you can create an animation where the rope is cut in the middle. (Think of the ending to *Indiana Jones and the Temple of Doom*.)

3. Try creating a rope ladder that dangles from a helicopter.

4. Try to devise a setup where the hair constraints are attached to the planks. This may require the use of a script such as rivet.mel, which you can download from www.highend3d.com.

Maya Fur: The Miracle Lawn

A commercial for a lawn treatment product requires the miraculous transformation of a lawn. The grass will transform from a sickly brown scraggly mess to a healthy green and well-trimmed lawn. The transformation will start from the center of the lawn and radiate outward. To accomplish this, we'll use Maya Fur combined with animated textures. What's more, we'll be creating all the textures in Maya.

Maya Fur is a bit like Paint Effects in that it has lots and lots of controls. We only need to work with a few of these controls to achieve our effect. Once you have a feel for how they work, you should be comfortable enough with Fur to experiment on your own.

Creating Ramps for the Animated Textures

We'll use some simple animated Ramp textures to control the transformation of the lawn. However, since Maya Fur does not allow you to apply an animated procedural texture directly to the Fur attributes, we'll have to generate some animated file textures of our own and apply them to the fur.

1. Start with a new, empty scene in Maya. Choose **Create > NURBS Primitives > Plane**. This will be the starting point for the lawn.

2. Rename the plane "lawn." Open its Channel Box and under the makeNurbs-Plane1 node, set **Patches U** and **PatchesV** to 24.

3. Set **ScaleX** and **ScaleZ** to 24 as well.

4. Assign a surface shader to the plane and name the shader "lawnControl."

5. Open the Attribute Editor for lawnControl. In the **Out Color** channel, click the checkered button to assign a texture. From the Create Render Node panel that opens, choose the Ramp texture.

6. The Attribute Editor will switch to the new ramp texture. In the Ramp field. type **lengthControlRamp**.

7. In the Ramp Attributes rollout, set **Type** to **Circular Ramp** and **Interpolation** to **None**.

8. Click on the blue box to the right of the ramp to delete the blue color marker.

9. Click on the green circle to the left of the ramp to select the green color marker. Click on the green square next to **Selected Color** to open the Color Chooser. Set the color to white; make sure the V slider is set to 1.

10. Do the same for the red color marker, but set the color to a dark gray; make sure the V slider in the Color Chooser panel is set to 0.4 (Figure 8.14).

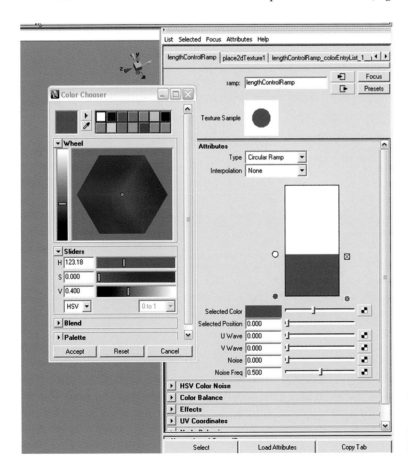

Figure 8.14:
The colors are changed on the lengthControl-Ramp.

11. Open the Hypershade and switch to the Textures tab. Select the lengthControlRamp, and from the Hypershade menu, choose **Edit > Duplicate > Shading Network**.

12. Rename the duplicate ramp "colorControlRamp." Open the Attribute Editor for colorControlRamp and change the white color to a dull greenish brown and the dark gray to a dark but pleasant green, the kind of color you associate with nice healthy lawns.

Animating the Ramps

We'll set some keyframes to animate the ramps. Just to make life a bit easier, we'll have the animation of the lengthControlRamp control the colorControlRamp so we only have to keyframe one ramp.

1. Open the Hypershade and switch to the Textures tab. MMB drag the lengthControlRamp on top of the colorControlRamp. From the pop-up menu, choose **Other** to open the Connection Editor.

2. In the Connection Editor, expand the **Color Entry List** attribute on the left and the right. Expand **Color Entry List**[0] on the left and right. Connect the **Color Entry List**[0].**Position** on the left side to the right (Figure 8.15); do the same for **Color Entry List**[1].

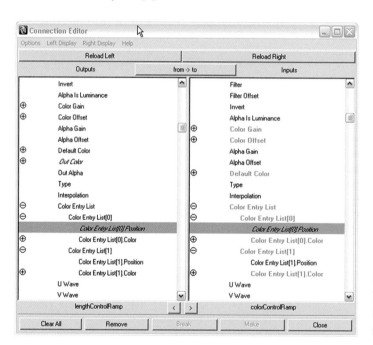

Figure 8.15:
The Color Entry List[0].Position on the left is connected to the same attribute on the right.

3. Open the Attribute Editor for the lengthControlRamp; leave the Hypershade open as well. In the Attribute Editor, select the white circle to the left of the ramp and move it up and down. In the Hypershade, you should see both the lengthControlRamp and the colorControlRamp update accordingly—the circle should expand or contract depending on which way you move the white marker.

4. Set the Timeline to 60 frames and rewind to the beginning.

5. In the Attribute Editor for the lengthControlRamp, set **Selected Position** to 0.01. The ramp should be all white. Right-click over the field and choose **Set Key**.

6. Move to frame 60 on the Timeline and set the **Selected Position** of the white marker to 1. Set another key.

7. 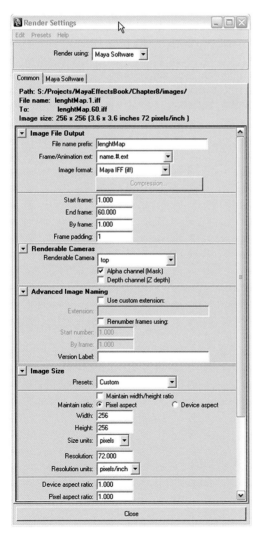 When you play the animation, you should see the gray dot expand and cover the lawn object. To see a version of the scene so far, open the lawn_v01.mb scene from the Chapter 8 folder on the CD.

Rendering the Ramps

Now we can render the ramps to create our animated textures for the lawn.

1. Choose **Windows > Rendering Editors > Render Settings** to open the Render Settings panel.

2. In the File Name Prefix field under the Image File Output rollout, type **lengthMap**. Set the **Frame/Animation Ext** setting to **name.#.ext**.

3. Set **End Frame** to 60.

4. In the Renderable Cameras panel, choose the top camera.

5. Set **Width** and **Height** in the Image Size rollout to 256 (Figure 8.16).

Figure 8.16:
The render settings for the length map

6. In the viewport, switch to the top camera. From the **View** menu in the viewport, choose **Camera Settings > Resolution Gate**. In the viewport, zoom in so that the edges of the lawn object match the resolution gate (see Figure 8.17).

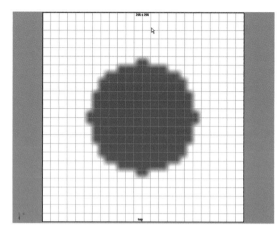

Figure 8.17:
The top view camera is positioned so that the lawn object fills the resolution gate.

7. Save the scene and start a batch render by switching to the Rendering menu set and choosing **Render > Batch Render**. The render shouldn't take very long.

8. When the rendering is complete, open the Hypershade and graph lawnControl. Open the Attribute Editor for lawnControl. From the Textures tab in the Hypershade, MMB drag the colorControlRamp over the **Out Color** channel on the lawnControl in the Attribute Editor. This will replace the lengthControlRamp with the colorControlRamp. The lawn object should change to the green and brown version of the ramp. The animation of the ramp should be the same as the animation of the lengthControlRamp.

9. Open the Render Settings panel. In the **File Name Prefix** field, change the setting from **lengthMap** to **colorMap**. Save the scene and do another batch render.

Creating the Lawn

Now that we have our two animated textures, we can create the lawn object itself.

1. Switch to the perspective camera in the viewport. Select the lawn object and give it a Lambert shader. Make the color of the shader dark brown.

2. Switch to the Surfaces menu set. Choose **Edit NURBS > Sculpt Geometry Tool**.

3. Use the Sculpt Geometry tool to make some small hills and valleys in the lawn surface; nothing too drastic, just a little shape to make it more interesting (Figure 8.18).

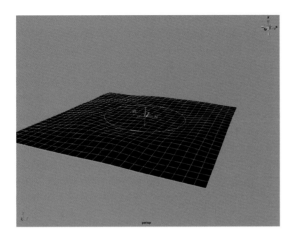

Figure 8.18:
Use the Sculpt Geometry
tool to create some low hills
and valleys on the plane.

Adding Grass to the Lawn

We can take advantage of the Fur presets that come with Maya to easily create the grass.

1. Click on the Fur tab on the shelf to access the Fur presets.

2. With the lawn object selected, click on the Grass preset. It's the seventh one from the left; use Figure 8.19 as a guide. You can look at the bottom left corner to see feedback concerning which preset your mouse is hovering over.

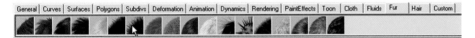

Figure 8.19: The grass preset is accessible through the Fur shelf.

3. Click the grass icon button to apply the preset to the lawn object. You'll see the lawn object become covered in green hairlike curves. This is a rough estimation of what the grass will look like. You need to do a test render to see how the grass actually appears.

4. Open the Render Settings window. From the Image Size rollout, choose the 640X480 preset and do a test render (Figure 8.20).

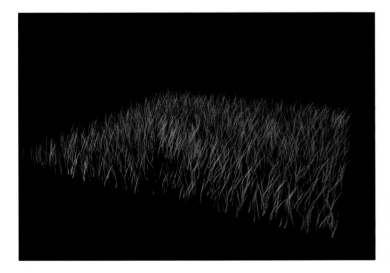

Figure 8.20:
The test render shows
the grass applied to the
lawn.

Adjusting the Grass Settings

Before we apply the animated textures to the grass, we'll alter the settings so that the lawn looks a little more natural.

1. In the Outliner, expand FurFeedback and select the Grass_FurFeedback node. Open the Attribute Editor and click on the Grass tab.

2. Set **Density** to 100,000 and **Global Scale** to 0.5.

3. Set **Baldness** to 1; this will make the grass fuller and less bald. (Seems like a setting of 1 should be more bald and a setting of 0 should be less bald, but what do I know?)

4. Do another test render to see how the grass looks (Figure 8.21).

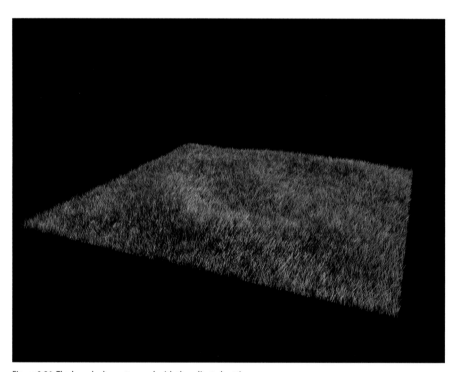

Figure 8.21: The lawn looks pretty good with the adjusted settings.

Animating the Length of the Grass

Now we have a nice starting point for our lawn. To animate the length of the grass, we will need to first apply the animated length texture and then bake the Length channel so that the Fur node updates correctly in each frame.

1. In the Attribute Editor for the Grass node, right-click over the field next to **Length** and choose **Create New Texture** (Figure 8.22).

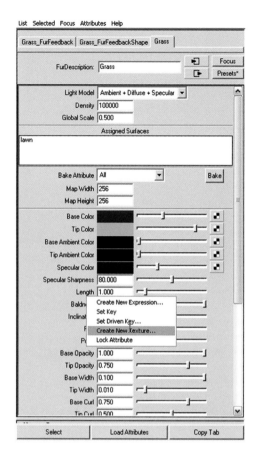

List Selected Focus Attributes Help

Grass_FurFeedback | Grass_FurFeedbackShape | Grass

FurDescription: Grass   Focus   Presets*

Light Model	Ambient + Diffuse + Specular ▼
Density	100000
Global Scale	0.500

Assigned Surfaces

lawn

Bake Attribute	All ▼	Bake
Map Width	256
Map Height	256
Base Color	
Tip Color	
Base Ambient Color	
Tip Ambient Color	
Specular Color	
Specular Sharpness	80.000
Length	1.000
Baldn	Create New Expression...
Inclinat	Set Key
	Set Driven Key...
F	Create New Texture...
P	Lock Attribute
Base Opacity	1.000
Tip Opacity	0.750
Base Width	0.100
Tip Width	0.010
Base Curl	0.750
Tip Curl	0.500

Select   Load Attributes   Copy Tab

Figure 8.22:
A texture can be applied to
the Length attribute.

2. Choose File from the Create Render Node panel. The Attribute Editor will switch to the new File1 node.

3. Click the folder icon next to Image Name. Use the File Browser dialog box to find the lengthMap sequence you rendered in the section "Rendering the Ramps" earlier in the tutorial. Select lengthMap.1.iff and click on the Open button to load the file (Figure 8.23).

Figure 8.23:
The lengthMap.1.iff
file is chosen for the file1
texture node.

4. In the Attribute Editor, check the box next to **Use Image Sequence**. This will load the 60-frame sequence. You won't notice much of a change in the perspective view, even if you play through the animation.

5. Open the Hypershade. In the Outliner, select the Grass_FurFeedback node. In the Hypershade menu, choose **Graph > Input and Output Connections**.

6. Move the cursor over the line connecting file1 to the Grass node; you'll see a pop-up label that reads file1.outAlpha and Grass.Length. We actually want the color of file1 to be connected to Grass.Length (Figure 8.24).

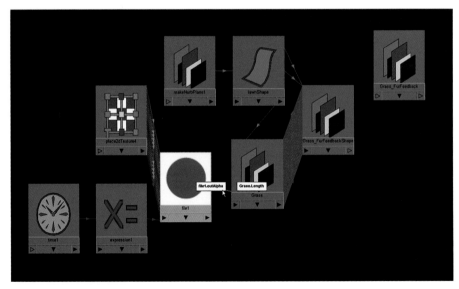

Figure 8.24: The outAlpha of file1 is connected to Grass.Length of the Grass node.

7. MMB drag file1 over the Grass node; choose **Other** from the pop-up menu to open the Connection Editor. On the left side of the Connection Editor, expand **Out Color** and highlight **Out Color R**; on the right side of the connection editor, highlight **Length**. Click the Close button once the connection is made.

Baking the Length Channel

The grass in the perspective view appears shorter but it's still not animated. To animate it, we need to bake the Length channel.

1. Select the Grass_FurFeedback node and open the Attribute Editor to the Grass tab. Under Assigned Surface, select Lawn.

2. Set the **Bake Attribute** menu to **Length**. Rewind the animation and click the Bake button in the Attribute Editor.

3. It will run through the animation, but you won't see much change. When it is complete, it will rewind the animation and the grass will appear longer. Now when you play the animation, you'll see a circle of short grass grow from the center.

4. Set the Timeline to frame 27 and do a test render. You'll see a circle of short grass at the center. It's not terribly dramatic; we'll fix this by animating the color channel (Figure 8.25).

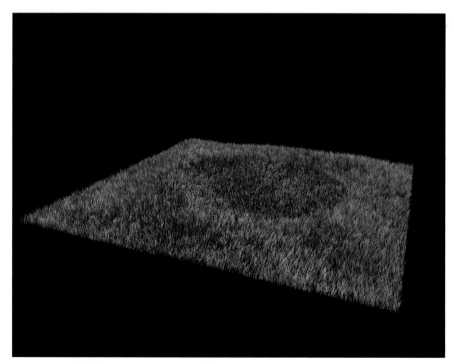

Figure 8.25: A circle of short grass appears at the center of the lawn.

Animating the Color of the Lawn

Animating the color of the lawn is easy, only slightly different from animating the length.

1. In the Attribute Editor for the Grass node, click on the checkered box next to the **Base Color** channel. Choose a file texture node and repeat steps 3 and 4 from the section "Animating the Length of the Grass," but load the colorMap texture instead of the lengthRamp texture. Make sure you click the box next to **Use Image Sequence** in the file2 Attribute Editor. In this case, you should not have to use the Hypershade to change the connections from file2 to the Grass.BaseColor channel. It should load correctly by default.

2. In the Attribute Editor for the grass node, select the lawn object from the **Assigned Surfaces** box, set the **Bake Attribute** menu to **Base Color,** rewind the animation, and click the Bake button in the Attribute Editor (Figure 8.26).

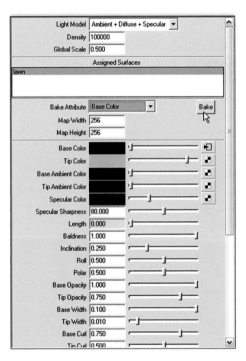

Figure 8.26:
The channels containing animated textures must be baked in order for them to work properly.

3. Repeat the steps in "Animating the Length of the Grass," but this time, plug the lengthMap texture into the Scraggle channel. Remember to bake the channel after applying the texture (Figure 8.27).

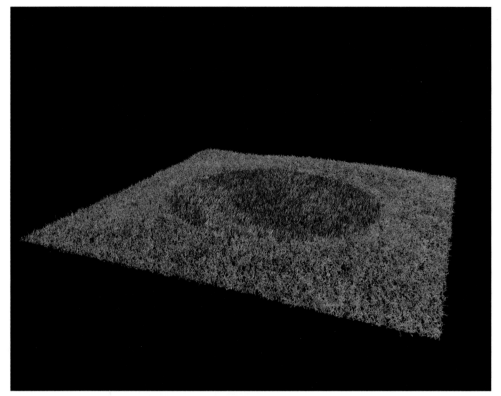

Figure 8.27: A circle of healthy green grass spreads across a scraggly brown lawn.

To see a rendered version of this scene, open the grass.mov file from the movies folder on the CD.

Further Study

Using Fur to create grass has a few advantages over using Paint Effects. It's very easy to apply animated textures to grass made from Fur, and you can also use the Artisan tools to paint Fur on an object. Fur also works on NURBS, polygons, and subdivision surfaces. With polygons and subdivision surfaces, you'll need to make sure that you do not have overlapping UVs for the Fur to behave correctly. Try expanding on the techniques of this exercise using these suggestions:

1. Animate an alien crop circle design by applying a more detailed map to the length channel of the fur node.

2. Try applying maps to other attributes such as **Baldness, Tip Curl, Clumping, Offset,** and **Base Width**.

3. Make a living room rug turn into a football field. Try applying a team logo file texture to the color attributes of the grass. Use the fBallField2.tif file in the sourceImages directory of Chapter 8 to create some of the gridlines on a section of the field.

Index

Note to the Reader: Throughout this index **boldfaced** page numbers indicate primary discussions of a topic. *Italicized* page numbers indicate illustrations.

A

Active attribute, 284, 287
active rigid bodies
    collisions, 265
    fissure effect, **284–285**
    spring constraint, 295–297
Add Attributes For Current Render Type
    option, 41
Add Dynamic Attributes menu, 50
Add Initial State Attribute option, 50
Add Per Particle Attribute option, 58
Add Selected Objects option, 111
Aim Vector setting, 166
alien nerve. *See* test tube nerve
Alpha Gain setting, 153, 155
Ambient Occlusion node, **32–37**, *32–33*, *35–38*
ampersands (&) in Expression Editor, 51
animated lighting effects with ramp textures,
    2–3, *2*
    alternative lights for, **9–11**, *10*
    geometry, **3–5**, *3–5*
    glowing, **8–9**, *9*
    shading, **6–7**, *6–8*
    UFO dome shading, **11–12**, *11*
animating
    3D audio meter, 54
    arrays of bricks, **144**, *145*
    bacterial pili, **200**, *200*
    bacterium movement, **38–43**, *38–43*,
        191–193, *192*
    blend shape transformations, **154–155**
    blend shapes, **150–151**, *151–152*
    blood cells. *See* blood cell animation
    curves, **95–97**, *96–97*, **209–210**, *210*
    eyes, **136**
    fissures. *See* fissure effect
    flying text effect, **304–305**, *304–305*
    force field, **61**
    IK spline offsets, 99, *99*
    interactive blend shape rigs, **143**, *144*
    lawn color, **334**, *334–335*
    mine detector paths, **175–176**, *175*
    Playblast, **201–202**, *202*
    pods, **133**, *133*, **135**
    probe, **173–174**, *174*
    ramps, **326–327**, *326*
    rope bridge, **322**, *322*
    rope cut, **313**, *313*
    scary tree, **179–181**, *180*
    sprites, **260–261**, *260*
    squashing effect, **116–118**, *117–118*
    tubes, **187–188**, *188*
    UFO. *See* UFO hovering animation
    vase sculpting, **126**
arrays
    of bricks, **144**, *145*
    in scripts, 292–293
Artisan tools
    blend shape weights, 131
    fur, 335
    magical field geometry, 228
Assign Paint Effects Brush To Toon Lines
    option, 160
Assign Unique Names To Child Nodes option
    interactive blend shape rigs, 142
    joints, 87
    mine detector effect, 172
    telescopic rig, 107
Attach Brush To Curves option
    mine detector effect, 174
    proximity display, 164
Attach Curves To Selected Surfaces option, 312
Attach to Motion Path option
    blood cell animation, 76
    probe animation, 173–174
attaching
    plank to rope bridge, **317–318**, *317–318*
    springs to particles, **245–247**, *246–248*
Attenuation setting
    blood cell animation, 77
    magical field geometry, 232–233
    particle springs, 249
    plasma ball effect, 71
    submarine collision effect, 268
    test tube nerve, 215
Attribute Spread Sheet option, 199, *199*
audio meter, **47**, *47–48*
    duplicating, **55–56**, *56*
    instancer for, **48–55**, *49–52*, *54*

audioMeter_v01.mb scene, *55*
Auto Create Curve option, *98, 115*
Auto Exposure setting
    and flicker, *9*
    magical field geometry, *242*
    streaking energy effects, *21*
Auto Parent Curve option, *115*
automated scaling control, **105–107**, *106–107*
Azimuth Max setting, *206*
Azimuth Min setting, *206*

B

back quotes (`) in Expression Editor, *293*
bacterium effect, **191**
    animating, **191–193**, *192*
    NURBS for, **200–201**
    particles with textures, **38–43**, *38–43*
    pili for, **194–197**, *195–196*, **200**, *200*
    Playblast for, **201–202**, *202*
    soft body object for, **193–194**, *193–194*
    surface offset for, **198–199**, *199*
    weeds stroke for, **197–198**, *198*
bacterium.mov movie, *202*
bacterium_v01.mb scene, *191*
bacterium_v02.mb scene, *194*
bacterium_v03.mb scene, *200*
bacterium_v04.mb scene, *202*
Bake Attribute menu, *334*
baking rigid bodies, **270–274**, *271–274*
Baldness setting, *330*
Base Color channel, *334*
Bend setting, *188*
Bevel Plus tool, *291*
Bind To setting
    curves, *95*
    tentacles, *90*
black holes, soda machine disappearing into
    lattices
        joints, **115–116**, *115–116*
        setup, **114–115**, *114*
    squashing effect, **116–118**, *117–118*
    twists, **118**, *119*
blend shapes, **121**
    in-betweens. *See* pods
    interactive. *See* interactive blend shape rigs
    with lattices, **122–129**, *122–128*
    layering. *See* bowl effect
Blinn shader
    fissure effect, *277*
    letters, *294*
    vase, *122*

Blobby Surface type, *245, 246*
blood cell animation, **75**
    blood for, **79–80**, *80*
    dynamic motion for, **77**
    particle rig, **75–78**, *76–79*
    rotation, **80–81**, *81*
    tuning, **79**
bloodVessel_v01.mb scene, *75*
bloodVessel_v02.mb scene, *81*
bomb from bowl. *See* bowl effect
Boolean operations, **275–278**, *276–278*
Bounciness attribute
    fissure effect, *285–286*
    submarine collision effect, *266*
bowl effect, **148**, *148*
    animating blend shape transformations for, **154–155**
    blend shapes for, **148–150**, *148–149*
    fractal textures for, **150–151**, *151–152*
    texture controls for, **152–153**, *153–154*
bowl_v01.mb scene, *148*
bowl_v02.mb scene, *155*
branches for test tube nerve, **206**, *206*
brick arrays, **144**, *145*
bridge_v01.mb scene, *311*
bridge_v02.mb scene, *312*
bridge_v03.mb scene, *318*
bridge_v04.mb scene, *318*
bridge_v05.mb scene, *323*
bridgePlanks.mel script, *321*
bridges. *See* rope bridge
Bright Color setting, *36*
brush for scary tree, **183–187**, *184–187*

C

caches
    bacterium effect, *201*
    dynamic curves, **323–324**
    magical field geometry, *236–237*
    particles, *46*
    rigid bodies, *271, 274*
    sprites, *260*
Camera And Aim option, *75*
cameras
    bacterium effect, *201*
    particle influence on, **75–81**, *75–81*
    vase, **123–124**, *124*
canvas for sprites, *256–257*
cars, telescopic. *See* telescopic car suspension rig
cells. *See* blood cell animation
Center Of Mass setting, *285–286*

Center Pivot setting
    flying text effect, 294
    telescopic rig, 109
Channel Box for UFO, 4, *4*
chasm spanning. *See* rope bridge
Check Topology option, 123
Chromatic Aberration setting, 239, *240*
Clear Color option, 256
climbing tentacle effect, **92–97**, *92–97*
Closest In Hierarchy setting, 95
clusters and cluster deformers
    proximity warning display, 164
    test tube nerve, 209–210, *210*
    vase, 124
Collide Cube option, 322
collisions
    flower effect, **62–63**, *63*
    flying text effect, 296
    particle. *See* force field effect
    plasma ball effect, **72–73**
    submarine effect, **265–268**, *266–267*
color
    animating, **334**, *334–335*
    scary tree, 182
    sci fi scanner, 34–35
    zombie hand, **29–31**, *30–31*
Color Balance rollout, 20
Color Entry List setting
    lawn effect, 326
    streaking energy effects, 18
Color Gain setting
    streaking energy effects, 20, 22
    tentacles, 89–91
Condition node, 169
Cone Angle setting, 182
Conserve setting
    blood cell animation, 77
    magical field geometry, 234
    particle springs, 246, *246*, 249
    particles, 43
    submarine collision effect, 269
Constraint Axes setting, 112
constraints
    flying text effect, 304–305
    objects to curves, 163–164
    rigging. *See* telescopic car suspension rig
    rope bridge, 317
    wheels, **109**
containment in plasma ball effect, **72**
Control attribute, 125
control curves for test tube nerve
    animating, **209–210**, *210*

converting to soft body objects, **210–214**, *211–214*
    creating, **207–208**, *208–209*
control segments, 79
Control Vertex setting, 124
control view camera, **123–124**, *124*
controls
    proximity warning display, **166–168**, *166–168*
    texture, **152–153**, *153–154*
Convert Paint Effects To Polygons option, 221
converting
    cube into soft body object, **229**, *229*
    curves
        to dynamic curves, **312**, *312*
        to soft body objects, **210–214**, *211–214*
Copy Into New UV Set option, 24
Copy UVs To UV Set option, 24
crack for fissure effect, **279–280**, *279–280*
Create Particle Grid option
    3D audio meter, 47
    blood cell animation, 76
crystal fissures. *See* fissure effect
crystal.mov movie, 288
crystal_v01.mb scene, 276, 277
crystal_v02.mb scene, 278
crystal_v03.mb scene, 280
crystal_v04.mb scene, 283
crystal_v05.mb scene, 285
crystal_v06.mb scene, 288
cubes
    3D audio meter, 47, 50
    converting into soft body object, **229**, *229*
    interactive blend shape rigs, 139
    magical field geometry, 227–228, *228*
cubic curves, 94
curl for scary tree, 179, 187
Current Solver setting, 105
Curve Attract setting, 208
Curve Degrees setting, 93
Curve Flow effect, 79
Curve Follow setting, 208
Curve Range setting, 14
Curve Tool Degree setting, 109
curves, 93
    animating, **95–97**, *96–97*, **209–210**, *210*
    constraining objects to, 163–164
    converting
        to dynamic curves, **312**, *312*
        to soft body objects, **210–214**, *211–214*
    dynamic. *See* rope bridge
    profile, 122, 124

test tube nerve, **207–208**, *208–209*
custom attributes, 90
cycle emission. *See* plasma ball effect
cycle for flower effect, **65–67**, *66*

D

DAG Objects Only option
    bowl effect, 150
    interactive blend shape rigs, 141–142
    path animation, 175
    proximity warning display, 162
    rope bridge, 314
    streaking energy effects, 16
daisies. *See* flower effect
Damping setting
    fissure effect, 285–286
    flying text effect, 296, 303–304
    magical field geometry, 233–234, *235*
    particle springs, 248–249
    submarine collision effect, 270
Dark Color setting, 34–36
Decay Rate setting, 182
Default Color setting, 28
deforming
    blend shape lattice, **127–128**, *127–128*
    proximity warning display, 164
    test tube nerve, 209–210, *210*
    vase, 124
dents. *See* submarine collision effect
Depth Sort for sprites, 252
Detach Skin option, 84–85
difference operations, 276–277, *276*
Disable Implicit Control setting, 271
disk caches
    bacterium effect, 201
    dynamic curves, **323–324**
    magical field geometry, 236–237
    particles, 46
    rigid bodies, 271, 274
    sprites, 260
Displacement Delay setting, 187
Display In Viewport setting, 13
Distance Between node
    mine detector effect, **169–171**, *170–171*
    proximity warning display, 166
Distance Scaling setting
    mine detector effect, 159
    proximity warning display, *165*
Distance tool, 140–141
distortion
    particle systems, **231–232**, *231–232*

scary tree, 183–185, *185*, 190
Divisions setting, 228
Dolly Track control, 181–182
dome shading, **11–12**, *11*
Draw As Mesh setting, 180
driven keys
    flying text effect, 304
    interactive blend shape rigs, 141
    offsetting, **305–306**, *305–306*
    telescopic rig, 107, *107*
Dropoff Rate setting, 90
drug commercial. *See* bacterium effect
Duplicate Input Graph option
    interactive blend shape rigs, 142, 144
    mine detector effect, 172
    tentacle, 87
Duplicate Surface Curves option
    telescopic car suspension rig, 111
    tentacle, 94
duplicating
    3D audio meter, **55–56**, *56*
    interactive blend shape rigs, **142–143**, *143*
    leg rig, **107–108**
    mines, **171–173**, *172–173*
    vibrating joints, 87, *87*
dynamic curves. *See* rope bridge
dynamic dents. *See* submarine collision effect
Dynamic Friction setting
    fissure effect, 286
    submarine collision effect, 266–267
dynamic particle motion, 77
Dynamic Relationships option, 73

E

Eccentricity setting, 238
Edit Oversampling Or Cache Settings option,
    53, 234, 245
Edit Ramp option, 253, *254*
Elevation Max setting, 206
Elevation Min setting, 206
Emission Attributes settings, 39
Emitter Type setting, 231
emitters
    particle springs, **244–245**, *245*
    particles, 38
    plasma ball effect, **69–70**
Enable Ray Tracing option, 222
energy effects, streaking. *See* streaking energy
    effects
EP Curve tool, 164, 311
Exact Shape Match setting, 312

expressions and Expression Editor
    3D audio meter, 50–54
    bacteria, 38–40, *40*
    flower, 67
    force field, 61
    magical field, 230
    plasma, 74
    scary tree, 180, *180*, 189
    sprites, 251, *255*
    syntax in, 292
    test tube nerve, 216
extendoLegCar_v01.mb scene, 100
extendoLegCar_v02.mb scene, 110
extendoLegCar_v03.mb scene, 113
eyes, pod. *See* pods

F

Facing Ratio setting, 240
Falloff setting, 34
field_v01.mb scene, 62
field_v02.mb scene, 68
fields
    force. *See* force field effect
    magical. *See* magical field geometry
    particles, 38
    soft body objects, **230**, *230*
Filler Color setting, 35
fingers. *See* zombie hand
fissure effect, **275**, *275*
    animating, **280–281**, *281*
    Boolean operations, **275–278**, *276–278*
    chunk visibility, **287–288**, *288*
    crystal separation, **283–284**, *284*
    dynamics, **282–283**, *282–283*, **285–287**, *285–287*
    fissure modeling, **279–280**, *279–280*
    gravity, **284–285**
Fixed Segment Length setting, 312
flickering with glow, 9
Flow Animation settings, 220
Flow Speed setting
    flower effect, 64
    test tube nerve, 218
flower effect
    collisions for, **62–63**, *63*
    flower for, **64–65**, *64–65*
    growth in, **67–68**, *68*
    object cycle for, **65–67**, *66*
flying text effect, **289–290**, *289–290*
    animating, **304–305**, *304–305*
    driven key offsets, **305–306**, *305–306*

    finishing, **306–307**, *307*
    renaming letters, **292–295**, *294–295*
    shelf button, **300–301**, *301*
    spring constraints, **294–296**, *295–296*
    spring rig, **297–300**, **302–304**, *302–303*
    text for, **290–291**, *291*
Focal Length setting, 181, *182*
force field effect, **56–57**, *57*
    animating, **61**
    force field for, **57–58**, *57*
    instances for, **60–61**, *61*
    ray gun, 57, **59–60**, *60*
    shield, **58–59**, *59*
forceField_v01.mb scene, 57
forces on test tube nerve, **207**, *207*
fractal textures
    animating blend shapes with, **150–151**, *151–152*
    for tentacles, 85
framing scary tree scene, **181**, *182*
Free Tangent Weight option, 133
Freeze Transformations option
    flying text effect, 295, 299
    rope bridge, 311
    telescopic rig, 101, 105, 109–110, 112
friction
    fissure effect, 286
    submarine collision effect, 266–267, 269–270

G

geometry
    energy, **14**, *14*
    lighting effects, **3–5**, *3–5*
    magical field. *See* magical field geometry
Get Settings From Selected Stroke option
    mine detector effect, 174
    proximity warning display, 164
    scary tree, 190
Glow Intensity setting, 9, 242
Glow Spread setting, 242
glowing edge, **240–243**, *241–243*
glowing lights, 2–3, **8–9**, *9*
glows for streaking energy effects, **12–14**, *13*, **21**, *22*
glowTypes.mb scene, 12, *13*
Goal Weight setting
    bacterium effect, 193
    blood cell animation, 77, 79
    magical field geometry, 229–230, 233
    particles, 38

soft body curves, 211, **215–218**, *216–218*
goalPP attribute, 41
goals for particles, 38
Graph Network option
    glowing lights, 8
    sci fi scanner, 34
grass. *See* lawn effect
grass.mov movie, 335
gravity
    bacterium effect, 200
    fissure effect, **284–285**
    flower, 62
    scary tree, 179–180
    submarine collision, 265–267, 272
grids
    particle, 47
    telescopic rig, 102
growth
    flowers. *See* flower effect
    pea pods. *See* pods
    test tube nerve, **218–220**, *219–221*

H

hair and fur effects, **309–310**
    dynamic curves. *See* rope bridge
    lawn. *See* lawn effect
hair constraints, **313–314**, *314*, **318–321**
Hair module, 323
hairy bacterium. *See* bacterium effect
hallucinations. *See* scary tree
halo
    lighting, 9
    magical field geometry, 242
    streaking energy effects, 21
hand, zombie. *See* zombie hand
Hide Non-Soft Object option
    bacterium, 193
    magical field geometry, 229
    test tube nerve, 211
hovering UFO. *See* UFO hovering animation
Hypergraph, 211–212, *211*, 214, *214*
Hypershade
    bowl effect, 150, *152*, 153
    glowing lights, 8
    lawn effect, 326, 332
    magical field geometry, 240–241
    mine detector effect, 170
    plasma ball effect, 74
    proximity warning display, 162–163, 168
    scary tree, 181
    streaking energy effects, 16–17, *17*, 20

tentacles, 89
zombie hand, 25–27, 31

I

IK handles, **105**, *105*
IK (inverse kinematic) splines
    activating, **98–99**, *98*
    for curves, **92–97**, *92–97*
    for lattices, **114–119**
    offset for, **99**, *99*
images for sprites, **256–259**, *256–259*
in-betweens. *See* pods
In Tan Type setting, 10
Incandescence channel, 3
Incandescence setting
    glow, 9
    magical field geometry, 241–242
    sci fi scanner, 34
    test tube nerve, 221
infection, zombie hand, **25–28**, *25–28*
Inherit Velocity option
    flower effect, 63
    force field effect, 59
    plasma ball effect, 72
Input And Output Connections option, 15
Input Curve attribute, 162, *163*
inputs, listing, 128
instanceMe attribute, 52–53, *52*, 67
instancing
    force field effect, **60–61**, *61*
    Paint Effects. *See* flower effect
    particles. *See* 3D audio meter
interactive blend shape rigs, **139**, *139*
    array of bricks for, **144**, *145*
    blend shape for, **139–140**, *140*
    duplicating, **142–143**, *143*
    editing animation for, **143**, *144*
    interactive control, **140–141**, *141–142*
    working with, **145–147**, *146*
interactive control
    blend shape rigs, **140–141**, *141–142*
    proximity warning display, **166–168**, *166–168*
Interactive Sequence Caching Options rollout, 258
interactiveBlendShapeRig.mb scene, 147
Intermediate Object setting, 277
Interpolation setting
    bacterium effect, 197, 200
    interactive blend shape rigs, 143
    magical field geometry, 241
    scary tree, 180

Interpolation setting, *continued*
    streaking energy effects, 15
    test tube nerve, 207
    UFO dome, 11
    zombie hand, 31
intersection operations, 276, *276*
inverse kinematic (IK) splines
    activating, **98–99**, *98*
    for curves, **92–97**, *92–97*
    for lattices, **114–119**
    offset for, **99**, *99*

J

joints
    curves, **94–95**, *95*
    deforming blend shape lattice with, 127
    lattices, **115–116**, *115–116*
    rigging. *See* telescopic car suspension rig
    tentacles, **85–87**, *85–87*, **97–98**, *98*
    vibrating, **85–87**, *85–87*

K

Keep Faces Together attribute, 4
Keep Image option, 186
Keep Image In Render View option, 13
Keep Unbaked Keys setting, 271
key framing
    fissure effect, 286
    stroke growth, **219–220**, *220–221*
Key Selected option
    fissure effect, 280, 287
    particle springs, 244
    rope bridge, 313
Krandle Productions logo. *See* flying text effect
krandle_v01.mb scene, 294
krandle_v02.mb scene, 296
krandle_v03.mb scene, 304
krandle_v04.mb scene, 307

L

Lambert shader
    3D audio meter, 47
    fissure effect, 278
    scary tree, 183
lattices
    bacterium effect, **191–193**, *192*
    blend shapes with, **122–129**, *122–128*
    converting into soft body object, 230
    joints for, **115–116**, *115–116*

    setting up, **114–115**, *114*
    squashing effect, **116–118**, *117–118*
    twists, 118, *119*
lawn effect, 324, *324*
    color animation, 334, *334–335*
    grass for, **329–333**, *329–332*
    lawn for, **328**, *329*
    ramps
        for animated textures, **324–326**, *325*
        animating, **326–327**, *326*
        rendering, **327–328**, *327–328*
lawn_v01.mb scene, 327
Layered Texture option, 29–30, *30*
layering
    blend shapes. *See* bowl effect
    multiple UV sets. *See* zombie hand
leafless tree. *See* scary tree
LED audio meter display, 47, *47–48*
    duplicating, **55–56**, *56*
    instancer for, **48–55**, *49–52, 54*
Leg_Car.mb scene, 100
legs, telescoping, **100–101**, *101*
    duplicating, **107–108**
    IK handles for, **105**, *105*
    placing, **108–109**, *108–109*
length of grass, **330–333**, *331–332*
letters for flying text effect
    creating, **290–291**, *291*
    renaming, **292–295**, *294–295*
lifespan
    blood, 79
    force field effect, 60
    magical field geometry, 231
    plasma ball effect, 72–73
    sprites, 251
lighting
    with ramp textures, **2–3**, *2*
        alternative lights for, **9–11**, *10*
        geometry, **3–5**, *3–5*
        glowing, **8–9**, *9*
        shading, **6–7**, *6–8*
        UFO dome shading for, **11–12**, *11*
    scary tree, **182–183**, *183*
lightning, 204–205, *205*
Line Color setting, 35
Line Width setting, 159
List of Input Operations dialog box, 128
Local Displacement setting, 180
Local Occlusion setting, 159
Lock And Hide Selected option, 302
Lock Selected option, 102
logo. *See* flying text effect

M

machine_v01.mb scene, 69
magical field geometry, **226–228**, *226–228*
   cube conversions, **229**, *229*
   distortion, **231–232**, *231–232*
   fields, **230**, *230*
   glowing edge, **240–243**, *241–243*
   initial state, **236–237**, *236*
   radial field, **232**, *232*
   rendering, **237–239**, *238–240*
   soft body springs for particles, **233–234**, *233–235*
magicSword.mov movie, 243
Magnitude setting
   blood cell animation, 77
   plasma ball effect, 71
Maintain Offset setting
   rope bridge, 317
   submarine collision effect, 265
   telescopic rig, 103, 112
Make Attribute Keyable option, 302
Make Brush Spring option, 203
Make Collide option
   flower effect, 63
   force field effect, 59
   plasma ball effect, 72–73
   submarine collision effect, 269
Make Copy Soft option, 229
Make Live option, 93
Make Non-Soft A Goal option
   bacterium, 193
   magical field geometry, 229
Make Paintable option
   bacterium effect, 196
   scary tree, 185, 190
   test tube nerve, 205
masks
   spreading infection, **25–28**, *25–28*
   streaking energy effects, **15**
Mass setting, 286
Matte Opacity setting, 47
Max Clip setting, 175
Max Count setting, 39
Max Distance setting, 34
Max Influences setting
   curves, 95
   tentacles, 90
Max Pixel Width setting
   mine detector effect, 159
   proximity warning display, 165

Maya Unlimited version, hair and fur effects, **309–310**
   dynamic curves. *See* rope bridge
   lawn. *See* lawn effect
MEL scripts
   flying text effect, 289–290, *290*
      renaming text letters, **292–295**, *294–295*
      rig, **297–300**, **302–304**, *302–303*
      shelf button, **300–301**, *301*
   hair constraints, **318–321**
mental ray
   Ambient Occlusion node, **32–37**, *32–33*, *35–38*
   fissures, 276
   test tube nerve, 221–222
meters, **47**, *47–48*
   duplicating, **55–56**, *56*
   instancer for, **48–55**, *49–52*, *54*
MidPoint setting, 267
Min Clip setting, 175, *175*
Min Pixel Width setting
   mine detector effect, 159
   proximity warning display, 165
mine detector effect, **158**, *158*
   Distance Between node for, **169–171**, *170–171*
   finishing touches, **176**, *176*
   mines for, **171–173**, *172–173*
   paths
      animating, **175–176**, *175*
      illuminating, **174**
   probe and mine display, **158–161**, *159–161*
   probe animation, **173–174**, *174*
   proximity warning display
      creating, **161–164**, *162–164*
      interactive control, **166–168**, *166–168*
      Paint Effects strokes, **164–165**, *165*
mineField_v01.mb scene, 158–159
mineField_v02.mb scene, 171
mineField_v03.mb scene, 173
mineField_v04.mb scene, 176
Minimum Corner setting, 47
MinMax creation method, 247
motion paths
   blood cell animation, 76
   probe animation, **173–174**, *174*
   streaking energy effects, **15–19**, *16–19*
   telescopic car suspension rig, **110–113**, *111–113*
multiple hair constraints, 318–321
multiple UV sets, layering with. *See* zombie hand
Multiply Blend Mode, 30

N

nerves, test tube. *See* test tube nerve
nesting script commands, 293
network systems, caches for, 46
nightmarish tree. *See* scary tree
noise
    bacterium effect, 200
    magical field geometry, 242
    scary tree, 179–180, 187
    zombie hand, 29
Normal Direction setting, 205
Normalize UVs option, 6, 6, 24
Num Particles setting
    blood cell animation, 76
    flower effect, 63
    force field effect, 59
Number Of Spans setting, 94
NURBS
    bacterium effect, **200–201**
    energy geometry, 14
    scary tree, 181
    Shatter effect, 286

O

object cycle for flower effect, **65–67**, *66*
Object Index setting, 68
ocean floor, denting, **268–269**, *268–269*
offset setting
    bacterium effect surface, **198–199**, *199*
    driven keys, **305–306**, *305–306*
    IK splines, **99**, *99*
    joints, 116
    UFO dome, 12
Original Particle Dies option
    flower effect, 63
    force field effect, 59
    plasma ball effect, 72
Oscillate setting, 143
Out Color setting
    lawn effect, 328, 333
    mine detector effect, 170
    streaking energy effects, 21
Out Glow Color setting
    streaking energy effects, 21
    UFO, 3, 8
Out Tan Type setting, 10
Out Transparency color, 21
Outliner
    streaking energy effects, 16
    UFO, 4, *4*
Outside Lattice option, 125

P

Paint Canvas, 256
Paint Effects, **157**
    flower. *See* flower effect
    scary tree. *See* scary tree
    soft body dynamics. *See* bacterium effect
    sprites, 256–257, *256–257*
    test tube nerve. *See* test tube nerve
    toon lines. *See* mine detector effect
Paint Effects To Polygons option, 65
Paint Selection tool, 3
paintbrushes, particle objects as, **249–250**, *250*
painting
    blend shape weights, **131–132**
    sprites for. *See* sprites
Parameter Range setting
    curves, 94
    mine detector effect, 175
Parametric Length setting, 175–176
Particle Collision Event Editor, 62–63, 275
Particle Object To Instance option, 48
particle springs, **244**, *244*
    adjusting, **248–249**, *248*
    attaching, **245–247**, *246–248*
    emitters for, **244–245**, *245*
    for paintbrush, **249–250**, *250*
    sprites for. *See* sprites
    turbulence, **249**, *249*
particleId setting, 50
particles, **45–46**
    and cameras, **75–81**, *75–81*
    collisions
        flower effect, **62–63**
        force field. *See* force field effect
    cycle emission. *See* plasma ball effect
    distortion with, **231–232**, *231–232*
    instancing and expressions. *See* 3D audio
        meter
    magical field geometry, **233–234**, *233–235*
    Paint Effects. *See* flower effect
    soft body springs. *See* particle springs
    textures for, **38–43**, *38–43*
particleSprings.mov movie, 244, 261
particleSprings_v01.mb scene, 249–250
particleSprings_v02.mb scene, 255
particleSprings_v03.mb scene, 261
passive rigid bodies
    fissure effect, **284**
    flying text effect, 295, 297
    submarine collision effect, 265
patches for lawn effect, 325
Path Attract setting, 206

Path Follow setting, 206
paths
    mine detector effect
        animating, **175–176**, *175*
        illuminating, **174**
    motion. *See* motion paths
pea pods. *See* pods
peaPod_v01.mb scene, 129
peapod_v02.mb scene, 137
perspective view for profile curves, 124
PhaseX setting, 43
pipe for climbing tentacle, 92–97, *92–96*
plank for rope bridge, **316–318**, *316–318*, 322, *322*
plasma ball effect, **68–69**, *69*
    collisions, **72–73**
    cycle emission, **70–71**
    emitter for, **69–70**
    particle containment, **72**
    polishing, **74**, *74*
    secondary particles, **72–73**, *73*
plasmaMachine.mov movie, 74
Playblast, **201–202**, *202*
Plug-in manager, 33
pods, **129**, *129*
    animating, **133**, *133*, **135**
    blend shapes
        sequence, **132–133**
        targets, **129–130**, *130–131*
        weights, **131–132**
    eyes, **136**
    rigging, **134–135**, *134–135*
    time lapse effect, **136–137**, *137–138*
Point Lock setting, 313
polishing, plasma, **74**, *74*
position attribute
    force field effect, 58
    ramps, 15
Post Infinity setting
    3D audio meter, *55*
    blend shape rigs, 143
    lights, 7, 10
    tentacles, 86
    UFO dome, 12
    vase, 126
pottery. *See* vase
Prefix Hierarchy Names option
    clusters, 210
    joints, 94, 97
    telescopic rig, 103
probe
    animating, **173–174**, *174*
    mine detector effect, **158–161**, *159–161*

probe.mov movie, 176
profile curves, **122–124**
Profile Lines setting, 159
proximity warning display
    creating, **161–164**, *162–164*
    interactive control, **166–168**, *166–168*
    Paint Effects strokes for, **164–165**, *165*

R

Radius setting
    magical field geometry, 231
    particle springs, 250
    plasma ball effect, 70, 72–74
    springs, 245, *246*
rain cloud, 62
ramp textures
    animated lighting effects with, **2–3**, *2*
        alternative lights for, **9–11**, *10*
        geometry, **3–5**, *3–5*
        glowing, **8–9**, *9*
        shading, **6–7**, *6–8*
        UFO dome shading for, **11–12**, *11*
    particles, **39–43**, *39–43*
ramps for lawn effect
    for animated textures, **324–326**, *325*
    animating, **326–327**, *326*
    rendering, **327–328**, *327–328*
random actions
    blood cell animation, 79
    force field effect, 58
    magical field geometry, 230
    particles, 46
    plasma ball effect, 72
Rate (Particles/Sec) setting, *57–58*
ray gun, 57, **59–60**, *60*
raytracing
    magical field geometry, 237–238
    scary tree, 181–182
    test tube nerve, 222
Rearrange Graph option
    bowl effect, 150
    streaking energy effects, 17
Rebuild Type setting, 94
reconnecting tentacles, **89–90**, *89*
Reflectivity setting, 238
Refractions setting, 238, *239*
Relationship Editor, 25–26, *26*, 29, 73
renaming flying text letters, **292–295**, *294–295*
Render View window, 13, 186
rendering
    magical field, **237–239**, *238–240*

rendering, *continued*
    ramps, **327–328**, *327–328*
    sprites, **260–261**, *260*
    test tube nerve, **221–222**, *222*
Resolution Gate option, 328
Rest Length setting, 303–304
Reverse Surface Direction setting, 205
revolving surfaces, **122**, *122–123*
rgbPP attribute, 58
rigging, **83**
    flying text effect, **297–300**, **302–304**, *302–303*
    interactive blend shape. *See* interactive blend shape rigs
    inverse kinematic splines. *See* inverse kinematic (IK) splines
    joints and constraints. *See* telescopic car suspension rig
    lattices, **114–119**
    pods, **134–135**, *134–135*
    tentacles. *See* tentacles
Rigid Bind option, 127
rigid body effects, **263**
    animated fissures. *See* fissure effect
    soft body combinations. *See* submarine collision effect
    spring constraints. *See* flying text effect
rigid body spring constraints, 226
rigidSpringRig.mel script, 300
robot_v01.mb scene, 13
robot_v02.mb scene, 21
robotic extension legs. *See* telescopic car suspension rig
Roll setting, 118
Root On Curve setting, 115
rope bridge, **310**
    animating, **322**, *322*
    curve conversions, **312**, *312*
    cut animation, **313**, *313*
    finishing, **323**
    hair constraints, **313–314**, *314*, **318–321**
    plank, **316–318**, *316–318*, **322**, *322*
    ropes for, **311**, *311*
    stick constraint, **314–315**, *315*
rotation
    blood cell animation, **80–81**, *81*
    deformers, 127–128
    lattices, 118, *119*
    rope bridge, 317
    scary tree, 184, 188
    telescopic rig, 103, 105
    UFO dome, 11
    vase, 126

Runge Kutta Adaptive method, 267
Runtime Before Dynamics Expression option
    3D audio meter, 50
    blood cell, 80
    flower, 67
    force field effect, 58
    particles, 42
    sprites, 255
    test tube nerve, 216

S

saucer.mov movie, 9
saucer_v01.mb scene, 2
saucer_v02.mb scene, 10
saucer_v03.mb scene, 12
Save Snapshot option, 257
SC solver, 105
scale
    bacterium effect, 191, 198, 201
    blood cell animation, 80
    fissure effect, 277
    flower effect, 62
    lawn effect, 325
    magical field geometry, 227
    mine detector effect, 174
    proximity warning display, 161
    rope bridge, 316
    scary tree, 178–179
    sprites, **252–255**, *254*
    squashing effect, **117–118**, *117–118*
    telescopic rig, 102, *102*, **104–107**, *104*, *106–107*
    test tube nerve, 206
scanners, sci fi, **32–37**, *32–33*, *35–38*
scary tree, **177–178**, *177–178*
    adjusting, **179**
    animating, **179–181**, *180*
    framing, **181**, *182*
    lighting, **182–183**, *183*
    smear brush for, **183–187**, *184–187*
    tube animation for, **187–188**, *188*
    variations, **188–190**, *189–190*
scaryTree_v01.mb scene, 178
scaryTree_v01.mov movie, 188
scaryTree_v02.mb scene, 183
scaryTree_v02.mov movie, 189
scaryTree_v03.mb scene, 188
scaryTree_v03.mov movie, 190
scaryTree_variation1.mb scene, 188
scaryTree_variation2.mb scene, 189
scaryTree_variation3.mb scene, 189

sci fi scanners, **32–37**, *32–33*, *35–38*
Screenspace Width setting
    mine detector effect, 159–161, 174
    proximity warning display, 165
scripts. *See* MEL scripts
Sculpt Geometry tool
    lawn effect, 328, *329*
    magical field geometry, 228
secondary particles
    distortion with, **231**, *231*
    plasma ball effect, **72–73**, *73*
seed setting
    force field effect, 58
    particles, 40, 46
Segment Length setting, 312
Select Face Component option, 3
Select Shell option, 23
Selected Color option, 325
Selected Position setting
    lawn effect, 326–327
    streaking energy effects, 15
semicolons (;)
    for commands, 51
    in Expression Editor, 292
Separate Duplicated Faces option, 4
Separate Extracted Faces option, 283
Set Control Curves option, 208
Set Current UV Set option, 24
Set Driven Key window
    flying text effect, 304
    interactive blend shape rigs, 141
    telescopic rig, 107, *107*
Set For Selected option, 58
Set Key option
    bowl effect, 151
    tentacles, 85
shader glow
    flickering with, 9
    scary tree, 186
shaders and shading
    glowing effect, 2–3
    sci fi scanner, **34–35**
    UFO animation, **6–7**, *6–8*, **11–12**, *11*
Shading Network option, 325
Shake Dimmer setting, 90–91, *91*
shakers for tentacles, **87–89**, *88*
Shape setting, 62
Shapes Display option, 162
Share One Brush option
    bacterium effect, 197
    proximity warning display, 165
    scary tree, 186, 190

Shatter effect, 286
shelf button, **300–301**, *301*
Shelf Editor, 301
Shelves dialog box, 301, *301*
shield, force field, **58–59**, *59*
simulating magic. *See* magical field geometry
Sketch Particles option, 76
skull, scanner for, **32–37**, *32–33*, *35–38*
skullScan.mov movie, 35
skullScan_v01.mb scene, 32
skullScan_v02.mb scene, 35
smear brush, **183–187**, *184–187*
Smooth option
    blend shape weights, 132
    joints, 115
Smooth Over Time And Space option
    bacterium effect, 200
    scary tree, 180–181
    test tube nerve, 207
Snap Curve To Root option, 98, 115
soda machine disappearing into black hole
    effect
    lattices
        joints, **115–116**, *115–116*
        setup, **114–115**, *114*
      squashing effect, **116–118**, *117–118*
      twists, **118**, *119*
sodaMachine_v01.mb scene, 114
soft body curves, **215–218**, *216–218*
soft body dynamics. *See* bacterium effect
soft body objects
    converting control curves into, **210–214**,
      211–214
    converting cubes into, **229**, *229*
    fields for, **230**, *230*
    and rigid body combinations. *See* submarine
      collision effect
soft body springs, **225–226**
    geometry for. *See* magical field geometry
    with particles. *See* particle springs
Solver Method option, 267
spanning chasms. *See* rope bridge
Sparse Curve Bake option, 271
Specular Color setting, 238
Specular Roll Off setting, 238
Spike interpolation setting
    magical field geometry, 241
    UFO dome, 11
    zombie hand, 31
spin for vase, **125–126**, *126*, 128–129
Spiral settings, 181
splats, **257–260**, *258*

splines, IK. *See* inverse kinematic (IK) splines
splotch for zombie hand, 26–27, **29**
spookyHand.mb scene, 36
spreading zombie hand infection, **25–28**, *25–28*
spring constraints. *See* flying text effect
Spring Release attribute, 304–307
Spring Rest Length setting, 296
springs
    flying text effect, **297–300, 302–304**, *302–303*
    geometry for. *See* magical field geometry
    particle. *See* particle springs
    submarine collision effect, **269–270**, *270*
sprites
    attributes, **250–255**, *252–255*
    creating, **251–252**, *251*
    images for, **256–259**, *256–259*
    rendering, **260–261**, *260*
sprouting flowers. *See* flower effect
squashing effect, **116–118**, *117–118*
Stamp Density setting, 186
startWeight setting, **39–42**, *40*
Static Friction setting
    fissure effect, 286
    submarine collision effect, 266–267
Stats fields, 19
stick constraint, **314–315**, *315*
Stiffness setting
    flying text effect, 296, 303–304
    magical field geometry, **233–236**, *235*
    particle springs, 248–249
    rope bridge, 312
    submarine collision effect, 270
streaking energy effects, **12**
    energy geometry, **14**, *14*
    energy shader, **20–21**
    glows, **12–14**, *13*, **21, 22**
    masks for, **15**
    motion path output value, **15–19**, *16–19*
stroke growth for test tube nerve
    controlling, **218–219**, *219*
    key framing, **219–220**, *220–221*
Stroke Time setting
    flower effect, 64
    test tube nerve, 218
Studio Clear Coat node, 242
Subdivisions settings
    fissure effect, 277
    magical field geometry, 227
submarine collision effect, **264–265**, *264–265*
    baking, **270–274**, *271–274*
    collision simulation, **265–268**, *266–267*

denting surfaces, **268–269**, *268–269*
finishing, **274**, *275*
springs for, **269–270**, *270*
submarine_v01.mb scene, 264
submarine_v02.mb scene, 268
submarine_v03.mb scene, 270
submarine_v04.mb scene, 274
subsegments, 79
Surface Curve option, 94
Surface Offset attribute, **198–199**, *199*
surfaces
    animated fissures on. *See* fissure effect
    denting, **268–269**, *268–269*
    revolving, **122**, *122–123*
suspension rig. *See* telescopic car suspension rig
swimming bacteria, **38–43**, *38–43*
sword. *See* magical field geometry
sword_v01.mb scene, 226
sword_v02.mb scene, 232
sword_v03.mb scene, 234
sword_v04.mb scene, 243

T

telescopic car suspension rig, **100**, *100*
    car motion, **110–113**, *111–113*
    creating, **102–104**, *102–104*
    front and rear controls, **109–110**, *110*
    leg, **100–101**, *101*
        duplication, **107–108**
        IK handles for, **105**, *105*
        placement, **108–109**, *108–109*
    scale limits, **104**, *104*
    scaling control, **105–107**, *106–107*
    wheel constraints, **109**
tentacle_v01.mb scene, 84
tentacleClimb_v01.mb scene, 92
tentacles, **84**, *84*
    climbing curves for, **92–97**, *92–97*
    disconnecting, **84–85**
    joints for, **85–87**, *85–87*, **97–98**, *98*
    reconnecting, **89–90**, *89*
    shakers for, **87–89**, *88*
    vibration, **85–87**, *85–87*, **90–91**, *90–92*
test tube nerve, **204**, *204*
    appearance, **205–206**
    branches and twigs for, **206**, *206*
    control curves
        animating, **209–210**, *210*
        converting to soft body objects, **210–214**, *211–214*
        creating, **207–208**, *208–209*

INDEX

creating, **204–205**, *204–205*
forces on, **207**, *207*
Goal Weights, 211, **215–218**, *216–218*
rendering, **221–222**, *222*
stroke growth
    controlling, **218–219**, *219*
    key framing, **219–220**, *220–221*
testTube_v01.mb scene, 204
testTube_v02.mb scene, 210
testTube_v03.mb scene, 217
testTube_v04.mb scene, 222
text, flying. *See* flying text effect
Texture-Centric option, 25
texture effects, **1**
    Ambient Occlusion, **32–37**, *32–33*, *35–38*
    controls for, **152–153**, *153–154*
    layering with multiple UV sets. *See* zombie
      hand
    particles, **38–43**, *38–43*
    ramp. *See* ramp textures
    streaking energy effects. *See* streaking energy
      effects
thrashing tentacle. *See* tentacles
3D audio meter, **47**, *47–48*
    duplicating, **55–56**, *56*
    instancer for, **48–55**, *49–52*, *54*
3D hallucinations. *See* scary tree
Threshold setting
    bowl effect, 153–155, *154*
    magical field geometry, 242
    plasma ball effect, 74
    streaking energy effects, 21
time lapse effect, **136–137**, *137–138*
Time Range setting, 273
Time Tolerance setting, 273
Tolerance setting, 273
toon lines. *See* mine detector effect
Trace Depth setting, 73
transformations
    blend shape, **154–155**
    flying text effect, 299
Translate setting
    3D audio meter, 54
    blood cell animation, 78
    fissure effect, 277, 279–281
    particle springs, 249
    rope bridge, 311, 317
    submarine collision effect, 265
    telescopic rig, 103, 105, 107
    tentacles, 86
    UFO, 4
Translate Frame settings
    lights, 7, 10

zombie hand, 27
Transparency setting
    magical field geometry, 227, 238
    scary tree, 183
    sci fi scanner, 34
    tube nerve, 221
trees, scary. *See* scary tree
Tube Width setting, 179
tubes, animating, **187–188**, *188*
Turbulence setting
    bacterium effect, 200
    blood cell animation, 77
    magical field geometry, 230, *230*
    particle springs, **249**, *249*
    particles, 42
    plasma ball effect, 71, 73
    scary tree, 180–181, 188
    test tube nerve, 207, *207*, 215
twigs, **206**, *206*
twists
    lattices, **118**, *119*
    sprites, 252–253

U

U settings
    mine detector effect, 175, *175*
    proximity warning display, 163
    rope bridge, 314–316, 319–320
    sci fi scanner, 35
    streaking energy effects, 16, 18–19, *18*, 22
    zombie hand, 26–27
UFO from bowl. *See* bowl effect
UFO hovering animation, **2–3**, *2*
    alternative lights, **9–11**, *10*
    dome shading, **11–12**, *11*
    glowing lights, **8–9**, *9*
    light geometry, **3–5**, *3–5*
    light shading, **6–7**, *6–8*
union operations, 276, *276*
Up Vector, 166
Use Image Sequence option, 332, 334
Use Interactive Sequence Caching option, 258
Use Per-Spring Damping option, 233
Use Per Spring Rest Length option, 233
Use Per-Spring Stiffness option, 233
UV faces for lights, 11
UV sets, layering with. *See* zombie hand
UV Texture Editor
    for lights, 6, 10
    for zombie hand, 24, 26–27, *27*

V

V Width setting, 35
vase, **122**, *122*
    blend shape controls, **124–125**, *125*, 127
    control view camera, **123–124**, *124*
    deforming blend shape lattices, **127–128**, *127–128*
    profile curves, **122–123**
    revolving surfaces, **122**, *122–123*
    sculpting animation, **126**
    spin, **125–126**, *126*
vibrating rig. *See* tentacles
Visibility Of Shape Nodes, 205
Visibility setting
    blend shape rigs, 142
    fissure effect, 287–288
    pod eyes, 136
    streaking energy effects, 12
    submarine collision effect, 264
    telescopic rig, 105
Visor
    bacterium effect, 195–196
    flower effect, 64
    mine detector effect, 160
    scary tree, 177, *178*, 185
    sprites, 256
    test tube nerve, 204

W

Walk Length setting, 233

weeds stroke, **197–198**, *198*
Weight setting
    bowl effect, 150
    magical field geometry, 229
    telescopic rig, 103
weighted tangents, 133
wheels, constraining, **109**
Width Scale settings, 206
wiggle
    plasma ball, 75
    scary tree, 179, 187
Wire Walk Length setting, 270
Wireframe On Shaded option, 49
wireframes
    magical field geometry, 233
    submarine collision effect, 270
World Centroid setting, 78, 81
World Space setting
    proximity warning display, 162
    test tube nerve, 213, *214*

Z

zombie hand, **22–23**
    color, **29–31**, *30–31*
    mask for spreading infection, **25–28**, *25–28*
    multiple UV sets for, **23–25**, *24*
    splotch, 26–27, **29**
zombieHand_v01.mb scene, 22
zombieMutantPottery_v01.mb scene, 128